This book is dedicated to the memory of Arthur Dunn,
whose example inspired his contemporaries and
future generations of amateur footballers.
And to all those who have organised, participated,
won and lost in the Arthur Dunn Cup
over the last 100 years.

THE CENTENARY HISTORY
OF
THE ARTHUR DUNN CUP

WRITTEN AND COMPILED

BY

DAVID ROY, IAN BEVAN & STUART HIBBERD

DESIGN AND PRESENTATION

BY

MICHAEL GILBERT WITH GEOFF KENTFIELD

ACKNOWLEDGEMENTS

We are grateful for the considerable assistance we have received from participating schools, former players and many others who have contributed to this book, with apologies and thanks to anyone we have omitted.

We are deeply indebted to the following for supplying either illustrations or information during our research:

Susan Andrew (Merton History Centre), David Barber (Football Association), Ned Boldero (Grandson of Arthur Dunn), Jennifer Booth (Rossallian Club), Martin Cannings (Ardingly College), Shirley Cork (Charterhouse), Dr N T Croally (Head of Classics, Dulwich College), Graham Dalling (Enfield Library – Local History Unit), Mark Dickson (Shrewsbury School), Wendy Doyle (Cambridge Family History Society), Christopher Gosling (Grandnephew of R C Gosling), Steve Handy, Penelope Hatfield (Archivist – Eton College), Mike Highstead (St Albans College), Kevin Kelly, Chris King (Sister of Donald Shearer), Ken Kiss (Crystal Palace Museum), David Lawrence (Sport England), Theodore Mallinson (Highgate), Tony Money (Radley College), Philip Morgan (Old Johnian Society), Timothy Morgan-Owen (Grandson of M M Morgan-Owen), Dr Jonathan Oates (Ealing Archivist), Brian Pearce, David Pearce (Berkhamsted College), Graham Peck (Ipswich College), Janet Pennington (Lancing College), Hugh Petrie (Barnet Archives), Norman Rosser (Malvern College), Karen Sampson (Group Archivist – Lloyd's Bank), Jane Sawyer (Granddaughter of Arthur Dunn), Ros and Mary Smalley (Kirby Lodge – Little Shelford), Mike Stones (Old Reptonian Society), Vince Taylor (Groundtastic), Eddie Smith (Westminster School), Mrs Suzie Rae (Winchester College), E Bruce Williams (Old Bradfieldian Society), Martin Williams (Hurstpierpoint College) and Cassandra Wright (Essex CCC).

We are also very grateful for the fantastic contributions received from:

Nigel Bennett (Lancing Old Boy), Richard Brightwell (Old Brightonian), Ian Brown-Peterside (Lancing Old Boy), Robin Burn (Old Eastbournian), Andrew Butler (Old Harrovian), George Chesterton (Old Malvernian), Mike Cockcroft (Old Reptonian), Mark Dickson (Old Etonian / Old Salopians FC), Hubert Doggart (Old Wykehamist), Mike Fawcett (Old Cranleighans), Francisco Ferrari (Old Millhillian), Mike Green (St Edmund's Canterbury Old Boy), Richard Hall (Old Aldenhamian), David Honychurch (Old Salopian), Chris Horne (Old Etonian), John Kilmartin (Old Brentwood), Giles King (Old Malvernian), Frixos Kyriacou (Old Cholmeleian), Bill Maddison (Old Forester), Simon Marriott (Old Wellingburian), Bertie Mawer (Old Witleian), Alastair Mercer (Lancing Old Boy), Keith Michel (Old Bradfieldian), David Miller (President, Old Carthusians FC), Guy Morgan (Old Cholmeleian), John Morley (Old Forester), Robin Moulsdale (Old Salopian), Russell Muir (Old Reptonian), Howard Olivere (Old Cholmeleian), Ian Payne (Old Reptonian), Richard Peck (Old Wellingburian), Oliver Pollard (Old Forester), Peter Rolfe (Old Reptonian), Ian Ryder-Smith (Old Malvernian), David Scrivener (Old Chigwellian), Malcolm Shepherd (Old Brentwood), Colin Smith (Old Forester), Chris Southgate (Old Citizens), Mark Stretton (Old Reptonian), Andrew Sweet (Old Chigwellian), Chris Sydenham (Old Chigwellian), Jeremy Tomlinson (Old Reptonian), Joe Ullman (Old Carthusian), Dale Vargas (Old Harrovian), Mike Wadsworth (Old Cholmeleian), Doug Wainwright (Old Cholmeleian), Tom Walker (Old Carthusian), Bruce Williams (Old Bradfieldian), Tony Williams (Old Malvernian), Michael Wills (Old Malvernian) and Fred Woolley (Old Harrovian).

A special tribute to David Roy for his dedication to the Arthur Dunn Cup and for his help, guidance and support during the production of this book. (Ian Bevan, Stuart Hibberd & Michael Gilbert).

Cover Design by Geoff Kentfield.
FRONT: OLD CARTHUSIANS 1949. BACK: OLD SALOPIANS 2003.

Published by

Replay Publishing Limited, 130 Aylesford Avenue, Beckenham, Kent BR3 3RY.

© David Roy, Ian Bevan, Stuart Hibberd & Michael Gilbert 2003.

Printed by
Cravitz Printing Company Limited, 1 Tower Hill, Brentwood, Essex CM14 4TA.

ISBN 0 9536663 1 X

CONTENTS

PRESIDENTS

1902	Lord Kinnaird (OLD ETONIAN)
1921	Norman Malcolmson (OLD ETONIAN)
1928	N V C Turner (OLD REPTONIAN)
1929	R T Squire (OLD WESTMINSTER)
1946	A G Bower (OLD CARTHUSIAN)
1963	A T Barber (OLD SALOPIAN)
1982	R Sale (OLD REPTONIAN)
1987	K F Boustred (OLD CHOLMELEIAN)

HON. SECRETARIES

1902	Norman Malcolmson (OLD ETONIAN)
1909	Hugh Hughes-Onslow (OLD ETONIAN)
1920	N V C Turner (OLD REPTONIAN)
1928	J Stewart (OLD BRADFIELDIAN)
1948	A R V Barker (OLD WYKEHAMIST)
1950	R S Blundell (OLD BRADFIELDIAN)
1973	J Sangster (OLD MALVERNIAN)
1976	D A Roy (OLD WESTMINSTER)

Foreword by JANE SAWYER
GRANDDAUGHTER OF THE LATE ARTHUR DUNN

I never met my grandfather, Arthur Dunn, but he has had a powerful influence on our family and undoubtedly on generations of amateur footballers. It is remarkable that the Cup competition that was set up in his name has now been going for 100 years.

It has been my privilege to present the Cup to the winning team for the last 44 years following a tradition started by my grandmother, Helen Dunn, and continued by my mother, Mary Shirley.

I am very pleased to see that the Centenary of the Arthur Dunn Cup is being marked by this publication which records my grandfather's short life, the establishment of the Cup, the participants and the history of the competition from 1902 to the present day.

David Roy has been a stalwart of the Arthur Dunn Committee for the last 27 years and without his dedication as secretary the competition would not be as successful as it undoubtedly is.

He and his collaborators, Ian Bevan, Michael Gilbert and Stuart Hibberd have compiled a comprehensive history which will no doubt bring back evocative memories of campaigns past.

Jane Sawyer

Introduction by *DAVID MILLER* <small>(PRESIDENT, OLD CARTHUSIANS FC)</small>

Sportsmanship is not yet dead. Some cynics and pessimists might argue to the contrary, supported by the evidence of many professional sports. We have drug cheats who corrupt the Olympic Games, and hardly a major football match passes without some conspicuous incident of attempted manipulation of the outcome by one or more wantonly expedient players. Yet sportsmanship and fair play are instinctive to human nature. The two-year-old playing "snap", the five-year-old playing draughts or the ten-year-old beginner at tennis, having to call the lines, spontaneously knows the difference between fair and unfair. As a traditional home for a century of honest play in football, the Arthur Dunn Cup competition is therefore as valid an example of honourable behaviour today as it was when it began in 1902/03 on the initiative of Arthur Tempest Blakiston Dunn, an Old Etonian who had been a prominent member of Cambridge University teams in the mid-1880s and subsequently the founder of Ludgrove Preparatory School. Sadly, he died prematurely after suggesting the idea to Norman Malcolmson, an old school colleague, who launched the competition in his memory.

Contemporary Dunn players conceding or taking advantage of penalty kicks, an ordinary enough occurrence, are unlikely to know that the advent of the penalty kick, originally proposed by the Irish Football Association in 1891, was a catalyst in the arrival of the Dunn Cup. The introduction of the new law, in conjunction with the absence of affiliation to a recognised competition by what were known as *"scratch"* teams, led to argument with The Football Association and deep resentment. Many die-hard amateurs regarded the principle of the penalty kick as an affront to the code of unspoken ethics in which they played the game. A penalty kick might be something necessary for stop-at-nothing professionals, but not to genuine amateurs – who, of course, had already implemented the formation of the FA Amateur Cup in 1894.

The rift between amateurs and professionals at the turn of the century was deep indeed, as witnessed by the lack of enthusiasm among the four British Associations for the creation of FIFA, from which international organisation they were later to withdraw for a while. Yet the separation of the gentleman old boys teams from the proletarian, increasingly powerful professional sides was to the long-term disadvantage of both. In spite of the limited success of Corinthian FC in the FA Cup for another decade or so, the amateurs had separated themselves from the rising technical level of the game, while the professional clubs tended to lose the restraining hand of the amateurs in matters regarding code of conduct.

For a while, the best of the amateurs could still command a place in the full national XIs of England, Scotland, Wales and Ireland. Such was the loyalty of some old-boy players to their team that they would even elect to play in the Dunn Cup rather than for England, as did Claude Ashton, one of three brothers for victorious Old Wykehamists, alongside Gilbert and Hubert, who in 1920 won the first of eight Dunn titles in fourteen finals. The inaugural final, played at Crystal Palace in 1903, ended in the title being shared, following a replay, between the Old Carthusians and Old Salopians, two clubs which, together with Old Malvernians and Old Reptonians have dominated the competition with double-figure victories each from their more than twenty final appearances.

If Dunn Cup football clung to old-fashioned manners, the clock has been put back in recent years, with players from the schools from which the competition evolves once again reaching international standard: Quinton Fortune of Forest and Frank Lampard of Brentwood, for example, though both left school for the professional ranks and respective full international caps with South Africa and England, before they could savour the rare exhilaration of Dunn Cup football.

Down the years there have been many notable players, from the Morgan-Owen brothers for Salopians, both Welsh internationals, and England's centre-half Charles Wreford-Brown and centre-forward G O Smith for Carthusians in that first final; the Ashtons for Wykehamists followed post WWII by Tony Pawson, England amateur international and the last amateur to play both first class football and cricket, for Charlton and Kent respectively; Howard Fabian, inside-forward for Cholmeleians pre-war in three losing finals and in a semi-final for Derby County in the FA Cup; Reg Vowells, England amateur international, for Brentwoods in their first of five titles in 1955; John Tanner, successor to G O Smith for Carthusians and match winner for Pegasus in the FA Amateur Cup triumph over Bishop Auckland in 1951; Robin Trimby of Foresters and Jan Illaszewicz of Malvernians. All of them have upheld the principle that, as much as the result, the game's the thing.

ARTHUR TEMPEST BLAKISTON DUNN WITH HIS FAMILY. LEFT TO RIGHT: ARTHUR HOLDS MARY, WIFE HELEN, MARGERY AND LAYING DOWN IN FRONT JOHN.

Chapter 1

ARTHUR DUNN

Keen, keen, keen, keen! Arthur Dunn was keen on sport, keen on games, keen on singing and keenest on all his friends, unceasing in his efforts - a human dynamo! But who was this Arthur Dunn? After all, for the majority, he is completely unknown. Yet, we have been remembering his name in the Cup competition now for 100 years. Well, Arthur Dunn was simply the finest and most accomplished footballer of the 1880s.

Arthur Tempest Blakiston Dunn was born in Whitby, North Yorkshire on 12th August 1861. He was descended from the Tempests, who gave their name to the House of Londonderry and from the Blakistons, who were owners of coalmines.

His mother, Helen Bowen, was the daughter of the Vicar of West Lynn. His father, John Dunn, was a mathematics professor at Cambridge University and hence the family settled at Little Shelford, five miles south of Cambridge.

EDUCATION

When he was old enough, although his parents struggled to pay the fees, he went to Eton. He joined Tarver's House for the Michaelmas term in 1874 and stayed until the summer of 1878. Though diminutive in stature relative to his peers, Arthur was actively involved in sports, particularly football, and deserved the award of his House colours. He was also academically capable, though less interested, and went on to Cambridge University.

At Cambridge, he was more interested in socialising and sport than academic study, and much to the disappointment of his father, gained only a third class honours degree. At football, however, he excelled and played for the University. He never lost his attachment for his old school and if ever there was a conflict of interest between the University team and Old Etonians, it was always the school that claimed his services.

OLD ETONIANS

This was the era when the amateur teams could still match the professionals. In 1879 Old Etonians won the FA Cup defeating Clapham Rovers by 1 - 0. It was reported that at the match Canon Norman Pares, who had played with Arthur for Tarver's at Eton, was recruited from among the spectators to take the place of a missing player!

Three years after leaving Eton, Arthur was considered proficient, if not large enough, to play first-class football. When he appeared for Old Etonians in a match against Clapham Rovers, there was an enquiry whether a boy still at school could play for the Old Etonians!

The following year, in 1882, Arthur was playing for the Old Etonians in a famous Cup Final, when they defeated the mighty Blackburn Rovers. The Daily Telegraph reported on 31st March 1882

"... a most determined rush was made by the light blue forwards and, Dunn conducting the ball skillfully down the ground passed it to Anderson who sent it between the posts. This feat was greeted with the most deafening cheers".

In the opinion of N L "Pa" Jackson: *"Arthur practically won the tie against Blackburn Rovers with a lovely centre all along the ground".*

Old Etonians were not so successful in the 1883 final against Blackburn Olympic. Early on, Arthur Dunn sustained a knee injury, and so the Etonians had to carry on with ten men. It was a draw at full-time but Kinnaird (the Old Etonian captain) had already agreed that extra time would be played (to save the Blackburn club the additional expense of a second trip to the Oval). So, 30 more minutes were played with Blackburn Olympic getting the winning goal.

In the Press, it was said that *"Dunn, until injured, played a capital game and it is undoubtedly to his absence that the Etonians owe their defeat".*

LEFT: ATBD A CLASSIC PORTRAIT.

BELOW: SCHOOLBOY ARTHUR AT ETON.

LEFT: 'KIRBY LODGE' THE DUNNS' HOUSE IN LITTLE SHELFORD. A PHOTOGRAPH FROM THE FAMILY ALBUM TAKEN IN THE 1880S, AND BELOW THE HOUSE TODAY.

BELOW: THE OLD ETONIANS IN THE 1880S.

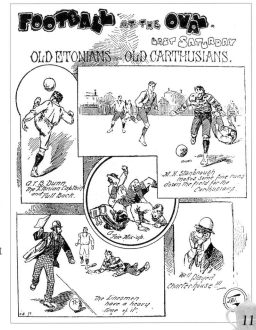

ARTHUR TEACHES AT ELSTREE

When Arthur left Cambridge he initially became a tutor for the Dunville family in Ireland and then he accepted the post as a master at Elstree school under Rev Lancelot Sanderson. *"These were happy and strenuous days for a young Master who was also playing for England. To keep fit, Arthur began systematically to over-train. As though daily games were insufficient he used to get up early and cover long tracts before morning school"* (Shane Leslie).

FOOTBALL ACHIEVEMENTS

Arthur spent seven happy years at Elstree and his football career was uninterrupted. He collected three volumes of press cuttings that preserve the scores and details of long-forgotten games. He played in over 500 matches and was constantly being mentioned in the match reports of the time. In 1886, he played outside right for the Corinthians when they beat Newcastle and Everton and drew with Middlesbrough. Playing for St Albans on November 23, 1887, he made a famous kick *"from almost the boundary line and to the utter astonishment of all the onlookers the ball went between the posts"*.

RIGHT: ARTHUR AND A COLLEAGUE, DEMONSTRATING THE TACKLE. (FROM A GUIDEBOOK ON ASSOCIATION FOOTBALL IN THE BADMINTON SERIES, PUBLISHED IN 1896).

"Dunn at full back gained a hearty cheer when he headed the ball out from under the goal, the goalkeeper having for a moment deserted his post".

men of easy and gentlemanly demeanour and they found their captain a very sociable companion".

Even as his football career was coming to an end, his exploits were still being reported. In 1892, Old Etonians were again grateful for his presence when, in a game against the Crusaders,

He played in the opening game at the Queen's Club ground when the Corinthians defeated Oxford University and in such obscure contests as London versus Sheffield and the South against the North.

At the end of 1888, the Old Etonians played five matches in six days. The Press asked *"how many goals will Dunn obtain?"*. Against the Household Brigade, he scored seven out of nine. In the game against Clapham Rovers, the ball burst and they used a rugby ball during the second half.

He played three times for England against Ireland; he also captained England against Wales and Scotland. Against Scotland, he (an amateur) once captained a team of ten professionals and the Press recorded that *"it was thought that his position would be irksome, but, as it happened, these particular professionals turned out to be*

Yet, he never basked in the glory of these occasions. In fact, it was characteristic of his sporting modesty that he slipped away one morning without telling his wife that he was going to captain England.

His last appearance in a big match was in a team of Old Internationals against Charterhouse at Queen's Club. Typically, he scored both the goals for his side.

ARTHUR DUNN THE CRICKETER

Arthur was an all-round sportsman and was a particularly good cricketer; he was a *"neat and determined left-handed bat and a fast round-arm bowler"*. With more time and opportunity for practice, he would certainly have appeared in first-class cricket and played with the greats of his day – W G Grace, C B Fry, etc.

Nevertheless, he did find time to raise the fortunes of the local Little Shelford cricket team, even coaching them to victory over the County of Cambridge. Once, on a tour in Ireland he related how he once took five wickets in an over, when overs contained five balls.

BELOW: A PHOTOGRAPH FROM THE SAME BOOK SHOWS ARTHUR DEMONSTRATING ADVANCING INTO THE PENALTY BOX. (GOALMOUTH MARKINGS WERE INTRODUCED IN 1892 IN THE SHAPE OF TWO SEMI-CIRCLES SIX YARDS FROM THE GOAL, THIS WAS CHANGED IN 1902 TO THE RECTANGULAR MARKINGS WE HAVE TODAY.

LUDGROVE SCHOOL

Arthur greatly enjoyed his time at Elstree but there was a problem. Elstree prepared boys chiefly for Harrow, and Arthur believed that his true vocation would be to prepare boys for Eton. So, with the help of Mrs Sanderson, he found a promising site for a new school at Ludgrove on the Bevan estate at Cockfosters. In May 1892, he opened the school with T R Pelly as his only pupil. He soon acquired five more, and with limited funds he recruited three maids and one assistant master, Henry Hale. By now he had married the love of his life, Helen Malcolmson, who proved a staunch support to him. Many of the traditions from Elstree were transferred to Ludgrove; Ludgrove life included *"some enjoyment of boyhood. Keenness was taught as a subject and games were given full scope. It was something to be taught football by a captain of England"*.

He was intolerant of leisure for himself or others. On the walls at Ludgrove there was a text from the ninth chapter of Ecclesiastes, which summed up his attitude:
"Whatsoever thy hand findeth to do, do it with all thy might; for there is no work, nor device, nor knowledge, nor wisdom; in the grave whither thou goest".

Any boy or even master not automatically keen was classed as a "scug", and he was banished to a corner in the school yard. Arthur was not satisfied unless they glowed in all weathers.

LEFT: LUDGROVE SCHOOL AT COCKFOSTERS.

ABOVE: LUDGROVE SCHOOL IN 1902.

BELOW: LUDGROVE TODAY.

LEFT: THE MASTERS AT LUDGROVE IN 1901 INCLUDED G O SMITH, SEATED FAR LEFT AND W J OAKLEY, STANDING BEHIND AD (SEATED) IN THE CENTRE.

Ten happy years passed; Arthur and Helen were blessed with three children – John, Margery and Mary. Gradually however, Arthur could play less football and he confided to friends that he wished that he had given his time to cricket which one can play into middle-age.

BELOW: LUDGROVE PUPILS AND MASTERS, POSE FOR THE SCHOOL PHOTOGRAPH IN 1901.

ARTHUR DUNN, THE MAN

RIGHT: ARTHUR AS A YOUNG MAN WITH HIS GRANDFATHER T DUNN.

One of his first pupils at Ludgrove (Shane Leslie) describes him thus: *"His small head was finely set. He would have given Michelangelo an ideal model for his stripling David.*

His proportions were like chiseled ivory and all of one piece. No limb seemed to have been added as an afterthought.

BELOW: ARTHUR PHOTOGRAPHED WEARING ENGLAND STRIP.

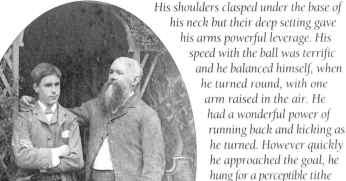

His shoulders clasped under the base of his neck but their deep setting gave his arms powerful leverage. His speed with the ball was terrific and he balanced himself, when he turned round, with one arm raised in the air. He had a wonderful power of running back and kicking as he turned. However quickly he approached the goal, he hung for a perceptible tithe of time to direct aim.

Overtaking was a remarkable feature of his play. He delighted in pursuing a fast forward and parting him from the ball at full speed".

Apparently, he was a fierce tackler, and yet he was severely injured only three times - against Blackburn Olympic in that 1883 final, against Bolton playing for the Corinthians in 1885, and against the North playing for the South in 1887. This was a remarkable record for one playing two or three matches per week for eleven years against every type of player.

He was reputed to have a beautiful singing voice but he had little literary interest. Apart from the Bible, he supposedly regarded the reading of a novel in an armchair as *"the rank and rotten in behaviour".*

ARTHUR'S EARLY DEATH

The workload at Ludgrove was intense because Arthur bore total responsibility for the school. He did all the administration; he taught in class and he joined in the football. *"He floated and swerved round the school like a falcon unceasingly".* He was wearing himself down.

He lived on his nerves (he was constantly in fear of a fire at the school) and by the end of each term he was always utterly exhausted. It is not surprising that he became irritable sometimes, but it is that nervous energy which drove him to *"electrify"* the Masters and the boys.

His happiest days were those when the Old Boys returned from Eton to play the school. The first Old Boys' match marked the opening of the new ground at Ludgrove in 1896.

Arthur enjoyed only five more Old Boys' matches. On February 18th 1902, he played a game of hockey on the ice at Trent Park, the hospitable home of the Bevan family. For the first time in his life, he had complained that he felt slow; others had noticed this as well. The next day was to be his last. He spent it in London with a parent, Colonel Kenyon Slaney MP, who took him to the House of Commons. He returned to Ludgrove very tired but not too tired to visit "Jo" (G O) Smith, who was ill in bed in the Cottage. *"One captain of England was saying farewell to another that night, though neither knew it".*

Arthur went to bed without saying how badly he felt. At eleven o'clock, his wife got up and opened a window. During those few moments that she was away from his side he sighed deeply and died.

Two days after his death, the Inter-varsity football match was played at Queen's Club. Arthur's name was printed on the match card as an official; he had intended to act as a linesman. The Cambridge eleven and the Oxford captain wore mourning bands in his memory. It was a tribute never given before or since.

The Times said:
"it would be difficult to find another man of his age and position whose premature loss has been more widely and genuinely mourned".

A memorial service, attended by the boys and staff of the school, was held at Christchurch, Cockfosters. Later that day, Arthur Dunn was buried in his home village of Little Shelford, Cambridgeshire.

Among those at the graveside were Lord and Lady Kinnaird, Messrs G O Smith and W J Oakley (who jointly took over the headship at Ludgrove) and R C Gosling.

Floral tributes were received from Cambridge University AFC, Old Etonians FC, Old Foresters FC, Old Carthusians FC, Eton Ramblers, Charterhouse football and cricket elevens, the Casuals FC, Forest school, and the executive committee of the Navy League.

LEFT: ARTHUR RELAXES IN THE GARDEN AT LUDGROVE.

BELOW: ALL SAINTS, LITTLE SHELFORD, CAMBRIDGESHIRE.

LUDGROVE. *Arthur Dunn acquired Ludgrove from the Bevan family in 1892. Here, the school grew and developed. He started with just one pupil, T R Pelly, but by the time Dunn died in 1902, the school had a waiting list for the next eleven years. Dunn had recruited a number of able and famous footballers to help him with the running of the school, notably Henry Hale. Later, he was joined by G O Smith and W J Oakley, both famous Corinthians and England players.*

When Dunn died so tragically, Smith and Oakley took over the running of the school, assisted by Frank Henly. This team carried on through the First World War, though the numbers were down.

After the War, G O retired and W J took over as headmaster. In 1929, W J's godson and nephew, Tim Shaw arrived after his time at Oxford. He soon enticed a friend, A T Barber to do the same. Alan Barber had been captain of cricket and soccer at Oxford, and captained Yorkshire CCC in the summer of 1930, and in that autumn he joined the staff at Ludgrove.

The school was thriving again but there were problems on the horizon. The expansion of the underground system and the subsequent suburban sprawl meant that Ludgrove was in danger of being swamped. So thoughts turned to moving the school to a more rural location.

A school called Wixenford, near Wokingham, Berkshire was soon identified as a possible target and an amalgamation was mooted. But it was only after considerable negotiation and refurbishment that the 131 acre site was rented and Ludgrove arrived in September 1937 (the Wixenford name was dropped and the boys became part of the Ludgrove complement).

By this time, W J had retired (1934) and then Frank Henly, who had taken over, gave up the post in 1937. So Tim Shaw and Alan Barber took the school to its new home and these two ran the school through the Second World War and up until the late 1960s. (Shaw retired in 1968 and Barber in 1972).

At this time, the School and surrounding acres were bought and the business was turned into a charitable trust with a board of Governors – there were now 128 boys at the School. When A T B retired, his son Gerald and an Oxford friend, Nichol Marston became joint heads and Gerald still runs the school to this day.

The Arthur Dunn traditions live on. There is still inter-house football when the whole of one house (35 boys) take on the whole of another, with three footballs in play at once and three referees. The final of this is the highlight of the Christmas term. There is also an annual dribbling competition which each boy has to enter. There are three age groups and a Cup is awarded to the best senior dribbler of the year. Arthur Dunn would have been proud indeed!

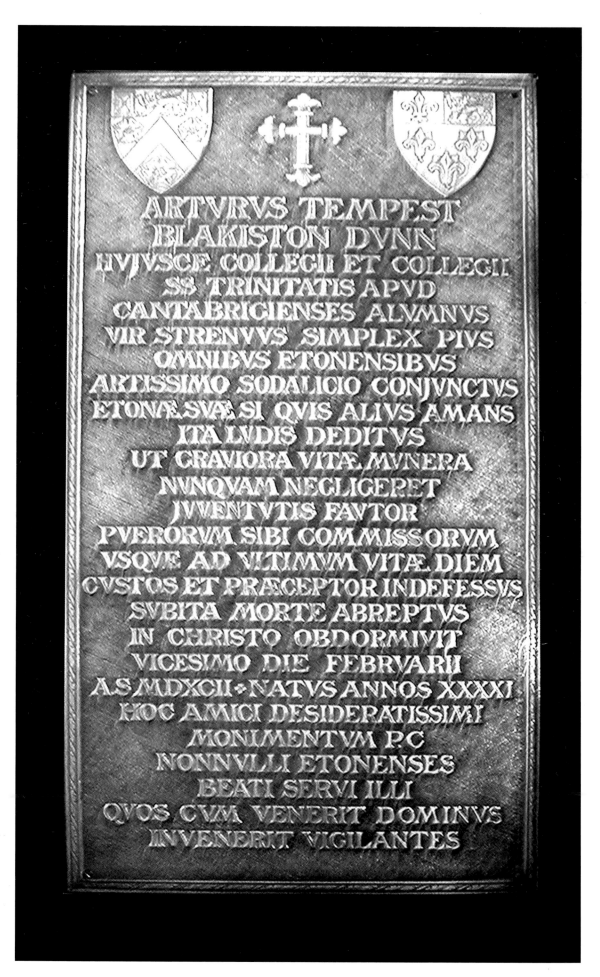

THE PLAQUE DEDICATED TO ARTHUR DUNN IN THE CHAPEL AT ETON.

ARTHUR TEMPEST BLAKISTON DUNN

**An alumnus of this college
and of the college of the holy Trinity[1]
in Cambridge.
An energetic, straightforward and pious man.
Joined in the most elaborate friendship
with all Etonians.
No other person of his Eton,
lovingly so dedicated himself to games
that he might never neglect
the more desirable gifts of life.[2]
A supporter of youth,
a guardian and indefatigable teacher
of the boys in his care
right up to the last day of his life.
Taken away by a sudden death
he went to sleep in Christ
on the 20th day of February
1902,[3] at the age of 41.
Some Etonians ensured the building of
this monument[4] for a much beloved friend.
Happy are those servants whom the Lord
finds awake when he comes[5].**

1. The abbreviation SS (line 2) stands, for 'sanctissimi' (most holy). This is Trinity College.
2. This is the only sensible way to translate this phrase, which literally means 'If any other person ...' but with no main clause.
3. The abbreviation A.S. stands for 'anno salvatoris' (in the year of the saviour). The date has been inscribed as MDXCII (1592) it should be MCMII (1902).
4. The abbreviation P.C. stands for 'ponendum curaverunt' which literally means: 'took care to be placed'.
5. This final couplet is a quotation from Mark's gospel.

Translated by
Dr. N T Croally (Head of Classics, Dulwich College).

ARTHUR TEMPEST BLAKISTON DUNN.

BORN, AUGUST 12TH, 1861.
DIED, FEBRUARY 20TH, 1902.

This must indeed be a sad number of Ludgrove "Notes." "Ten years ago next May, Mr. Dunn started with one boy: when he died he left an entry list full to overflowing till 1911." That is a brief, but telling account of his work at Ludgrove. When the terrible blow first fell on the school, one was reminded forcibly of the well-known lines :-

> *All within is dark as night:*
> *In the windows is no light:*
> *And no murmur at the door,*
> *So frequent on its hinge before.*
>
> *Close the door, the shutters close,*
> *Or thro' the windows we shall see*
> *The nakedness and vacancy*
> *Of the dark, deserted house.*

It seemed as if Ludgrove without Mr. Dunn was an impossibility. But the grand old motto, "Think and Thank" is well illustrated by such a case as this, and, during this period of trial, there has been much for which to be thankful. Second thoughts suggested that such a work, begun and developed but not nearly completed, must be continued. So Ludgrove is still to go on, always depending, it is hoped, on what has been so well described in a letter from a parent as the "Arthur Dunn Tradition." With Masters, Boys, and Members of the Household all combining to keep the machine in motion, and encouraged by Masters and Old Boys at Eton, time has been afforded for arrangements to be made. Mention, too, must be made of the cordial support so readily given by Parents. Now one thinks of the bright outlook, which will, however, always have a shadow thrown on it by a cloud that can never be entirely effaced. And yet this cloud may have its silver lining, and may serve as a constant reminder of the noble example that has been set, and of that beautiful text, which has been so happily described as Mr. Dunn's life motto: "Whatsoever thy hand findeth to do, do it with thy might." Beautiful appreciations of Mr. Dunn have appeared. There is no necessity to add more; but this is perhaps a fitting opportunity for expressing the sincere and heartfelt gratitude of all at Ludgrove for the ever-ready, helpful, tactful kindness shown to them by Mrs. Dunn. It is their fervent wish that she may in due time receive comfort, and they feel that no greater solace could be afforded her than the knowledge that they will strive to advance in that direction to which their beloved master and friend himself would have pointed.

THE OBITUARY REPRODUCED ABOVE, WAS PUBLISHED IN THE LUDGROVE SCHOOL MAGAZINE IN THE SUMMER OF 1902.

Dear N.
one might write for ever on this. I think golf is partly responsible, but largely so because one has to play such a lot of hoppers.

There's nothing in it but an 'Old Boy' association, but who has the time to start it?

Yours
A T B Dunn

THE ARTHUR DUNN CHALLENGE CUP. (INSET) ARTHUR DUNN'S NOTE TO NORMAN MALCOLMSON IN 1901.

THE CHALLENGE CUP

On 12th October 1901 an article appeared in a newspaper headed *"Amateur Clubs and the English Cup"*. It began: *"It has been said that amateur football is on the decline, that it is not what it was, and that its ultimate insignificance is, in fact, merely a matter of time"*. This reflected the growing impression that amateur football was doomed and when Arthur Dunn read this, he was so moved that he wrote a brief note to another Old Etonian, Norman Malcolmson, as follows:

Dear N,

One might write for ever on this. I think golf is partly responsible, but largely so because one has to play such a lot of hoppers.

There's nothing for it but an "Old Boy" association, but who has the time to start it?

Yours, ATBD

Arthur did not have time to follow this thought through but on March 12th 1902, just three weeks after his untimely death, an informal meeting of Old Boys interested in amateur football was convened by Norman Malcolmson and held at the Sports Club. At this meeting the following resolutions were passed:

1. That, in the opinion of this Meeting, an annual competition, under Association Rules, in the form of a cup contest, confined to the representatives of the chief Public Schools, is desirable;

2. That a trophy, to be called *"The Arthur Dunn Memorial Cup"*, or by some such title, be provided for competition, to be held by the winners for one year;

3. That the following schools be invited to appoint one representative to act on the General Committee: *Bradfield, Brighton, Charterhouse, Eton, Felsted, Forest, Harrow, Lancing, Malvern, Radley, Repton, Rossall, Shrewsbury, Westminster and Winchester, the competition to be for the Old Boys of the above schools.*

Those present also expressed the view that any surplus profits from the competition should be given to charity.

This informal meeting was followed, three weeks later, by a formal one, at which the chair was taken by no less a figure than C. Wreford-Brown, a pillar of the Corinthians and capped four times for England in full internationals. The motions passed by the informal meeting were unanimously confirmed, and then officers were elected as follows:

President: Lord Kinnaird (Eton). *Vice-Presidents:* R C Guy (Forest), R C Gosling (Eton). *Committee:* R T Squire (Westminster), G O Smith (Charterhouse), W J Oakley (Shrewsbury), C Wreford-Brown (Charterhouse), R E Foster (Malvern), W M Cowan (Brighton), J R Mason (Winchester). *Hon. Secretary:* N Malcolmson.

C WREFORD-BROWN - OLD CARTHUSIAN

Charles Wreford-Brown was one of a dynasty that had a continual presence at Charterhouse for over a century.

Like so many of his generation, Charles was a genuine all-rounder. At Charterhouse, he captained the cricket as well as the football elevens, and after he had been awarded his Blue for cricket as well as for football, only a badly split finger kept him out of the Varsity match at Lords. This let in Lord George Scott who retained his place. While at Oxford, it is claimed that he invented the word "soccer" to distinguish the kicking game from other versions.

During his England days in the 1890s, at centre-back, his tireless tackling and scientific feeding of his forwards made him outstanding among such masters of that position as John Holt of Everton, Tom Crawshaw of Sheffield Wednesday and James Crabtree of Aston Villa.

When Arthur Dunn died, and Norman Malcolmson was promoting the idea of a memorial trophy, it was to Charles Wreford-Brown that he turned for support and Charles was very much involved in the setting-up of the competition. He then played in the first three finals for the victorious Old Carthusians. On two of these occasions, his brother, O E, was in the same team.

He went on to become a leading administrator of the game, being prominent in the formation of the AFA and latterly becoming Chairman of the Football Association.

He was manager of the 1936 England Olympic team, and forbade them to give the "Nazi Salute".

During the next few weeks a special committee drew up the rules of the competition (See part four). Meanwhile, the actual trophy was presented by R C Gosling; and thus, within 14 weeks of Dunn's death, the vision had become a reality. Six months later the Arthur Dunn Challenge Cup competition was well and truly launched, the schools taking part in the first season being:

Bradfield, Brighton, Charterhouse, Eton, Felsted, Forest, Harrow, Lancing, Malvern, Repton, Rossall, Shrewsbury, Westminster and Winchester.

Radley College decided not to participate at this stage.

ROBERT CUNLIFFE GOSLING - OLD ETONIAN

Well over six feet in height and weighing nearly thirteen stone, Robert Cunliffe Gosling left his mark at both inside-right and inside-left, with his speed, passing and shooting from all angles that underline the dribbling skill he had acquired from Eton's Field Game. He was one of five Gosling brothers (picture above) who attended Eton at the same time.

His unselfishness and finesse no doubt gave him the wonderful knack of knowing how to keep his line together, a quality which England's selectors recognised when they picked him for his first international against Wales in 1892. He played in five internationals and captained the side in his last – against Scotland in 1895. It was said that he was "the richest man who ever played for England at the side of a professional". Of course, Gosling generously donated the trophy for which the teams compete in the Arthur Dunn each year.

LORD KINNAIRD (1847-1923) - OLD ETONIAN 1ST ARTHUR DUNN CUP PRESIDENT

Alfred Kinnaird was one of the most influential pioneers in the early history of the Football Association. Tall and bearded, Kinnaird was highly respected as a player, taking part in an unsurpassed total of 9 FA Cup Finals and winning 5 Cup winners' medals (with Wanderers and Old Etonians). Subsequently, he became a prominent member of the FA, rising eventually to the post of president. His unique contribution to the game was marked in 1911 when the second FA Cup itself was given to him.

Lord Kinnaird was made the first president of the Arthur Dunn Cup competition in 1902 but was forced to relinquish this post temporarily when the split between the professionals and the amateurs made his position tantamount to a conflict of interest. The breach healed, he returned and held the post until 1921.

Matches were played over a period of 5 months culminating in a final to be held in March 1903. After initially considering an offer to host the final from Queen's Club, Kensington, it was eventually decided to accept an offer from the Crystal Palace Company to hold the final on the FA Cup Final ground at the Crystal Palace. The net receipts were shared between the Crystal Palace Company and the Arthur Dunn competition.

By process of elimination, the two teams left to fight out the final on 28 March 1903 were Old Carthusians and Old Salopians. In a keen and close game, the result was a draw (2 - 2) even after 20 minutes extra time and it was decided to replay at Ealing on Wednesday April 1st. Coincidentally, this game too ended in a 2 - 2 draw, and so it was then decided that the cup should be held jointly by these two clubs, six months each.

THE FIRST SEASON

FAR RIGHT: THE FRONT AND BACK OF M M MORGAN-OWEN'S OLD SALOPIAN MEDAL, COMMEMORATING THE 1903 INAUGURAL FINAL.

The draw for the first round of the competition was made at the Committee Meeting at City University Club on Thursday 25th September 1902 and published on October 1st as follows:

Old Rossallians	v	Old Felstedians
Old Salopians	v	Old Harrovians
Old Etonians	v	Old Foresters
Old Carthusians	v	Lancing Old Boys
Old Reptonians	v	Old Westminsters
Old Brightonians	v	Old Wykehamists

Old Malvernians and Bradfield Waifs (Old Bradfieldians) each received a bye through to the second round. The venues for each game were to be decided by the teams drawn first.

Among the famous players taking part in this memorable final were the Morgan-Owen brothers for Old Salopians, both full Welsh internationals, while the Old Carthusians included the Wreford-Brown brothers and the incomparable G O Smith.

This result was a foretaste of the next 50 years, for in the period from 1903 to 1955 these two clubs between them appeared in 29 of the 40 finals and won 22 of them.

From the beginning, the Old Carthusians dominated the scene, winning outright five of the first eight finals.

RIGHT: OLD CARTHUSIANS JOINT HOLDERS 1903.

(back row)
O T NORRIS, CAPT W SIMPSON, C H WILD, C F RYDER, A R HAIG-BROWN, T S ROWLANDSON.

(front row)
O E WREFORD-BROWN, W U TIMMIS, W F H STANBROUGH, G O SMITH, C WREFORD-BROWN, M H STANBROUGH.

THE ARTHUR DUNN CUP.

The competition, instituted as a memorial to the late Mr. A. T. B. Dunn, reached its final stage on Saturday when, at the Crystal Palace, the Old Carthusians and Old Salopians met and played a drawn game, each scoring two goals. In a bright, interesting match, there was little to choose between the teams, which contained many famous University and international players. Strong defence marked the play throughout, the backs kicking with wonderful accuracy considering the wet ball and slippery turf. Up to half-time heavy rain caused a further hindrance to good football, while the wind always blew strongly down the ground. As the game progressed the weather improved, and the work of both teams became better, the combination among the forwards reaching a high standard during the 20 minutes extra time that was played in the hope that a deciding goal might be obtained. G. E. Wilkinson and T. S. Rowlandson, the goalkeepers, did well, the former's smart saves in the first half and late in the game being largely responsible for the Old Salopians averting defeat; for the splendid fight they made H. A. Lowe, M. Morgan-Owen, and J. D. Craig, the half-backs, were chiefly responsible. They tackled splendidly, and constantly broke up the attacks made by the strong Carthusian forwards—M. H. Stanbrough, C. F. Ryder, G. O. Smith, W. F. H. Stanbrough, and A. R. Haigh-Brown. G. O. Smith showed much of his former skill in passing and shooting, and Ryder dribbled and shot splendidly. The Salopians' forwards occasionally combined cleverly, and H. Morgan-Owen opened the game beneficially for his wing men. In this way the first goal was scored. H. N. Edwards took a long pass from the centre, and, after a smart run down the left, shot a fine goal. Haigh-Brown equalized through an error of the goalkeeper, who ran out and missed his kick, the Corinthian merely having to run through the goal with the ball. Before half time H. Morgan-Owen got another splendid goal for the Old Salopians. He took a long pass by J. S. D. Rider, and scored with a hard left-foot shot. Nearly half an hour had elapsed in the second half before Ryder got the second goal for the Carthusians, and there was a most exciting struggle for a winning point. C. L. Alexander once almost scored, but on the whole the Salopians had to do most of the defending, and in the latter part of the extra time they were very hard pressed. About 1,000 people watched the match, which, it is expected, will be replayed on Wednesday, April 8. Captain Simpson was referee.

CRYSTAL PALACE GROUND (1903)

The original Crystal Palace was of course built to house the Great Exhibition of 1851. After the Exhibition closed, the building was moved to a new site in South London and became the focal point of a "theme park", opened in 1854.

ABOVE: THE CRYSTAL PALACE, CUP FINAL FOOTBALL GROUND.

FAR LEFT: THE REPORT OF THE 1903 FINAL FROM THE *TIMES*. NOTE THAT THE REPLAY ACTUALLY TOOK PLACE ON APRIL 1ST.

The football ground was created in 1894 when two large fountain basins in Crystal Palace Park were filled in and turned to grass to form a vast sports arena. One half of this area was turned into a football ground and in 1895 this became the venue for the FA Cup Final. This continued for 20 years until the outbreak of the First World War.

The Crystal Palace Company attracted many other footballing and sporting activities to Crystal Palace Park. When the Arthur Dunn competition was first organised, the Company offered the use of the ground for the first Arthur Dunn Final provided the proceeds were shared. This was agreed by the Arthur Dunn Committee.

ABOVE: W G GRACE WAS A SPECTATOR AT THE FIRST FINAL.

LEFT: OLD SALOPIANS JOINT HOLDERS 1903.

(back row)
W J OAKLEY, P JOHNSON, C L ALEXANDER, J D CRAIG, J S D RIDER, H N EDWARDS.

(front row)
H MORGAN-OWEN, H A LOWE, M M MORGAN-OWEN, G E WILKINSON, C W ALEXANDER, S EVANS.

DID YOU KNOW?
*"OWING TO THE BOAT RACE,
WHICH, BY THE WAY SEEMED A
RATHER INADEQUATE REASON, THE
START WAS DELAYED UNTIL FIVE
O'CLOCK. NO OPPORTUNITY
REMAINED FOR EXTRA TIME, IT BEING
ALREADY HALF PAST SIX WHEN CAPT.
SIMPSON BLEW HIS WHISTLE".*

EALING FC GROUND
(1903 REPLAY & 1911)

The exact location of the ground at Ealing is not known.

The Ealing Football Association was formed in the 1890s and used a pitch on Ealing Common.

From 1894, several grounds to the north of Gunnersbury Lane were used. It is likely therefore that the Arthur Dunn Cup replay in 1903 and the 1911 final were played on one of the pitches in this location.

THE FIRST ARTHUR DUNN CUP FINAL REPLAY
by F. J. Kittermaster

Wednesday April 1st found a goodly number of Old Boys from Shrewsbury and Charterhouse assembled at the Ealing F.C. ground to witness the replaying of the match which had ended in a draw of 2 goals all on the previous Saturday. The ground was wet and heavy after several hours rain, and we prophesied inferior play and prepared to make excuses for any short comings. Never were prophets so wide of the mark. Both sides showed extraordinary form all the way through, and the pace of the game was tremendously fast. Many of us O.S.s who were looking on were strangers to one another, but that there were plenty of us who "thought the things of Shrewsbury" was evident when the shouting began. It was like a Challenge Match on Kingsland, and I think the cries of "Shrewsbury" and "Charterhouse" were about as evenly matched as the two teams.

From the very start it was evident that G.O. Smith was in great form and that, once he was within reach of our goal, we should have an anxious time of it. Time after time he set his wings going with himself, as he alone knows how to do, and time after time our backs pulled them up in beautiful style. To prevent a goal being scored for 20 minutes against such passing as the Carthusians showed was no mean feat. Then "G.O." after some tricky play obtained just the extra second that he wanted, of which some of us knew by experience, and high in the right-hand corner of the net flew the ball. But during this time the Carthusians had not by any means had the game all their own way: our forwards had many openings made for them by the halves, and any number of good runs were made: but unfortunately everything - even the good corners kicked by Ryder - just went wrong at the critical moment. So the game went on, fast and evenly fought, till half-time. We had two uncomfortable alarms, once when W.F. Stanbrough shot through but was given offside, and again when another shot at close quarters seemed bound to score but Wilkinson pounced upon it with his left hand and pinned it to the ground, just against the goal-post - a magnificent save.

The Carthusians went off with a rush after the interval, and in less than a minute had scored again. G.O. Smith was almost facing his own goal when he received a short pass: he was round and had shot hard into the net in far less time than it takes to describe. Then there was much despondency, as Xenophon has said. But it seemed to have no discouraging effect on the O.S. team: they continued to play the same hard persevering game as before. "I don't think much of Craig" said another O.S. to me at the beginning of the match. "You wait a bit," I answered. We did not wait in vain. Though Craig was not so good as M. Morgan-Owen and Lowe in the first half, he afterwards played splendidly, both in attack and defence, and it was from him that came the dribble and centre which gave H. Morgan-Owen his chance: and how the latter used his opportunity a wild Salopian cheer soon showed. But there was a still wilder one to come a few minutes afterwards, when another good centre by Craig put the ball right in front of the Charterhouse goal and C.W. Alexander managed to get it into the net. It is not the part of a wise man to break his own umbrella, but there was an excuse for it, wasn't there? Did the echo of that shout reach you at Shrewsbury, I wonder?

There is little more to add: the game went on to the end in the same ding-dong fashion, both sides trying hard to score again. Perhaps it was too much to hope for a further success: at any rate the score of two all gives an excellent idea of the day's play. Such was the end of one of the very best games I have ever witnessed. Every man on the side played well: the full-backs were wonderfully steady and safe, and forwards all showed cleverness and dash. But without grudging them the praise they deserve, it was the half-back trio that pulled us through: their play was very near faultless. Craig I have already mentioned. M. Morgan-Owen, though suffering from a chill, was indefatigable and gave G.O. Smith no rest. Lowe led his forwards beautifully and emerged successfully from many tussles with Haig-Brown, both in tackling and sprinting. Wilkinson - but then you all know Wilkinson. In goal si recte, ne labora.

In conclusion allow me to congratulate the O.S. Football Club on its formation, its formers and the form it has shown in its first season, and to hope that its subsequent career may be as successful as its beginning. And that, of course, depends on you who are still at Shrewsbury.

WILLIAM J OAKLEY - OLD SALOPIAN

Oakley did not have the typical physique for a back; he was built for speed rather than for resistance. His speed would have helped his back-play but it was his judgment and his pluck that set him apart from his contemporaries. It is said that "when he went out to meet a forward he knew precisely what he was to do…". And in a match for England against Scotland at Celtic Park, he sustained a head injury. Yet he continued even though he was so concussed that, at the end, he did not know the result of the game (England lost heavily!).

Oakley played for Old Salopians but due to an injury had already retired from playing by the time the Arthur Dunn Cup was started. He did however continue as coach to the team and is shown with the team in the photograph before the 1903 final.

Like his friend G O Smith, Oakley played for Corinthians and England, and he joined the staff at Dunn's Ludgrove School. When Dunn died so tragically, G O and W J Oakley shared the responsibilities of running the school. When G O retired after the First World War, W J assumed sole control and remained headmaster until he too retired in 1934. Tragically, he died in a car accident shortly after.

DISPUTE WITH THE FOOTBALL ASSOCIATION

Unfortunately, during this opening season, an acrimonious conflict arose between the Arthur Dunn Competition and the Football Association. Firstly, the FA alleged that the referees in the Arthur Dunn competition were not officially registered. Secondly, the Arthur Dunn clubs objected to FA rule relating to the penalty kick; they regarded it as being contrary to their code of conduct.

There was also a demand by the FA that all Arthur Dunn clubs should become affiliated to a recognised association, a step which several of the clubs were reluctant to take. The Press fanned the flames of the conflict. Indeed, if it had not been for the diplomatic skills of Norman Malcolmson, the situation might well have become so intolerable that the competition would have died in infancy. Malcolmson smoothed over the main difficulties by means of a series of conversations with F J Wall, the Secretary of the FA.

The Association, however, refused to ratify these verbal agreements, and a complete rupture seemed imminent, but was finally averted by the appearance, at a full Council meeting, of three Arthur Dunn representatives, who successfully defended their committee against all charges of misdemeanour.

As a result, the FA Council passed a resolution which, though vague and liable to misinterpretation, was nevertheless understood by the Press and the public to mean that the Old Boys had won their case. This impression was confirmed, and at the same time better relations were established in the following year by the nomination of Malcolmson to serve on the FA Council as representative of the public schools.

GROUND PROPOSALS

The Committee also had to debate other proposals. Various grounds were used for the early rounds of the competition e.g Norbury Park, the Greyhound at Dulwich and Queen's Club. It was now suggested that the Essex County Cricket Club ground at Leyton should be rented in a joint agreement with Corinthians. This ground would then be used for matches by participating teams; the Arthur Dunn Competition would then benefit from any profits from the event. A meeting was held on January 16th 1904 but no minutes were kept because the Secretary and many others *"were detained in a characteristic London fog and never reached the meeting"*. However, a joint sub-committee was set up and before long an agreement had been reached and the ground was used by participating teams. In the meantime, an agreement was reached with Queens Club for the final (on the same terms as that with the Crystal Palace company i.e. to share the net receipts).

FAR LEFT: F J WALL, THE SECRETARY OF THE FA.

BELOW: FOGBOUND HOUSES OF PARLIAMENT.

QUEENS CLUB (1904-8; 1920 & 21)

When Prince's Club (Cadogan Square) and Lillie Road Sports ground closed in 1886, there was a distinct lack of multi-sport complexes for the sons of the wealthy in London. In response to this, Hon Evan Charteris, Colonel George Francis and the Hon Algernon Grosvenor (all presumably members of Prince's) decided to establish a club and set about finding a site. They acquired an area of land covering Vereker, Palliser, Gladstones and Comeragh Roads in Baron's Court.

With a capital of £60,000 the Queen's Club Limited was formed and Algernon Grosvenor became Chairman of the Board of Directors. Within a few years, Queen's Club had collected a list of vice-presidents that included one marquis, 14 earls, a viscount and numerous other gentlemen, the sons of titled or prominent men in the world of sport, business and private life.

The new ground was opened on 9th November 1887 when the Corinthians played a match against Oxford University. The Corinthian team included one Arthur Dunn. It took about 18 months to complete the Club buildings which were opened in January 1888. Near the Palliser Road entrance was the football pitch which was used for soccer or rugby. By the 1890s, Corinthians had adopted Queen's as their home where they remained until 1914.

After lengthy negotiations before and after the Dunn competition started, Queen's Club was used for the Dunn Final for five years before further disagreement caused the Committee to look elsewhere. Ground scarcity in 1920 forced them to return to Queens Club for the 1920 and 1921 finals.

CARTHUSIANS
MAKE THE CUP THEIR OWN!

In the second season, the competition was increased by the entry of Old Cholmeleians and Old Cranleighans, but once again it was Old Carthusians who raced to the final where they met Old Rossallians. This time the game was held at Queen's Club and despite some good half-back play from Old Rossallians, the superb efforts of

G O Smith (at centre-forward) and Vassall (on the right wing) led to a Carthusian victory by two goals to nil. It was however a very clean game, there being only one foul given throughout the whole game by the referee Captain Simpson.

At a meeting in November 1904, it was decided to drop the word "Challenge" from the name of the competition and ever since it has been known as just the "The Arthur Dunn Cup".

In 1904/05, Old Johnians and Old Citizens joined the competition but again it was Old Carthusians who won the final (again by the margin of 2 - 0), this time by beating Old Reptonians. However, there was apparently little to choose between the two teams. The Times report stated:

"The competition this year has been most interesting. A number of teams entered, and although 4 or 5 of these were certainly in a higher class than the rest, there were some very good matches even in the earlier rounds, while it is probably that the final tie brought the two best elevens together".

When the time came for the Committee to consider the entry for the 1905/06 competition, applications from Old Aldenhamians and Old Wellingburians were accepted. Aldenhamians reached the semi-final in their first season but lost to Old Carthusians, who went on to beat Old Reptonians in the final again by 2 - 0.

It would have pleased Arthur Dunn to have read the Times report of that final:

"It has been gratifying to see the large attendances at several of the matches, as it shows that interest in amateur football is not dying out".

The Cup was presented to the winners at the already customary dinner at the Trocadero in the evening after the game.

THE SPLIT

A further skirmish with the FA took place in 1906, this time on the subject of payments made to charity and to the promotion and welfare of amateur football. No sooner had Malcolmson surmounted this difficulty than the historic *"split"* occurred between the FA and a body of amateurs, united under the title of the Amateur Football Defence Association. The Arthur Dunn Clubs unanimously pledged their support to the Defence Association but, as a result, the competition was deprived of its first president, Lord Kinnaird,

GILBERT OSWALD (G O) SMITH
OLD CARTHUSIAN

There are few people that are so well-known as to be recognisable solely by their initials. However, there is no doubt that the letters W G relate to Dr W G Grace, the greatest of all cricketers. So it is with G O.

He was the finest centre-forward of his day - the 1890s - and some might say the greatest of all time. He had wonderful balance, which gave him superb dribbling and swerving powers. He rarely headed the ball because he kept it on the ground, both in dribbling and shooting. Adept at positioning, he made as many goals for his colleagues as he scored himself. He scored 115 goals for Corinthians in 131 matches and played 20 times for England between 1893 and 1901, scoring 11 goals and captaining the side on 14 occasions.

G O was the star player of the Old Carthusian side that played in the first season of the Arthur Dunn Cup. Of course, this team reached the final drawing 2 - 2 with Old Salopians. In the replay, Smith scored both goals for his side but the teams were still tied so the Cup was shared.

On the early death of Arthur Dunn, he retired from international football and took over the joint headmastership of Ludgrove School with another amateur, Corinthian, Oxford and England International, William Oakley. He did however take part in the Arthur Dunn Cup for Old Carthusians and played in the first three Arthur Dunn Finals. His last appearance was in 1905.

who was compelled to resign by the dictates of the FA, and also of its representation on the Council of the Association in the person of Malcolmson.

Nevertheless, rather than jeopardizing the existence of the competition, this attitude appears to have enlisted even greater support, for the number of competing clubs was raised by the entry of Old Radleians, and more were to follow.

CARTHUSIANS DEFEATED – AT LAST!

From the enlarged competition beginning in the autumn of 1906, Old Reptonians survived to reach the final again in March 1907. However, Carthusians were not to join them on this occasion. Old Brightonians had the distinction of being the first team to beat Old Carthusians in the Arthur Dunn Cup (in the third round).

In a high-scoring game that was drawn 3 - 3 at full-time (including a goal by the Old Brightonian goalkeeper B W King), Brightonians eventually won 5 - 4 after extra time. Despite another good win in the semi-final against Old Cholmeleians (4 - 2), the final was a great disappointment for them. Old Reptonians were a far better side and outplayed Brightonians to win 4 - 1. The referee for this game was R E "Tip" Foster.

REGINALD ERSKINE FOSTER OLD MALVERNIAN

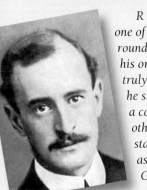

R E Foster was one of the greatest all-round sportsmen of his or any era. It is truly amazing that he should have been a contemporary of other such out-standing talents as C B Fry and G O Smith.

Foster is unique in being the only man to captain England at both cricket and football. His cricketing record is exceptional.

He scored 287 to win the Test match in Sydney in 1903; this remains the highest score by an Englishman in a Test in Australia. He was also an exceptional slip fielder.

Foster, however, only gained five caps at football due to injuries and work commitments; he was a stockbroker. An old boy of Malvern College, he played for Old Malvernians and later Corinthians.

Tragically, "Tip" Foster died from diabetes at the early age of 36.

INCREASED INTEREST IN THE COMPETITION

In 1907, the number of competing clubs was increased again, now up to 24, with applications from Old Berkhamstedians, Old Ipswichians and Old Albanians being accepted. Still, the Old Carthusian bandwagon rolled on; they had not given up the title for long! Yet again, they reached the final in 1908 and this time came up against Old Wykehamists, who put up a creditable performance and by all accounts deserved a draw.(Carthusians won 2 - 1).

The continued pressure of applications to take part led to the idea of forming a second tier; but in view of the uncertainty of the immediate future, it was decided to leave such a step to be taken by the Amateur Association, if formed.

A new venue (Leyton) was chosen for the 1909 final and this time Old Salopians who had shared the first title fought their way to the final. On a very heavy and rather slippery surface, the Old Malvernians proved too good for Old Salopians. Even with the Morgan-Owen brothers in their line-up, Salopians were easily beaten by 3 - 0.

Yet another venue was used in 1910 - Weybridge Football Club's *"pretty, if rather inaccessible"* ground. It was some distance from London and so the attendance for the final was low (200 - 300). The Old Rossallians played some good football in the first half and were a goal up at half-time. However, in the second half they tired rapidly and Old Carthusians scored two goals to take the Cup for the fifth time in eight years. After the game, the usual dinner was held at the Trocadero restaurant, attended by both teams and some members of the Amateur Football Association.

The competition over the winter of 1910 and into 1911 was rather closer than usual and a lack of good forwards meant that the defences of most teams prevailed. When it came to the final, it was yet again the Old Carthusians who ran out onto the pitch at Ealing. With Lord Alverstone, himself an Old Carthusian, there to watch them (and their success to date), they might have been forgiven for believing that the Cup was theirs for the taking. Ignoring however a very good Old Reptonian team.

MORGAN MORGAN-OWEN OLD SALOPIAN

Morgan Maddox Morgan-Owen DSO TD was born in 1877 and was educated at Shrewsbury and Oriel College, Oxford. In 1897, he was a member of the Association football team in the Oxford v Cambridge match and in the following year, along with his brother "H", played for Wales.

One of the great centre half-backs of his day, he captained the famous Corinthian team that once beat Bury, winners of the FA Cup, by 10 goals to 3, On another occasion he and his brother both withdrew from a full Welsh international side chosen to face England in order to play for the Old Salopians in the final of the Arthur Dunn Cup, an action that was echoed in later years by C T Ashton, of Old Wykehamists.

Morgan Morgan-Owen was prominent in the formation of the Arthur Dunn Cup. He and his brother were in the Old Salopian team that shared the trophy in its inaugural season and they were members of the team that reached the 1909 final only to lose 3 - 0 to Old Malvernians. After his playing days, Morgan sat on the Arthur Dunn Cup Committee for many years.

BELOW: THE TROCADERO RESTAURANT, VENUE OF THE AFTER-GAME DINNER.

LEYTON GROUND (1909 & 1922)

In the early years of the 20th century, Essex County Cricket Club owned the Leyton cricket ground and played a number of their county matches there. In the winter, the ground off Leyton High Road was used for football.

Many clubs played at Leyton, especially Corinthians, and a number of Old Boys teams used it as their home ground in the London area. Early rounds of the Arthur Dunn Cup were held there and, on one occasion, in 1909, the Arthur Dunn Cup Final.

After the 1921 cricket season, Essex CCC sold the ground to the Army Sports Council, although Essex continued to play there until 1933. In this era when the Arthur Dunn Cup Final did not have a permanent home, the Leyton ground was used for a second time in 1922.

WEYBRIDGE FC GROUND (1910)

The 1910 Dunn Cup Final was played on the ground owned by Weybridge Rose FC. This was located in Walton Road, Weybridge and was described in the reports about the final as "pretty". However, as it was so far from London, the game did not attract a large crowd; the final did not return the following year.

Weybridge Rose FC was quite successful for a period before the first World War and undertook a number of improvements to its ground between 1908 and 1912. However, after 1918 the team went into terminal decline, probably due to the success of other local teams such as Hersham and Walton. Weybridge FC, as it was now called, was disbanded in July 1930.

MERTON FC GROUND (1912 & 1914)

Merton Football Club were based at the John Innes Sports ground in Watery Lane, Merton Park when their pitch was used for two Arthur Dunn Cup Finals, in 1912 and 1914. The ground had been provided by John Innes, who was Lord of the Manor from about 1867 until his death in 1904.

TWICKENHAM RFU GROUND (1913)

The ten-acre ground at Twickenham, West London, was acquired by the Rugby Football Union in 1907 in order to give the England rugby team a permanent home.

It had previously been a market garden and was initially known as "Billy Williams' cabbage patch" (after the RFU Committee member who proposed its purchase). Subsequently, and ever since, it has been known simply as "headquarters". The Twickenham ground was used for only one Arthur Dunn Cup Final - in 1913.

On the afternoon's play, Reptonians deserved their 1 - 0 victory.

The holders Old Reptonians made it to the next final on March 30th 1912 at another new venue – Merton, but they were trounced by an impressive Malvernian team (4 - 0). The goals were scored by the brothers Day (S H and S E) who each got one and L A Vidal who got two.

OLD BRIGHTONIANS WIN THE CUP

The 1913 competition threw up two of the lesser fancied teams to contest the final. Nevertheless, Old Aldenhamians had a reasonable record since they had joined the competition in 1906 and Old Brightonians had reached a final in 1907. Brightonians had met Foresters in the second round (at Leyton) and on a wet and muddy pitch, with the light far from good, they fought out a 2 - 2 draw. At the replay on the same ground, Brightonians then trounced Foresters 10 - 3. After further wins, over Old Wellingburians and then Old Malvernians, the final was held in April 1913, this time at the home of Rugby Union, Twickenham.

There was an additional complication because *"there were only two Association balls on the Rugby enclosure, both of*

RIGHT: OLD BRIGHTONIANS 1912/13 WINNERS OF THE ARTHUR DUNN AND SUSSEX AFA CUPS.

(LEFT TO RIGHT) BACK ROW: W MCCOWAN (HON. SEC.), G M DAWBARN, A R G ROBERSON, G BELCHER, L F DOWER, A H BELCHER (CAPT.).

SEATED: A J MURDOCK, P HAVELOCK-DAVIES, M H CLARKE, C E HOFFMEISTER (ACT. CAPT.), R W DOWER, A D CAVE (INSET).

IN FRONT: C R SHALLOW, W S ROSS.

very bad shape" (Brighton College Magazine). Aldenhamians took the lead when Deakin, the Aldenham forward, got the ball jammed awkwardly between his legs, nearly falling over but still managed to walk the ball into the net. However, in the second half, Brightonians scored two good goals to take the trophy.

Some were contemptuous of this final. As the Sportsman reported:

"There are those who declare the presence of the Old Brightonians and Old Aldenhamians in the final of the Arthur Dunn Cup was due to a decline in the football at Charterhouse, Malvern and Westminster, who used to have things very much their own way, rather than to an improvement in the football of the smaller Public schools". The periodical continued:

"I have never seen so much hefty charging in one afternoon. Men were bowled over like ninepins. And very wisely the referee, W E Greenland, did not worry about trifles. He 'let her rip'. The whistle was not blown more than three times for a free-kick, and then only in cases of off-side.

"It was a stimulating match altogether, an antidote to much anaemic Soccer of an ultraclever kind. Even the roars of the spectators were refreshing. Shrill treble was blended with basso profundo, and the croak of the youth whose voice is breaking with the bleat of the Old Boy who is really old. And it was good to hear those School cries so wholeheartedly given".

There was already a trend away from football to rugby. One correspondent in the Rossallian magazine pointed out that in the Liverpool and Manchester areas there were only three teams with which Public Schools could be associated - *"there are no nice soccer clubs outside London".*

In June 1913 Old Ipswichians withdrew from the competition for just that season; as a result, Old Aldenhamians received a bye in the first round of the 1914 competition.

Again, it was Old Reptonians who survived to reach the final in March 1914. On this occasion, they met the Old Cholmeleians appearing in

their first final. The more experienced side were too good for the newcomers and ran out the winners 3 - 0.

THE OLD BOYS COMPETITION

After the initial discussions in 1906/7 about the formation of a separate Old Boys' competition the matter was left in abeyance. However, in 1913, the Old Boys' League, under the auspices of the now-established AFA, undertook to form an Old Boys' Cup Competition under the patronage of the Arthur Dunn Competition, by whom the trophy was presented. Eight teams entered the competition in the first year:

Old Alleynians – Alleyn's School, Dulwich

Old Brentwoods – Brentwood School, Essex

Old Burians – King Edward VI School, Bury St Edmunds

Old Chigwellians – Chigwell School, Essex

Old Framlinghamians – Framlingham College, Suffolk

Old Hurst Johnians – St John's College. Hurstpierpoint

Old Lawrentians – St Lawrence College, Ramsgate

Old Tridents – Trent College, Nottingham

The draw for the first round was as follows:

Old Alleynians v Old Tridents
(played at North Dulwich)

Old Framlinghamians v Old Lawrentians
(played at the Universities and Public Schools
Athletic Club, Wembley)

Old Burians v Old Brentwoods
(at Brentwood School)

Old Chigwellians v Old Hurst Johnians
(at Chigwell School)

The first winners of the cup, in 1914, were Old Hurst Johnians, who were invited to enter for the Arthur Dunn Cup the following season, though their actual appearance was deferred for five years by the First World War.

THE OLD BOYS CUP

In 1913, the Arthur Dunn Committee had received so many applications for entry to their competition that they decided to set up a new competition on the same lines as the Arthur Dunn. This competition was to be called the "Old Boys Cup".

The new competition was under the direct control of the Arthur Dunn Committee until 1926 when the Football Association drew attention to the fact that an FA Rule stated that one competition could promote and manage a second competition if it was restricted to members of the promoting competition. As a result, the independent Old Boys Cup Competition came into being at a meeting held on 10th June 1927.

Over the years, a number of winners of the Old Boys Cup have later been invited to join the Arthur Dunn, notably, Old Hurst Johnians and the Old Brentwoods. The Old Boys Cup retains a link with the Arthur Dunn Cup because every year since 1986, the winners of the Old Boys Senior Cup challenge the winners of the Arthur Dunn Cup for the Vic Merrett Trophy.

A B Kingsley (Old Wykehamist) and N W Beeson (Old Malvernian) contest the ball during the 1938 final.

BETWEEN CONFLICTS

In the 20 years between the two World Wars, the Arthur Dunn competition was dominated by four teams. Three of them – Old Carthusians, Old Malvernians and Old Wykehamists – each won the trophy three times in a row (between 1921 and 1931). The only other team to get their hands on the trophy in these years was Old Salopians.

This was only a foretaste, because the Salopians won the trophy on four more occasions in the 1930s. The only other team to make any impact was a splendid Old Aldenhamian side, led by Donald Shearer, that won the trophy in 1934.

THE ATTRACTION OF THE OVAL BALL?

Initially though, the future was not guaranteed. As soon as possible after the war, Norman Malcolmson set about reviving the competition. An informal meeting of the clubs was held at the Holborn Restaurant on 16th June 1919. Radleians, Rossallians and Berkhamstedians could no longer raise teams as their schools had converted to rugby. And although the initial entry for 1919/20 was an encouraging 22 teams, a few more withdraw due to the difficulty of finding players, so that the first round draw consisted only of a series of walkovers.

THE BREACH HEALED

There was some encouraging news because the end of the global hostilities coincided with the healing of the rift between the FA and the AFA.

To demonstrate the improved relationship, the Arthur Dunn Committee was again invited to nominate a representative of the public schools to sit on the FA Council.

The first nominee was G N Foster, centre-half in the Old Malvernians winning team of 1912, and the Hon. Secretary of the famous Corinthians. He held the post at the FA for the next four years and was succeeded for a similar period by A G Bower, another Corinthian who was also capped five times for England. (He also played in the victorious Old Carthusians side in their three successive victories between 1921 and 1923).

In 1933, Major J Stewart (Old Bradfieldians), the Hon. Secretary and later chairman of the Arthur Dunn competition, succeeded Bower as the public schools representative. He was then in 1952 to become a vice-president of the FA. This had the unfortunate effect of depriving the competition of its representative on the Council. The FA independently decided to consult the Headmasters' Conference and the Incorporated Association of Headmasters. This body nominated Dr A W Barton, former Repton master who later became the headmaster of the City of London School, but not a member of the AFA, on the grounds that he represented the interests of a larger number of schools than those embraced by the Arthur Dunn competition.

MALCOLMSON BECOMES PRESIDENT

Norman Malcolmson's period as Hon. Secretary came to an end in February 1920. He had launched the competition with immense skill and energy since he first set out to realise Arthur Dunn's wish, expressed in that brief note 18 years previously.

He was succeeded by N V C Turner, and in the following year was elected president, a post that he held until 1928 when Turner again succeeded him.

Malcolmson's death, on 20 February 1929 – exactly 27 years after that of Arthur Dunn – ended a fine record of service to amateur football. The office of Hon. Secretary then passed to Stewart, who took the competition into a second post-war era until his resignation in 1948.

RESUMPTION OF THE CUP COMPETITION

After all the withdrawals, 16 teams were left to compete in a revised Second round as follows:

Old Wykehamists v Old Albanians

Old Reptonians v Old Carthusians

Old Salopians v Old Aldenhamians

Old Hurst Johnians v Old Wellingburians

Old Malvernians v Old Foresters

Old Citizens v Old Bradfieldians

Old Cholmeleians v Old Westminsters

Old Felstedians v Lancing Old Boys

From now on the participants in the competition remained remarkably consistent. The draw in 1939/40 included eleven of the fourteen founding member teams from 1902/03.

1920
WYKEHAMISTS' FIRST WIN

The first post-war holders of the Cup were Old Wykehamists, who played Old Malvernians at the Queen's Club. Prince Henry, who shook the hands of all the players at the conclusion of the game, presented the trophy.

NORMAN MALCOLMSON OLD ETONIAN

Norman Malcolmson was the son of Rev Lancelot Malcolmson who ran Elstree School. Inevitably, Norman attended the school and was a member of the football eleven.

In 1887, Norman went to Eton where he won his "field" (football eleven) in 1893. When he left Eton he naturally joined the Old Etonians, of which he became honorary secretary.

By virtue of the fact that Arthur Dunn married his sister, Norman Malcolmson was Arthur's brother-in-law. No doubt, they discussed the subject of football many times and it is not surprising then that it was to Norman that Arthur voiced his concerns about the sport.

Of course, Norman, in conjunction with C Wreford-Brown started the Arthur Dunn Cup in 1902. He went on to represent the Arthur Dunn and the public schools on the FA Council, where his negotiating skills were respected.

ABOVE: G N FOSTER, OLD MALVERNIAN.

The stars of this game were the three Ashton brothers. Hubert scored the first, and Claude (C T), still at Winchester at this point, scored the second. The third was a remarkable family affair. C T collected the ball on half-way, drew two defenders to him and found Gilbert. He, in turn, drew in the two full backs and bisected them with a pass to Hubert, who dribbled the ball into the net. Hubert then completed his hat trick with an unstoppable shot. In goal for Wykehamists was one Douglas Jardine, who brought off some remarkable saves.

The appearance of Claude Ashton in this final led in 1922/23, to an alteration of the rules.

The newly-formed Headmasters' Conference decided that past members of schools only would be allowed to play.

Claude Ashton made a notable contribution to the history of the competition, and not only by leading Old Wykehamists to victory in three consecutive seasons. On one of these occasions, he even withdrew from an England team to play for his old boys. In doing so, he emulated a similar sacrifice by the Morgan-Owen brothers, who gave up appearances for Wales to play for Old Salopians.

OLD CARTHUSIANS: ROARING INTO THE TWENTIES

The 1920/21 Wykehamist team was without its major stars and so a good Aldenhamian team was able to dispatch them in the Second round. Unfortunately, Aldenhamians were themselves weakened for the final and Old Carthusians beat them 2 - 0 in a skilful match. Injuries and the unavailability of L E Partridge, their right-winger (because he was to run in a hurdles race for Cambridge) denied Aldenhamians their strongest

DOUGLAS JARDINE OLD WYKEHAMIST

Douglas Jardine was born on 23rd October 1900 and after preparatory school at Horris Hill near Newbury, he progressed to Winchester College. Here, he showed early promise at both football and cricket; he captained the cricket side. He was always a determined person and one of his contemporaries said of him: "he was never young. He had a confidence and self-sufficiency beyond his years. As captain of Lords (the Winchester XI) he went his own way and argued down such eminent cricket masters as Hary Altham and Rockley Wilson".

Of course, Jardine will always be remembered for his captaincy of the England Cricket team in Australia for, what came to be known as the "Bodyline" series. He made a deep study of Donald Bradman's batting and concluded that he was vulnerable to the lifting ball. So, positioning most of his fielders on the leg side and then getting his bowlers Larwood and Voce to bowl at pace to this field, Bradman was neutralised and the Australian batting destroyed. For ever after, Jardine was vilified, probably unfairly, for the tactics.

Away from cricket, Jardine always played football for Old Wykehamists and was present in the Old Wykehamist eleven that played in the 1920 Arthur Dunn Final.

team. The winners celebrated at the Café Royal. The gate receipts amounted to £32.47.

This win for Carthusians was the start of their three-win sequence. The 1922 final played on 1st April at the Army Sports ground at Leyton was a repeat of that in 1921. After Williams' opening goal for Carthusians, Sainsbury brought Aldenhamians level before half time. The winner came from the man of the match, R J Thorne-Thorne. His brilliant goal followed a run from his own half after beating three men. The game was played in front of a crowd of around 1,000.

In 1923, Old Carthusians completed a second hat-trick in the competition. They had already won three successive finals (in 1904, 1905 and 1906). They had a remarkable record having taken

CLAUDE THESIGER ASHTON - OLD WYKEHAMIST

Claude Thesiger Ashton was the all-round player who excelled at both football and cricket. After Winchester, he won Blues at Cambridge for hockey as well as the traditional leading summer and winter games. He gained his only full England cap in 1926 against Northern Ireland. He also played on twelve occasions for his country as an amateur. He played for the Corinthians in their famous 1927 FA Cup tie at the Crystal Palace against Newcastle United. Although United won 3 - 1 they had only drawn level with 14 minutes to go. Ashton's goal in this game was one of over a hundred that he scored for Corinthians.

Along with his two brothers, Gilbert and Hubert, he played for Old Wykehamists in their tremendous run in the Arthur Dunn in the 1920s. It is said that when all three brothers turned out for Cambridge University that the team was then dubbed "Ashton Villa". In all, he played in seven Arthur Dunn Cup Finals, four times on the winning side.

Claude was also an accomplished batsman and fielder and played for Essex before the war. Sadly, he died in 1942 in a plane crash whilst serving as an acting Squadron Leader with the RAF.

part in ten finals with only one defeat (in 1911, when the Old Reptonians beat them 1 - 0). This game was played at the Old Spotted Dog ground, Forest Gate, and Carthusians' opponents were Old Malvernians. Better finishing and team work from Carthusians led to their victory by five goals to one. H R H Williams distinguished himself with a hat trick.

RETURN TO THE CRYSTAL PALACE

In 1922, the Corinthians and the Casuals had taken a tenancy on the football ground at the Crystal Palace. Of course, there were close connections between the Arthur Dunn teams and the Corinthian club, including the Corinthians secretary, Geoffrey Foster, who was the FA public schools representative. It was almost inevitable therefore that the Arthur Dunn competition should make use of the facilities. For the next decade or so, the two football grounds at the Crystal Palace were used for early rounds in the competition as well as the final.

So, for the 1923/24 season, the final returned to the Crystal Palace after an absence of 21 years. The Arthur Dunn Committee agreed to spend £5 in total advertising the game and each of the competing teams - Old Malvernians and Old Reptonians – received six complementary tickets for the game. It is worth noting that the referee received a fee of 11/6 (57.5 pence) for officiating at the game.

Although Old Reptonians started as favourites, in the end, the Old Malvernians were deserved

THE OLD SPOTTED DOG GROUND FOREST GATE (1923)

The club is now the last surviving founder member of the Isthmian League, which was formed in 1905.
The ground was the venue for the Arthur Dunn Final of 1923.

The Old Spotted Dog ground, in Upton Lane, Forest Gate is the East London home of Clapton FC. The club were one of the country's leading amateur sides winning the FA Amateur Cup on five occasions up until 1925. They moved to the ground in September 1888.

ABOVE: THE PUBLIC HOUSE THAT GAVE ITS NAME TO THE GROUND.

OLD WESTMINSTERS
MAKE IT TO THEIR FIRST FINAL

Old Westminsters at last made it to a final in 1924/25 but they were no match for Old Malvernians who romped to a 3 - 0 victory. This was a fourth victory for Malvernians, at the time only Carthusians had participated in more finals. The Times correspondent was particularly impressed by the goalkeepers. They *"so shone and so resembled each other that they might have been called "The Two Macs".* For Westminster, McBride had the more to do, and, with the possible exception of the first goal, it was not his fault that his side was behind, for he made many good saves. (The Malvernian goalkeeper was MacKinnon).

Ultimately it was superior finishing by Malvernians that led to their victory.

The tensions between the professional and amateur game were evident in The Times match report. Contrasting the game with the previous week's FA Cup semi-finals their reporter commented,

"not only the players but the spectators too, gave a demonstration of what behaviour, both on or off the field, should be during a decisive football match. The play on the field was keen and clean: the enthusiasm off it was great, but restrained… such a crowd as this could make even a bad match pleasant and it made Saturday's good one seem even pleasanter than it was".

Not that the supporters from the public schools were anything less than partisan. At the final, Old Westminsters were without some of their usual supporters. *"These might fittingly be called their 'railing' crowd, for not only do they cling tenaciously to the outside of the railing at*

winners. N W Beeson, the Old Malvernian captain and centre half, was the man of the match, due to his marking and distribution. The Partridge brothers scored the goals, N E after seven minutes and G B in the second half from a shot that went in off the underside of the bar. For the first time, Mrs A T B Dunn was invited to present the trophy to the valiant winners. This was Malvernians' third victory and the first of their three-win sequence.

LEFT: *OLD MALVERNIANS WINNERS 1925.*

(back row)
E R T HOLMES, A E MACKINNON, C G W ROBSON, H A PRIDHAM, W R T PICTON-WARLOW.

(middle row)
G B PARTRIDGE, G F MORICE, N W BEESON, W C STUART-LOW, G L MILLER.

(front row)
D J KNIGHT, N H STONE.

Vincent Square whenever there is a match, but sometimes, it is to be feared, they are more occupied in railing at players who do not meet their fancy than in attending to the finer points of the play. On the whole, it does not seem that they were missed very much".

OLD MALVERNIANS
COMPLETE THEIR HAT-TRICK

Old Malvernians achieved a third consecutive victory in 1925/26. They had beaten Old Wykehamists

in a thrilling semi-final (5 - 3). Meanwhile, their opponents, Old Salopians, had overcome Old Wellingburians.

In the final, Old Malvernians won against the run of play. In the game at the Crystal Palace, Malvernians went ahead and then slipped to 2 - 1 behind. A brilliant combination move by Stuart-Low, Holmes and Robson resulted in Robson equalising, Holmes then found the winner three minutes after half time. The opposing centre-halves stood out in an exciting game; G B Partridge for Old Malvernians and L B Blaxland for the Old Salopians. *"The whole match was, to a great extent, almost an individual contest between these two players".*

HON. TREASURER APPOINTED

At the Annual General Meeting in June 1927, the Arthur Dunn Cup Committee decided to appoint its first Hon. Treasurer N W Beeson of the Old Malvernians – after the accounts had been properly audited.

There was also a consideration of the new booklets to be issued after the 1927/28 season.

MALVERNIANS DEFEATED

Old Salopians were to become the team of the thirties but they also won an exceptional final against Old Malvernians

ABOVE: N W BEESON.

in the cold and the rain in April 1927 at the Crystal Palace. This was a repeat of the previous final but Old Malvernians were prevented from a fourth successive win by some sterling play from the Salopians. At full time, with the scores level at 2 - 2, the captains agreed to play a further half hour. Newton scored for Salopians and Picton-Warlow replied for Malvernians. All square going into the last 15 minutes Newton, Bush and Lewis helped clinch the game 6 - 3. After two hours of Cup Final football, there had only been one free kick: the offence - offside.

Yet, the Malvernians continued their dominance of this period with a 3 - 2 victory in the 1928 final. They however needed extra time to dispatch Old Wykehamists. Their opponents were weakened after twenty minutes by the recurrence of an old injury to C T Ashton, who limped through the rest of the game. He, however, scored a goal but then reverted from centre forward to centre back. He had only been playing at centre forward as he was recovering from influenza. This was Wykehamists' only defeat of the season.

TURNER RESIGNS AS SECRETARY

The Committee meeting in April 1928 was the occasion of Noel Turner's resignation as Hon. Secretary, to be succeeded by Major Stewart. The minutes of this meeting were written in Turner's typical erudite and amusing style as the following will illustrate:

N V C TURNER
OLD REPTONIAN
PRESIDENT 1928-1931

Noel Turner appeared as a goalkeeper for Old Reptonian team that reached the final of the Arthur Dunn Cup three times before the First World War. In 1911 and 1914, Reptonians won the Cup (against Carthusians and Cholmeleians respectively) and Turner kept a clean sheet on each occasion. In 1912, they lost 4 - 1 to old Malvernians. After the War, Turner returned to the team for the 1920 Dunn campaign.

The side unfortunately lost to the successful Old Wykehamist side which included the Ashton brothers and went on to win the trophy by beating Old Malvernians 5 - 0.

Turner regularly kept goal for Corinthians and also earned one Amateur international cap for England against Belgium in 1920.

After his playing days were over, Turner became Public Schools representative on the FA Council and was appointed Hon. Secretary of the Arthur Dunn Cup when Norman Malcolmson was appointed President. He subsequently succeeded Malcolmson to the Presidency in 1928. Sadly, Noel Turner died the following year.

CRYSTAL PALACE
CYCLE TRACK GROUND (1924-1936)

When the fountain basins at the Crystal Palace were filled in to create a Sports arena, a cycle track was created in the northern basin (cycling being a very popular sport at the end of the nineteenth century). Inside this was placed an athletics track for local athletics meetings.

After the First World War, when the Corinthians and the Casuals arrived at the Crystal Palace and adopted the old FA Cup Final ground as their home, there was so much amateur football organised at the ground that this other ground also began to be used for football. So while Corinthians might be playing a major League side in an FA Cup match on the main ground, Old Salopians could be using the northern ground for a Dunn match.

By the 1930s, the Arthur Dunn Cup Final itself returned to Crystal Palace and was played on this northern ground.

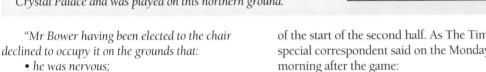

BELOW: OLD WYKEHAMISTS WINNERS 1931.

(back row) A D GARROW, G S GRIMSTON, G R M RICKETTS, J L T GUISE, G I BARTY-KING. (middle row) A R V BARKER, P G T KINGSLEY, C T ASHTON, J F T TOPPIN, C R V BELL. (front row) M B S BOWER, J W M MANSEL.

"Mr Bower having been elected to the chair declined to occupy it on the grounds that:
- he was nervous;
- he was not sufficiently in touch with matters arising from the competition;
- he was too accustomed to occupying it in his own home.

The Hon. Sec. suspects that his refusal was on the grounds of economy in order to evade payment of drinks all round usually associated with this high office".

WYKEHAMISTS MAKE IT
THREE OUT OF THREE

The 1928/29 final saw Old Wykehamists beat Old Carthusians by three goals to nil. Old Wykehamists were faster to the ball, passed and finished better, in a disappointing game, played on the Cycle Track ground at the Crystal Palace. Mrs Arthur Dunn again presented the cup.

In 1930, the Cup again went to Winchester with a 4 - 1 win for the Wykehamists. In a disappointing game, played partly in heavy rain, Old Salopians went four down within 15 minutes

of the start of the second half. As The Times special correspondent said on the Monday morning after the game:

"the Old Wykehamists were the better side all round, quicker on the ball, more clever individually and – in spite of the fact that A T Barber was on the other side – more pertinacious in their tackling, and nowhere was their superiority more marked than in the half-back line".

Old Wykehamists completed their hat trick of victories on 28 March 1931 again at the Crystal Palace. It was the first and only appearance of the Old Citizens in the final and they seemed to be completely overawed by the occasion, losing by five goals to one. C T Ashton, although closely marked, scored the first two Old Wykehamist goals.

BILL BLAXLAND & JOHN S O HASLEWOOD OLD SALOPIANS

Bill Blaxland was the secretary of the Old Salopian Football Club from 1921 to 1937. He was responsible for much of the success of the Old Salopians in the inter-war years by his influence and organisation, as well as his appearances as centre-half. He first appeared in the Arthur Dunn Final of 1926 when Old Salopians lost to Old Malvernians in a thrilling match at the Crystal Palace. The following year, he was captain of the team that got its revenge by beating Old Malvernians 6 - 3 after extra time. In all, Blaxland appeared in seven finals including the "Team of the Thirties" that won the trophy four times in six years (1932-37). He even scored a goal in the 6 - 1 defeat of Old Reptonians in 1932.

He was an Oxford blue (1919-21) and later appeared for Blackburn Rovers, and for Corinthians. He played cricket for Derbyshire in the summer holidays from Repton where he was housemaster. He gave outstanding service to Repton, running both cricket and football, and when the groundsman was called up for War service, he took over that work as well.

John Haslewood was a critical element in the Old Salopian "Team of the Thirties" led so majestically by Bill Blaxland. He was a prolific goal-scorer and got a goal in each of the five finals in which he played (1930, 1932, 1933, 1935 and 1937).

In 1935 John and Alan Barber both played for the Old Salopians in the Arthur Dunn Cup Final when they defeated the Old Wykehamists 3 - 0, the following week they both played for the Old Salopians in the final of the Halford Hewitt but were beaten by the Old Carthusians.

ABOVE: ACTION FROM THE 1933 FINAL.

OLD SALOPIANS: THE TEAM OF THE THIRTIES

The most consistent side during the thirties were the Old Salopians, winners four times in six years. After losing the 1930 final 4 - 1 to the Old Wykehamists they won the competition in 1932, 1933, 1935, and 1937.

The most convincing victory was in 1932 when they defeated Old Reptonians, 6 - 1. This was a magnificent performance by the Salopians with the half-back line of Barber, Blaxland and Waye *"at the top of their form"*. The Salopians were 3 - 0 up after thirty minutes, Skelton opening the scoring when a shot by Moxon was only parried by the goalkeeper, Haslewood heading in Skelton's cross for the second and Moxon adding the third from Barber's through-ball. Pouring rain made conditions treacherous in the second half, but Blaxland added a fourth and Moxon completed a hat-trick to complete a most impressive performance. This game was played at the Crystal Palace and was preceded by a minute's silence in memory of H Hugh-Onslow, President and founder-member of the AFA.

The 1933 final was also played at Crystal Palace. Despite playing poorly in the first half, Salopians' teamwork saw them through 3 - 1 against Old Chomeleians. After going behind, Skelton, Haslewood and Moxon with a header in the last minute, were the Salopian scorers.

CRYSTAL PALACE NO LONGER AVAILABLE

At the Committee meeting on 30th January 1933, there was a lengthy debate about a proposal to form an Arthur Dunn League. In the end, the idea was rejected – only to resurface 30 years later.

There was also a problem because the Crystal Palace authorities decided that the two grounds at Crystal Palace would no longer be available for the early rounds of the competition. This meant that those teams that made use of these facilities had to make other arrangements.

Further, the Arthur Dunn Committee meeting on 16th February 1934 then learned more bad news in a letter from the General Manager of the Crystal Palace. He said he could no longer offer the Arthur Dunn competition any facilities, given that the Corinthians no longer played at the Crystal Palace.

However, both the 1935 and 1936 finals were subsequently played at the Crystal Palace albeit on the second (Cycle track) ground – the main football ground had now been transformed into a speedway track.

ABOVE: ACTION FROM THE 1934 FINAL.

RIGHT: THE PRESENTATION OF THE CUP TO THE OLD ALDENHAMIAN CAPTAIN, DONALD SHEARER 1934.

DONALD SHEARER OLD ALDENHAMIAN

Donald Shearer OBE CBE was one of the finest footballers to play in the Arthur Dunn Cup. His off-the-field career was equally distinguished. Shearer excelled at sports, primarily as an exceptional centre-forward and a fine batsman. He represented Britain at football in the 1936 Berlin Olympics and played for 20 years for Ireland at cricket. In 1951, he became the first Irishman to score a century at Lord's.

In the Arthur Dunn Cup, Shearer captained the Old Aldenhamians to victory in the 1933 final against the Old Wykehamists. He played and scored for the Casuals in their 1936 FA Amateur cup victory against Dulwich Hamlet. He was also a key player in the Irish League side against the Football League in both 1935 and 1936.

He served in Africa during World War II, and was for a time the Commander of the garrison at Tobruk. He was awarded the OBE at the conclusion of the war.

He was the first chairman of the Northern Ireland Sports Council. He was from 1960 to 1969 honorary ADC to the Queen. His services to Northern Ireland were recognised in 1974 when he became a CBE.

victory in the competition. With only one player with an established reputation, the amateur international centre forward, E D R Shearer, they won a notable victory 6 - 2 against Old Wykehamists. Donald Shearer had an outstanding game, scored a goal, and was involved in four of the others.

OLD SALOPIANS - AGAIN!

In the 1934/35 final, the Salopians played Old Wykehamists yet again. Once ahead, The Times correspondent could not see them being defeated because of their defensive strength. They ran out 3 - 0 winners.

The Old Salopians' ascendancy was all the more remarkable given they did not play regularly together during the season as they only formed a team for their Arthur Dunn fixtures. Their strength and cohesion was in the main due to a solid phalanx of P S Snow and A G Strasser at the back, and R Waye, L B Blaxland and A T Barber at half back.

BELOW: ACTION FROM THE 1935 FINAL.

Six months after the 1936 final, the great glass edifice itself went up in flames and the association of the Arthur Dunn with the Crystal Palace came to an end – for the moment!

OLD ALDENHAMIANS BREAK THE SEQUENCE

Following the withdrawal of Old Harrovians (1931) and Old Hurst-Johnians (1932), Old Ardinians were invited to join the 1933/34 competition. It was, however, Old Aldenhamians who sprang a surprise in 1934 final. The game was played on a beautiful afternoon in front of a good crowd, who witnessed Aldenhamians' first

BRADFIELDIANS REACH THEIR FIRST FINAL

The 1935/36 final was between Old Carthusians and Old Bradfieldians. A large crowd witnessed Bradfieldians first appearance in the final.

They had managed to knock out the holders, Old Salopians, in their semi-final. P H Williams, the Old Bradfieldians centre half, was the man of the match, and towards the end, he went to the centre forward position to try to get his team back in the match. It was to no avail as Carthusians won 2 - 0.

LEFT: MRS ARTHUR DUNN PRESENTS THE CUP TO L B BLAXLAND THE OLD SALOPIAN CAPTAIN, 1935.

ABOVE TOP: ACTION FROM THE 1936 FINAL.

ABOVE: THREE CHEERS AT THE PRESENTATION 1936.

J G Dunbar scored both goals, one in each half.

The Times reported that he *"… hurled himself cheerfully and to no little effect against anyone or anything between himself and the ball"*. Sports' reporting was more prosaic in those days!

This is how The Morning Post's report started:

"Although the Old Carthusians were clearly fast enough to have run off with the Arthur Dunn Cup before the match without fear of being caught by Old Bradfieldians, they preferred to put themselves to the trouble of taking the trophy by lawful means, after all, it is as well to have an alternative scheme in reserve, and it would have been a pity rashly to disturb the halcyon charm that a precocious March had bestowed upon the scene of such a stern if bloodless conflict, graced by the presence of Mrs Arthur Dunn".

PICTURES RIGHT-HURLINGHAM. MATCH ACTION AND THE CUP IS PRESENTED TO THE JOINT WINNERS 1938.

THE FINAL MOVES TO HURLINGHAM

A new team went into the draw for the 1936/37 competition. Old Chigwellians now joined the 15 other teams. There was also a change to the rules in 1937. It was now agreed by the Committee that fixtures could be played up to fifty miles from the centre of London (as opposed to twenty-five miles previously). Neutral linesmen were also introduced for the final.

Because of the demise of the Crystal Palace, a new ground was needed for the 1937 final. On this occasion, the Number 1 Polo ground at Hurlingham was offered. So on 20 March in perfect spring weather, Old Salopians and Old Bradfieldians contested the final at Hurlingham.

Old Salopians won 4 - 1, although Old Bradfieldians were only 2 - 1 behind with less than ten minutes to go. The Old Salopians had scored their first two goals (by Haslewood and Roberts) when Old Bradfieldians were down to ten men, their centre forward Fussell having suffered an attack of lumbago. Just when Bradfieldians looked like they might equalize, Singleton got a third goal and then Roberts added a late fourth.

Lord Athlone presented the trophy to Bill Blaxland the victorious captain.

CUP IS SHARED FOR THE SECOND TIME

The 1937/38 final was again played at the Hurlingham club. In true tradition, with a 2 - 2 draw after extra time, it was decided that Old Malvernians and Old Wykehamists should share the trophy. It was an even end to an even game. Wykehamists played all the good football in the first half and established a two-goal lead.

HURLINGHAM GROUND (1937-39)

Hurlingham, in south-west London, was originally part of the Fulham Palace estate, the summer residence of the Bishops of London. By the twentieth century, this ground had become a popular venue for sporting events. It hosted polo and rugby as well as association football. After the demise of the Crystal Palace, the Arthur Dunn Final migrated to Hurlingham and the last three finals before the Second World War (1937, 1938 and 1939) were played at this exclusive venue.

GERRY HOLLEBONE OLD CARTHUSIAN

Gerry Hollebone was captain of the Old Carthusian side that won the Arthur Dunn Cup on two occasions just before the Second World War. He was a friend of the Dunn family and was encouraged by Mrs Helen Dunn in the mid-1930s to get involved in organising Carthusian football. Carthusians had not had much success in the previous few years.

So in 1934 Hollebone began running the Old Carthusian Football Club and success was not long in coming. In 1935, they were drawn against the powerful Old Aldenhamian side led by Donald Shearer. They drew 2 - 2 in the first match and were 0 - 4 down in the replay. At half-time, Carthusians changed tactics and put the two Moss brothers, who were very fast, on the wings, and their crosses caused havoc in the Aldenhamian defence. Carthusians won 5 - 4 and went on to lift the trophy by defeating Old Bradfieldians. This was the first Old Carthusian success for twelve years. Three years later, the Carthusian team led by Hollebone did it again and beat Old Cholmeleians 2 - 1 in the 1939 final.

Although Gerry Hollebone went on playing for the Carthusian cricket team for some years after the War, he gave up football after 1945 as he did not feel that he could maintain the fitness. He did however maintain his involvement with the Arthur Dunn by joining the Cup committee.

TOP: ACTION IN THE GOALMOUTH DURING THE 1939 FINAL.

ABOVE: THE 1939 PROGRAMME.

LEFT: THE PRESENTATION OF THE CUP BY MRS ARTHUR DUNN TO GERRY HOLLEBONE, CAPTAIN OF THE CARTHUSIANS, 1939.

Malvernians came back in the second half with an own goal by Simson and a close range success by Jacomb. Both teams attacked in turn during extra time and Wykehamists struck the bar.

CARTHUSIANS' ELEVENTH WIN

The eleventh Old Carthusian Arthur Dunn victory was in March 1939. On the same day, Portsmouth beat Huddersfield in an FA Cup semi-final, on their way to holding that trophy for the next seven years. Strong March winds spoiled both games, which were played at Highbury and Hurlingham respectively. Old Carthusians went into an early 2 - 0 lead. With the wind behind them, Wreford-Brown drove the ball into the top corner of the net after a goalmouth scramble. Fields then beat Stebbings with a half volley. In the second half, Old Cholmeleians, with the wind at their back, battered the Old Carthusians defence, which managed to hold out until Webster scored with ten minutes remaining. Old Carthusians held on to win 2 - 1.

Six months later, the world was plunged into war yet again. So, like so many leisure activities, the Arthur Dunn competition was prorogued for the duration. The draw for 1939/40 was made but was not used until the 1946/47 competition. By this time, Old Citizens had succumbed to the oval ball game, to be replaced by Old Brentwoods.

R T SQUIRE - OLD WESTMINSTER PRESIDENT 1932-1944

Ralph Tyndall Squire was born in Marylebone on 10th September 1863. During his time at Westminster School, he played in the first eleven between 1880 and 1882. After this early promise, he blossomed into a versatile full-back / half-back, equally capable in either role.

At Cambridge, he became secretary of the CUFC and got a blue in 1884 and 1886, but sadly missed out on the 1885 varsity match. Subsequently, he joined Old Westminsters, Clapham Rovers and Corinthians (1886-92), acting as Corinthians' Treasurer for many years from 1903.

A critic in the 1890s described him as "strong and not lacking in pace he has a sure kick, and with any amount of dash sticks to his opponent unflinchingly".

THE 1950 SEMI-FINAL BETWEEN OLD CARTHUSIANS AND OLD REPTONIANS.

PEGASUS SPREADS ITS WINGS

There was one team that was ineligible to enter the Arthur Dunn Cup and yet it had an immense influence on the Competition. Pegasus FC was formed in 1948 and achieved dramatic success, particularly in the FA Amateur Cup. Many of those who played in the team – Ken Shearwood (Salopians), H A Pawson (Wykehamists), J D P Tanner (Carthusians), etc – also played for their Old Boys teams and contributed to the achievements of these teams in the Dunn during the 1950s. Later, some of these individuals, notably Shearwood, Saunders and Dutchman helped to nurture the next generation at their chosen schools and this led to the success of Lancing OBs, Malvernians and Chigwellians in the 1970s, 1980s and 1990s. But all that was in the future.

POST-WAR
RESUMPTION OF THE COMPETITION

As Britain returned to some form of normality after six years of war, it was unclear whether the Arthur Dunn competition would continue.

The first Committee meeting after the War was held on 18th June 1946, attended by: B M Adams (Old Reptonians), G T Hollebone (Old Carthusians), R G S Banks (Old Wykehamists), J Stewart (Hon. Secretary – Bradfield) and N W Beeson (Hon. Treasurer – Malvern).

It was announced that a number of significant members had been lost in the War. C T Ashton was killed in action in 1942, R T Squire, the President, and G O Smith had also died during the War years.

The Hon. Secretary announced at the meeting that he had sent a letter to all Clubs on 6 September 1945 to ask whether to resume the competition. In response, there was strong agreement to restart in 1946/47 *"whatever the difficulties"*. The Times reported that *"this is indeed welcome news. There is nothing keener or more enjoyable to be seen in a season of football than these Arthur Dunn matches, which for so long have contrived to keep the spirit of the amateur game alive in the public schools"*. It was agreed that the draw made for the 1939/40 season should be used for the first competition after the war.

Due to the shortage of grounds around

London, it was arranged for the final in 1947 to be held at the Lloyd's Bank ground at Beckenham. Discussions were opened to increase the radius around London, stated in Rule 14, to over 50 miles.

Almost inevitably, it was Old Carthusians who progressed majestically to the final in April 1947 where their opponents were old adversaries, Old Reptonians.

The Old Carthusian side was spearheaded in the campaign by one J D P Tanner who operated on the right wing, making killing crosses that worried opposing defences and gave numerous opportunities for the Carthusian forwards. There was also a further devastating tactic because Tanner was often switched to the centre-forward position later in games and was very capable of scoring himself. For example in the second round against Old Wykehamists he provided the passes for two of the Carthusian goals and then scored himself from the centre-forward position. His brilliance continued in the semi-final against Old Salopians and then in the final he scored two goals (Wreford-Brown got the other) to help defeat Reptonians.

A J WREFORD-BROWN
OLD CARTHUSIAN

A J Wreford-Brown followed in the great tradition of the family in going to Charterhouse, playing football for the school and subsequently progressing to the Old Carthusian team. His father, Charles, was of course a leading figure in the formation of the Arthur Dunn competition and played in the first three finals. His uncle, O E, also played in the first two finals. A J was a member of the victorious Dunn side that won the trophy in 1936 and scored a goal to gain another victory in 1939. Then, after the Second World War, whilst a master at Charterhouse, he was a member of the winning sides of 1947 (in which he again scored a goal) and 1949.

TOP: *GOALMOUTH ACTION DURING THE 1947 FINAL.*

ABOVE: *THE OLD CARTHUSIAN CAPTAIN, R M HOLLIS RECEIVES THE CUP FROM MRS ARTHUR DUNN.*

LLOYDS BANK GROUND BECKENHAM (1947)

Lloyds Bank acquired the Sports Ground at Copers Cope Road, Beckenham in 1921 when the Bank merged with the Capital & Counties Bank. By the purchase of additional land from the adjoining Cator estate, the ground was expanded to 25 acres, with twelve tennis courts, and one netball, three cricket, three rugby, four football and two hockey pitches. In 1925, the pavilion (left) was rebuilt to designs by E A Stone.

The 1947 Arthur Dunn Final was held at the Lloyd's Bank ground. However, this was the only year that it was held there as an agreement was shortly made with Tooting & Mitcham FC for the final to be located on their ground. In 1999, Lloyd's Bank decide to close the facility at Beckenham, citing a fall in usage and the prohibitive cost of refurbishment. The ground has now been sold for redevelopment.

A G BOWER (1895-1970)
OLD CARTHUSIAN
PRESIDENT 1947-1963

Alfred George Bower, known to everyone as "Baishe", was indeed a legend in his own lifetime. He was the last amateur to captain a full England side and attained this honour without having been a member of the Charterhouse First XI. In all, he obtained five full England caps between 1924 and 1926, and 13 amateur caps between 1921 and 1928. He also played in the old Carthusian side that won the Arthur Dunn Cup three years running from 1922.

After leaving Charterhouse, he served in the Army throughout the First World War, and played an appreciable amount of football during this time. After the War, he was soon playing for old Carthusians, for Casuals in the Isthmian league, and of course, for many years in the Corinthians, who were virtually the leading amateur side in England at that time.

Baishe was in the Corinthian side that played in the FA Cup which, in their first year in the FA Cup, beat Blackburn Rovers and were only just beaten by Newcastle United. He played successfully for Chelsea for several seasons, and became a considerable favourite with the crowds, where he was known as the man who never committed an intentional foul.

He was President of the Arthur Dunn Cup competition from 1947-1963.

On 18th June 1947, A G Bower was elected President in place of the late R J Squire. There was, however, some doubt about the election of the secretary. Major J Stewart wanted to retire and G T Hollebone (Old Carthusians) was nominated as his successor. Hollebone could not give a definite decision and so Major Stewart agreed to carry on for the moment. It seems that a number of people decided to resign and Major Stewart found himself taking on the Chairmanship and the Competition's representative on the FA Council (as well as continuing as Secretary).

WYKEHAMISTS DOMINANT

The competition in 1947/48 led to a final at a new ground, the home of Tooting and Mitcham FC. This time it was Old Wykehamists who snatched the trophy for the sixth time.

Wykehamists' path to the final began with a convincing win over Old Aldenhamians at Aldenham. Apparently, the initial stages of the game were not of a very high standard but with the arrival of a new and heavier ball, more fully inflated, the game improved. Aldenhamians put up a good fight but Wykehamists had a very strong side featuring Pawson, R Hornby and the incomparable G H G Doggart.

After a second round routing of Bradfieldians (4 - 1), the semi-final was against Old Salopians. *"It was a very good game played between two very strong sides of at least equal strength to the better pre-war Dunn Cup sides"* (The Wykehamists – March 1948). The correspondent not only recognised the quality of both sides but also commented on three Wykehamists supporters from Winchester *"whose attendance was once again greatly appreciated"*. He was also at pains to thank *"Shearwood, Pawson and J W Hornby for all the arrangements made, including those for the tea"*!

In the final, their opponents were Old Cholmeleians but Wykehamists, with the *"intelligent passing of Doggart and Hornby and the speed of Abbott and Pawson"*, were far too good. Wykehamist's ran out winners by 5 - 1. This was Wykehamists' tenth appearance in the final and their sixth victory, including a tie in 1938.

BELOW: A H FABIAN (CAPTAIN, OLD CHOLMELEIANS), TOSSES THE COIN WATCHED ON BY J L EDWARDS, THE REFEREE AND M R F SIMSON (CAPTAIN, OLD WYKEHAMISTS), TO START THE 1948 FINAL.

FAR RIGHT AND RIGHT: MATCH ACTION DURING THE 1948 FINAL.

BELOW: M R F SIMSON, CAPTAIN OF THE OLD WYKEHAMISTS IS PRESENTED WITH THE CUP BY MRS ARTHUR DUNN.

CARTHUSIANS WIN AGAIN

Carthusians were not to be denied ownership of the trophy for long. In 1949, they won the Cup for the thirteenth time. Their opponents were their old rivals, Old Salopians. It was not one of the better finals because apparently players tried to achieve too much on their own, and the tackling was so keen that cohesive movements were few. *"But everyone enjoyed the hearty scrambles for the ball, and it was all grand fun"*. Despite being without their star, Tanner, Carthusians were the better side. In the second half, the

LEFT: PLAY DURING THE 1949 FINAL.

BELOW: THE VICTORIOUS OLD CARTHUSIANS SIDE OF 1949. (FROM L.TO R.) J G LARKING, P B H MAY, D L BENKE, A J WREFORD-BROWN, A HASTINGS, V R GOODRIDGE, R M HOLLIS (CAPT), P BENNETT, K R DOLLEYMORE, M J RIMELL AND P C G LARKING.

On 9 June 1948, the Committee was notified that one of their members, R G S Banks had recently died on the cricket field. In his memory, a donation was made to the Working Men's College in which Banks was greatly interested.

Three Committee members were nominated to the Old Boys Committee but poor old Major Stewart could still not get someone to take on the role of secretary. At the same meeting, following on from previous discussions, it was agreed that Rule 14 should be changed to state that games should be held within *"70 miles of London"* with grounds to be decided by the Committee after the first round. Negotiations were opened with Surrey CCC with a view to playing Dunn Cup games at the Oval and this was *"agreed in principle"* but only games played before February.

PEGASUS ARE FORMED

At the AGM held on 17 June 1948, it was noted that a new amateur club had been formed, uniting the football clubs of Oxford and Cambridge Universities. This club was to have a brief but spectacular life, with starring roles for Old Boys, like Ken Shearwood and J D P Tanner, who also competed in the Dunn.

In October 1948, Major Stewart was finally able to resign as secretary to be succeeded by A R V Barker (Old Wykehamists) but Barker was forced to resign in 1949 due to ill-health. It was agreed that Bartry-King (Old Wykehamists) should be approached. He subsequently declined the offer and in August 1949, the issue was finally settled when R S Blundell (Old Bradfieldians) took on the role – which he was to fulfil for the next 20 years.

Salopians improved, particularly when Ken Shearwood, the Oxford University and Pegasus centre-half, previously the Salopian's best defender, adopted an attacking role, and Crawford moved from centre-forward to outside-left. But at the end of the day, Old Carthusians were victorious.

HOLDING THE CUP IS CAPTAIN R M HOLLIS WHO PLAYED IN THE 1939 FINAL AND CAPTAINED THE SIDE IN FOUR OTHER FINALS (1947, 49, 50 AND 51) WINNING THREE TIMES.

P B H MAY - OLD CARTHUSIAN

Peter Barker Howard May was born on 6 December 1929 at Reading in Berkshire. He blossomed as a cricketer on the Green at Charterhouse and progressing to Cambridge, he won blues for football and cricket.

He went on to be the lynchpin of the Surrey and England batting during the golden era of the 1950s, his awesomely powerful driving complemented by an intense concentration under pressure. May came to be regarded as the finest post-war batsman in England.

He captained England in 41 Tests and led them to victory in 21 of them a record.

Peter May, like so many of his contemporaries, was able to participate at a reasonable level in more than one sport. Though he is famous for his cricketing exploits he was also a capable footballer. He was a key member of the Old Carthusian team that dominated the Arthur Dunn competition just after the Second World War. He played in three consecutive finals – 1949 and 1951 which Carthusians won, and the losing final of 1950.

Sadly, on 1st July 1949, Mrs Arthur Dunn, who had presented the Cup for so many years, died. She was laid to rest next to her husband in the churchyard at Little Shelford. Her daughter, Mrs Andrew Shirley, agreed to carry on the family tradition.

FAR RIGHT AND RIGHT: OLD CARTHUSIANS (ON HOME GROUND) BEAT OLD REPTONIANS 2 - 0 IN THE 1950 SEMI-FINAL.

FAR RIGHT: THE STAND WAS PACKED FOR THE 1950 FINAL.

BELOW: THE CAPTAINS AND THE REFEREE AWAIT THE OUTCOME OF THE TOSS.

RIGHT: A CLEARANCE BY THE CARTHUSIAN GOALKEEPER.

which eventually fell through. They however came up with a report (August 1949) that recommended the formation of a limited company to raise capital for the purchase and operation of a ground for the benefit of member clubs. In June 1950, it was finally agreed that the Competition should not be involved in running its own ground.

At the same time, Rule 14 was modified again to state that all games should be played on school grounds wherever possible, and otherwise within 70 miles of London.

It was Carthusians yet again that fought their way to the final in April 1950; not that they were destined to win the Cup this time. Despite the efforts of Tanner and Larking and their team, they were no match for the likes of Tillard, Doggart, Pawson, Abbott and the other Wykehamists.

GROUND PROPOSALS

In 1950, Col. Morgan-Owen died and the following year C Wreford-Brown also died. A proposal that the Competition should secure a permanent ground led to the formation of a sub-Committee to look into this. They monitored a plan led by Lancing to purchase an old polo ground at Cobham, Surrey for their purposes –

RIGHT: THE WYKEHAMISTS ATTACKING THE CARTHUSIAN GOAL DURING THE 1950 FINAL.

PEGASUS

Pegasus Football Club was formed in 1948 from the amalgamation of the Oxford University Centaurs AFC and the Cambridge University Falcons AFC. The name, Pegasus, of course depicts the winged horse in classical mythology; this therefore represented the combination of the Centaur, the man-headed horse, and the Falcon, a bird.

At the inaugural meeting at the East India and Sports Club, St James' Square, London, the Rev Kenneth Hunt was elected president, Graham Doggart became the Hon. Treasurer and the founder, Dr H W Thompson (Tommy), became the secretary.

LEFT: DR H W THOMPSON, FOUNDER OF PEGASUS.

The club's rise was nothing short of sensational. "The winged horse…prepared for its first flight to the stars through the clouds of a Cup adventure" (Edward Grayson – Corinthians and Cricketers). Granted exemption from the first three qualifying rounds of the FA Amateur Cup (because of the Varsity commitments), the team suffered only one defeat – when they were narrowly beaten in the closing stages of a thrilling quarter-final at Oxford by the ultimate winners, Bromley; the game was watched by over 11,000 people. Edward Grayson, a spectator at the game, recalled that "the Pegasus performance against one of the most consistently successful amateur clubs in southern England since the War was truly amazing, and the result could easily have gone the other way".

Two years later (in 1951) Pegasus won the FA Amateur Cup by defeating Bishop Auckland at Wembley. Of this team, Brown, Cowan, Shuttleworth, Saunders, Pawson, Tanner and Potts were capped for England.

The success of Pegasus was due to a number of factors. They received considerable assistance and expert coaching from the likes of George Ainsley, the former England professional, who was also coach at Tottenham Hotspur. The team also benefited from the fact that many of the players had gone to the Varsities later than was usual (due to the War). However, this flood of talent was threatened because of a dispute that was ultimately to cause its demise. Traditionally, Corinthian-Casuals had claimed the right to call upon services of players who had been down for more than one year. Unfortunately, this would immediately deny Pegasus of the services of Ken Shearwood and others. So in 1951, the ruling was withdrawn much to the chagrin of Casuals. It became very acrimonious when both teams were drawn against each other in the third round of the 1953 FA Amateur Cup campaign. In a scrappy game at the Oval, Corinthian-Casuals were swept aside by a Pawson goal.

Ultimately, Pegasus got to the final of the Cup that year and defeated Harwich and Parkeston with five members of the 1951 side – Brown, Shearwood, Saunders, Pawson and Carr. Shearwood particularly made a large contribution. Though he did not receive the deserved recognition, he was described as a brilliant stopper (He once said: "If we get to Wembley – then over my dead body!").

Pegasus did not reach these heights again but the team continued for several years. However, the seeds of disaster were always present. "Tommy" resigned as secretary in 1954. The Cambridge contingent tended to stick to the one-year rule and so fewer and fewer Cambridge players were involved with the team. "So what began as a combined football venture by Oxford and Cambridge undergraduates, inspired by Tommy, finally foundered on a difference of opinion that became apparent as early as 1949 when the one-year rule was rescinded" (Ken Shearwood in his book "Pegasus").

The last recorded match that Pegasus played was on 6th April 1963 against Marston United in the third round of the Oxfordshire Senior Cup, which they won by a single goal.

Members of the Pegasus team have had a considerable and long-lasting influence on the Dunn, first as players turned out for their Old Boys teams – John Tanner (Old Carthusians), Ken Shearwood (Old Salopians), Tony Pawson (Old Wykehamists), Reg Vowells (Old Brentwoods), Donald Carr (Old Reptonians) and then later Shearwood joined the staff at Lancing and inspired a new generation of Old Boy footballers. With similar effect, Denis Saunders went to Malvern and John Dutchman taught at Chigwell.

ABOVE: PEGASUS, FA AMATEUR CUP WINNERS - 1951.
(BACK L. TO R.): J PLATT, K A SHEARWOOD, J A DUTCHMAN, R COWAN, D F SAUNDERS (WITH CUP), J D P TANNER, B R BROWN, H A PAWSON, D B CARR.
(FRONT): J MAUGHAN, H J POTTS.
(BACK TO CAMERA), DR H W THOMPSON (HON. SEC.).

ABOVE: 1951, G R SCOTT (CAPTAIN, OLD WELLINGBURIANS), BILL CHIVERS (REFEREE) AND P BENNETT (CAPTAIN, OLD CARTHUSIANS), WAITING FOR THE PENNY TO DROP.

RIGHT: GOALMOUTH ACTION DURING THE 1951 FINAL.

RIGHT: THE OLD CARTHUSIANS CELEBRATE THEIR WIN IN 1951.

FAR RIGHT: MRS ANDREW SHIRLEY PRESENTS THE CUP TO P BENNETT, OLD CARTHUSIAN CAPTAIN, 1951.

BELOW: OLD WELLINGBURIANS RUNNERS UP 1951.
(BACK L. TO R.): J W L CHAMBERLAIN, E J BELTON, L E EDON, C H COOK, H K JOHNSON, J K GOTCH, B HUCKLE. (FRONT): D L MEAD, J L SCOTT, G R SCOTT (CAPT.), W B SHERET, J B RILEY.

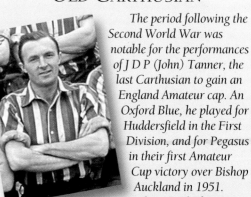

ABOVE: THE OLD WELLINGBURIANS TEAM OF 1951 AT THEIR REUNION IN 1991.

The Carthusians' grip on the competition was still strong, for in 1951 they reached the final yet again. This time, the opposition was a new name, Old Wellingburians, and the newcomers matched the old hands in every respect. *"In fact, it was only minutes, with victory at last assured by four goals to two, that the Carthusians were able to breathe freely again after an exciting Wellingburian rally had brought some warmth to the cold, windy afternoon in the second half".*

The conditions at Tooting and Mitcham that day were very difficult. A strong wind blew from goal to goal, and the ball, *"of an unexpected orange tint"*, was light and fickle, a combination sometimes sufficient to reduce even the masters of the game to mediocrity.

J D P TANNER
OLD CARTHUSIAN

The period following the Second World War was notable for the performances of J D P (John) Tanner, the last Carthusian to gain an England Amateur cap. An Oxford Blue, he played for Huddersfield in the First Division, and for Pegasus in their first Amateur Cup victory over Bishop Auckland in 1951.

He subsequently for many years served on the Committee of the Football Association. He played in three winning Dunn teams in 1947 (in which he scored two goals), 1951 and 1954, and the losing finalists in 1950. He, Peter May, May's brother J W H, D G W Goodliffe (who played for Millwall just after the War), and T R H Savill, formed the backbone of the Club' successes in those years.

GOLDEN JUBILEE

In 1952 the Old Etonians belatedly made their first appearance in the final – surprising for one of the pioneers of football! They came up against one of the stalwarts of the Dunn competition, Old Salopians, who showed no mercy. Etonians, as the underdogs, gained good support from the neutrals in the crowd but their success was not to be. Moulsdale opened the scoring from Pugh's pass and added a second after a goalmouth melée.

The Etonians pulled one back before half-time and began to look dangerous. The third goal was decisive, Rhys's neat flick putting Moulsdale through to complete his hat-trick and the Salopians took control with Rhys (2) and Clegg ensuring a comfortable victory by six goals to one. This was Salopians' seventh title.

As 1953 marked the Golden Jubilee of the inaugural Arthur Dunn Final it was agreed that there should be a dinner to mark the occasion – and this took place on Wednesday 22nd April 1953.

ABOVE: THE 1952 FINAL.

INSET LEFT: MRS ANDREW SHIRLEY PRESENTS THE CUP TO THE OLD SALOPIAN CAPTAIN ROBIN MOULSDALE, 1952.

LEFT: OLD SALOPIANS CELEBRATE THEIR VICTORY IN 1952.

THE ARTHUR DUNN CUP
1902 - 1953

PRESENTED BY R. C. GOSLING
FEBRUARY, 1902

JUBILEE DINNER
WEDNESDAY, 22ND APRIL, 1953
CONNAUGHT ROOMS · · W.C.1

PRESIDENT · · A. G. BOWER

LEFT: THE MENU FOR THE JUBILEE DINNER. THE SPEAKERS AT THE DINNER WERE: G A R GREEN (OLD SALOPIAN), R S BLUNDELL (HON. SECRETARY ARTHUR DUNN CUP), A L HILDER (HON. TREASURER ARTHUR DUNN CUP), AND SIR STANLEY ROUS (SECRETARY FOOTBALL ASSOCIATION).

TOOTING AND MITCHAM GROUND SANDY LANE (1948 - 1956)

Sandy Lane became the home of Tooting Town in 1922. They merged with Mitcham Wanderers in 1937 to form Tooting and Mitcham United, the new club played in the Athenian League until 1956, and then joined the Isthmian League. Sandy Lane hosted nine Arthur Dunn Cup Finals between 1948 and 1956. Tooting and Mitcham played their final game at Sandy Lane in April 2002 and have moved to a new ground in Bishopsford Road, Morden.

MEMORIES OF THE OLD SALOPIANS IN THE 50s
by A R B Moulsdale

A R B MOULSDALE
OLD SALOPIAN

Robin Moulsdale is another with a strong footballing lineage. His father, J R B Moulsdale was a member of the Corinthian team that defeated the mighty Blackburn Rovers in the FA Cup of 1924. Joining the Old Salopians after leaving school, Robin found himself leading a very good Salopian side in the early 1950s. He came into the side in 1947 and captained them to victory in the Dunn in March 1952. This feat was repeated in the Jubilee year of 1953, followed by another visit to the final in 1954 only to lose to the old enemy, Carthusians.

For the fourth successive year, Robin led Salopians to another Dunn Final. On this occasion, the opponents were Old Brentwoods and the result of a thrilling game was a 4 - 4 draw. Both teams held the trophy jointly for next year.

After a gap of nine years, Robin led a new team to the final again in 1964. They won 4 - 1 over Old Aldenhamians.

My first hazy memory of Arthur Dunn Cup football takes me back to January 1947. I had left school a few weeks before and struggled by stop-start train one cold, snow-filled day to Forest. Statistics have never been strong with me (nor memory now) but there were about nine Foresters present and seven Old Salopians. John Haslewood was a persuasive man, insisting that one of his team had come from Cornwall and another from Scotland, and no way could he get a team together the following week, so the referee agreed to start. Conditions were icy with snow showers drifting in thin wisps. After a very short time when we were leading 4 - 2, John said conditions were impossible and claimed the match.

Next in 1950, there was a game at Iffley Road against Carthusians, which we lost, and then an unforgettable match against Cholmeleians who included the great, but by then, venerable names of Taj Webster and Howard Fabian. We won 10 - 1. I can still see Howard Fabian when nine down running to take corners from both wings determined to find Taj Webster's head. By now, we were beginning to assemble a powerful forward line led by Dick Rhys certainly the best footballer I ever played with or against. In the 1952 final against Eton, Dick was surrounded by prostrate Etonians having dribbled around the penalty area and then slipped it to me to walk into the net. For the next four years (1951-55), we averaged four goals a game in sixteen matches.

I first captained the Salopians in 1951 and, in those pre-Arthurian League days, the great skill was to get the right players to the right ground at the right time. Too frequently we had to organise a delayed start while we watched our eleventh man bump up to the touch-line changing his boots in the car. In one memorable match against Eton they arrived with nine men, the tenth joining in after five minutes or so, but the eleventh hadn't arrived by half-time. Eventually he appeared, played a vigorous part on the wing, and then without a word disappeared. Apparently, his car had broken down, but he could neither ring up nor explain because he had interrupted a silent retreat at some monastery to turn out and not let his team down.

We had a lot of fun and laughed a lot, which is not to say the games were played with anything but the utmost determination and vigour. I have never tackled anyone in my life, but I do remember once coincidentally meeting shoulder to shoulder the great Reptonian centre-half, Dick Sale. To my surprise, he fell over but rose immediately firing imprecations at me and the referee. And the tackles were fierce. Johnny Clegg, our flying right wing, was often targeted and a mistimed tackle once broke his leg. Flying wingers were part of the tactical scene in those days, Pawson for Winchester and Tanner for Charterhouse.

But the game was very different in those days. No self-respecting winger tackled back, or spent time in his own half, no fullback ventured over the halfway line. We played the 'W' formation up front and thought we were wonderfully fit, but covered nothing like the ground that our successors do. And no self-respecting Salopian headed the ball – except Ken Shearwood. Ken was a magnificent header of the ball and had survived the water-absorbent leather balls and thick mud of Shrewsbury. He could dominate an England amateur centre-forward in a Wembley Cup Final, but the rest of us let it bounce.

In 1953/54 we lost the final to Tim Savill's Carthusians. Dick Rhys went sick on the morning of the match and we never found a way through an inspired Carthusian defence. The final of 1954/55 was an epic. Reg Vowells, an old Emmanuel mate of mine, was immense, his red hair the flying buttress of the Brentwood defence and his cultured feet prompting their attack. We still scored our four goals, but so did they and in the last minute of extra time with Johnny Clegg clean through at least a hundred miles an hour the Brentwood keeper blocked the shot. The press were poised to write up this great final, as indeed they covered most of the Dunn matches in those days, but the next day was the start of a long newspaper strike, so I never saw an account of the game.

I was away in 1956/57 and in the next two years with only Johnny Clegg and myself left from the forward line of those winning years, we lost in the first round each time 5 - 3 to a young but strong Malvern side. In the second of these (1959/60), we played at Malvern in the worst conditions I can remember and I conceded the game before the final whistle. It seemed an eminently sensible thing to do at the time and now seems incredibly feeble. It was one of those total rain days where the mud had turned to flood and our heavy shirts were filled with water when the wind turned east and it became bitingly cold. Dick Chadder of Malvern retired with hypothermia (it couldn't have been quite as young a side as I imagined) and my ageing fleshless bones were beginning to rattle. No way were we going to swim through the flood to score two more goals. "Enough", I said to the ref, and as I write it, again it does seem sensible.

FAR LEFT: THE TEAMS LINE-UP FOR THE PRE-MATCH PRESENTATION, 1953.

LEFT: MOULSDALE (OLD SALOPIAN CAPTAIN), BILL CHIVERS (REFEREE) AND DOGGART (OLD WYKEHAMIST CAPTAIN) AWAIT THE OUTCOME OF THE TOSS, 1953.

BELOW LEFT: 1953 ACTION FROM BEHIND THE WYKEHAMISTS GOAL.

BELOW: ONE OF THE THREE GOALS SCORED BY THE SALOPIANS, 1953.

FAR LEFT: THE PRESENTATION OF THE CUP BY MRS ANDREW SHIRLEY TO ROBIN MOULSDALE, THE OLD SALOPIAN CAPTAIN.

LEFT: HUBERT DOGGART THE OLD WYKEHAMISTS CAPTAIN, CONGRATULATES ROBIN MOULSDALE AFTER THE PRESENTATION OF THE CUP.

BELOW: THE OLD SALOPIANS HOLD THE TRADITIONAL CELEBRATION.

It was appropriate that 50 years after Salopians shared the first Arthur Dunn Cup with Old Carthusians, they should again get to the final. In fact, by their victory over the Old Wykehamists by three goals to one at Tooting and Mitcham, they emphasised their predominance in the competition during these first few years after the Second World War. *"And this was quite the best final since the war, full of constructive football, powerful shooting and desperately near misses"* (The Times). Playing into a strong wind, the Salopians conceded a goal in the opening minutes and then came under heavy pressure. *"To Charlesworth, for two or three vital saves in goal, and to Robinson, who clipped the dangerous Pawson's wings must go the honours"* (The Times).

MEMORIES OF AN OLD WYKEHAMIST
by Hubert Doggart

G H G DOGGART
OLD WYKEHAMIST

Hubert Doggart is the son of A G Doggart, another famous Wykehamist, who was one of the stars of the famous Corinthian team of the 1920s.

Hubert followed his father to Winchester and played football at school. He progressed to Old Wykehamists and became captain of the side just after the Second World War. With a strong team of players, Doggart led the team to victory in the 1950 Dunn Final over Old Carthusians.

He took the team to another final in 1953, the Jubilee Year of the Competition, only to lose to Old Salopians. And then the Wykehamists had to wait eight years before they had another chance. But in 1961, Doggart once again led the team to another victory (over Old Cholmeleians).

My scrapbook reminds me that Geoffrey Green paid us a pleasing tribute for our team-work against the Old Cholmeleians in the 1948 final. To come back from War service and be able to play in this wonderful event, so redolent of the Corinthian spirit of its founder, was a great delight. I seem to recall that the 2 Cholmeleian older-timers, Taj Webster and Howard Fabian, not surprisingly, tired a little towards the end, and that our greater youth and experience - four of our side, Tony Pawson and Rob Tillard for Oxford, Barry Abbott and I for Cambridge, had played at Dulwich Hamlet in the Oxford v Cambridge match of 1947 (and William Slack and Dick Hornby had played previously for Oxford) - helped us to win the day comfortably (5 - 1).

To have beaten Old Carthusians, Cup winners more often than any other school, 3 - 1 on that memorable March day in 1950 must count as our finest achievement since the Second World War. And the Times Association Football correspondent seems to suggest that we deserved to win, in part because of our control of the mid-field, in which William Slack, Tim Slack and Rob Tillard played such a sterling role, and in part because we were more inventive in attack. We had, in Tony Pawson, it should be remembered, a dribbler of a soccer ball of rare genius, and his counterpart for the Carthusians, John Tanner, was expertly held in check for much of the game.

It is, of course, the Finals that appear in the scrapbooks, so that we move on to 1961. We played successive sides that year from the London area, and I recall returning after a match not far from Hainault, in an earlier round, and buying, at a station bookstall, several copies of the Evening News that boasted a photograph, with a heading "Meet Tiny Simon", of Sue, my wife, and our first arrival..

It was an unalloyed pleasure to be playing again in a final at Wealdstone – on the same day that, not all that far away, England were beating Scotland 9 - 3, and to be captaining a young Wykehamist side all of whom had had me as Master-in-charge at school. I recall with satisfaction that, after going 2 goals up and losing that lead, we came again and scored twice, thereby winning 4 - 2. One of our 2 finest players, Barry Read, is still able to talk anyone who is prepared to listen through many of the moves in that game! I doubt whether the other, Ian Maclure, could do that, but he was a top-flight winger in the old mould.

BELOW: MRS ANDREW SHIRLEY PRESENTS THE CUP TO A DELIGHTED G H G DOGGART IN 1950.

It was an extra pleasure to be captaining in a final for the third time; and there are extant photographs showing me receiving the cup, on both occasions, from the Hon. Mrs Shirley, Arthur Dunn's daughter. I understand that this span - 1950-1961 - was exceeded by the Salopian Robin Moulsdale, and I think of no better rival, since our fathers played in the same great Corinthian sides of the 1920s, who themselves followed in the great tradition of the early Corinthian teams that included G O Smith and the great Arthur Dunn himself.

Scrapbooks, those lovely evokers of "time past", do not tell of the preliminary rounds, when we would go miles by car or by train - I recall a fine win at Shrewsbury after an interminable journey there - and revel in each other's company, and do our damnedest to win, but not at all costs. It was both an education and an enjoyment in equal measure, for which we must always be grateful..

DRAWN ARTHUR DUNN CUP FINAL

OLD BRENTWOODS FIGHT BACK IN TIME
Old Salopians 4, Old Brentwoods 4

Quite one of the best and certainly the most exciting of Arthur Dunn Cup finals of recent years was played on Saturday at the Tooting and Mitcham ground before a large and enthusiastic crowd. That it should end inconclusively in a draw after extra time is perhaps unsatisfactory, for in such an event there is no replay, each side holding the cup for six months in turn. But half a loaf is better than no bread and neither side deserved to leave such a game empty handed, for it was cut and thrust all the way.

Old Brentwoods, playing in the final for the first time in their history, have infused new life into the competition and it needed all the experience of the Old Salopians, finalists for the past four years, to hold off this fresh challenge. It will not be long before it is Brentwood's undisputed turn.

OLD SALOPIANS EQUALIZE

Space alone prevents individual mention of the game's heroes: rather let events tell their own story, for it was not long before the pattern of the game began to take shape. Old Brentwoods were the first to draw blood when in the eleventh minute Harrison, taking a free-kick just outside the penalty area, pierced the Salopian defensive screen with a low drive just inside the post. Within the minute Old Salopians had drawn level, for Malyon was fatally deceived by the flight of a high cross pass from Bretherton for the ball to bounce over his head and into the net.

Brentwood, however, quickly reasserted themselves and some eight minutes later restored their lead with a good goal by Skeate after Vowells and Horrex had combined on the right for Odammtten to supply the final pass. Moreover, they went further ahead shortly afterwards when Odammtten broke clear on the left to place his centre perfectly for Horrex to head home. They might even have scored a fourth goal but for a timely clearance by Robinson off his very goal-line and at half-time it seemed plan sailing for Brentwood.

With the change of ends Old Salopians, who had been quite unable to harness the wind to their advantage in the first half, soon struck their real form and scored three goals in the space of eight minutes to snatch the lead for the first time in the game. It was Roberts who showed the way to recovery with a long pass out to Pugh, whose centre Moulsdale crashed into the roof of the net. This was followed four minutes later with another move instigated by Pugh and carried on by Rhys for Moulsdale again to supply the final thrust. The Salopians were now on terms and Brentwood wilted under the onslaught; their rhythm deserted them and a fatal hesitancy in distribution was to be seen for the first time.

Minutes later the Salopians went ahead with a glorious goal by Rhys again after Pugh had made the earlier running. It seemed that Brentwood had shot their bolt but to their credit they came again and eight minutes from time Horrex, taking a cross pass from Corker in full stride, cut inwards to equalize with a rising shot off the underside of the cross-bar. And so to extra time, and, though the tempo slowed, the football in no way suffered. If anything, the excitement intensified as first Webb, in quite his best form, saved point blank from Odammtten and then Langridge somehow retrieved a header by Pugh from his very goal-line. Later Malyon made ample amends for his one mistake with fine saves from Rhys and Clegg to climax a memorable afternoon.

KEN SHEARWOOD - OLD SALOPIAN

Ken Shearwood has had a profound influence on amateur football both as a player and a motivator. Returning from war-service in the Navy with a DSC, he spent a period as a fisherman at Mevagissey. In 1947, he went up to Oxford to read history and went straight into the University football team, playing for 4 years in the matches against Cambridge. When the joint Universities team, Pegasus, was formed in 1948, Shearwood was a colossus at the heart of their defence, featuring in the teams that won the F A Amateur Cup in 1951 and 1953.

At the same time, Ken turned out for Old Salopians whenever he could. He appeared in three Dunn finals – 1949, 1952 and 1954. As a stopper centre-half, he "marshalled the defence around him with cheerful good humour, inspiring everyone with his determined example.

The fact that he scored from many a scorching back-pass was neither here nor there. Neither Bill Rhys nor Michael Charlesworth could ever possibly have been offended by these bullet-like own-goals such was the warmth strength of Ken's inevitable apology".

After his playing days were over, Ken became a master at Lancing College where he inspired so many young men at Lancing that they later provided the personnel for the successful Lancing Old Boys sides of the 1980s.

On April 3rd 1954, the old rivalry was revived. In a repeat of the inaugural final, Old Carthusians met Old Salopians but this time Carthusians forced a win, taking the trophy for the fifteenth time. The Cup was presented by Arthur Dunn's daughter, Mrs Andrew Shirley.

FAR LEFT: THE TIMES REPORT OF THE 1955 FINAL, WHICH WAS NEVER PRINTED DUE TO A PAPER STRIKE.

BRENTWOOD SHARE THE CUP

The Times described the 1955 final as *"quite one of the best and certainly the most exciting of Arthur Dunn Finals"*. A large and enthusiastic crowd at Tooting and Mitcham watched Old Salopians and Old Brentwoods share eight goals. Even after extra time, they could not be separated so the Cup was shared. As is the tradition, the Cup was held by each club for six months. This was the first time that Old Brentwoods had played in a final. *"It will not be long before it is Brentwood's undisputed turn"*.

BILL CHIVERS - REFEREE

Bill Chivers joined the Amateur Football Association in 1934 and soon became one of the most sought-after officials in the amateur game.

He officiated in several leagues and also the final AFA Senior Cup. It is said that Bill's greatest asset was "his extreme geniality at all times" and in twenty years of refereeing he never sent a player off the field.

He was so well-regarded that he was asked to referee five Arthur Dunn Finals in the early 1950s.

MEMORIES OF AN OLD WELLINGBURIAN
by Richard Peck

In January 1956, I had entered the Royal Military Academy Sandhurst. We were under strict military discipline, as you can imagine in those early years after WW2, when National Service still existed. In November, I had received an informal approach from Garnet Scott about my availability to play in the Dunn Cup match at Wellingborough in December. I was approaching the end of my first year and, as it was a two-year course, I was still in the junior year. it was no time for me to request leave, for this unusual reason, from a Saturday morning's Academy Parade! I suggested to Garnet that he should write to my Company Commander. He did and, to my surprise, I was granted leave from 10:00am.

I owned a small car, which had to be garaged outside the Academy; it was kept in a garage in Sandhurst village for 5 shillings a month. I called to see the owner, Jock Thompson, during the week to make arrangements to take the car out on the Saturday morning. On the day, having walked the mile or so from my room in very high spirits, you can imagine my feelings when I found the garage locked and bolted with not a soul in sight. We were still suffering the after effects of the Suez Campaign., which had left us on petrol rationing. Jock had run out of petrol and, as this was the major part of his business, he saw no point in staying open. He had completely forgotten that I was due to take my car out!

So, I could ring the school and explain my predicament, suggesting they find a replacement: I could walk or run to Camberley station, two miles away and hope to get train connections to Wellingborough; or perhaps I could hitch a lift towards London. If I was successful, I could judge the situation as I made progress. I could ring the School, at the appropriate time, either to suggest they find another player or to arrange transport from Wellingborough Station.

I decided on the third option and, soon afterwards, complete with my bag containing my football kit, I was on the pillion seat of a motor cycle, making my way along the A30. At some point (I think it was near Staines) I took my leave of the motor cyclist, thanking him as warmly as I could, and completed my journey to London by train. When I reached St Pancras, good fortune was with me. There was a train leaving shortly for Wellingborough, which would arrive at the time the match was due to start; so I bought a ticket, found a telephone box (a mobile phone would have been useful!) and rang the School. I was told a car would be waiting for me at the station. During the journey, I went to the w.c to change into my OW strip and boots, and returned to my compartment. This must have seemed an unusual occurrence to those with whom I shared it! The train was on time, the car was there and I arrived at the pitch three or four minutes after the kick-off. There was a good crowd of OWs and Old Malvernians on the touch-line, who had been informed of the situation, and I was given a warm hand as I joined the match. I had used a good deal of nervous energy in reaching Wellingborough but, after 12 months of military training at RMAS, I was very fit and ready for battle! Sadly, we lost!

At the Committee meeting on 19th January 1956, a proposal to enlarge the competition was rejected due to the lack of finance. And to raise additional funds, negotiations were opened with the Times to make a donation.

In the final of that year, on March 24th, Old Malvernians

regained the Arthur Dunn Cup after a span of 18 years when they defeated Old Wykehamists at Tooting and Mitcham. In a typically hard-fought and exciting contest, Malvern won by three goals to two after extra time. Wykehamists were without G H G Doggart and B L Reed and so they resorted to an open game in the hope that Pawson could exploit this. But the Malvern half-backs, Beeson and Chadder, held good control.

MOVE TO WIMBLEDON

The 1956/57 final was held at Plough Lane, Wimbledon, and Old Malvernians got there for the second time in a row. On the day that Manchester United (the Busby Babes) defeated Birmingham City to reach the FA Cup Final, Malvernians successfully held on to the Arthur Dunn Cup despite stiff opposition from Old Reptonians.

WIMBLEDON - PLOUGH LANE (1957 & 1958)

Plough Lane was the home of Wimbledon FC between 1912 and 1991. The 1957 and 1958 Arthur Dunn Cup Finals were played here. Formerly one of London's top amateur clubs, Wimbledon were elected to the Football League in 1977. They reached the top division in 1986 and in 1988 became the second club to win both the FA Amateur Cup (in 1963) and the FA Cup (1988).

The first to achieve this feat were Old Carthusians who won the FA Cup in 1881 and the FA Amateur Cup in 1897.

In September 1988, to celebrate the fact that Wimbledon had won both competitions, Old Carthusians and Wimbledon played a friendly match at Charterhouse.

But Reptonians were not to be denied for too long because the following year, they returned to Wimbledon. *"There is nothing quite like this competition in football today, for although to the purist it may lack some of the finer arts of the game it possesses a code and virility of its own which the more illustrious spheres would do well to emulate"* (The Times). Repton were in their eleventh final but had not won the trophy since 1914, and they were to be frustrated again for Old Cholmeleians, after four previous unsuccessful finals, were the better side on this occasion. *"This was a team victory, for Highgate were faster, fitter and stronger in the tackle than Repton and had they been less headstrong in front of goal the match should have been theirs for the asking before half-time"*. (The Times).

OLD CHOLMELEIANS – MEMORIES
by Mike Wadsworth

My only fixed and certain memory is that in the 1957/58 semi-final against Foresters it was my fate to be required to mark a chap called Trimby who was an England International or some such celebrity. I was told to forget any ideas of feeding our attack – as wing-half I usually regarded myself as the "linkman" and much preferred to do that than to actually mark my opposing inside forward!! – and simply to follow Trimby all over the field and "mark him out of the game". I proceeded to do this and succeeded only because the Forest team just didn't pass the ball to him; on the one (or almost one) occasion when someone thought fit to give him the ball he beat me effortlessly with a little jink and was off towards goal with me trailing behind him like a small spaniel trying to chase a greyhound! It has always puzzled me why the rest of his team didn't realise at that point what would happen if they gave him the ball again! My rather more general memories are:

1. Bill Knightley-Smith was an absolutely wonderful centre-half who had the rare talent of being at just the right place at the right time to deal with dangerous attacks. I certainly don't think we would have won either year without him.

2. Dick Greenslade was the arch exponent of the sliding tackle, which on a wet surface he would begin about 10 yards away from his intended victim! He was the scourge and terror of all right-wingers (generally a fleet-footed but frail bunch) and after encountering a couple of Dick's "specials" within the first 10 minutes his opponent was rarely seen actively seeking the ball again! I'm sure Dick won't mind me commenting that today he would probably last about 5 minutes before being invited to the dressing room by way of a red card but the fact is that he tamed some very good players by what I would describe as "assertive action" and was a real asset to the team.

3. Colin Drybrough was an accomplished player of all games (he subsequently captained Middlesex at cricket and played a blinder in goal for Oxford University against Cambridge after about 2 weeks' experience in the position!) and was a very quick left-footed sharp shooter who was useful to have cutting in from the left wing. Unfortunately, I can't remember a single goal in any match in either year so can't romance about some 30 yard thunderbolt struck by his deadly left foot! He is lurking in Perth, Western Australia where he has lived for many years.

4. Alan Murray was a particularly talented inside forward with a wonderful touch (rather like John White of Spurs) and I'm sure he made a big contribution. Like Bill K-S he unfortunately died young, being an innocent victim in an early M-way pile-up.

5. John Fawcett and David Hollinrake were both excellent centre-forwards of what I would describe as the bustling, direct style i.e. if they got the ball they made for goal and had a bang (no fancy mucking about).

AN OLD REPTONIAN'S MEMORIES
by Jeremy Tomlinson

I first appeared in an Arthur Dunn Cup Final in 1960. Reptonians had not won the Cup for 46 years and our opponents were Malvernians. It was these two teams who dominated the competition over the next 20 years but Reptonians were the team of the 60s.

The 1960s were the start of many fashions and with England winning the World Cup in 1966, football went through a popular period. However, the end of National Service in 1959 had the greatest effect on Dunn football as it meant that good players could progress immediately into Dunn sides. In addition, many players continued their football with College football almost exclusively at Oxford and Cambridge. In fact, in the early 60s pre-match publicity always listed the number of 'Blues' in a team. There were at least eight Blues in that 1960 final, whereas by 1979 there were none. Teams lined up in the two - three - five formation, which was gradually replaced by more fashionable line-ups. The school colours were replaced with exotic strips and the cricket sweaters were replaced by tracksuits for the pre-match kick-about.

One of the joys of Dunn football was the quality of the school pitches used. Although the start of the campaign in early December, just at the time pitches started getting heavy, was in marked contrast to the final, which was often played on a hard ground accompanied by a blustery wind. The most successful sides were those who could easily adjust their play to the conditions.In addition to the pitches another delight was the variety of clubhouses, pubs and hotels that both sides mixed together in after a match. Most teams had a hard core of supporters who joined in the match post mortems, renewed friendships and regenerated rivalry. There were not the motorway links of today and of hazardous journeys down a foggy M1 seemed to be all part of the fun!

In the early 60s, the Westminster Tavern, in the shadow of Big Ben, was a popular venue and no-one will ever forget distinguished committee men Dick Blundell and Alan Hilder standing on the steps leading down to the Dive Bar singing Bye Bye Blackbird and other songs late into the night after a Dunn final.

There was no real home for finals at this time. From 1960 to 1962, the final was played at Wealdstone FC, a club with a proud history in the Athenian League. The 1963 final was played on the Bank of England ground at Roehampton. An abiding memory of this final was when Rodney Hewitt (Old Ardinians) as a spectator, lowered his umbrella and headed a misdirected shot at goal 40 yards back into play at Roehampton.

Apart from Malvernians, there were other formidable opponents. Brentwoods had the best record winning three finals in the 20-year period from 1960 to 1980. Wykehamists won the Cup in 1961 and were probably the last side with the true Corinthian spirit. They turned out in cricket shirts, sleeves buttoned down, collars turned up and stroked the ball around the pitch. When they were good they were very good when they were bad they were awful. Hubert Doggart and Barry Reed were not only fine cricketers for England, Sussex and Hampshire respectively, but super footballers, John Patrick was an enthusiastic and prolific goal scorer and on the wing was Mervyn Greenway, who would engage spectators, opposition and his own team in conversation, interspersed with some wonderful mazy dribbles, the hallmark of a classic winger.

Carthusians won in 1962 and, at the time, had the best record in the competition, having won 16 times. They were a good all-round team led by Goodliffe, and the two Lees brothers were useful players. The vociferous Ants Allom kept goal and after back trouble curtailed his football career he could be heard from the touchline instead. It was a wonderful playing surface at Charterhouse with a beech hedge close to one touchline and more than one full back trained in Third Division North methods finished in that hedge attempting to tackle a fast and tricky winger.

Old Salopians beat Old Aldenhamians in 1964 to lift the Cup. Their success was built on fitness with David Sargeant and Jeremy Alexander examples of nonstop runners, however, it was the tactical skills of Robin Moulsdale that blended the side together to give them victory.

OLD CHOLMELEIANS DEFEND THE CUP

Old Cholmeleians successfully defended the Cup the following year (1959). *"It was further emphasised on Saturday that success in the Arthur Dunn Cup is bred at school, where tuition of the feet in winter is as important as net practice in summer. Old Cholmeleians, whose average age was probably under 21, contained only two players on the wrong side of 25"* (The Times).

The opponents were Old Brentwoods who scored first but were no match for Old Cholmeleians. *"Coull and Griffiths, whose voluminous shorts tried bravely to conceal an advance in years, had their moments in attack, but usually Knightly-Smith and Greenslade had the measure of them, and if they did get within range Clyde was agile and safe in goal"*, the final score was 3 - 1.

The 1959/60 season was marked by an incredible match in the first round when Old Wellingburians beat Old Chigwellians by eight goals to three. Richard Peck played in that campaign and reckoned that it was the probably the best football that he experienced in his 14 years in the team.

He recalled that marvellous match against Chigwellians. It was the first time that he had played with the stylish John Riley, who was rarely available for the Dunn because he was committed to league football in Nottinghamshire. *"On that day in December 1959, the OW team played with a cutting edge which contrasted with the normal over-elaborate and fussy style of previous years. John's vision was a revelation and his passes sliced through the Chigwellian defence. We scored 8 goals that day. John Riley was pure class. It was good win"*.

Unfortunately, Wellingburians progressed no further because in the next round they lost to Old Bradfieldians. When it came to the final itself, the two protagonists were Old Reptonians and Old Malvernians.

"Old Reptonians, finalists in the Cup three times in the past four years and winners in 1914, beat Old Malvernians at Wealdstone on Saturday after an exciting, full-blooded match which might so easily have gone the other way. But they were deservedly as much by their determination as their skill for they never hesitated in the tackle or stood on ceremony".

The 1960/61 competition proved to be another smooth campaign for Old Wykehamists. A comparatively easy first round against the Chigwellians had been followed by wins at Forest and Brentwood where in both games, an early lead had been established by simple goals scored after a kindly bounce or the unexpected twist of fortune. *"These had enabled the team to settle down to its new 4 - 2 - 4 formation and practice effectively the defensive covering and mid-field working which the new formation required, and to emerge with convincing wins in both games"*.

When Wykehamists ran out at Wealdstone for their 14th final, their opponents were their rivals in the 1948 final – Old Cholmeleians. But this was a much stronger Cholmeleian side and as a result, it was a most exciting game. The first goal went in 15 minutes after the interval (by Patrick) closely followed by a second for Wykehamists (Greenway), only for Cholmeleians to get two goals of their own. Eventually, however, hard work by Doggart, Woolley and Reed led to two further goals for Wykehamists, and the tie was settled. The Cup was presented by Mrs J.D.Ross, granddaughter of Arthur Dunn.

The 1962 at Wealdstone was a most exciting and enthusiastic affair. There was a strong wind straight down the pitch and with this at their backs Old Carthusians made the early running. For the first 10 minutes, the Malvern defence was uncertain in front of goal. But Carthusians were too hurried in their approach and Malvernians, under the steadying influence of Costeloe, soon settled.

Five minutes from the end, it seemed all over for Malvern when Martin mistimed an awkward bouncing shot from Savill and Old Carthusians were in the lead. This was far from the end of the story, for in virtually the last minute there was another goalkeeping error when Allom misjudged the flight of a shot from Costeloe which he allowed to pass just inside the post.

Extra time brought about the best football of the match and it was Carthusians who had more in reserve. They took the lead early on, against the wind, when Jakobson was at hand to score after Martin had mishandled a shot from Lees and they hung on to their lead until the end.

THE BIG FREEZE

The 1962/63 competition was played during the winter of the big freeze. Consequently, very little play took place between December 1962 and March 1963.

In the first round of the Arthur Dunn, the Old Westminsters were drawn against the Old Carthusians, the holders, at Vincent Square. The game was played on the third Saturday of December and resulted in a very exciting 2 - 2 draw.

Over the Christmas and New Year period, there were two very heavy falls of snow and then the temperature stayed below zero for about eight weeks. David Roy was playing for Old Westminsters at this stage and has clear

LOWER MEAD STADIUM WEALDSTONE (1960 - 62)

The Lower Mead Stadium was Wealdstone FC's home ground between 1923 and 1991. The club's honours included winning the FA Trophy in 1984/85, the FA Amateur cup in 1965/66 and the Conference in 1984/85. Three Arthur Dunn Finals from 1960 to 1962 were played at this ground.

BANK OF ENGLAND PRIORY LANE, ROEHAMPTON (1963)

Priory Lane, home of the Bank of England AFC whose teams play in the Southern Amateur league, has long been one of the finest playing surfaces in the country. The ground hosted the 1963 final.

HIGHGATE SCHOOL (1964)

The Far Field at Highgate School was used for the 1963 Dunn Final. It had been intended to use the new stadium at Crystal Palace, however, the development was still not complete. In the circumstances, Ken Boustred, who was a member of the Arthur Dunn Cup Committee, arranged for the pitch at Highgate to be made available.

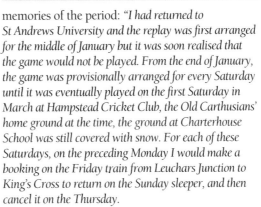

memories of the period: *"I had returned to St Andrews University and the replay was first arranged for the middle of January but it was soon realised that the game would not be played. From the end of January, the game was provisionally arranged for every Saturday until it was eventually played on the first Saturday in March at Hampstead Cricket Club, the Old Carthusians' home ground at the time, the ground at Charterhouse School was still covered with snow. For each of these Saturdays, on the preceding Monday I would make a booking on the Friday train from Leuchars Junction to King's Cross to return on the Sunday sleeper, and then cancel it on the Thursday. As long as I cancelled it 24 hours in advance I did not lose my money.*

Eventually, when the game was played, I think I was the only player on either side who had played any football during these two and half months. At St Andrews, the University soccer squad had played once a week on the frozen West Sands, it was freezing!".

The second round was then played in a rush. George Chesterton, an Old Malvernian and a master at the school, remembered being co-opted into the Malvernian team for their game with Carthusians.

"I was innocently sitting in the dining hall of my House (No 5) having lunch eating my cottage pie, when through the gate, visible from my seat, I saw Julian Davies the OM goalkeeper and he advanced up the drive. David Bailey on my right said: "I expect they want you to play this afternoon Sir". Hearty laughter all round. I went to the door, and blow me, that is exactly what they did want. It truly was a case of any port in a storm. Julian was injured, and there was no-one else!

DID YOU KNOW?
THE ARTHURIAN LEAGUE WAS STARTED IN THE 1962/63 SEASON, BUT THE FIXTURES WERE NOT COMPLETED DUE TO THE BAD WEATHER.

A T BARBER - OLD SALOPIAN
PRESIDENT 1963 - 1982

Alan Barber was an outstanding sportsman in many respects. He excelled at several sports. He went to Oxford and in 1929, he gained a double blue at both football and cricket. He also received a half blue for golf.

After university, he went on to play cricket for Yorkshire for several seasons and captained the side for one season. As a Fives player, he won the Kinnaird Cup in 1934 and 1936 and was a committed promoter of the game. He became President of the Eton Fives Association in 1973 and the Alan Barber Cup competition was founded in his honour.

He was also a member of the Old Salopian football club and competed in the Arthur Dunn Cup for many seasons between 1925 and 1939. In 1935 both Alan Barber and John Haslewood played for the Old Salopians in the Arthur Dunn Cup Final when they defeated the Old Wykehamists 3 - 0. The following week, they both played for the Old Salopians in the final of the Halford Hewitt but were beaten by the Old Carthusians.

In 1937, Alan (with Tim Shaw) became joint headmaster of Arthur Dunn's own school, Ludgrove. They ran the school until 1968 when Shaw retired and Alan continued until his own retirement in 1972. His son, Gerald, now runs the school.

In 1963, Alan Barber was elected President of the Arthur Dunn Cup, a post he held for nearly twenty years, until shortly before he died in 1982.

It was a Dunn match of the most exhilarating sort. At full time we had to cross over 3 - 3. Charterhouse went 4 - 3 up and all seemed lost, but two late goals saw the OMs scrape home. My only appearance in the Dunn!".

The final moved again in 1963; the venue on this occasion was the Bank of England ground at Roehampton. The game was played in driving rain and the surface was very slippery. In spite of this, however, both teams managed to play a coherent and at times, skilful brand of football. Old Reptonians were worthy victors in that they were better able to come to terms with the conditions and they played with more imagination.

In 1964, yet another final and yet another ground! Old Salopians won the Cup for the tenth time at Highgate School.

They fully deserved their success against Old Aldenhamians. They snatched an early lead, increased this before half-time, and completely consolidated their position in the second half before Aldenham were able to score a quarter of an hour before the end.

THE ARTHUR DUNN CUP FINAL 1964 Extracts from The Field, April 16,1964
Jeremy Alexander

The 50th final of the Arthur Dunn Cup, played on a Highgate school ground, was won by the Old Salopians. By beating the Old Aldenhamians 4 - 1 they recorded their 10th victory in the competition and their first since 1955.

It was the Salopians who settled down first. The Aldenham defence had still not come to grips with the Shrewsbury forwards switching position when, after ten minutes, Moulsdale found Burns on the left wing. Burns made ground and centred square to the near post. Murray in goal was indecisive and, as he and another defender half went for the ball with Sargeant in attendance, the latter somehow scrambled it over the line. It was not beautiful but it was vital.

After another Salopian attack was resisted, the ball was cleared but intercepted on the halfway line and Ker and Moulsdale were sent away down the right in a swift exchange of passes which ended in Moulsdale steering the ball past the advancing goalkeeper, from 15 yards out, into the far corner of the net. The value of the quick riposte to penetrate a defence momentarily off guard was never so clear, and the Salopians led 2 - 0 after only 16 minutes. So the score remained until half-time.

At the start of the second half an Aldenham siege lasted some 10 minutes, but no goals accrued, and as the game progressed the Salopians emerged from their beleaguered half to regain the initiative. A long free-kick from Osborne on the left was flicked on by Burns with his head, and Murray, from point-blank range, grabbed it excitingly at the second attempt. But in the 65th minute a corner from Ker was headed out straight and Walls, standing just outside the penalty area, volleyed the bouncing ball into the righthand corner of the net while the world stood still.

This heralded the most attractive phase of the game. Soon the Salopians drew blood again when Burns passed the ball on the outside of Sargeant, to the left of the goal, and Sargeant flicked it first time into the goal from the narrowest of angles. Aldenham pulled this one back within a few minutes. A clever through-ball found King for once free from the shackles of both Wright and Platt, and he made no mistake with only Parry to beat. It was a nicely executed goal and it showed that, given an inch, he would take a mile.

But it was not enough to inspire more nor daunt the buoyant Salopians who flowed down the right flank and battered down the left, defensive inhibitions cast aside. Victory was theirs and they knew it. It was a triumph of strategy. They summed up their resources and played according to them.

And then there was Moulsdale, sole survivor from the winning sides of the early 1950s. If he has lost stamina, he has assuredly gained in guile. He moves, as he always has, with a motion fluent yet slightly stiff and jerky, like some marionette. But it was he who was pulling the strings of this Salopian side, flitting ceaselessly about, prompting and probing, quietly inspiring. There was none more worthy this day to receive from Mrs. Jane Ross, grand-daughter of the late Arthur Dunn, the Cup which he first earned 12 years previously.

MEMORIES OF THE OLD SALOPIANS IN THE 60s
by A R B Moulsdale

I had hung up my boots – until 1963!! I don't remember who persuaded me out again. It was probably David Lanyon, but I do remember reluctantly taking the field at Vincent Square with an unpromising side, being soon one down and wondering what I was doing. And then John Burns scored from a distant free-kick, David Sargeant was put through and after one of his ball-bouncing dribbles notched the next and miraculously we walked off 3 - 2 winners.

The next match was away against Reptonians, certainly a much better side than us. I clearly remember in the changing room as I slowly tied my bootlaces the dread of facing the old enemy with the odds so much against us. But John Burns scored another free-kick (it was before the days of walls), and I can still see the red-headed blur of a defender, whose name I won't reveal because he knows it too well, committed to a tackle in the box. I was down and up again, putting the ball on the spot before the referee blew his whistle. Somehow we were three up at half-time. We scored once and then again miraculously at the start of the second half. Then the longest forty minutes of my life began. Reptonians scored two but no more and we were through to the semi-final.

ABOVE: THE OLD SALOPIANS WINNING TEAM OF 1964. (BACK L. TO R.) J S KER, D N SARGEANT, A J M WALLS, J L OSBORNE, D L WRIGHT, D J PLATT, J G ALEXANDER. (FRONT) J E BURNS, A R B MOULSDALE, F W COOPER, L G PARRY.

Now we had to take ourselves seriously and we devised a tactical plan that would inspire Alf Ramsey to create the wingless World Cup winners of 1966. The W formation had long been abandoned for lack of appropriate pieces, but we had plenty of stout defenders and forever runners. Long before 4-2-4 had entered our consciousness, let alone 4-4-2 we played 1-9-1. Graham Parry, the shortest goalkeeper to win an AD winner's medal, caught everything and threw it out to me at outside-left (static, but marginally nearer to the action than left outside). I stopped it and then slotted it through to any of our defenders strong enough to make a forward run. The plan was adaptable, as illustrated in one of the two semi-final matches against Cholmeleians, at Shrewsbury in deep mud. Jeremy Ker, normally a swift front runner, had been ordered to stay wide on the only patch of grass. He bravely did for most of the match, then disobeyed instructions, went into the middle and dribbled through for the winning goal. By now we had so much confidence in our system, and John Burns could always score from a free-kick, we felt we could beat anyone. We duly won the final 4 - 1 against Aldenhamians. We had one more try next year with the same system in the first round at Highgate. I can remember being through with only the keeper to beat (was this part of the plan?) and missing. We lost and the boots were burnt.

Looking back on those years (1947 - 1964), an historian - which I am not - might see them as a distinct period. We had heard of the Corinthians, were imbued - unconsciously - by their famous spirit, and certainly thought that the most important thing was to have fun. But we took penalties when awarded them and no-one would give up an international cap to play for their old school as two Salopians famously did for the first Arthur Dunn Final. There was no going back to those days despite the triumphant and brief Pegasus story. And we were stuck in a tactical dead-end. Was it the change in the offside rule of 1925 that introduced the stopper centre-half? Since then no-one had interfered with the 'W' formation, at any rate in Public School circles (when was the Revie plan?) and I can remember being outraged at Wembley in 1953 when a promising England move was ended by a Hungarian winger tackling back.

And we had Ken Shearwood, the best stopper centre-half in the competition, even if we could not always play him because of Pegasus duties. Stopper centre-halves were not like the great Corinthian attacking centre-halves and Ken was better in the air than on the ground. Somewhere we were playing on a ground which behind one goal dropped a long way down to a lower pitch. It was snowing - strongly. We had a free kick perhaps thirty yards out. We were not drilled or practiced so every one looked vaguely around wondering who should kick it. Suddenly a great shout from the snow storm and Ken appeared, hair and shirt sleeves flying; he smote the ball which soaring high over the bar like a rugger conversion disappeared into the storm and down into the depths. We recovered the ball, choked back the tears of laughter and Ken returned to defence.

OLD CHIGWELLIAN CAPTAIN, HOWARD BERNDES RAISES THE CUP AFTER THE 1980 FINAL, FLANKED BY ALAN BARBER (PRESIDENT) AND DAVID ROY (HON. SECRETARY).

RETURN TO CRYSTAL PALACE

The National Recreation Centre at Crystal Palace was designed to be a state-of-the-art sports complex that included an Olympic-size swimming pool, diving area, gymnasia and a modern athletics stadium to rival any in the world. The latter was built on the old FA Cup Final ground. The connection with football was not to be lost because the infield area could be used for team sports.

Discussions about a possible relocation of the Arthur Dunn Final to the Crystal Palace began in 1963. At the Committee meeting in May of that year, it was suggested that such a move would be beneficial not least because it would save the Hon. Secretary considerable effort near the end of each season in searching for a venue depending on which non-league ground was free. Also, the date of the final could be fixed at the beginning of the season and so it could be advertised well in advance.

Other benefits presented themselves – spectators would be seated, and there would be facilities for collecting an entrance fee. Neither of these features was available at the venues used in 1963 and 1964.

MOVE TO CRYSTAL PALACE DELAYED

It had been hoped that the new stadium would be ready for the 1964 final but it was not to be. In the event, the first football to be played on the ground was in August 1964 when Crystal Palace FC met West Ham in a pre-season friendly. The West Ham side included the likes of Bobby Moore, Geoff Hurst and Martin Peters, whose names were soon to be immortalized.

B J HARE (1939-2001) OLD REPTONIAN

John Hare was the ever-present captain of Old Reptonians during their successful run in the Dunn in the 1960s. Born in Yorkshire in 1939, John went to Repton and played football and cricket for the school. After a year out, John went up to Brasenose College, Oxford, where he got a soccer Blue (1961/62).

John played in five Dunn finals for the Old Reptonians captaining the side in 1963, 1965, 1966 and 1968 (winning in 1963, 1965 and 1968).

While following his teaching career – at Oswestry, Millfield, then in Kent, and eventually as Headmaster at Haileybury Junior School, John continued to play football. He captained the Repton Pilgrims regularly on their tour of the South Coast "where he encouraged his side not only to play with enthusiasm, but also to play to win". As a captain, "he led by example and expected 110%, which he himself always gave" (by his friend, Nigel MacLean).

John later became President of Old Reptonians. He sadly died in 2001.

REPTONIANS - TEAM OF THE SWINGING SIXTIES

If one looks at the 1960s as a whole, this was undoubtedly Old Reptonians' decade. Having won the trophy in 1960, they won it again in 1963, 1966, 1968 (joint-winners) and 1970. They also appeared in the 1965 final.

During this period, they had many fine players: – John Hare, Alan Basnett, Peter Rowland, Pat Vaughan and Jeremy Tomlinson.

Their opponents, in this first final back at the Crystal Palace, were their old rivals, Old Malvernians. In fact, these old adversaries would play against each other in three out of the next four finals.

NATIONAL RECREATION CENTRE CRYSTAL PALACE (1965 – 1981)

Sir Gerald Barry, formerly the Director-General of the 1951 Festival of Britain, was invited to submit a scheme for the redevelopment and it was he who proposed the building of a National Youth and Sports Centre. This was to include an outdoor sports stadium and an indoor centre. Work was started in 1960 and the Centre, designed by Sir Isaac Hayward, was officially opened on 13th July 1964 by HRH the Duke of Edinburgh. The building cost £2,750,000.

So, the football stands and the pavilion were finally swept away to be replaced by a modern all-seater stand for a new audience to watch athletics. Initially, the ground seated 12,000 spectators with 4,500 under cover in a single cantilever stand on the exact site of the previous pavilion and football stands. In 1977, the Queen Elizabeth II Jubilee stand was built on the other side of the ground, which could accommodate a further 4,500 people.

MALVERNIAN'S GOLDEN ERA

During the seventeen years at the Crystal Palace, Old Malvernians had a golden period in Arthur Dunn football. They played in eleven of the seventeen finals winning seven of them. This included five consecutive finals (between 1965 and 1969). A lot of their success must be attributed to Denis Saunders, the master in charge of football at Malvern for many years in the 1950s and 1960s. Denis Saunders had been the captain of Pegasus on the two occasions when they won the FA Amateur Cup in 1951 and 1953. They also had some excellent players in Dick Chadder, Jan Illaszewicz (Bridle), David Loader, Tony Williams and Ian Ryder-Smith.

Tony Williams expressed the view that he *"was lucky enough to be playing football at Malvern College when Denis Saunders, the ex-Pegasus captain arrived at the school to look after football and he quickly introduced the 'push-and-run' system that had been so successful for his Pegasus coaches, Arthur Rowe and Vic Buckingham, who had looked after Tottenham Hotspur in their consecutive championships of Division two and Division one.*

Denis Saunders and the Headmaster encouraged the school to take advantage of the Football Association's twinning scheme with our nearest Football League Club and we had weekly visits from Ronnie Allen of West Bromwich Albion and England fame, and occasional games with the full WBA squad that had finished as runners-up in Division one and finalists in the FA Cup at Wembley in 1954".

So at last, in 1965, the Arthur Dunn Final was held at Crystal Palace. The contenders were

ABOVE:THE REFEREE CHECKS WHO HAS WON THE TOSS BEFORE THE START OF THE 1965 ARTHUR DUNN FINAL, WHILE THE TWO CAPTAINS R H CHADDER OF MALVERNIANS (RIGHT) AND B J HARE OF REPTONIANS MARSHALL THEIR TROOPS.

RIGHT: DICK CHADDER IS HELD ALOFT WHILE GRIPPING THE CUP IN CELEBRATION OF A MALVERNIAN VICTORY IN THE 1965 FINAL.

RICHARD CHADDER - OLD MALVERNIAN

Richard Chadder has a fine footballing pedigree. He is the son of the remarkable Harvey Chadder, who was the scourge of professional teams like Newcastle United when he played in the great Corinthian teams of the 1920s.

Richard took his lead from his father who was master in charge of football at Malvern while Richard was a pupil. After Oxford, Richard joined the Old Malvernians and was a constant presence at the heart of the defence in the great OM teams of the 1960s.

Richard has an impressive record in the Dunn. In all, he played in nine finals. His first was in 1956, which Malvernians won, and then again in 1957. He was also in the teams that lost in 1960, 1962 and 1963. But it did not end there, for under his captaincy, Old Malvernians got to the final four times – winning in 1965 at the Crystal Palace, followed by two defeats (1966 and 1967). His last appearance was in 1968, when he captained the Malvernian team that drew with arch-rivals, Old Reptonians.

REPTON FALTER BUT ARTHUR DUNN CUP IS THEIRS

Old Malvernians 3, Old Reptonians 4

This year's final of the Arthur Dunn Cup was a repetition of last year in that again the two best sides in the competition faced each other to settle the issue. But this time Repton turned the tables on their rivals in an exhilarating match played on Saturday at the National Recreation Centre, Crystal Palace.

It was, however, a mighty close affair. At half-time Repton, with two clear goals in their pockets, which they stretched to a margin of three with barely half an hour of play remaining, seemed to be coasting to an easy victory but then Malvern surged back with such effect that for the final 20 minutes it was still anybody's game.

MIDFIELD TRIO

Repton, in the final analysis, just had the edge. Their defence was the more closely knit, they were well served in midfield by Hare, Vaughan and Gillard, and Malvern never quite found an answer to their flexibility in attack, mainly in the person of Barnwell. But Repton by no means had things all their own way and Theobald, Williams and Illaszewicz were always a thorn in their flesh.

After Repton had early missed an easy chance they opened the scoring at the quarter-hour with a splendid goal when Basnett beat Walton in his far top corner. They went farther ahead seven minutes from half-time when Tomlinson scored from close in

But with the resumption Malvern made their effort and reduced the lead within 10 minutes when Stevens scored after Ellis had cleared a shot by Williams off his goal line. Five minutes later Stevens headed firmly against a Reptonian post from Loader's free kick but within the minute Repton went farther ahead.

This was a tragedy for Malvern for Gillard intercepted a weak pass in defence to beat the gallant Walton inside his far post. Two minutes later Basnett beat Walton again and Repton looked home and dry.

However, soon afterwards Loader was upended in the penalty area on his way through and Ryder Smith duly reduced the arrears from the penalty spot. Malvern now crowded on all sail and five minutes later Illaszewicz scored from an angle to set the game alight.

OLD MALVERNIANS.—P. A. Walton ; A. W. Beeson. R. H. Chadder ; A. G. Theobald. J. M. Ellis. G. C. Turner ; P. H. Vaughan, P W. S. Rowland (captain). B. J. Hare ; L. M. L. Barnwell, A. P. Basnet.
OLD REPTONIANS.—D. C. M. Vaughan ; C. B. Costeloe. I. Ryder Smith ; H. D. Loader, J. W. Illaszewicz, A. K. Williams. P Hayden, C. W. Stevens. R. G. Gillard. J. J. W. Tomlinson, D. Harrison.
REFEREE.—A. W. Stockbridge (A.F.A.).

J J W Tomlinson, P H Vaughan, D C M Vaughan & A P Basnett
Old Reptonians

The successful Old Reptonian team of the 1960s was led by John Hare but he was supported by a number of able players. Jeremy Tomlinson appeared in all six finals with Reptonians between 1960 and 1970. Of these, he was on the outright winning side four times and the shared trophy of 1968.

One of the stars of the Reptonian team in the mid-60s was Alan Basnett. Jeremy Tomlinson described him as a "goalscorer of similar ability to Jan (Bridle)".

Other ever-present members of the team were the brothers Vaughan. Pat Vaughan was "one of the best footballers Repton produced, beautifully balanced, and a visionary passer. His brother David captained the Repton school team from the left wing yet had the ability to play in goal in three Dunn finals" (Jeremy Tomlinson). They both appeared in five finals between 1960 and 1970. Pat did not play in 1963 and David was not present in 1970.

PROFILE PICTURES ABOVE:
(TOP LEFT) JEREMY TOMLINSON,
(TOP RIGHT) ALAN BASNETT,
(BOTTOM LEFT) DAVID VAUGHAN,
(BOTTOM RIGHT) PAT VAUGHAN.

Old Reptonians and Old Malvernians but Reptonians started as favourites as they had scored 20 goals on their way to the final. However, in a very close game, Old Malvernians won 2 - 1. (Goalscorers: Malvernians - Theobald and Williams; Reptonians - Hare).

The Times commented:

"Malvernians won but with nothing to spare; that they did so was due to the way in which they scored their goals and then, as the game drew to a close, flung back the Reptonian attack".

Old Reptonians got their revenge the following year (1966) when they won 4 - 3.

LEFT: THE TIMES REPORT OF THE 1966 FINAL.

HARROVIANS
RETURN TO THE COMPETITION

In the 1966/67 season, Old Harrovians re-entered the competition after a gap of 36 years; they had last played in the 1928/29 season. This meant that for the first time since 1914, there would be more than sixteen teams in the competition and there would have to be a preliminary round.

England's success in the 1966 World Cup had led to considerable interest in football. A group of Old Harrovians had started playing football again in 1963 although football was not being played at the Harrow School and it did not start there again until 1977. The driving force behind the Old Harrovians was Fred Woolley, their current President.

AN OLD HARROVIAN'S MEMORIES
by Fred Woolley

On Saturday 5th October 1963, a 4 - 2 victory over Lancing Old Boys second XI had announced to the football fraternity, the return of the Old Harrovians after 33 years of hibernation – the original Club was founded in 1859 but folded in 1930. The spirit was willing but the flesh was evidently too weak.

As a result of the efforts of David Buik, Fred Woolley, Andrew Brodie, Alex de Grunwald and Roderick Hill devoted much time and energy to promoting this ambitious revival which the sceptics believed would soon burn itself out. In 1963/64, the first official season, Charles Jamieson emerged as a powerful force in front of goal and Peter Beckwith showed that skill could be accommodated in this pioneering effort. De Grunwald was clearly an outstanding goalkeeper, gaining representative honours with St Andrews and Dundee Universities. Don McNeill, slightly older and a master at Harrow, did much in these early days both on and off the field. His constant encouragement and optimism became a feature of the Club for many years to come. His ability as a player commanded the respect of Harrovians and opponents alike.

FRED WOOLLEY
SPEAKING AT THE
ARTHUR DUNN
CENTENARY DINNER
ON THE 14TH MARCH
2003.

For the 1966/67 season, Old Harrovians, founder members in 1902, received an invitation to re-enter the Arthur Dunn Cup competition thereby increasing the number of clubs in the draw to 17. Owing to the ground difficulties, home advantage against Old Brentwoods had to be surrendered and the tie was played at Burland Road, Brentwood. Harrovians lost 2 - 3 in the last seconds of extra time and Brentwoods went on to win the Cup. The match was as close as the score-line suggests and Harrovians did well to subdue the flair of Peter Clements and company, and survive the awesome defensive qualities of the Brentwoods left-back, Andrew Lowe.

In season 1969/70, the enthusiastic captaincy of Garth Bearman and regular training directed by the FA coach Jackie Goodwin, resulted in the Club's first Dunn victory, 2 - 1 at John Lyons School over Old Westminsters. In the second round, again at John Lyons, a titanic battle took place with the eventual losing finalists, Old Foresters, whose substitute was Robin Trimby, a man who gained full amateur international honours. Given the strength of the visitors, the final score-line was certainly no disgrace: Harrovians 3 Foresters 4.

In 1970/71, the Club again drew Old Foresters. In the dressing-room prior to the match, Jimmy Cox pulled a hamstring while lacing up his boots and was unable to take the field. Beckwith, attending as a spectator and looking under-nourished, was called into action. Jackie Goodwin was not retained for the 1971/72 season but arranged for a posse of FA trainee coaches to attend with notebooks the Arthur Dunn Cup first round tie at Eton. This was to be a day of disappointment for the Club, losing the match 0 - 1 with the Hon. Secretary cautioned for "persistent infringements in late tackling" after only five minutes play.

Mike Keenan became first XI captain for the 1973/74 season and commanded regular support from the younger players amongst whom Nigel Hughes, Myles Thompson and Robert Worthy were to become prominent in the future. Sadly, in the Dunn against Brentwoods at Hampstead Cricket Club, the very promising and talented Willie van Straubenzee broke a leg and never played for the Club again. The Club was deprived of the services of a gifted footballer who would have contributed much to this new era.

The next few years were to see Harrovians involved in some titanic encounters in the Dunn. Under a new captain, Geoff Harrow, in 1974/75 the Club came up against Old Salopians. A 3 - 3 result at Shrewsbury was followed by an exciting 4 - 4 draw at Hampstead and the matter was finally resolved back at Shrewsbury where Salopians won 6 - 3. The following year, the team lost to Lancing 2 - 3. The game was marred by an injury to Keenan, an outstanding player, who had interrupted his honeymoon in order to play. He was carried off with an unidentified injury – possibly exhaustion! In 1976/77 the Club drew 2 - 2 with Foresters in the first round (Fred Woolley scored for both teams in extra time) only to lose 4 - 1 in the replay.

The highlight of these years came in 1983/84. For the first time in its history, Old Harrovians reached the advanced stages in the Dunn. After wins over Old Etonians and then Old Chigwellians, the prize was a home draw against Lancing Old Boys in the semi-final. Though Harrovians raced to a 3 - 0 lead, Lancing then managed to find an extra gear and ran in winners 5 - 3.

ARTHUR DUNN CUP

PENALTY GIVES VICTORY TO BRENTWOODS

Old Malvernians 2, Old Brentwood 3

Down the years Brentwood have produced man fine footballers but they reached true fulfilment on Saturday at the National Recreation Centre, Crystal Palace, by winning the Arthur Dunn Cup outright for the first time in their history.

They shared this trophy with Old Salopians in 1955 after extra time, and in 1959 they were beaten in the final, but this was only the third occasion when they have won through to the final.

By contrast, their opponents Old Malvernians, have dominated the Arthur Dunn Cup in the past 10 years. Seven times in finals and three times winners, they seemed likely to add another victory to their impressive record this year.

The pundits gave Brentwood only an outside chance and only then, if they could score an early goal. But it was Malvern who took the initiative, missed two simple chances, Stevens heading wide of the near post and Illaszewicz firing over the top from close range, in the opening 10 minutes.

Reprieved from early disaster Brentwood began to settle down and hold the dashing Malvernian forwards. But in the fortieth minute Malvern at last broke through when Illaszewicz struck Loader's cross from the right into the roof of Guyver's net.

However, Malvern were not ahead for long. Just before half time Brentwood equalized with a fine goal, Clements and Allen pulling the Malvernian defence out of position for Francis to sweep the ball inside the far post.

Soon after the interval Ryder-Smith hit the Brentwood crossbar, but within minutes Allen put Brentwood in the lead for the first time when he steered a chip by Francis past Bailey. With half an hour remaining Williams went up into the attack, renewing his partnership with Illaszewicz, and Brentwood were hard pressed. Yet they survived until 10 minutes from the end, when Williams was brought down heavily in the penalty area for Ryder-Smith to score from the spot.

It now seemed that Brentwood could lose, but they kept their heads in the crisis. Five minutes later Malvern were penalized in the area for a less obvious handling offence and Thomas coolly placed the ball past Bailey to give Old Brentwoods a victory they fully deserved.

OLD MALVERNIANS.—D Bailey; R. H. Chadder, A. W. Beeson; I. Ryder-Smith (captain), A. K. Williams, P. Hayden; H. D Loader, R. W. Tolchard, J. W. Illaszewicz, P. M. Townend, C. W. Stevens.

OLD BRENTWOODS.—A. Guyver; B Maguire, A. Love; J. Churchill (captain), P. Thomas, T. Russell; P. Clements, P. Francis, P. Allen, G. Harvey, G. Bowman.

REFEREE.—R O. Hounsell (A.F.A.)

BRENTWOODS WIN THEIR FIRST FINAL

Old Harrovians did not progress too far in their first season back in the competition and when it came to the later stages, it was Old Brentwoods and Old Malvernians (again) that made it through to the final. It was a hard-fought final finally decided by a penalty taken coolly by Pete Thomas, which gave Brentwoods a 3 - 2 victory.

The success of Old Brentwoods marked a significant change in the history of the competition. Although Brentwoods had shared the Cup with the Old Salopians in 1955, and Old Cholmeleians had won in 1958 and 1959, this was the beginning of a period when the big five (Carthusians, Malvernians, Salopians, Reptonians and Wykehamists) no longer dominated the competition.

BRENTWOODS AND MALVERNIAN RIVALRY

The 1967 final was also the start of an amazing sequence. Between season 1966/67 and 1979/80, Old Malvernians either won the Cup or were beaten by the Old Brentwoods, either in the final or in an earlier round. This happened every year except season 1969/70 when the Old Salopians beat Old Malvernians 4 - 0 in the first round.

In the twenty seasons between 1964/65 and 1983/84, Old Brentwoods and Old Malvernians met on seventeen occasions, the Old Brentwoods won nine times to the Old Malvernians' eight. (See part 4, records section for a full list of these statistics).

ABOVE: THE TIMES REPORT OF THE 1967 FINAL.

OLD MALVERNIANS
by Ian Ryder-Smith

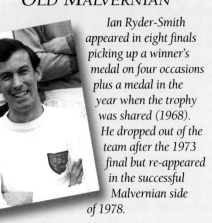

I RYDER-SMITH
OLD MALVERNIAN

Ian Ryder-Smith appeared in eight finals picking up a winner's medal on four occasions plus a medal in the year when the trophy was shared (1968). He dropped out of the team after the 1973 final but re-appeared in the successful Malvernian side of 1978.

In 1962, I played in my first Dunn game and will always remember the great encouragement from Geoffrey Partridge, of West Bromwich Albion fame, who was then our President.

Over the next nine years, the Club had a purple patch. As Ivor Norton reminded us when he resigned as OM Chairman in 1971 (having been in the post for ten years), we had been Arthur Dunn Cup finalists eight times in those ten years and AFA Senior Cup finalists in another year. Plainly we had one bad year!

In the eight years following the inception of the Arthurian League, the Club won the senior league five times and, since the inauguration of the Arthurian League Junior Cup, the second eleven had won this twice. In fact, from 1955/56 to 1975/76 we won the Arthur Dunn Cup no less than eight times, the Junior Cup three times and the Junior Division twice.

Memories return of Tony Beeson leading by example from right-half. Richard Chadder tough as nails – who would want to tackle him? We were always short of goalkeepers and when we had one, David Bailey, he managed to break his wrist a week before the Dunn final. However, what a rock he was in our great run to the AFA Senior Cup Final in 1964.

At this time, a schoolboy of unusual talent left Malvern; this was Jan Illaszewicz (Bridle). His technique was that of a professional player, and I believe he was the difference between us and other sides. Under pressure, we would belt the ball to Jan and shout "you're on your own" and off he would go for a few seconds, before returning and lining up at the centre-spot again, with a shy grin on his face.

Bill Stevens scored the winner in our AFA semi-final replay against Midland Bank, after drawing 4 - 4 at the Polytechnic at Chiswick. Midland Bank hit every bit of our woodwork that day, but they were not prepared for Bill's lone run midway through the second half. We should have won the final against Old Camdenians at Dulwich Hamlet, on a pitch devoid of grass. However, it was not to be and we went down 3 - 2 in an exciting game. The feat of getting to the AFA Final put Arthurian League teams on the map again, and I believe increased the respect in which other amateur clubs held the Arthurian League teams.

As the great OM teams of the 60s began to age a little – Williams, Theobald, Irvine, Costeloe, Dogsie Martin, wee Davy Loader, Roger Tolchard, Phil Hayden, Nick Stockbridge, Mike Murphy, other players were coming through to bridge the 60s to the 70s. Ian Murray was already established, as was Peter Townend, but in the mid 1970s a new crop headed by Chris Williams, Nick Williams and the Denham brothers came together to support Richard Wilson, Mike Byers, Nick Stockbridge, Richard Whateley and the evergreen Jan Bridle. The two Murphy brothers also played their part, and the Dunn was won in 1975, 1976 and 1978.

DAVID LOADER
OLD MALVERNIAN
DAVID LOADER HAD A LONG CAREER IN THE DUNN. HE PROBABLY PLAYED IN MORE DUNN GAMES THAN ANYONE ELSE – OVER 500 GAMES. HE FIRST APPEARED IN THE FINAL IN 1960 AND WAS PRESENT IN THE MALVERNIAN TEAM THAT REACHED EIGHT MORE FINALS UNTIL 1973.

MALVERNIANS AND REPTONIANS
SHARE THE CUP

The 1968 final was the fifth occasion that Old Malvernians and Old Reptonians had met in a final since 1960. (Old Reptonians won in 1960, 1963, 1966 and the Old Malvernians in 1965). On this occasion, the game ended in a 1 - 1 draw after extra time. Although the Times correspondent thought Malvernians were the better team, Reptonians played the whole of extra time without Rolfe, and so they probably deserved to share the spoils. In the old tradition, the Cup was therefore shared. This would be the last time that this would happen because the rule was changed at the 1969 AGM.

In 1969, three of the less fancied teams – Old Bradfieldians, Lancing Old Boys and Old Westminsters – reached the semi-finals but again it was Old Malvernians who went on to appear in their fifth consecutive final and defeat the Old Bradfieldians 1 - 0.

Bradfieldians were unlikely finalists. One of the team members, Keith Michel remembered:

"The 1968/69 season began with no real expectation and no inkling of what was in store. A comfortable win over the Wykehamists in the first round led to an encounter with the Aldenhamians which resulted in a close 1 - 1 draw. The second round replay was a dramatic end to end affair culminating in

OLD BRENTWOODS
by John Kilmartin

In the late 1960s and early 1970s, Brentwood school had a highly successful team and a number of the players added a new dimension to the club when they joined the Old Brentwoods. Stalwart and talented Old Brentwoods, who had considerable Arthur Dunn Cup experience, such as Peter Clements, Tim Russell, Peter Thomas, Pat Francis, Peter Allen, George Harvey, Geoff Bowman, Barry Maguire, Andrew Love, Alan Guyver and John Churchill were joined by the outstanding talents of Brian Baker, Jimmy Harris, David Anderson, Howard Maguire, Phil Needham, Neil Harris, Don Cameron, Nigel Bunter, Michael Tack, Simon Boon, Michael Walker and Richard Baker. There were, of course, many other players as well.

The talent shone through and the team became a very good Cup side and during the 1960s and 1970s, the Old Brentwoods played in the final eight times – a superb achievement! We won the Cup in 1967, 1972 and 73. We were runners up in 1971, 74, 76, 77 and 79.

Happy, happy times when you win, despair when you lose and in particular when the team should have won! My abiding memory of such a game was the first final in which I played against Foresters in 1974. They were, of course, huge local rivals and because of this we knew it was going to be the survival of the fittest! It was tense, it was hard and, just when we thought the game would go into extra time, they were awarded a dubious penalty! I say "dubious" because I was involved in the penalty!

The referee translated a brave dive to get the ball at the feet of Colin Smith as a penalty. Everyone who knows Colin will know that this was not a sensible thing to do on my part, unless you were confident that you were going to get to the ball first. I was confident! The referee didn't see it like that and, of course, the referee is always right! Colin scored from the penalty. Game over. Who'd be a goalkeeper?

The second final I played was against Malvernians in 1976. A great club and another with a very successful heritage of playing in the Arthur Dunn Cup. Over the years we have had so many memorable encounters with Malvernians and the final in 1976 was no exception. Two good sides played in ideal conditions at Crystal Palace and with twenty minutes to go we were leading 3 - 1. We were well on top and I am sure all the team were so very confident that it was going to be our day. Everyone was playing well and, from my position in goal, it was a joy to watch.

But disaster was just a few minutes away! Malvernians scored from a corner, 3 - 2, equalised three minutes later, 3 - 3. You could feel the confidence draining away and within the final five minutes our dream was shattered. They scored two more goals and we lost 5 - 3. A massive disappointment, but all credit to Malvernians for coming back from what looked like a lost cause and not for the first time in the history of their football club they won a game from the jaws of defeat.

All in all, I played in three Arthur Dunn Cup Finals and ended up on the losing side on each occasion and there are one or two other Old Brentwoods who share the same unenviable memory. But, for me, the real memories are of the competition itself, the titanic battles; the excitement and expectation; the elation of winning whether it be in the preliminary round or in the final; the celebrations that followed every Cup game and the admiration of your fellow competitors. Names too many to mention, but they were very special both on and off the field and many still remain good friends to this day.

a narrow 5 - 4 victory, the winner being scored by David Shilton, a fearsome striker of his day.

With the semi-final draw against Westminsters at Vincent Square, a final appearance seemed to the optimists perhaps within reach. It was not however achieved without another close-fought contest and the Club had once again to thank Shilton for the final goal in a 2 - 1 win.

With victories in the Arthurian League, the Club approached the final against the Malvernians to be played at the Crystal Palace Sports Centre with anticipation and confidence. Supporters came from far and wide and were not disappointed at yet another closely contested game. Everyone thought the Old Brads had a chance.

Some said that the team that day might have been as good as their distinguished predecessors in the 1930s. Certainly there was no lack of skill or ability. In goal was Graham Roope, arguably the finest all-round sportsman ever produced by the school, already

an established Surrey cricketer and later to play in some 20 cricket Test matches for England. Chris Gorringe would later replace his captaincy of the Club with many years service as Secretary of the All-England Tennis Club at Wimbledon. John Gregory, one of the finest mid-fielders of the decade had played several years for the Sheffield Falcons and was an internationally renowned rock climber and mountaineer. Most of the rest of the team had senior amateur experience at representative or university level including Ian Buckley, captain of Southampton University and myself, a Cambridge Blue.

Underdogs the Club may have been but most believed that there was a real chance to strike silver on the sideboard for the first time. Sadly, it was not to be. Almost inevitably, the game was decided by the odd goal. Reports of the day showed that there was little to choose between the two teams, the only goal being scored in the second half by Mike Driver from a pass by Ian Ryder-Smith, a towering player "in

ARTHUR DUNN CUP   GEOFFREY GREEN

Galvanized by spirit of C B Fry

Old Reptonians 2, Old Foresters 1

What with a Times team of newsmen and photographers manfully chasing Russian embassy footballers all over Kensington Gardens and occasionally getting a touch of the polka-dot ball, and the Old Reptonians turning apparent defeat into victory in the last half-hour over the Old Foresters, at the Crystal Palace National Recreation Centre, to win the Arthur Dunn Cup for the eighth time, the day was both a gay trip and a sentimental journey.

Nor was that all. There were generous dollops of cameraderie to follow—measure for measure as the Russian hosts were more closely challenged in the vodka stakes; and later champagne flowing from the Arthur Dunn Cup itself in the early hours as a nightingale sang in Berkeley Square. It did the old heart, if not the legs, good.

If Forest were to have turned their first half superiority into more lasting terms they should have transplanted to this other Eden of Sydenham the chestnut trees that once skirted their own school grounds of long ago. These used to be "in play" and could be skilfully used by a clever player. They needed them now. As it was

they lost themselves in their own wood, running out of steam over the last stages in spite of the persistent stoking of their boiler by Wilson, Wheeler and Beschizza.

It was stamina, plus team spirit, plus the calm mounting of a counter challenge by Vaughan, Tomlinson and Harrison as they pushed the ball about, that saw Repton home in the end, deservedly· though at the interval, I for one, would not have wagered even an extinct half a crown on their chances.

If Forest were ever to have won their first Dunn final in history, they should perhaps have done so in the opening 20 minutes, as Beschizza and Wheeler twice went desperately close; and when Rogers, clean through, squandered a fine opening by Wheeler before at last he actually scored following a corner and move down the right.

That goal lead at the interval, however, was not enough in spite of all the signs and the heady encouragement of their followers, led by a young blood who persistently shattered the damp afternoon air with a hunting horn. Far from awakening the dead, that battlecry in due course merely awoke Repton. A beautiful rainbow suddenly painted the sky and as the drizzle glistened through a pale sun, we knew there was a fox's wedding somewhere near at hand.

So was a Repton victory. The

spirit of C. B. Fry suddenly galvanized his young heirs as first Gill firmly headed in Rolfe's corner, and then the lanky Tomlinson followed suit as he nodded home the winner 12 minutes from the end, from a clever move between Whitehead and Vaughan.

One or two of us older drones, slightly in our cups perhaps, swore that in our day we would have beaten both lots put together. But that is our privilege, to dream. Yet what was a positive affront to the ear was the dull plop of a suet pudding of a ball—an old leather relic resurrected, it seemed, from some distant past, when Aston Villa and Preston North North End were the invincibles of the nineteenth century.

Both sides complaining bitterly, could certainly have done with the plastic variety which the gentlemen of The Times, tongues hanging out, had hunted so bravely all over Bayswater in the morning. But you cannot have everything Vodka, champagne, rainbows and that nightingale were enough for one day in the life of any Printing House square.

OLD REPTONIANS.—M. Stockdale: B. J. Hare, A. C. Borrett (sub.: P S. Rowland), P. Vaughan, P. N. Gill. A. C. Whitehead. P. W. Rolfe. J. W. Tomlinson. G. C. Turner, J. D. Harrison. P. R. Smith
OLD FORESTERS.—G. Peacock.: R. Hayes, R. Dunn. G. Green. C. Smith. R. Wheeler. L. Beschizza, D. Wilson. R. Marshall. M. Rogers, S. Duncombe.
Referee.—P. G. F. Lancaster (A.F.A.).

ABOVE: GEOFFREY GREEN'S REPORT IN THE TIMES OF THE 1970 FINAL.

great form in mid-field". There were late chances to equalise but in the end it was only the outstanding brilliance of Roope in goal who denied the legendary Illaszewicz from widening the score-line".

SUBSTITUTES
USED FOR THE FIRST TIME

At the 1969 Annual General Meeting, it was agreed that in the event of a drawn final, there should be a replay. Also, the subject of allowing a substitute for an injured player was discussed at great length. Unfortunately, there was a certain amount of confusion because the ruling was interpreted differently by the clubs. In the first round game between Old Etonians and Old Cholmeleians, both teams had scored when the Old Etonian wing-half, Peter Lowndes, was cut down by a late tackle. A twelfth man was ready to come on when the referee stated that he had no instructions to allow a substitute. So, with only ten

men, Etonians went down 4 - 1. They later appealed to the Committee for a ruling. It was evident that the rule was not clear, so the teams were asked to replay the match and, at the same time, the rule on the use of substitutes was changed to allow a substitution at any time in a match and for any reason.

In the next final (April 1970), Old Reptonians became the first side to use a substitute in a final when Peter Rowlands replaced A C Borrett at half-time. Their opponents were Old Foresters, one of the original teams, appearing in their first final. Geoffrey Green (Old Salopian and Times correspondent) reported that *"if Forest were ever to have won their first Dunn Final in history, they should perhaps have done so in the opening 20 minutes, as Beschizza and Wheeler twice went desperately close; and when Rogers, clean through, squandered a fine opening by Wheeler before at last he actually scored following a corner and a move down the right.*

That goal lead at the interval however was not enough in spite of all the signs and the hearty encouragement of their followers, led by a young blood who persistently shattered the damp afternoon air with a hunting horn. Far from awakening the dead, that battle-cry in due course merely awoke Repton. A beautiful rainbow suddenly painted the sky and as the drizzle glistened through the pale sun, we knew there was a fox's wedding somewhere near at hand.

So was a Repton victory. The spirit of C B Fry suddenly galvanised his young heirs as first Gill firmly headed in Rolfe's corner, and then the lanky Tomlinson followed suit as he nodded home the winner 12 minutes from the end, from a clever move between Whitehead and Vaughan".

Two years after their last victory, it was Old Malvernians who took the trophy in 1971. However, they first had to battle through an intense semi-final against Lancing Old Boys. Tony Williams remembered that the game was held at Lancing and *"they had a very good side at the time, and over-confidence probably saw to it that we faced a three goal deficit within 20 minutes. But somehow we won 5 - 4 with an opening goal coming after Loader and I had actually produced a move we had practiced from a throw-in, and the winning goal being scored by our inspirational captain Ian Ryder-Smith, who probably had covered every blade of grass twice over during the game, admonished all our players whom he knew could cope with a blast, and kicked most of the opposition to show that he didn't have any individual grudges. No game was ever lost until the final whistle as far as the skipper was concerned. His six-foot four frame, thrashing around in mid-field and towering bravely in for the last minute headers from corners and free-kicks, was an asset any side would treasure".*

In the final, Old Malvernians gained revenge for their defeat by Old Brentwoods in 1967 by defeating them 4 - 2. Norman Creek reported in the Times:

"In a match of rather hesitant play in defence, the two fastest players on the field – Bridle and Loader – virtually won the Cup for Malvernians. The first half was a hard, even struggle. Williams dived to head the first goal for the Malvernians: Brentwoods equalised when Stevens had the misfortune to head a swerving free-kick past his own goalkeeper: and then Ryan equalised again with the last kick of the first half.

With the wind behind them, Malvernians controlled the second half. They plied Bridle and Loader with the ball at every opportunity, and Bridle obliged with two thrilling goals".

In 1972 they defeated the Old Salopians 1 - 0. Brentwoods coped better than Salopians with the windy conditions at Crystal Palace. They took the initiative from the start and might have scored more goals but for a sound Salopian defence. In the event, it was a corner by Thomas that led to Brentwoods hitting the bar and Harris forcing in the rebound.

The 1973 final was a very exciting game when Brentwoods defeated Old Malvernians 3 - 2 after extra-time. Norman Creek reported in the Times:

"It was a fluctuating match of good and bad football, with dull periods suddenly interspersed with dashing constructive play leading to rousing goalmouth incidents. If Malvernians looked the more experienced and methodical, Brentwoods had the advantage in midfield, where Anderson, Baker and Francis tackled and opened up the game to good purpose.

The man of the match, as in several previous finals, was Malvernian's Bridle. He was as strong, fast and tenacious as when he played for England's schoolboys against Scotland 15 years ago.

The game got off to a flying start, even if Walker-Smith in the Malvern goal did not.

LEFT: THE SALOPIAN GOALKEEPER, JEREMY SALE, DEALS WITH AN AERIAL CHALLENGE DURING THE 1972 FINAL.

BELOW LEFT: THE VICTORIOUS "DUNN" TEAM. (Back row) R DEASLEY, J HARRIS, P WRIGHT, A GUYVER, D ANDERSON, T RUSSELL AND B BAKER. (Front row) N HARRIS, P THOMAS, H MAGUIRE, R BAKER & P CLEMENTS.

BELOW: THE TIMES REPORT OF THE 1972 FINAL.

Third Arthur Dunn win for Brentwoods

By a Special Correspondent

Old Brentwoods, losing finalists last year, won the Arthur Dunn Cup for the third time in their history by defeating Old Salopians 1—0 at the National Sports Centre, Crystal Palace, on Saturday.

A strong cross wind denied both sides the opportunity of playing football. However, Old Brentwoods coped with the difficult conditions the better.

Old Brentwoods won the initiative from the start and only sound handling by J. Sale in the Salopian goal prevented an early score.

Salopians could make progress only individually, and, although W. Tutton had won his spurs in the Salopian defence, Brentwood might have been comfortably in the lead by half-time.

On the resumption G. B. Kendrew replaced J. G. Alexander, the Salopian captain, and their attack increased in mobility. But it was Brentwood who always threatened to open the scoring and after H. Maguire had clipped the far post with a strong cross shot they went ahead in the 60th minute when P. Thomas headed a corner from the right against the bar and J. Harris forced the rebound through.

With the last quarter remaining Salopians were still in the game with an outside chance. With P. Thomas, the Brentwood spearhead, hurt in a tackle and substituted by P. Wright, Salopians threw everything into attack and three clear chances in injury time so nearly won them a reprieve.

OLD BRENTWOODS: A. Guyver, R. Deasley, J. Harris, T. Russell, R. Baker, D. Anderson, B. Baker, H. Maguire, P. Thomas (sub. P. Wright), P. Clements, N. Harris.
OLD SALOPIANS: J. Sale; R. A. Weetch, A. J. Walls, W. Tutton, R. H. Gilkes, I. R. Short, J. G. Alexander (sub. G. B. Kendrew), S. K. Jones, R. Tudor, P. St J. Worth, C. J. Rowlinson.
Referee: W. H. Evans.

MEMORIES OF TWO OLD FORESTERS
by John Morley & Colin Smith

JOHN MORLEY AND COLIN SMITH OLD FORESTERS

John Morley's first game for Old Foresters was in the second round in the 1960/61 season against Old Wykehamists. His last was in the same 1974/75 final against Old Malvernians. During that period, he missed only two games – the semi-final and the losing final in 1969/70 – due to a cartilage injury.

Colin Smith played his first game for Old Foresters in 1958. In a game against Old Bradfieldians, he broke a collar bone and was taken to hospital. He then appeared regularly until his last game in the Arthur Dunn Final of 1974/75, when he came on as a substitute.

John Morley and Colin Smith were contemporaries in the Old Forester teams of the 1960s and 1970s, a time when Old Foresters at last established themselves as serious contenders in the Dunn competition.

"For many years, the Arthur Dunn Cup was like the Holy Grail so far as the Foresters were concerned. Founded 25 years before the Cup competition started, we had already had our golden period and indeed are the only school to have had both its Old Boys team and school team playing in the FA Cup in the same year. However, we had never won the Dunn or even reached the final and in the days of friendly-only football, our competitive season ended each year with elimination from the Dunn.

In those years, Reptonians and Malvernians seemed to dominate the competition and although I do not think they or any other club liked playing Foresters, we were always burdened with the fact that we had never won and perhaps we wanted to win too badly. However, we did not have either the tradition of winning or possibly the strength in depth which many other clubs seemed to have. Whilst we could bring in Robin Trimby, who was an Oxford Blue and amateur international, and David Wilson, who was a Cambridge Blue and an Olympic trialist at the age of 16, Malvernians and Reptonians in particular, could bring in a complete tram of Blues just for the Dunn. Games in those days were hard but generally fair. I do not recall any player having his name taken and certainly none sent off but I also believe that referees were told that the Dunn was played in this way and they should take this into account. Certainly, I remember the crowd counting my sixth foul in succession before I was fouled to further cheers!" (John Morley).

The first glimmer of hope came in the 1962/63 season. Foresters reached the semi-final but as Colin Smith recalled: "we were beaten in a very close match by Malvernians but it is the only time I saw Robin Trimby lose his cool with the referee for a match-turning decision". The following year, Foresters returned to Malvern and beat them 3 - 0 "in a game where we had only four shots, the other hitting the post" (John Morley). Colin Smith remarked that "Richard Dunn, who sadly died two years ago, played a magnificent game at centre-half, completely closing down Tony Williams and his colleagues". However, "the loss in the next round to Cholmeleians was particularly galling; the game was played on a snow-covered pitch which made the game a lottery".

In 1964/65, Old Foresters lost in the second round away at Repton "where last minute injuries forced us to call in one of our spectators from the bar" (JM). And this was followed by defeats in the early rounds to their Essex rivals – Chigwellians or Brentwoods.

At last, in 1969/70, Foresters got to another semi-final and a straightforward win over old Cholmeleians. "The loss against Reptonians was a bitter pill having led for 80 minutes and to lose by two headed goals in the dying minutes was particularly difficult, having by mutual agreement out-played them for most of the game. I remember taking a bottle of champagne into the Reptonian dressing room and Gerry Tomlinson, the Reptonian skipper, remarking how unlucky we had been" (CS). John Morley remarked that "Reptonians perhaps had that tradition of winning, which we had not".

"In 1973/74, we eventually achieved what we had been striving for since the competition started. The most significant game, however, was not the final but the semi-final away at Repton. Perhaps knowing that I had not many years left, gave the game an added edge but Reptonians were still a formidable side with a number of very experienced players. However, after early pressure, I am sure that the experience of the older players, Dave Wilson, Colin Smith and myself enabled us to win comfortably in the end and also ensured that we kept our nerve in the final against a talented and experienced Brentwood team. The League was also won to give us the double" (JM).

In the first minute he was completely bamboozled by a high floating free-kick taken by Francis from the edge of the centre circle, and the ball flopped into the net five yards behind him. Three minutes later, Bridle equalised when he dribbled past two Brentwood defenders, drew out the goalkeeper, and shot into the open goal.

Harris, a useful substitute, headed Brentwoods into the lead after half-time, but Malvernians quickly equalised through Andrew, and two tiring teams had to play extra-time.

Just when it seemed that the trophy would have to be shared, and after innumerable goal-mouth incidents, the tall Thomas thumped a powerful header past the stranded Malvern goalkeeper and the holders had been successful once again. It was in every sense a worthy final".

OLD FORESTERS FIRST WIN
AFTER ONLY 71 YEARS!

As one Old Forester said after the game *"It's taken us 71 years to do it"* – and a narrow squeak it was too! At last, the Old Foresters won the Cup for the first time in 1974 by defeating their Essex rivals 2 - 1 in a very close game in which the central defenders of the Old Foresters, Geoff Green and John Morley, were outstanding. The Old Brentwoods were appearing in their fourth consecutive final and had been hoping to make it a hat-trick of wins.

In 1975, Old Foresters returned to the final and although Mike Hassid headed them into the lead they lost 2 - 1 to Old Malvernians. Later, Mike Hassid became a referee and, in 1990, he ran the line and then refereed the 1993 final.

MALVERN AND BRENTWOOD MEET AGAIN

In the 1976 final, Old Malvernians met Old Brentwoods for the fourth time since 1967 and won a superb game 5 - 3. With twenty minutes remaining, Old Brentwoods were winning 3 - 1 but in a rousing finish Old Malvernians scored four goals. First, a corner from the left, and a mix-up in the Brentwoods goal-mouth led to an own goal that made it 3 - 2 to Brentwoods with 11 minutes left. Then a Murray shot was deflected past the unhappy Kilmartin, and it was 3 - 3.

"Malvernians now sensed it was their day, A ferocious Saunders volley put them in front, and then the perseverance of Whateley had its reward. He rounded the goalkeeper and slid the ball precisely into the corner of the net to complete a wonderful fight-back" (The Times).

The Annual General Meeting in July 1976 agreed that in future, the draw should be made only for the preliminary and first rounds; the other rounds were to be drawn when the participants were known. This was put into effect for the 1976/77 season.

Old Carthusians reached the 1977 final. This was their first appearance in the final since 1962 and their opponents were Old Brentwoods. Old Carthusians had been in free scoring mode on the

Arthur Dunn Cup Final
MALVERNIANS RECOVER WELL

Malvernians 5, Brentwoods 3

Malvernians retained the Arthur Dunn Cup on Saturday, at Crystal Palace but vanquished Brentwoods were the better team in the first half.

Needham scored for Brentwoods after 35 minutes following a corner, but Malvernians equalised through Murphy just before half-time.

In the second half, Walker headed a Brentwood goal, then Deasley crashed in the ball from close range – 3-1.

Malvernians fought back hard. A corner from the left, and a mix-up in the Brentwoods goal-mouth led to an own-goal that made it 3-2 to Brentwoods with 11 minutes left. Then a Murray shot was deflected past the unhappy Kilmartin, and it was 3-3.

Malvernians now sensed it was their day. A ferocious Saunders volley put them in front, and then the perseverance of Whateley had its reward. He rounded the goalkeeper and slid the ball precisely into the corner of the net to complete a wonderful fight-back.

LEFT: *THE TIMES REPORT OF THE 1976 FINAL.*

way to the final scoring seventeen goals. Much of this was due to their two very quick and clever forwards, Peter Godby and Alan Stewart. At the other end, they conceded only three goals in three games but there was a feeling that they had really not been tested.

By contrast, Old Brentwoods, had defeated Old Etonians 4 - 3 in a very close game in the preliminary round. They then gained revenge for their defeat in the 1974 final by beating their local rivals, Old Foresters. In the semi–final, they defeated Old Malvernians 1 - 0 and so Brentwoods were the favourites to defeat Old Carthusians.

However, the game did not go to plan. After five minutes, Micky Walker missed a penalty for Old Brentwoods and then, Old Carthusians played some superb fast and direct football to win 3 - 0. It was very appropriate that one of the first winners of the Arthur Dunn Cup should win the final in their Centenary Year.

The 1978 final was between Old Malvernians and Old Bradfieldians but the outstanding match in this season's competition had been the semi-final between Old Brentwoods and Old Malvernians.

Malvernians won 5 - 4 after extra-time.

JAN BRIDLE - OLD MALVERNIAN

Jan Bridle (formerly J W Illaszewicz) was born in 1942, the son of a Polish pilot killed in the War. He went to Malvern from 1956 – 61 and was an outstanding all-round athlete, being in the Football XI 1959/60, the Cricket 2nd XI 1960/61, the Swimming team 1958 – 61 and captain of Rugby football. He later played cricket for Dorset.

Jan played in thirteen finals for the Old Malvernians between 1961/62 and 1977/78, being on the winning side seven times. This surpasses the record set by T S Rowlandson (Old Carthusian) between seasons 1902/03 and 1909/10.

Bridle's full record is as follows:
Winning years: 1964/65, 1967/68, 1968/69, 1970/71, 1974/75, 1975/76, 1977/78.
Runner-up years: 1961/62, 1962/63, 1965/66, 1966/67, 1972/73, 1981/82.

In his report on the 1973 AD final, Norman Creek said in the Times, that "the man of the match, as in several previous finals, was Malvern's Bridle. He was as strong, fast and tenacious as when he played for England's schoolboys against Scotland 15 years ago". Bridle was never a powerful kicker but he had a remarkable ability to emerge from a series of tackles still balanced and with the ball at his feet, whereupon he would place the ball just inside the post, or unselfishly pass it to a colleague who was in a better position to score. In a celebration of 100 years of Old Malvernian football, in the AFA Record (March 1997), Tony Williams wrote: "Bridle was possibly the best goalscorer not to be capped in the old amateur international days. He once scored twice when an AFA XI drew 2 - 2 with the full England Amateur XI (disguised as an FA XI) and regularly played for Bournemouth Reserves. He holds the record for Arthur Dunn Cup Final appearances, and played in a record seven winning sides out of thirteen finals".

Ian Ryder-Smith was unable to play for the Old Malvernians as he was away on business, so he sent a telegram, *"Good luck but watch Phil Needham"*. This was presented to the Old Malvernian team at half-time, by which time they were 3 - 0 down and Phil Needham had scored all three.

In the final, Old Malvernians were too strong for Old Bradfieldians and won 4 - 1. This victory meant that Jan Bridle (Illaszewicz) had played in seven winning Old Malvernian sides.

The Old Malvernian victory in 1978 was the start of another trend in the history of the Arthur Dunn Cup. In the six years from 1978, six different teams won the Cup. This was probably because the standard of play of all sides had improved gradually since the start of the Arthurian League in 1962/63. Consequently, one or two sides could not dominate the competition at certain periods, as they had done in the past.

ALDENHAM WIN THE CUP – THEN LOSE IT!

When Old Brentwoods reached the 1979 final, it was anticipated that this would be their year. Having lost in 1976 and 1977, they reached the final again having had three home ties. In the second round, they had been victorious in another close game against Old Malvernians 3 - 2. In the final, their opponents would be Old Aldenhamians, who had also had three home ties. Old Aldenhamians had not reached the final since 1964 but they had won the Arthurian League Championship in 1976/77.

It was not the Old Brentwoods' day. John Baugh, in the goal for the Old Aldenhamians, was rarely troubled as Andy Clare had organised the Old Aldenhamian defence very well and Phil Smith, who had played in the Old Aldenhamian side in 1964, dictated the play from midfield. It was very appropriate that Donald Shearer, who had captained the Old Aldenhamians in 1934, was present at the final as a guest of Alan Barber, the President of the

Arthur Dunn Cup Committee. Richard Hall was in the Aldenhamian team and recalled:

"It was decided that we would all meet at the School on the morning of the match as Mike Hetherington had arranged to take the team in the School minibus and also take us to his sister's house in Beckenham for soup and a sandwich lunch. At the time, I only lived about half an hour from Crystal Palace, but made my way up to Aldenham. Besides the 12 we also had David Latchman as our sponge man who had supported the side for the past 2 years.

We arrived at the ground with less than half an hour to spare and changed into our brand new kit. I then noticed that I had left my pair of football boots back at the School. Steve Hitchins loaned me a pair of his boots which were size 10 (I have a petite size 8). A couple of pairs of socks later, I just made the photocall.

Not the best of matches, but a superbly taken goal by Dave Pickett secured the result for the OAs. We had excellent celebrations at Crystal Palace starting with half bottles of sparkling Blue Nun in the changing rooms before the team headed back through Central London to the Three Horseshoes. On the way back in the minibus, the orange plastic bucket used by the spongeman, became the indoor toilet. While going through the West End, the back door was opened and the contents deposited on an astonished couple in a Ford Escort.

Back at the Three Horseshoes, we celebrated the win well into the night. I will never forget the sight of Phil Kerr giving a good exhibition of lap-dancing – a day never to be forgotten. And after it was all over, we discovered that the trophy had been left behind at Crystal Palace".

Luckily when Andy Clare rang up the Sports Complex the next day, the Cup was in safe hands.

One has to feel very sorry for Don Cameron of Old Brentwoods, as he had played in five finals – 1971, 74, 76, 77 and 79 – and lost them all. On the only occasion in this period that Old Brentwoods won the Cup (1972/73), he was not available!

ABOVE: JAN BRIDLE AFTER THE FINAL OF 1978.

THE RISE OF CHIGWELL AND LANCING

Once again, the influence of Pegasus had an impact on the Dunn. Both John Dutchman and Ken Shearwood had played in the all-conquering Pegasus team. They subsequently became masters at Chigwell and Lancing respectively and coached the school sides. It was not surprising therefore that the Old Boys teams should eventually benefit culminating in 1980 when Old Chigwellians and Lancing Old Boys reached the final. Neither of these clubs had previously reached this stage. Indeed, only once before (in 1913, Old Aldenhamians v Old Brightonians) had the final been contested by two teams that had not appeared before.

Lancing Old Boys, although one of the founder members of the competition, had only previously reached the semi-finals three times (in 1928/29, 1937/38 and 1968/69). Jamie Wood had put together a very good, young side based on the many good Lancing School sides coached by Ken Shearwood.

Nigel Bennett, who played in this team, reckons that *"Lancing would not have achieved its Dunn successes of the 1980s without Ken Shearwood or the inspired direction of the Lancing captain of the time, Jamie Wood, to help him out. Ken brought two vital ingredients to our success at that time - organisation and the bringing together of the best Lancing footballers at that era - Nigel Bennett, Nigel Pitcher, Martin Wyatt, Nick Triggs, Martin Todd and Chris Sutherland among many others. The faith he had in skilful attacking football at school was perhaps best illustrated by his decision to pick a tiny, frail 13-year-old (called Nigel Bennett) against the strong wishes of other teachers many of whom thought the selection to be ill-considered".*

In their first round match against the Old Cholmeleians, Lancing Old Boys played some amazing football in very wintry conditions and won 5 - 1. They then defeated Old Foresters 4 - 1 at Forest and, in a very close game, defeated Old Brentwoods 4 - 3 at Brentwood in the semi-final. Old Chigwellians got to the final by defeating the Old Aldenhamians 2 - 1, Old Bradfieldians 1 - 0 and Old Salopians 2 - 0 at Shrewsbury.

CHIGWELLIANS FIRST SUCCESS

In the final the Old Chigwellians won a gripping game 4 - 2 after extra-time. The Daily Telegraph reported:

"Chigwellians deservedly won the Arthur Dunn Cup for the first time when they overcame Lancing in extra time of an exciting final.

Redrup opened the scoring for Chigwellians after 25 minutes when he hit the ball in from close range, after a goal-mouth melée.

Dutchman was fouled inside the area and scored from the penalty spot to put the Chigwellians two ahead, just after the interval. At this stage, Lancing took control of midfield and Pitcher headed in from the corner. Lancing battled away for the equaliser, and with five minutes to go substitute Brooking headed firmly into the net.

Chigwellians went into the lead in the first period of extra time when Redrup headed past Sutherland, then in the dying minutes of the game Dutchman ran through to score and seal the match".

THE FIRST REPLAY SINCE 1903

The 1980/81 season marked a revival in Old Reptonian fortunes. Richard Body was now in charge, assisted by Scottie Cheshire (Mark Stretton described these as Reptonians' very own *"Clough and Taylor"* managerial partnership).

Reptonians began the campaign with a preliminary round game against Old Westminsters, who were convincingly beaten 5 - 0. *"In the following round, the team converged on Highgate where their unfamiliarity was apparent in the initial period of the game. Within the first 10 minutes there was a lucky escape, a Cholmeleian shot beat Ballinger, hit one post, rolled along the goal line, onto the other post and was then thankfully cleared. Having survived the early pressure the ORs gradually took control to win 3 - 0.*

The semi-final at Charterhouse was a classic, blood and thunder game in which there was some excellent football played by both teams. The lead changed hands on numerous occasions and with the score at 3 - 3 the game could have gone either way. It was the ORs who scored the important 7th goal with 10 minutes to go and subsequently killed off the Carthusian challenge, when a flowing move the length of the pitch ended with Martin Beckett rounding two Carthusians to tap the ball into the empty net. Thus ensuring a 5 - 3 victory and a place in the final against old rivals Malvernians". (Mark Stretton).

Malvernians also had a tough journey to the final. In the semi-final, they had a hard-fought match against Lancing Old Boys. Nigel Bennett played for Lancing in this game and remembered that he and his colleagues raced to a 3 - 1 lead, but *"Malvernians overwhelmed us in the second half to win a great game 4 - 3".*

The last final at the Crystal Palace was therefore between the two teams that had appeared in the 1965 final, the year that the Dunn final had returned to the Crystal Palace. The game itself was a tense one and resulted in a 3 - 3 draw. Thus, for only the second time in the history of the Arthur Dunn Cup competition, there would have to be a replay. How ironic it was that the rule allowing a replay had been changed as a result of the drawn final between Malvernians and Reptonians in 1968.

Mark Stretton recalled: *"Like the semi-final, the final was a high scoring game which ended 3 - 3 after extra time. In the replay the ORs were more dominant than the eventual 1 - 0 scoreline suggests and even had a legitimate goal disallowed. The win was secured from a rehearsed free-kick which Body chipped around the defensive wall to Stretton, who fiercely volleyed into the net. Richmond High Street was caught somewhat unawares as the OR celebrations began late on a midweek evening".*

LEFT:
MARK STRETTON
IN 1981.

THE STAND AT MOTSPUR PARK.

Chapter 6

TO MOTSPUR PARK
VIA DULWICH

After 16 settled years at the Crystal Palace, the Arthur Dunn Cup Final was on its travels again in 1982. The National Recreation Centre at Crystal Palace was now to be restricted exclusively for athletics so another venue had to be found. With the help of Derek Goodliffe, who had played in the Old Carthusian team that had won in 1954 and 1962, the final was moved to Champion Hill, East Dulwich, the home of Dulwich Hamlet FC. Derek's family had very good connections with the Isthmian League Club.

THE FIRST FINAL AT DULWICH HAMLET

There were two remarkable games before the final of 1982. In the second round, there was a repeat of the previous year's semi-final between the Old Carthusians and the Old Reptonians, once again played at Charterhouse. Old Carthusians gained their revenge by thrashing the holders 7 - 1; they were four goals up after only twenty minutes.

Old Carthusians were a very exciting, attacking side and the key players in the forward line were Alan Stewart, who played up front on the left and Peter Godby as a striker.

In the semi-finals, Old Malvernians played Lancing Old Boys again – a repeat of the previous year – but this time the venue was Malvern. Once again, Lancing Old Boys managed to lose a game which they should have won. Lancing were leading 3 - 1 with 12 minutes of extra-time remaining but ultimately lost 4 - 3.

So, the first final at Dulwich Hamlet was between Old Carthusians and Old Malvernians. Old Carthusians won 3 - 0 by playing simple direct football; the goals were scored by Oulton, Pratt and Stewart. They also had a sound defence made up of the veteran Easton, and Herbert-Smith.

RICHARD SALE - OLD REPTONIAN
PRESIDENT 1982 - 87

Dick Sale was a "larger than life" character. He went to Repton, becoming Head of School, captain of football and played in the Cricket XI for two seasons. At Oxford, he won blues for cricket and fives before and after the War, in which he served as a major.

After the War, he returned to Repton to teach. Dick was a real 'schoolmaster of the old school', as was to be expected of an Old Reptonian and son of a Shrewsbury housemaster. But Dick was also an outstanding 'all-round' games player. He played in the Derbyshire cricket team in the 1950s, and for the Old Reptonians in the Arthur Dunn.

In 1966, Dick became Headmaster at Brentwood School where his combination of firmness with an impish sense of humour won him respect from parents, staff and boys. During this period, Old Brentwoods achieved their greatest successes in the Arthur Dunn Cup. And it was this widely-held respect that led to Dick Sale being invited to become the President of the Arthur Dunn Cup competition in 1982.

This success in the Arthur Dunn was the second part of a remarkable treble for Carthusians. They had already won the Cricketer Cup in the previous summer, then on Saturday 3rd April 1982, the Arthur Dunn Cup and the following day they won the Halford Hewitt (the Old Boys Golf Competition). Thus, Old Carthusians were holders of the three major Old Boys Trophies at the same time.

DICK SALE ELECTED PRESIDENT

In the Summer of 1982, Alan Barber resigned as President due to illness and so at the AGM in June, Dick Sale, an Old Reptonian and the Headmaster of Brentwood was unanimously elected President of the Arthur Dunn Cup competition.

CHAMPION HILL - DULWICH HAMLET

(1982 - 1986)

The Champion Hill ground has been the home of Dulwich Hamlet FC since 1912. The old ground was demolished in 1992 and replaced by a modern stadium. As well as hosting the Arthur Dunn finals from 1982 to 1986 the old ground held a crowd of 20,744 for the 1933 FA Amateur Cup final between Kingstonian and Stockton.

MEMORABLE MATCHES
by Nigel Bennett

NIGEL BENNETT
LANCING OLD BOY

After playing football in the school first XI (from age 13), Nigel then got two Blues at Oxford University, scoring in both games, which Oxford won.
Nigel also had a trial for Wolverhampton Wanderers but did not make the first team squad. He did however partner Andy Gray up front in the reserve team.
Nigel was ever-present in the Lancing OB team that won the Arthur Dunn Cup three times in succession (1983 - 85), scoring in 1983 and 1985 (2). In all, Nigel appeared in six finals, firstly in the losing team in 1980, and later he retained a place in the Lancing team during the 1990s. By this time, he had become a goalkeeper and in this role he played in the successful finals of 1993 and as recently as 2000.

ABOVE: 'NIGEL, THE GOALKEEPER' IN THE 2000 FINAL.

A) THE GOOD

i) Semi-final vs Harrovians 1984

Won 5 - 3 but 3 - 0 down with 19 minutes to go against a side a division below us was not a good position to be in. Against the run of play Harrow led 1 - 0 at half time scoring direct from a corner. Having needlessly conceded a penalty (handball) early in the second half Harrow scored again, against the run of play, with an outrageous shot from about 30 yards. 0 - 3 – Oh dear! We needed to score in the first five minutes of the re-start. We did and quite improbably, given the time left to play, it never seemed in doubt from that moment that we would win.

ii) Semi-final vs Malvernians 1985

Won 3 - 0 away at Malvern on a very heavy pitch. Satisfying for two reasons. Firstly, for gaining revenge after two horrible defeats by Malvern in previous years. Secondly, for totally dominating one of the stronger teams of the day to the extent that they were lucky to have only lost 3 - 0.

iii) Preliminary Round vs Foresters 1986

We had beaten Foresters 5 - 0 in the final the previous year and I suppose that they were less than happy to draw us away from home in the next year's first round. This was an extraordinary game. Lancing were missing several players (N Bennett, N Pitcher, N Triggs) for various reasons, injury and otherwise, which was always going to make this game much more even than the previous year's final and for Foresters Chris Elliott and, particularly Nicky Francis who scored four goals were outstanding. Foresters were ahead, in scoring, throughout the match and only a superb goal from Martin Wyatt took the game into extra time at 2 - 2. Foresters continued to lead the scoring 3 - 2, 3 - 3, 4 - 3, 4 - 4, 5 - 4 until with eight minutes to go a corner to Lancing. The ball was headed down and Simon Bennett, a magnificent player for Lancing but mainly (and rather annoyingly for him) out-shone by his younger brother, scored the winner with a fierce left foot drive. Amazingly, there was still time for Foresters to miss an open goal before the referee ended the game. There are not many times when I have felt sorry for the Foresters but this was one of them!

B) THE BAD

i) Final vs Chigwellians 1980

I'm sure the Chigs see this very differently and indeed they deserved to win on the day (4 - 2). For Lancing both Wyatt and Bennett were injured, shouldn't have played but did play (badly) because it was a final on a rotten, rock hard pitch at Crystal Palace. A massively below-par performance by us.

C) THE UGLY

i) Semi-final vs Malvern 1981

This I remember was a great game except that our defending was so fragile at that time (like West Ham used to be) that even if we scored three we weren't guaranteed to win. 3 - 1 down at one stage Malvern overwhelmed us in the second half to win a great game 4 - 3.

ii) Semi-final vs Malvern 1982

This time round we were determined not to make the same mistake as in 1981. A tough game which, at 1 - 1 after 90 minutes, went into extra time. 3 - 1 up with only 12 minutes to play should have been enough but again a jelly-like collapse at the back (goalkeeping error, great goal by Bridle and then the "inevitable" winner as our heads dropped) – 4 - 3 to Malvernians. The darkest hour before the dawn and probably the incentive we needed to train harder, get fitter and be more competitive as well as more skilful.

LANCING'S TREBLE WINNING SEQUENCE

At the culmination of 1982/83 season, Lancing Old Boys once more reached the final. Their opponents were Old Chigwellians, who had defeated them in the final in 1980. On this occasion, Lancing Old Boys were successful and in so doing won the Cup for the first time in their Centenary Year.

This was an excellent Lancing Old Boys side as was demonstrated when they became the first side to win the Cup in three successive years since Old Wykehamists achieved the feat before the Second World War.

They were very well captained by Nigel Pitcher and among the many outstanding players were Nick Triggs – a sweeper, Robin Brodhurst in midfield and a front line of Martin Wyatt, Nigel Bennett and Nigel Pitcher.

In the keenly-contested final, the goals were scored by Bennett and Pitcher. *"There was an element of luck in Lancing's first goal, a cross from Wood in the 15th minute being deflected onto the head of the grateful Nigel Bennett, who made no mistake from close range.*

But Lancing had the edge in all departments with S Bennett and Triggs sound in defence and Beale, Brodhurst and Todd gradually gaining midfield superiority over the determined Chigwellians of whom Phelps was outstanding.

Inch and Dutchman tried hard to inspire a Chigwellian revival in the second half but they lacked the support they deserved. Chigwell's hopes were shattered in the 75th minute when a poor backpass by Conolly let in Pitcher for the second goal". (Daily Telegraph).

With Lancing Old Boys winning the cup in 1983, it meant that for the first time six different

teams had won the cup in six years. This season's competition was also notable for a remarkable game in the preliminary round when a young Old Bradfieldian team surprisingly defeated the Old Foresters 6 - 3.

Lancing did not have an easy run to the next final in 1984. They had to come from behind in two of the early matches, In the first round, they were losing 2 - 1 to Old Cholmeleians with five minutes to go but eventually won 5 - 3 after extra-time; in the semi-final, Old Harrovians were leading 3 - 0 with 20 minutes to go but once Lancing Old Boys had scored the first, they quickly scored another four.

Their opponents in the final were Old Carthusians. Thus, the two most successful teams of the period were pitted against each other. The outcome was an excellent final, which

ABOVE: A JUBILANT LANCING AFTER WINNING THE CUP IN 1983.

LEFT: THE LANCING OLD BOYS CAPTAIN NIGEL PITCHER HOLDS UP THE CUP AFTER THE PRESENTATION IN 1983.

NIGEL PITCHER, MARTIN WYATT AND NICK TRIGGS
LANCING OLD BOYS

Nigel Pitcher and Martin Wyatt formed part of the striking trio that were so successful for Lancing in the early 1980s, the other was Nigel Bennett. They both appeared in the 1980 final which Lancing lost 4 - 2 to Old Chigwellians. This three-some were then the strike force that won the trophy three times between 1983 and 1985. Bennett described Nigel Pitcher as having "great ball control and athleticism allied with great courage, he never hid in a game and would always run hard at defenders and commit them". Pitcher scored in each of the four finals in which he played.

Of Martin Wyatt, Nigel Bennett said that "there was one quality that set Martin apart from his OL contemporaries - supreme goal-scoring ability whether with the head, left foot or right foot, he could, and did, score goals of extraordinary opportunism". Wyatt scored a goal in the 1984 and 1996 finals.

In the centre of the defence for Lancing at this time was Nick Triggs. He too appeared in four finals (1980, 1983, 1984 and 1985). Nigel Bennett said of him that "his distribution from the back was outrageously good and routinely balls were played thirty or forty yards accurately to team-mates, with the outside of either foot when necessary".

PROFILE PICTURES:
(FAR LEFT TOP)
NIGEL PITCHER,
(FAR LEFT BOTTOM)
NICK TRIGGS,
(BELOW)
MARTIN WYATT.

Lancing Old Boys won 2 - 0. The goals were scored by Pitcher and Wyatt and no matter how hard Godby and Stewart tried for Old Carthusians, they were unable to score.

Nigel Bennett (Lancing Old Boys) described Al Stewart as *"simply a class act. His balance and ball-control were exceptional. Two-footed, deceptively strong and fast (not electrically quick, thank goodness!) he would have been a fabulous asset for us!"*.

The Daily Telegraph reported: *"Pitcher, Lancing's most dangerous forward, gave them the lead in the 28th minute, heading home Hodgkinson's accurate cross off the far post. The second half was fast and furious. Godby used his speed well down the flank, but Lancing went further into the lead when Wyatt burst through, beat two defenders and drove the ball into the net off a post"*.

OLD CITIZENS RETURN TO THE FRAY

In season 1984/85, two new sides entered the competition. Old Citizens were re-entering as they had played between 1904/05 and 1938/39. After the Second World War, the school had played rugby but then changed back to football in the 1980s.

The other team was the Old Boys of St Edmund's Canterbury. Mike Green was a leading light in the St Edmund's team and recalled:

"It all began with Julian Ironside, a bright, talented individual who not only captained the school side but went on to Cambridge, where he captained the University side for 2 years! Near the end of his time at Cambridge, he got in touch with me, full of youthful enthusiasm and good intent, persuading me that we should enter the Arthur Dunn Cup, convincing me that he (and I) would find a youthful enthusiastic squad who would want to do this. My younger brother, Oliver, and I ran the Old Boys' sport for quite a long time, which included the

Old Boys versus the School cricket match, and also the Brewers Cup, which was the equivalent of the Cricketers' Cup for the smaller schools. We also arranged a series of hockey games, playing under the name of the Cossacks.

I was approaching 40 at the time and my brother only two years younger, and felt a little apprehensive. Nevertheless we entered, and to our dismay we were first drawn against Lancing Old Boys, who were doing very well in the competition. Although drawn at home, we were no match for them, and of course Julian Ironside could not play! However, we were not deterred and entered again the following year when we were drawn against Old Harrovians.

This game has now become folklore! We were struggling to get the Superstars out as Julian said that he could not play – in fact he only played in one or two games! I had jokingly told my brother, who teaches at a prep school in Hampshire, to bring his boots. We met and had a good lunch neither of us expecting to play.

On arriving at the school, it was clear that we had problems with car breakdowns etc., so we lined up with a strong, somewhat robust back four, with no speed or mobility, but lots of experience. With a strong wind behind us, we went ahead, but they equalised shortly after half-time. In defence, we were bombarded and the keeper, Andrew Barrett, as well as the back four of M Green, Jordan, Taff and O Green, held a solid uncompromising line. A well-taken breakaway goal, and being able to withstand the pressures, meant that we claimed our only and famous victory!!".

Unfortunately neither side remained in the competition for long – Old Citizens played for only five seasons and St Edmund's Canterbury for six. St Edmund's Canterbury did not run a regular old boys football team as the majority of their old boys played for their hockey team.

LANCING MAKE IT A HAT-TRICK

Lancing Old Boys reached their third consecutive final and won easily – they defeated the Old Foresters 5 - 0. The goals for Lancing Old Boys were scored by Nigel Bennett, who scored two, one a brilliant volley from 35 yards, Gavin Sheridan, Chris Beale and Nigel Pitcher. *"Chris Elliott proved Foresters' liveliest player, but after conceding three first-half goals and having a Richard Harnack penalty saved by Chris Sutherland in the 43rd minute they faced a hopeless task"*. (Daily Telegraph).

This was a contrast to the earlier rounds. Lancing only managed to defeat the Old Carthusians after two replays and, in the semi-final, they at last beat their bogey side the Old Malvernians 3 - 0 at Malvern.

This was a remarkable run for Lancing Old Boys. Not only had they won the Arthur Dunn Cup for the third time in succession but they had also won the Arthurian League in these three years. This was a very strong side with some fine players and

BELOW: RICHARD HARNACK, OLD FORESTER, HIS FIRST APPEARANCE IN A FINAL 1985.

BELOW: THE MATCH REPORT FROM THE DAILY TELEGRAPH AND THE COVER OF THE PROGRAMME, 1985.

LANCING ON FOR DOUBLE

By A Special Correspondent
Old Foresters 0, Lancing OB's 5

Lancing completed a hat-trick of Arthur Dunn Cup victories and are now poised to claim a remarkable feat of Arthurian League and Cup double for the third successive season.

Nigel Bennett played a captain's role in the Cup success at Dulwich Hamlet on Saturday. He scored two one a 35-yard volley and created another for Gavin Sheridan with a 40 yard run to the by-line before pulling the ball back Chris Beale and Nigel Pitcher were the other scorers.

Chris Elliott proved Foresters liveliest player, but after conceding three first half goals and having a Richard Harnack penalty saved by Chris Sutherland in the 43rd minute they faced a hopeless task.

ARTHUR DUNN CUP FINAL

13TH APRIL 1985

OLD FORESTERS

v

LANCING OLD BOYS

AT

DULWICH HAMLET FOOTBALL CLUB

KICK-OFF 3 P.M.

Presentation of cup by Mrs. Jane Ross granddaughter of the Late Arthur Dunn.

Children: 50p

ADULTS: £1

thoroughly deserved its success. Much was owed to the assistance provided by Ken Shearwood, the Old Salopian, who coached and encouraged them. (He had been master in charge of football at Lancing College between 1955 and 1977).

OLD BRENTWOODS' RARE WIN

Lancing Old Boys' magnificent run came to an end in the 1985/86 season when they lost to their arch-rivals at this time, Old Carthusians. In a second round tie, they were defeated 1 - 0 after a replay. Unfortunately, at the end of the previous season, Nigel Bennett had sustained a nasty injury and it would be a few years before he was able to play again. But before this defeat, Lancing Old Boys had played an amazing game in the preliminary round against the Old Foresters winning 6 - 5.

Old Carthusians were then beaten in the semi-final, also after a replay, by Old Brentwoods, who went on to win the final by defeating Old Cholmeleians 1 - 0. It was a very good final which Old Brentwoods deserved to win with the goal being scored by Dixon.

Old Brentwoods had last won the cup in 1973 and Phil Needham, a very nippy centre forward and a wonderful scorer of goals, played in both the 1973 and 1986 winning teams, and in the other four finals in which Old Brentwoods had played during that period. Old Cholmeleians, who were appearing in the final for the first time since 1961, played splendidly throughout the match.

Frixos Kyriacou appeared for Cholmeleians and looked back on the campaign as follows:

"After narrowly defeating Aldenhamians at Highgate in the preliminary round,

ABOVE: PHIL NEEDHAM OLD BRENTWOOD, WAS ONE OF THE MOST DANGEROUS GOAL-POACHERS PLAYING IN THIS ERA. HE PLAYED IN EIGHT FINALS, WINNING IN 1973 AND 1986.

LANCING OLD BOYS

Chris Sutherland: ('Col Blink') Lancing's regular No.1 goalkeeper for a number of years. Dunn winner 1983 and 1984. Hobbies - Food and Kitchens. (Kitchen designer) Age: 28

Jim Todd ('Toddy') Younger brother of M. Todd (an OL Stalwart). Very consistent and classy full-back. Dunn winner 1984. Hobbies - Gauloises & Ken Livingstone. (Journalist) Age: 24

Simon Bennett: ('Beef') Elder brother of the Captain. Tough and uncompromising centre-half. Dunn winner 1983. Hobbies - Food and more food. (Accountant) Age: 27

Nick Triggs: ('Twiglet') Very skilful player and superb organiser in defence. Dunn winner 1983 and 1984. Hobbies - Leather and Lace. (Accountant) Age: 26

Robert Stallibrass: ('Stobby') Has had a good season and claimed the left-back position. Dunn winner 1984. Hobbies - Amsterdam and Crystal Palace F.C. (Sales) Age: 25

Gavin Sheridan: ('Spike') Just finished at Exeter University. Very fit midfield player or defender. Dunn winner 1983 and 1984. Hobbies - Wide boy cars and flowery shirts. (Future Merchant Banker) Age: 21

Nigel Bennett: ('The Doog') Captain; ex-Oxford University and Wolves Reserves. Reknowned best player in the league. Dunn winner 1983 and 1984. 14 goals this season. Hobbies - Food especially cakes. (Chartered Surveyor) Age: 25

Robin Brodhurst: ('Mary Decker') Stalwart midfield player and good striker of the ball. Dunn winner 1983 and 1984. Hobbies - Glenda Hoddle and Spurs F.C. (Lloyds Broker) Age: 26

Chris Beale: ('Basher') Ex-3rd battallian Paras. Dunn winner 1983. Very fit, fast winger and midfield player. 4 goals this season. Hobbies - Jazz, fast cars and slow women. (Lufthansa Cargo) Age: 24

Martin Wyatt: ('The Capitalist' or Mulligan or Metgod') Ex-Hull university. Dunn winner 1983 and 1984. Phenomenal goal poacher. 23 goals this season. Hobbies - money and goals. (Advertising) Age: 25

Negel Pitcher: ('Yogi') Ex-skipper. Dunn winner 1983 and 1984. Aggressive, speedy forward. 15 goals this season. Hobbies - Beer and music. (Banking) Age: 27

Nick Bell: ('Bodger') Skilful forward or midfield player. 5 goals this season. Dunn winner 1984. When bearded known as Sutcliffe! Hobbies - A football at his feet or pizzas on his plate. (Advertising) Age: 24

John Wills: ('Curly') Youngest member of the squad, and has performed admirably when selected. Very quick. Hobbies - 'The Surprise'. (Chauffeur) Age: 21

Phil Stallibrass ('Dad') Senior member of the squad and his skill has played a major part in the Club's success recently. Dunn winner 1984. Sweeper, or midfield player. Hobbies - 'Big Macs and fish and chips. (Director of travel company) Age: 30

LEFT: THE PEN PORTRAITS OF THE 1985 LANCING OLD BOYS, AS PRINTED IN THE PROGRAMME.

MARK N STRETTON
OLD REPTONIAN

Mark Stretton has been a stalwart of the Old Reptonian team of the 1980s, through the 1990s and into the new millennium. After a distinguished career in School football, notably as captain of the School team in 1978/79 and 1979/80, he progressed quickly to the Old Reptonians and played in the team that won the Arthur Dunn Cup in 1981 (in a tough tussle with Old Malvernians, who held them to a 3 - 3 draw, before losing 1 - 0 in the replay).

Mark played for Leek Town for a season (1983/84) but he returned to the Reptonian team and captained their run of successes when they won the Arthur Dunn in 1986/87, scoring in the first game and in the replay (against Old Cholmeleians), in 1990/91 against Old Carthusians (Mark scored the opening goal in the replay). Mark also scored in the 1989/90 final against Old Chigwellians (which Chigwellians won). He also played in the Old Reptonian teams that were runners-up in 1992/93 and more recently in 2001/02.

In all, he has appeared in 6 Arthur Dunn Cup Finals and scored five goals.

ABOVE: MARK POSES FOR THE TEAM PHOTO BEFORE THE 1993 FINAL.

OLD REPTONIAN MEMORIES
by Mark Stretton

In the 1981/82 season, we were the Cup holders and the Carthusians got their revenge in the first round for the previous year, winning 7 - 1. And so began a few wilderness years with early exits. During this period, the northern emphasis was becoming less pronounced. The London Arthurian League side began to benefit from the arrival of new players from the successful school teams of the late 70s and early 80s: Batey, Blakesley, Brownhill, Frost, Miller, Proctor, Stretton, Smith and Wale. They joined the likes of Eifion-Jones and Walford to ensure that the nucleus of the Dunn side was playing together on a weekly basis.

The 1986/87 season saw wins over Ardinians 1 - 0, and Harrovians 5 - 0, leading to a semi-final on a snow-bound San Hall against the Malvernians. A very professional performance with an orange ball, ensured a 2 - 0 victory and a celebratory Red Lion lock-in! Thus to the final where our opponents were Old Cholmeleians. Victory was snatched from the ORs grasp on two occasions. The Cholms equalised in the final minute of both normal time and extra time to force a replay.

The second meeting was somewhat different with the ORs gaining a 3 - 0 cushion with goals from Stretton, Eifion-Jones (pen) and Cowell. There was however an anxious last 10 minutes as the margin was reduced to 3 - 2 but a last minute equaliser thankfully did not happen for a third time! This time Chelsea was the scene for the OR celebrations, as Eddie Wale orchestrated renditions of "I want to be a Repton Ranger", which reverberated long into the night.

Additional silverware was to follow at the start of 1987/88 in the Vic Merrett Trophy, the "Super Cup" equivalent against Old Parkonians, winners of the London Old Boys Cup. A determined defensive performance was the highlight of this game, which ended 1 - 1 after extra time and was won 5 -3 in the penalty shoot-out. In the Dunn easy wins against Harrovians 5 - 2 and Westminsters 4 - 0 were followed by a 1 - 3 defeat in a quarter-final replay with Brentwood.

1988/89 commenced with another victory over Harrovians 4 - 0. In a scoreless quarter-final, the ORs were denied a penalty in the dying minutes away at Malvern and subsequently lost the replay 1 - 2.

MOTSPUR PARK (1987 - 2000)

Motspur Park was built as a sports complex for London University. It was opened on 27th May 1931 with the Annual University Athletics Championships. In 1932, a covered stand, changing rooms and areas for hockey, tennis and netball were added. Since that time, the ground has been used for many sporting activities, including football, but particularly athletics. It was considered for some time to have the best cinder track in England. It was the venue for the Surrey County Athletics Championships from 1933 to 1985.

In 1999 Motspur Park was purchased by Fulham FC and is now used as their training ground.

The Arthur Dunn Cup Final was first held at Motspur Park in 1987 and continued to be used until 2000 when doubt about its availability on match days necessitated a move to a new venue.

Old Cholmeleians struggled initially to defeat Old Westminsters who started the game with only 10 men. Westminsters' numbers were bolstered after 30 minutes when one of their supporters, who appeared to be at least 60 years old, agreed to join the fray. Despite a full compliment, the Old Cholms were worthy winners at 3 - 0.

With the benefit of Gary Stempel as coach, and the lethal forward combination of Mark Walton and Andrew Savva, there was a growing belief amongst the Old Cholms that they could actually get to the final. Stempel's organisational skills, coupled with a goalkeeper playing as a reserve sweeper, meant the Old Cholmeleians did not concede a goal in the first two games. It became customary for the Club's President, Ken Boustred, to visit the changing room before all home Dunn games to wish us luck.

In the second round, which was away, the Old Cholms faced an unknown quantity in St Edmund's OBs. However, despite going behind early in the game the Old Cholms regained their confidence and played some sparkling football, eventually running out worthy winners at 6 - 1.

The semi-final against Malvernians was a robust game played at Highgate. Malvernian's Denham brothers figured strongly at both ends of the pitch matching the exploits of the Old Cholms Savva and Gray brothers. Andy Savva and Al Denham were inseparable for most of the game and got rather too close on more than one occasion. However, honours were shared at full time. During extra time, the fitness of the Old Cholmeleians told, thanks to Stempel's vigorous training routines and the Old Cholms won the match 5 - 3. At last, the Old Cholms had got to the final.

The final itself was held on an overcast day on a very muddy pitch. True to form, our opponents, Old Brentwoods arrived by coach in blazers looking very business-like. However, nobody (quite possibly in the history of the Cup itself) could match the arrival of Paul Davies, the Club's former Chairman, who had flown back from Brunei for the weekend to watch the match.

The final was a rather dour affair with Brentwoods content to limit the Old Cholms playing their usual flowing game. The tactics however worked and the Old Cholms were restricted to very few chances. The game was won by a spectacular goal scored by Dixon, which deserved to grace a slightly more entertaining affair.

The facilities were excellent, particularly the baths, and the result, though important, was put to one side after the game allowing the Old Cholms to savour the achievement of being the first OC side to reach the Dunn Final in 30 years".

THE MOTSPUR PARK ERA

The 1986 final was the last to be played at Dulwich Hamlet. The venue had to be changed as a firm date for the Arthur Dunn Cup Final could not be guaranteed due to Dulwich Hamlet's league commitments.

The 1987 final was therefore moved to the London University's ground at Motspur Park, where it would remain for fourteen years – until 2000.

The season was first marked by the entry of Old Haileyburians but when it came to the later stages of the competition it was the Old Reptonians and Old Cholmeleians who ran on to the pitch at Motspur Park.

In a hard-fought game, Old Reptonians took the lead twice, first by Mark Stretton, only to have it erased by a Cholmeleian score. In the 90th minute, Mark Halstead scored an equalising goal and took the game into extra time. Then after a further Reptonian goal by Eddie Wale, Mark Walton made the scores level right at the end of the extra 30 minutes.

In the replay, Old Reptonians took a three-goal lead but Old Cholmeleians scored two goals in the last ten minutes.

Doug Wainwright captained old Cholmeleians at this time and remembered the 1986/87 season:

"This season turned out to be our most successful in many a year, culminating in our second successive year in the Dunn Cup Final. Our team was fortunate enough to be blessed with youth, good looks and a couple of old war-dogs to steady the ship.

The OCs first round opponents were Lancing and although on paper we were probably expected to win it proved to be a classic Cup tie. Having dominated the match and led 2 - 1 with 10 minutes to go, we conceded a goal which allowed them to have another crack at the whip. The return leg turned out to be another similar encounter. This time the OCs emerged deserved 3 - 2 victors. Somewhat of a relief, having endured three years of the Lancing Golden period!

The second round saw us take on a dogged Carthusian team. We took an early second-half lead but failed to capitalise on our pressure and put the tie out of the Carthusians reach and the last few minutes saw the ball hit the crossbar and stay in our 6-yard box till the final whistle.

In the semis, our opponents were Chigwellians, who gave us our hardest test on our way to the final – we fell behind early in the first half but levelled the score minutes later. The OCs broke the deadlock after a period of stalemate, with a late second-half goal.

The final against Reptonians was one of mixed fortunes. Having won the League by beating Reptonians two weeks prior to the final, we were in a quietly confident mood. On the day, the pitch and weather were a great leveller. This combined with a physically determined Reptonian side made for a close Cup tie. Any dreams of a fast-flowing and skilful game were swiftly dashed and sunk in the mud pools of Motspur Park. Vinnie Jones would have been in his element!!! The Reptonians maintained a 2 - 1 lead until the dying moments, when we managed to level the game and force extra time, with neither team breaking the deadlock. The replay was fought under conditions in complete contrast to put

KEN BOUSTRED - OLD CHOLMELEIAN PRESIDENT 1987 - 2002

Ken Boustred was passionate about football. He played at Highgate School and it was material that on leaving school, he would join Old Cholmeleians. In fact, for the rest of his life, he was very involved in Amateur Football.

When he joined Old Cholmeleians Football Club, he soon became team secretary and in so doing guaranteed himself a game each Saturday. After the Second World War, he started rebuilding the Old Cholmeleian FC, which had been a wandering Club before the War, and so with redoubtable tenacity Old Cholmeleians acquired the ground in Hendon Wood Lane, Totteridge, and got the Clubhouse built.

He became Hon. Secretary of the OCFC in 1951, a position which he held until 1974. He saw them through many good times; they won the Arthur Dunn Cup in 1958 and 1959 and were finalists again in 1961. He was, along with Peter Watkins and John Gilbert, instrumental in starting the Arthurian League in 1962/3. The Old Cholmeleians were always one of the stronger and successful clubs and the pinnacle of their success came in 1971/2 when Old Cholmeleian teams were champions of all four divisions of the Arthurian League.

In the mid-1960s, he was involved in the start-up of the Cholmeleian six-a-side tournament, for Arthur Dunn Cup teams, which took place on a Sunday in mid-September just after the start of the season.

Once he relinquished his position as Hon. Secretary of the Old Cholmeleian FC, he soon took other positions. He was President of the Arthurian League between 1975 and 1984, President of the Amateur Football Alliance (1983 – 85), President of the London Legal League, and President of the Arthur Dunn Cup Committee from 1987 until his death. For many years, he was also Hon. Solicitor to the Amateur Football Alliance.

Ken was a great lover of and believer in Amateur Football and for most Saturdays every season, except towards the end of his life, he would be watching the Old Cholmeleians, an Arthur Dunn game or an AFA game.

VIC MERRETT TROPHY
THE VIC MERRETT TROPHY WAS STARTED IN 1986 AS A TRIBUTE TO A RESPECTED OFFICIAL OF THE OLD BOYS CUP COMPETITION. AT THE BEGINNING OF EACH SEASON, THE WINNERS OF THE ARTHUR DUNN CUP ARE INVITED TO PLAY A ONE-OFF GAME AGAINST THE WINNERS OF THE OLD BOYS CUP. THE FIRST DUNN TEAM TO PARTICIPATE WERE OLD BRENTWOODS IN 1986.

the game out of our reach. We managed to claw a second goal back in the last 15 minutes which put the capacity crowd on the edge of their seats. The elder Gray came on as a substitute but immediately pulled a hamstring and went off again!!! But Reptonian defence held out and they deservedly lifted the Cup to the euphoria of their supporters. Thus the double eluded the OCs – 'twas only a game!!!".

It was appropriate that Old Reptonians should win the Cup in this year in memory of the President Dick Sale, Old Reptonian, who had died suddenly in the February of 1987.

KEN BOUSTRED ELECTED PRESIDENT

At the Annual General Meeting in 1987, Ken Boustred, an Old Cholmeleian, was appointed the new President. It was also fitting that in his first year as President, Old Cholmeleians should win the 1987 final by defeating Old Brentwoods 2 - 1. It was the first time since 1959 that Old Cholmeleians had won the Cup, and it was third time lucky for this generation of Old Cholmeleians, as they had lost the two previous finals. Old Brentwoods scored first through Allden but Halstead equalised for Old Cholmeleians in the first half and Walton

scored the winning goal towards the end of the game.

Howard Olivere recalled this momentous season for Old Cholmeleians:

"The team entered the 1987/88 competition in a very determined mood. We had been defeated narrowly in the final the previous two years and we hoped it would be third time lucky. The team had few changes from the earlier finals and it was the same as the League side. Most agreed that this was the strongest Old Cholmeleian side for many years with a mix of subtlety and aggression aided by some Greek and Swedish lineage. The addition of Mark Collins, recently returned from America, was also a key to success in the competition.

Old Citizens enjoyed the full force of our determination in the first round and we ran out 6 - 1 winners. This left us with the daunting trip to Lancing where few OC sides previously had emerged victorious. This proved to be a cracking Cup tie as there was always an edge to our meetings. The tie was won by a header from the smallest player, Frixos Kyriacou, who flung himself to score a diving header in the closing minutes. It was a superb goal and the faces on the Lancing supporters contrasted our reaction perfectly.

The trip to Shrewsbury was undertaken with rather more confidence. On paper, we felt we were expected to win and saw the third final looming large. However, the semi-final was a stern test on a day when we did not produce our best football. They say the sign of a great team is when it plays poorly and emerges with a win. This was true that day and we were mighty relieved to beat an Old Salopian side who missed a penalty near the end. I felt this moment was significant and that our name was on the Cup.

The preparation for the final was handled superbly by our coach, Gary Stempel. He was running the youth team at Millwall and the team benefited from his knowledge (self-defence training was not included). Arrival at Motspur Park brought back vivid memories of the year before. We had lost to Reptonians after a replay and there was a mood of real determination to succeed this time. The opponents were Brentwoods who had beaten us narrowly two years prior. It was clear it would be a tight game and so it turned out.

Brentwoods opened the scoring in the first half when our jet-lagged goalkeeper Martin Smith was a little slow off his line to meet a cross. We were awarded a penalty soon afterwards and Mark Halstead scored to calm the nerves. It remained that way at half-time. The sides were equally matched with Simon Doran a constant threat on the Brentwood left-wing. With five minutes to go, a clearance found our centre-forward Mark Walton in the clear. A slight loss of control ended in a collision with the Brentwood goalkeeper, who actually broke his wrist. Whilst on the ground, Mark Walton eased the ball into the corner of the net. To quote from the Telegraph: 'at the final whistle, joy was unconfined'. After a 30-year absence, our name was finally on the Cup".

The 1989 final was between the arch-rivals of the 1970s, Old Brentwoods and Old Malvernians. This final was just as hard-fought. In a first-class match, Old Malvernians eventually won 3 - 1 after extra-time. For Phil Needham of Old Brentwoods, this was his eighth final!

Malvernians' success meant that they had won the cup in every decade except the three years of the competition in the late 1940s. Unfortunately, they could not maintain this as they failed to win the cup throughout the 1990s.

LET'S PUT THE LID ON IT!

The 1989 final was marked by the start of a mystery that was to go unresolved for six months. As is the tradition, the Cup was held by the winning team for the year. Then, in readiness for the 1990 final, the Hon. Secretary collected the Cup from the Old Malvernian goalkeeper, Mike Wills, only to notice, as he was cleaning said Cup, that the lid was no longer part of the ensemble. Quel Dommage! Where was the lid?

No-one seemed to know where it had gone. Mike Wills said that the team had held a farewell party for the Cup the previous Saturday but could not remember seeing the lid. So at the 1990 final, the Cup was presented without the lid!

And then a flash of inspiration! David Roy remembered that Old Malvernians had held a dinner at the Connaught Rooms in January 1990 and the Cup had been on show. A quick phone call to the Connaught Rooms *"Have you got a spare lid for a tureen? One that does not seem to fit? You do! I'll be round!"*. There, amongst the lids for the vegetable tureens was the lid of the Arthur Dunn Cup!

ABOVE: THE ARTHUR DUNN CUP "TUREEN LID".

BELOW: THE 1989 OLD MALVERNIAN TEAM.

"I remember as if it was yesterday"

I remember it well, the winter of 88,
An all night party, I'd got in very late.
Suddenly beside me, the telephone did ring,
It was the bloody skipper – an extraordinary thing.

"Willsy we need you, Ardingly at home,
Hammer's disappeared, can't get him on the phone"
A South Ken meet in Ian's little car.
Now where's my kit? Damn – I've left it in a bar.

Now a great big headache all the way to school
Listening to Bob Dylan and Al Denham's drool.
I bought new kit, it wasn't very funny,
Didn't get my knees dirty – what a waste of money!

Still, we were through, Repton next to play,
A "nil nil" draw on a very windy day.
Off to the replay, Temps in Clunty's car,
"World outside my window", our favourite song by far.

Can't remember the score, but we won of course,
Sammy on the touchline, shouting himself hoarse!
All the way to London, singing Tinita's song
Straight to the Cross Keys, it didn't take that long.

Semi-final approaching, Charterhouse away
A nice flat pitch, suiting our style of play.
Let through an early one, but I didn't mind,
They had the "flying pig", and that was being kind.

An Ian Denham hat trick, even one with his head,
Saw us through in a great game, when all was done and said.
Time for celebration, now the game is over
Head out of the sunroof of my new Range Rover!

Now we're in the final, I remember my secret fear –
Don't stuff it up now, for this will be our year.
The confidence, the certainty, that we were good enough
That no matter what, no matter how tough.

And so it was but strangely, I remember little about the game
Except poor Boonie's broken leg, and Temps' moment of fame.
The cup collected, smiles all round, it's now time for beer,
Except that I am flying off – to Australia I fear.

So as you all gathered round, drinking your dinner wine,
Revenge is sweet, so they say and it shall be mine.
"Eight pints by eight" was my task, I never shall forget
And you are all fined the same – no arguments, no sweat.

So on this day in March, when you are gathered round
Spare a thought for Willsy, he is Hong Kong bound,
Have one for me, or two or eight, anything will be fine
And I will raise a glass to you the team of 89.

Michael Wills – Old Malvernian goalkeeper 1989
(the last Malvernian side to win the Cup).

OLD SALOPIAN DAVID HONYCHURCH IS CLOSED DOWN BY ANDREW LUTWYCHE LANCING OLD BOYS, DURING THE 1999 FINAL.

Chapter 7

ANOTHER TIER
ON THE
WEDDING CAKE

The year 1990 marked the start of five years of dominance by the Old Chigwellians; they won the cup in 1990, 1992 and 1994. Old Wykehamists reached the semi-final for the first time since 1977 and gave Chigwellians a very hard game but in the end the Essex side won through.

The 1990 final turned out to be an epic struggle. Chigwellians opponents were Reptonians. One of their stars, Mark Stretton, remembered that *"…Chigwellians, … went behind just before half time. The ORs had shackled the dangerous Chigwellian attack. However, with 15 minutes to go, Willatt, the ORs central defensive colossus, broke a leg. Chigwellians thereafter*

equalised (with a goal by Richard Tapper) forcing extra time. Despite creating a number of opportunities (in this period) the ORs were unable to score a winner (final score 1 - 1).

"Again a replay was necessary. However, on this occasion, the ORs suffered a similar fate to the Cholms in the 86/87 final, going 0 - 3 behind early in the game but running out of time despite scoring two second half goals and exerting frantic pressure in the final minutes".

On this occasion, the Cup was presented by Ken Boustred, President of the Arthur Dunn, and for the first time, medals were presented to the finalists and the officials.

ABOVE: FOR THE FIRST TIME IN THE HISTORY OF THE DUNN FINALS, THE THREE OFFICIALS WERE FROM COMPETING CLUBS IN THE ARTHUR DUNN CUP.
(L. TO R.) M HASSID (OLD FORESTER), B D HARVEY (OLD BRENTWOOD) AND D M DUNN (OLD CHOLMELEIAN).

AN OLD CHIGWELLIAN'S MEMORIES
by Chris Sydenham

Chris Sydenham started playing for the OCs in 1981 on leaving school. He first took part in the Arthur Dunn Cup in the 1982/83 season but was left out of the Chigwellian team that lost to Lancing in the final. Thereafter, he became a regular in the team which was ultimately successful in 1990. He recalled:

"In 1989/90, we turned the tide and defeated Cholmeleians 3 - 2 at home in the first round and then overcame Wellingburians away and Wykehamists away before meeting Old Reptonians in the final. I can clearly remember the final to this day and it was a massive occasion for the Club. Mike Partridge was our captain and he reverted the dress requirements back to usual match-day wear, although our senior players such as big John Conolly insisted on wearing a jacket and tie.

CHRIS SYDENHAM
OLD CHIGWELLIAN.
CHRIS PLAYED IN THE 1990, 92 AND 94 FINALS, HE WAS ON THE WINNING SIDE ON ALL THREE OCCASIONS.

Telegrams were there to greet us in our changing room at Motspur Park and to give some idea of the importance of the final to us, we even employed the services of a professional physiotherapist for the day as a number of us were struggling with ankle injuries and the like.

Mark Stretton was the Reptonian captain that day and he scored the first goal in a 1 - 1 draw. Reptonians were an excellent side as their record in the Dunn over the next couple of years proved but our forwards, Ian Grover, Richard Tapper and Andrew Jefcoate backed up by our greater fitness and team spirit finally proved too much for them in the replay and we triumphed 3 - 2. I am sure the fact was most of our players had played at Motspur Park for the Arthurian League Representative side helped us to settle into the surroundings.

BELOW: THE ARTHUR DUNN MEDAL.

The following year, 1990/91 as holders we distinguished ourselves by being thrashed 6 - 3 by the Old Foresters in the preliminary round, who in turn promptly lost in the next round to the eventual winners, Old Reptonians.

The year after, 1991/92 we thrashed Cholmeleians 7 - 1 in the first round (with Ian Grover scoring 4 goals) after they had defeated the Wykehamists 7 - 0 in the preliminary round, before seeing off Old Aldenhamians and Old Salopians at home, to take us through to a final with the Old Etonians. This was another memorable occasion for us under Greg Bryce's captaincy and we came out worthy winners 3 - 1".

EASTBOURNIANS AND WITLEIANS JOIN

RIGHT: DAVID ROY (HON. SECRETARY) WAITS TO TAKE THE TEAM PHOTOGRAPHS IN 1991.

In season 1990/91, two new sides, Old Eastbournians and Old Witleians, entered the competition. There was an amazing start to the season when in the preliminary round, the holders, Old Chigwellians were beaten 6 - 3 by their near neighbours, Old Foresters. It was a closer contest than the score suggests as until the last few minutes the Old Foresters led 4 - 3.

In the second round, there was another epic battle between Old Brentwoods and Old Malvernians which the Old Brentwoods won 5 - 4.

The final was between the Old Reptonians and Old Carthusians. In another drawn game (1 - 1) Mark Kerevan scored for Old Carthusians and Eddie Wale for Old Reptonians. In the replay, after a goal-less first half, Old Reptonians played superbly in the second half, scoring four goals with Peter Gillespie and Mark Stretton outstanding.

ARTHUR DUNN CUP FINAL

OLD CARTHUSIANS

V

OLD REPTONIANS

at

London University Ground, Motspur Park

on

6th April 1991

Kick-off 3.00pm

Presentation of cup by Jane Ross
Granddaughter of the late Arthur Dunn.

Adults £1   Children 50p

The proceeds from today's final will be given to charity

For the second year running, in season 1991/92, the holders were defeated in their first game. Lancing Old Boys defeated Old Reptonians 3 - 2 and gained revenge for their defeat in the semi-final the previous season. The final was between Old Chigwellians and Old Etonians.

Old Etonians, who very ably led by James Scobie, had reached their first final since 1952 having defeated the Old Carthusians 4 - 3 where they had been leading 4 - 1 with 10 minutes to go but Old Carthusians nearly snatched a draw. They

THE OLD SALOPIAN FC AND THE ARTHUR DUNN CUP IN THE 90'S
by David Honychurch

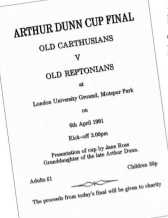

After nearly 30 years in the wilderness, Old Salopian football was revived partly by the inspiration, commitment and skill of David Honychurch.

The team's first European tour in 1990 was the basis for galvanising a mixture of youth and committed senior players into a fighting force to compete with the best. However, it took four years for the fruits of these efforts to be seen. As David recalled:

"The '94 draw …gave us the possibility of two home ties against teams from the First Division of the Arthurian League, where we were currently residing. Our home ground - Senior at Shrewsbury - we hope gives us a strong advantage more for the town's geography and the M6 difficulties than our style of play and so we were optimistic of progress! Our hopes were met and we advanced to a fixture at Charterhouse so glamourous that it attracted the BBC cameras - not Match of the Day but those for a documentary about the role of the Public Schools in originating the Rules of the Game. This would have been the seventh consecutive semi-final the club would have lost so Lady Luck was probably ours that day. I can still feel the sense of elation as I watched team-mates such as Bowden, Saunders and Goodman sink to their knees in joy, demonstrating the competitors feeling for this grand old competition. A logistical problem presented itself in that we had grown so used to our losing streak that the Club's annual London dinner had been arranged for the eve of the game - That evening my captain's responsibilities were changed to those of a nanny.

The final presented by far our toughest hurdle playing Old Chigwellians twice winners in the recent past and a team sprinkled with AFA and Arthurian League representatives. The 44th minute saw us pleasantly surprised to hold a 2 - 0 lead - the 45th witnessed the Motspur Park stand engulfed in claret smoke flares and game on at 2 - 1. More San Siro than suburban Surrey I remember thinking. By the end we were on the ropes and relying on the not inconsiderable Angus Pollock professionalism (no doubt learnt in his three Blues fixtures at Wembley), goalposts and the bar to keep us in the game as Greg Bryce mis-aimed a 25 free kick! If we had maintained the two goal lead at half time the Cup should have been ours but we knew an excellent Chigwell would not give up lightly. When the groundsman cancelled extra-time it was our opponents who were disappointed.

Two weeks later and not on the Show Pitch we were overrun - the 5 - 1 defeat, still the heaviest of all my Arthur Dunn games. Close but still no cigar and by now 31 seasons had passed since the OSFC last won the Arthur Dunn - how many plinths would it have by the time we next saw it? The challenge of the cup is quite extraordinary. Two post-match beers and the despair of 94 had turned to the challenge of 95. Retirement had been postponed by Pollock and Dyke, the two elder statesman - and I was well aware of the identities of several key figures from Mark Dickson's all-conquering school team.

Persuasive conversations during the summer led to more new faces on the pre-season tour and more importantly to three key new Arthur Dunn debutantes - Cooke (times two) and Ellis, the Worcestershire cricketer with an all round sporting prowess taking "5 for 59" against the West Indies.

then beat Lancing Old Boys 3 - 2 at Lancing. Unfortunately, they were not allowed to reproduce this form in the final where they lost 3 - 1 to Old Chigwellians.

The 1992/93 final was between Lancing Old Boys and Old Reptonians. The young Lancing Old Boys side, which was master-minded by Alastair Mercer, had at last reached the final; they had lost in the semi-finals in the previous two seasons. In a very close game, Lancing OBs won 1 - 0, the only goal being the result of a quickly-taken free kick which released Pete Alcock, who ran through and scored.

Lancing Old Boys had a very tight game against the Old Chigwellians in the semi-final and

only won 3 - 2 after extra-time.

It was very nice that Nigel Bennett was playing again for Lancing Old Boys. When he had recovered from his nasty knee injury, his knee was not strong enough to play in the outfield so he converted himself into a goalkeeper. After playing many games for Lancing Old Boys second eleven, he was eventually promoted to the first eleven and by playing in the 1993 final, it meant he had played in four victorious sides.

NO EXTRA TIME!

The early stages of the 1993/94 competition were marked by the defeat of Lancing Old Boys, the holders, in a replay after two very

ARTHUR DUNN CUP FINAL
OLD CHIGWELLIANS
V
OLD ETONIANS
at
London University Ground, Motspur Park
on
4th April 1992
Kick–off 3.00pm
Presentation of cup by Jane Ross
Granddaughter of the late Arthur Dunn.
Children 50p
Adults £1
The proceeds from today's final will be given to charity

DAMIAN LEWIS - OLD ETONIAN RUNNERS UP 1992 (V CHIGWELLIANS). AS SOAMES FORSYTE IN 1TV'S 'THE FORSYTE SAGA' 2002 AND AS LIEUT. RICHARD WINTERS IN BBC MINI-SERIES 'BAND OF BROTHERS' 2001.

LEFT: MIKE HASSID (OLD FORESTER), THE ONLY MAN TO HAVE PLAYED IN A FINAL (1975 & 1985) AND REFEREED A FINAL (1993).

The first round saw a pre-Christmas visit to Surrey again to play Jason Golder and his Carthusian team mates (never a game for the faint-hearted) for a re-run of the previous season's semi-final - no cameras this time but another deserved victory - 1 - 0.

My ever-increasing trips to the South Bank of London to Sea Containers House, the home of the AD draw, this time paired us against old rivals from the school circuit - Malvern. Even by Shrewsbury standards the heavy, cloying mud was desperate. To use a well worn Salopian footballer adage "we defended the deep end in the first half" and captured a 2 - 1 win in the last few minutes. That night saw one of the great traditions of the cup where the teams enjoy a quiet couple of drinks together and it was excellent to enjoy the company of Ed Gilbert, Sam Harris and Giles King all pleased to remind us that they, unlike us, were ex-winners.

Although we enjoyed the feeling of being in the semi-finals again, that night we were well aware that Essex was strongly represented with Chigwellians and Foresters, the firm favourites for the final.

We drew the former at Roding Lane in a memorable game. Our young and old players gelled to form a solid team and a Dave Arthur headed "wonder goal" meant we surprised a lot of people and gained revenge for the previous year's final.

From that moment, the team believed in themselves and we relished the visit to Motspur Park again although once more we would start underdogs. Foresters were the runaway winners of our division and also won the Essex cup. Straightaway they proved their quality when David Pratt (the former Spurs player's son) scored a second-minute free kick. This was only the second goal we had conceded in the competition and the first time we had gone behind, so now we would need to show different qualities. We maintained our composure and equalised mid-way through the first half, and took the lead early in the second.

Twelve months on and the identical scoreline with about the same time remaining in the final - had we learnt from the previous year? Outstanding defensive performance from James Skelton (postponing his stag weekend!) Mark Lascelles, Hugh Raven and Man of the Match Phil Deans ensured we had and as the whistle went two hundred or so Salopian supporters could look forward to the evening. It is a sign of the quality of this competition that although it takes only 4 or 5 games to win it, it is so difficult to do so. In the 31 years since our last win, we had numerous talented teams and players but the cup had eluded them and thus the 95 team's achievement was considerable - the XI Salopian team to win the cup. Although clearly the Forest team felt hard done by, it was obvious they would have their day as we would quickly find out! But for us I felt the team we had created, with three Arthur Dunn campaign debutantes, was as strong as we could have hoped for. It is fitting that it reached its peak on its most important day, the eleven never playing together again. Several of the elder players were able to confirm their retirement from Arthurian duties sound in the knowledge they had joined an exclusive club of Salopian sportsmen.

The Old Salopian Football Club was, therefore, the proud holders of one of the oldest Amateur trophy still being competed for entering a new Millennium. The targets we would have set ourselves on that evening in Amsterdam were surpassed with a symmetrical record during these 10 seasons of twice being winners, twice runners-up and twice losing semi-finalists.

However on reflection, although the results were all important at the time, it was just satisfying to compete in the Arthur Dunn, playing at some fine venues, against fierce opponents but nonetheless all of whom had a similar awareness of the competition's heritage".

exciting games against the Old Carthusians. Once Lancing Old Boys had been defeated, Ken Shearwood came to the semi-final between the Old Carthusians and Old Salopians at Charterhouse to encourage the Old Salopians; the Old Salopians won 2 - 1. The deciding goal was scored by David Honychurch when he broke through the Old Carthusian defence from the halfway line.

RIGHT: THE COVER OF THE 1994 REPLAY PROGRAMME.

When it came to the final, the protagonists were Old Chigwellians and Old Salopians. But there was one unusual feature of this final. For the first time, (as far as the Hon. Secretary can remember) the 1993/94 final nearly did not take place on the due date. The weather at the end of March and early April had been very wet and it rained hard on the Friday before the game. After long discussions between the groundsman at Motspur Park and the Hon. Secretary, it was agreed that the game could be played but no extra-time would be played if it was required.

The Hon. Secretary explained this to the two sides and they both agreed to play with this small provision. The pitch was very wet but a very exciting final was played between the Old Chigwellians and Old Salopians.

Old Salopians, as the underdogs, nearly caused a major upset as they scored two goals in the first 30 minutes; the pace of David Honychurch always caused problems

BELOW: DAVID HONYCHURCH SLOTS THE WINNING GOAL PAST THE OLD FORESTERS KEEPER.

for the Old Chigwellian defence. But just before half-time, Ian Grover, who played extremely well throughout the game, scored one goal and then another one midway through the second half. Almost inevitably, the game ended in a draw (2 - 2) and of course there could be no extra time!

In the replay, Old Salopians were not allowed to play the fast football which they had played in the first game and Old Chigwellians deserved their 5 - 1 victory.

In the first round of the 1994/95 competition, Old Witleians recorded their first victory when they defeated the Old Etonians 1 - 0. And in the semi-final the Old Salopians had gained their revenge over the Old Chigwellians when they defeated them 1 - 0 at Chigwell.

So, the 1995 final was between Old Salopians, who had last won the cup in 1964, and Old Foresters who had achieved their only success in 1974. Old Salopians, who won 2 - 1, needed a lot of resilience in order to win the cup for the eleventh time. Early in the game, David Pratt scored for Old Foresters with a free kick from just outside the penalty area. Although Old Foresters always looked dangerous when attacking, they were unable to score again.

Midway through the first half, David Honychurch broke through the middle of the

ARTHUR DUNN CUP FINAL

REPLAY

OLD CHIGWELLIANS

v

OLD SALOPIANS

at

London University Ground, Motspur Park

on

23rd April 1994

Kick-off 3.00 p.m

Presentation of cup by Ken Boustred
President of the Arthur Dunn Cup Committee

Adults £1.00   Children 50p

****

The proceeds from today's final will be given to charity

ARTHUR DUNN CUP FINAL

OLD FORESTERS

V

OLD SALOPIANS

at

London University Ground, Motspur Park

on

1st April 1995

Kick-off 3.00 p.m.

Presentation of cup by Jane Sawyer
Granddaughter of the late Arthur Dunn

Adults £1.50   Children 50p

****

The proceeds from today's final will be given to charity

RICHARD HARNACK AND CHRIS ELLIOTT OLD FORESTERS

Richard played for four years in the same School First XI as Chris Elliott. He then played in the Public Schools team for two years.

After leaving school in 1984, Richard progressed to the Old Foresters and was a member of the team for 18 years. In that time, he has appeared in 40 Dunn games, scoring five goals (from mid-field).

Like Chris Elliott, Richard has played in five Dunn finals – in 1985, 1995, 1997, 1998 and 2000.

Having been an essential part of the school first XI for four years, Chris left school in 1983 and played in the Public Schools team for two years (with Richard Harnack), followed by three years in the Cambridge University team, including three wins over Oxford. He had the distinction of scoring in one of those matches at Wembley. Chris then played for Old Foresters FC for 19 years and won the Club's top scorer trophy nine times.

He made 42 appearances in the Dunn, scoring 27 goals, including four hat-tricks. He was present in each Old Foresters team that got to the final of the Dunn five times, firstly in 1985 and on four occasions between 1995 and 2000. This included two victories – in 1997 (over Old Brentwoods) and then again in 1998 (over Old Salopians).

Old Foresters defence and holding off a strong tackle placed the ball past the goalkeeper. Early in the second half, he fastened onto a loose ball in the penalty area and scored with a fierce drive. For the remainder of the game the Old Foresters were striving for the equalising goal but Old Salopians held on to win thanks to some good defending from Phil Deans, Hugh Raven and Mark Lascelles and a little bit of good fortune.

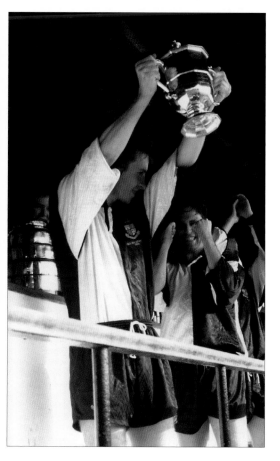

LEFT: TEENS, TWENTIES & THIRTIES: SCOTT ELLIS, DAVID HONYCHURCH AND DAVID ARTHUR. THE 1995 OLD SALOPIAN TEAM WAS SELECTED FROM SEVERAL GENERATIONS.

FAR LEFT: OLD SALOPIAN SKIPPER DAVID HONYCHURCH LIFTS THE CUP IN CELEBRATION 1995.

BELOW: THE 1995 OLD SALOPIAN WINNING TEAM.
(Back row): SCOTT ELLIS, TOM COOKE, MARK LASCELLES, HUGH RAVEN, SIMON GOODMAN, JAMES SKELTON & ROB COOKE.
(Front row): PHIL DEANS, DAVID ARTHUR, DAVID HONYCHURCH, ANGUS POLLOCK & PHIL DYKE.

Old Boys played some fine fast attacking football which resulted in four first class goals, two scored by Ian Brown-Peterside and one each by James Wyatt and Pete Alcock. In the Times, Ivo Tenant commented that Lancing's victory *"owed much to the skill of Ian Brown-Peterside and the coaching of Ken Shearwood, a figure as distinctive on a football ground as the school's most famous former pupil and supporter, Sir Tim Rice".*

ABOVE: CUNNINGHAM FOR LANCING EVADES A BRENTWOODS TACKLE. FAR RIGHT: LANCING OBS PLAYED FAST ATTACKING FOOTBALL DURING THE 1996 FINAL.

In season 1995/96, Old Haberdashers entered the competition. And there were two major shocks in the early rounds. In the preliminary round, the holders, Old Salopians, were beaten 1 - 0 in a very close game at Shrewsbury by their old rivals, Old Reptonians. Then, in the second round Old Foresters, the losing finalists from the previous season, were beaten 2 - 1 by Old Bradfieldians. In this game, Old Foresters were attacking for the majority of the game and were denied by a superb performance by the Old Bradfieldian goalkeeper and the woodwork, which must have been hit at least half a dozen times.

RIGHT: OLD BRENTWOODS REFLECT ON ANOTHER NET LOSS IN THE FINAL. (THE TIMES).

So the two sides which reached the final were Lancing Old Boys and Old Brentwoods. The latter were a young team whereas Lancing Old Boys were a mixture of experience and youth. Quite a few of their side had played in the final in 1993 and James Wyatt was playing in his fifth final, having first played in 1980. The first half was very even and the only goal was scored by Sullivan of Old Brentwoods when his long shot was deflected past the goalkeeper. In the second half, Lancing

RIGHT: LANCING CELEBRATE IN STYLE, 1996.

In the 1996/97 season penalty shoot-outs were introduced to decide drawn replay matches, it was used to decide the second round match between Old Salopians and Old Chigwellians at Shrewsbury. The first game had ended 1 - 1, the replay 0 - 0 and Old Salopians won the penalty shoot-out 5 - 4. In the final, Old Foresters played Old Salopians, which was a repeat of the 1995 final.

Although Salopians took the lead through David Cookson, Old Foresters deservedly won 3 - 1, as they played some very good football. Nick Francis and Chris Elliott scored two first class goals; the third goal was scored by John Gray. It was very appropriate that this generation of Old Foresters won the Cup as Nick Francis, Chris Elliott, Richard Harnack and Mark Robinson had all played in the final in 1985 when Old Foresters lost to Lancing Old Boys. This was the first time that a father and son had played in a winning side (but for different schools) as Nick Francis is the son of Pat Francis who played for the Old Brentwoods for many years and played in the winning teams of 1967 and 1973.

This year was the Old Malvernians Centenary season and it was appropriate that they should reach the semi-final having had a few years without success.

Arthur Dunn Cup deserves its place in football folklore, says **Bryon Butler**

Old boys meet again for slice of 'wedding cake'

NOT many mortals have a football trophy named after them. It may be a rung below a personally labelled comet, city or ballpoint pen, which sets apart chaps like Halley, Lenin and Biró, but it is still a serious distinction.

The old World Cup was known as the Jules Rimet Trophy; Europe's nations play for the Henri Delaunay Trophy; and the Alan Hardaker Trophy is awarded to the man of the match in the Coca-Cola Cup final.

Then, of course, there is Arthur Tempest Blakiston Dunn, whose big annual moment came again on Saturday, at Motspur Park, beside the Kingston by-pass, in south-west London. His cup, it should be added, is older and bigger than any of the above.

The Arthur Dunn Cup is 94 years old and 2½ feet tall — and still growing — a silver plaque honours every winner, and when one deck is full, another is added. It looks like a wedding cake, and, at their moment of triumph, victors are obliged to hold it aloft in four different parts.

The Arthur Dunn Cup also happens to be one of the smallest and most quixotic of English football's national tournaments. It is competed for by the old boys' teams of fewer than two dozen public schools. Entry is by invitation only, and no guests or ringers are allowed. It is exclusively for 'former pupils' and is the only closed competition of its kind in football. All proceeds go to charity.

It is not, however, a tournament that the big professional clubs should be sniffy about. Their debt to the Old Etonians, Old Harrovians, Old Carthusians, Old Westminsters, Old Reptonians and their like, is considerable.

The old boys of these public schools, then embracing muscular Christianity and becoming something more than spartan kennels for the pups of the privileged and wealthy, were the pioneers of organised football in mid-Victorian England. They founded the Football Association, and launched both the FA Cup and international football.

The big cities and towns eventually discovered that football was a pretty good game, formed their own clubs, and, in a decade or so, their professionals were winning all the major trophies. This, in turn, led to the birth of the Arthur Dunn Cup.

Dunn, an Old Etonian and full England international, noted the decline of the amateur and declared that something should be done. He died soon afterwards, at the age of 41, but his words were taken to heart.

Within six months, a tournament for old boys was under way. The cup, named after Dunn, was presented by another full international, Robert Cunliffe Gosling, the oldest of five brothers who had been at Eton at the same time — known as Max, Ma, Mi, Min and Quint.

Among the players who took part in the first final in 1903 were Charles Wreford-Brown, yet another England international, and the man who first coined the word 'soccer', and a fellow Corinthian, G O Smith, who by general consensus was the finest centre-forward of his time. R C Robertson Glasgow said he was "the finest hero of them all".

W G Grace watched the first final, and among other cricketers of somewhat more than average ability, who later played in the tournament, were G N Foster, D R Jardine, E R T Holmes and P B H May.

All of which brings us to 1997 and the 84th final — between Old Salopians, who had won the cup 11 times, and Old Foresters, whose one and only previous triumph was in 1974.

The old boys of Forest School, near Snaresbrook, London, E17, the only school to have played in the FA Cup, deservedly won 3-1. The Old Salopians looked better organised to begin with, despite a wind which played havoc with good intentions, and took the lead after only four minutes through Robert Cooke.

But the Old Foresters proved more innovative, with their experienced captain, Nick Francis, in outstanding form. A crowd of 300 saw them score through Francis himself, a wicked volley from 20 yards, Chris Elliot, a deflected header, and the lively John Gray after enterprising work by Elliot. The Old Salopians conceded that the better team won.

David Roy, the tournament's secretary for 21 years, said later: "What makes it work so well is loyalty, pride, old comradeship and the simple joy of playing against one another. That's why it will always matter."

The cup was presented by Jane Sawyer, the granddaughter of Arthur Dunn.

Old Foresters: M Butler; J Banks, C Hossain, N Francis, M Kendall; J Gray, L Douris, R Harnack, P Risby (A Heyes, 83), C Elliot, M Robinson (S Yankson, 62). **Sub:** A Smith. **Goals:** Francis (27), Elliot (43), Gray (55). **Booked:** Harnack.

Old Salopians: P Hollands; H Raven, M Lascelles, T Cooke; R Cooke, P Deans, D Cookson (M Bailey, 85), T Onions (D Saunders, 58), P Dyke; S Ellis, D Honychurch. **Sub:** A Clarke. **Goal:** R Cooke (4). **Booked:** Lascelles.

Referee: P R Burrowes.

Final flourish . . . Old Foresters' Lee Douris (right) is tackled by David Saunders   Picture: PHIL SHEPHARD-LEWIS

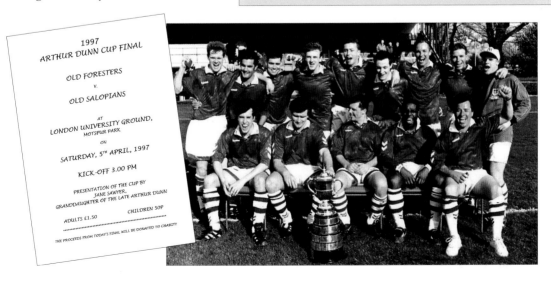

ABOVE LEFT: ROBINSON THE OLD FORESTERS PLAYER/COACH RUNS OUT TO CONGRATULATE THE TEAM AFTER THE FINAL WHISTLE.

LEFT: OLD FORESTERS SHOW DELIGHT AT WINNING THE CUP, 1997.

FULL OF EASTERN PROMISE!

1998
ARTHUR DUNN CUP FINAL

OLD BRENTWOODS
v.
OLD FORESTERS

AT
LONDON UNIVERSITY GROUND,
MOTSPUR PARK
ON
SATURDAY, 4ᵗʰ APRIL, 1998

KICK-OFF 3.00 PM

PRESENTATION OF THE CUP BY
JANE SAWYER,
GRANDDAUGHTER OF THE LATE ARTHUR DUNN

ADULTS £2.00   CHILDREN 50P

THE PROCEEDS FROM TODAY'S FINAL WILL BE DONATED TO CHARITY

The 1998 final was between the arch local rivals Old Brentwoods and Old Foresters; they had met once before in a final, in 1974, when Old Foresters won 2 - 1. Again, Old Foresters were successful, winning 3 - 1, and became the first team to retain the Cup since Lancing Old Boys won it in 1983, 84, 85.

The final was an exciting game but the strong wind made the playing conditions very difficult. Old Foresters got off to a very good start with two early goals scored by Sid Yankson and Chris Elliott, but Andy Sansome scored a fine individual goal to bring Old Brentwoods back into the game. Just before half-time, Old Foresters increased their lead when Phil Risby ran through from the halfway line to score.

The two sides to reach the 1999 final were Lancing Old Boys and Old Salopians - two of the four sides which had dominated the 1990s (the others were the Old Chigwellians and Old Foresters). Although Old Salopians were appearing in their fourth final in six years and Lancing Old Boys their third final in seven years, this was the first time that these two sides had ever met in a final.

Old Salopians took the lead early in the first half when Phil Westerman headed home. After this goal, the Old Salopian defence and midfield controlled the game and repelled every effort Lancing OBs made to equalise until, midway

through the second half, Ian Brown-Peterside created an opening for himself and scored with a low cross shot. This equalising goal spurred Old Salopians into greater effort and within

IAN BROWN-PETERSIDE LANCING OLD BOY

Ian was at Lancing from 1985 to 1990. He made his first XI debut in January 1987 (while in the fourth Form) and earned a regular place in the team when in the fifth form. He also became a prolific goal-scorer for the school. Ian represented the independent schools at under-16 and under-19 (both for the south and the national team). He went to the end of the season counties tournament with the national independent schools twice while in the lower 6th, scoring 3 times. He also played for Lewes a couple of times, while still at school, and also for the Sussex County side.

Ian was a member of the successful Lancing team that got through to four Arthur Dunn Cup Finals between 1993 and 2000. He scored six goals and this contributed to the team in winning three of these finals.

RIGHT: A TUSSLE FOR THE BALL BETWEEN IAN BROWN-PETERSIDE, BEN EVANS (LANCING) AND DAVID HONYCHURCH (SALOPIANS).

ten minutes they had scored twice, first by Piers Curran following a good run on the left by David Cookson and Scott Ellis scored from the edge of the penalty area and so Old Salopians won 3 - 1.

In the second round, Old Salopians had defeated Old Foresters 3 - 2 and ended the Old Foresters effort to win the trophy three years

in succession. In the semi-final Lancing OBs had played a very determined Old Wykehamist team at Winchester and were very lucky to draw 2 - 2, but won the replay 2 - 0. Old Millhillians entered the competition this season but unfortunately only played for two seasons as they could not encourage younger leavers to join their club.

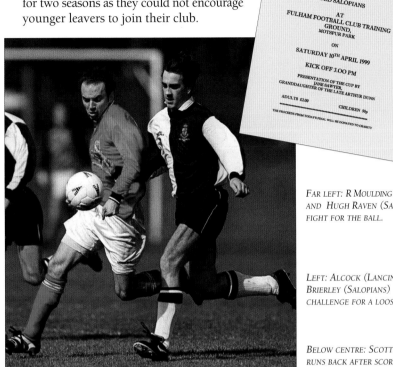

1999
ARTHUR DUNN CUP FINAL

LANCING OLD BOYS

V.

OLD SALOPIANS

AT
FULHAM FOOTBALL CLUB TRAINING
GROUND,
MOTSPUR PARK

ON

SATURDAY 10TH APRIL 1999

KICK OFF 3.00 PM

PRESENTATION OF THE CUP BY
JANE SAWYER,
GRANDDAUGHTER OF THE LATE ARTHUR DUNN

ADULTS £2.00

CHILDREN 50p

THE PROCEEDS FROM TODAY'S FINAL WILL BE DONATED TO CHARITY

FAR LEFT: R MOULDING (LANCING) AND HUGH RAVEN (SALOPIANS) FIGHT FOR THE BALL.

LEFT: ALCOCK (LANCING) AND BRIERLEY (SALOPIANS) CHALLENGE FOR A LOOSE BALL.

BELOW CENTRE: SCOTT ELLIS RUNS BACK AFTER SCORING SALOPIANS THIRD GOAL.

ABOVE: HONYCHURCH (SALOPIANS) AND KELSEY (LANCING) TUSSLE FOR THE BALL.

FAR LEFT: THE SALOPIAN CAPTAIN, HUGH RAVEN LIFTS THE CUP IN CELEBRATION.

LEFT: WATERMAN, ELLIS AND CURRAN POSE WITH THE ARTHUR DUNN CUP.

Lancing Old Boys again reached the final in 2000 where their opponents were Old Foresters. This was the second time they had met in a final (the previous occasion had been in 1985 when Lancing Old Boys won 5 - 0). This time Lancing Old Boys won 3 - 0. Three players - Chris Elliott and Richard Harnack of Old Foresters, and Nigel Bennett of Lancing Old Boys - played in both finals. All three had given tremendous support to their clubs. Nigel Bennett was playing in his sixth final and had been victorious on five occasions.

FAR RIGHT: THE TIMES REPORT BY JOHN GOODBODY OF THE 2000 FINAL.

RIGHT: IAN BROWN-PETERSIDE, LEFT, SCORER OF ALL THREE GOALS IN LANCING OLD BOYS' VICTORY, TAKES THE BALL PAST JAMES BANKS, OF OLD FORESTERS IN THE ARTHUR DUNN CUP FINAL. (THE TIMES 2000).

ABOVE: A ADOMAKOH OLD CARTHUSIAN, HAS PLAYED IN FOUR DECADES OF ARTHUR DUNN CUP FOOTBALL,1970S, 1980S, 1990S AND THIS CENTURY.

The difference between the two sides was Ian Brown-Peterside who scored a hat-trick, the first since 1952. It brought his goal tally to six in the four finals in which he had played. In the earlier rounds, Old Foresters had had two very exciting matches firstly in the second round they beat Old Westminsters 5 - 3 after extra time and then in the semi-final defeated Old Reptonians 2 - 0 at Repton. Unfortunately, Old Ardinians withdrew from the competition this year. They had been struggling for a few years to raise a side but this was very sad as they had been great supporters of the competition since they entered in 1933/34. (Their most successful period had been in the 1960s when they reached the semi-finals in 1963, 64 & 65).

Lancing round off week to remember

| Lancing Old Boys | 3 |
| Old Foresters | 0 |

By John Goodbody

FEW football competitions in Britain have such an entrancing history as the Arthur Dunn Cup, the first final of which, in 1903, featured G. O. Smith, winner of 20 full England caps, and a man described by the cricket writer, R. C. Robertson-Glasgow, as "the finest hero of them all". Another player in that match was Charles Wreford-Brown, the man credited with inventing the word "soccer".

For the first 76 years of "the Dunn", this annual competition was dominated by the old boys of Charterhouse and Malvern, who between them won the trophy 33 times.

Peter May appeared for Charterhouse in the competition as did Douglas Jardine, his predecessor as England cricket captain, who represented Winchester before leading England in the notorious Bodyline series.

However, since 1979, Charterhouse and Malvern have been less successful and Lancing, Old Foresters and Chigwell have become increasingly prominent, together with Shrewsbury. Lancing Old Boys have benefited from a regular flow of talented players from a school where Ken Shearwood and Chris Metcalf have been inspiring as coaches. The most intriguing member of their team at Motspur Park, Surrey, on Saturday was Nigel Bennett, who scored twice as an outfield player for Oxford against Cambridge in the 1980 Varsity Match but on Saturday was the goalkeeper in his sixth final in the competition.

Adam Pierce, the Lancing captain, said: "The real difference between the two teams was Ian Brown-Peterside. He gave us the speed and finishing up front." His hat-trick was conclusive in an otherwise even game.

Four years ago, Brown-Peterside scored twice when Lancing beat the Old Brentwoods 4-1 in the final and on Saturday he formed a partnership with Will Rum, who captained Lancing to victory in the Boodle and Dunthorne Cup for independent schools three years ago. He scored the first in the 25th minute and the second in the 58th minute before confirming victory seven minutes from time. It rounded off a good week for Lancing, who also won the Londonderry Cup old boys squash competition by beating Gresham's.

LANCING OLD BOYS (4-4-2): N Bennett — J Simpson, J Davis, D Gurney, B Evans — A Rum (sub: J Forbes-Wilson, 88min), A Cunningham (sub: S Kelsey, 88), A Pierce, A Mercer — I Brown-Peterside, W Rum (sub: P Alcock, 83).

OLD FORESTERS (3-5-2): M Butler — A Smith, A Heyes, B Barnett (sub: P Alexander, 69) — N Keaveney (sub: B Murphy, 57), J Banks, R Harnack, L Douris, J Dunn — S Yankson (sub: P Hooper, 71), C Elliott.

Referee: R Hannerson.

A NEW MILLENNIUM AND COBHAM

Motspur Park had now been bought by Fulham Football Club and it proved difficult to ensure that the ground was available for the Arthur Dunn Final. So the 2001 final was moved to Cobham.

There were many shock results in the 2000/01 season. The first minor shock occurred in the preliminary round when Old Wykehamists beat Old Chigwellians at Winchester. The first major shock happened at Lancing where the holders were defeated 2 - 0 by Old Witleians and then Old Westminsters travelled to Malvern and beat

IMPERIAL COLLEGE SPORTS GROUND COBHAM (FROM 2001)

The ground was opened in the mid 1950s as Charing Cross Hospital's Sports Ground. After a merger with Westminster Hospital it became the Westminster and Charing Cross Hospital Sports Ground in 1980. In 1997 it became the Imperial College Sports Ground.

Old Malvernians 3 - 0. But the biggest surprise was the Old Bradfieldians 3 - 1 victory after extra time over Old Brentwoods. They had been one of the favourites this season as they had won the Arthurian League the previous season. Old Bradfieldians continued to cause shocks because in the second round they defeated Old Reptonians 4 - 0 at Repton. Also in the second round, Old Westminsters defeated Old Foresters 2 - 1 with a goal in the last minute of extra time, and Old Harrovians thrashed Old Cholmeleians 8 - 2, the game being played the day after the Old Harrovian annual dinner.

In the semi-finals, normality returned and Old Bradfieldians and Old Carthusians easily made it into the final. Old Carthusians were appearing in their twenty-fourth and Old Bradfieldians their fifth final. They had been unsuccessful in the previous four and so they were again as Old Carthusians won 4 - 1. The Old Carthusians were always a little quicker and Jason Golder, Matt Mitten and Henry Nash all scored before half-time to give the Old Carthusians a 3 - 0 lead. In the second half, Leigh Webb completed the scoring. So, Old Carthusians, having been the joint first winners in 1902/03, became the first team to win the cup in the new Millennium. The only decade that they failed to win the cup was the 1990s.

CHIGWELLIAN RESOLVE

The 2002 final was between Old Chigwellians and Old Reptonians which Old Chigwellians won 2 - 0. This was the Old Chigwellians' fifth victory achieved from six final appearances. It was a very clean game and the only booking was of a vociferous dog that argued with the referee!

Old Reptonians squandered many chances in the first half. Richard Basnett, who came closest to scoring for Reptonians,

said: *" we controlled the first half and if we had scored first we would have gone on to win comfortably".*

Eventually, Paul Landsman and Jon Mahoney scored two good goals late in the second half for Old Chigwellians to gain a well-deserved victory as they had adapted better to the windy conditions. The Chigwellian captain, Don Cathcart commented: *"….we got our rewards without playing well. They gave us problems early on but after that I felt we were comfortable".*

In the semi-final, Old Chigwellians had had to defend well to achieve 1 - 1 draw against Old Salopians at Shrewsbury but easily won the replay 3 - 1. The holders, Old Carthusians were defeated 3 - 2 by Old Harrovians in the second round. Old Harrovians were three goals up at one time but Old Carthusians fought back to make it 3 - 2, which meant that Old Harrovians had to defend valiantly for ten minutes at the end of the game.

In the first round there was a very exciting game between Old Brentwoods and Old Westminsters which ended 4 - 4, in the replay Old Westminsters won 7 - 0.

2002
ARTHUR DUNN CUP FINAL

OLD CHIGWELLIANS
V.
OLD REPTONIANS

AT
IMPERIAL COLLEGE SPORTS GROUND
COBHAM, SURREY

ON
SATURDAY 6TH APRIL 2002
KICK OFF 3.00 PM

PRESENTATION OF THE CUP BY
JANE SAWYER,
GRANDDAUGHTER OF THE LATE ARTHUR DUNN

ADULTS £2.00   CHILDREN 50p

THE PROCEEDS FROM TODAY'S FINAL WILL BE DONATED TO CHARITY

ABOVE: THE CHIGWELLIAN GOALKEEPER REPELS A REPTONIAN ATTACK.

ABOVE: JANE SAWYER, GRANDDAUGHTER OF THE LATE ARTHUR DUNN, CONGRATULATES DON CATHCART, OLD CHIGWELLIANS CAPTAIN, 2002 WINNERS.

LEFT: OLD CHIGWELLIANS CELEBRATE WITH THE ARTHUR DUNN CUP AFTER WINNING THE 2002 FINAL.

Salopian Ben Chesters slips between Carthusians Henkes and Mitten during the 2003 Centenary final.

CENTENARY SEASON

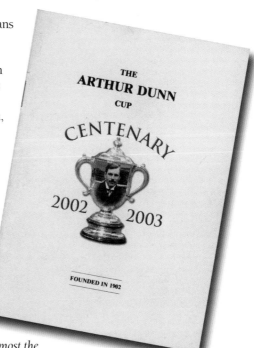

A century has passed since it was decided to remember Arthur Dunn with the Cup competition set up in his honour, a century since 14 teams were entered in the draw for the first season, one hundred years since Old Carthusians and Old Salopians contested the first Arthur Dunn Cup Final at the Crystal Palace.

And one hundred years later, the winning of that same piece of silverware was the target for 20 teams in the 2002/03 season. (Of these, eleven teams were present in that first season).

The draw for the opening rounds of the competition resulted in the following:

PRELIMINARY ROUND:

Old Wellingburians v Old Haberdashers (1)

Old Eastbournians v Old Reptonians (2)

Old Bradfieldians v Old Wykehamists (3)

Old Chigwellians v Old Cholmeleians (4)

FIRST ROUND:

Old Aldenhamians v Old Brentwoods

Old Haileyburians v Old Witleians

Old Harrovians v Lancing Old Boys

Old Malvernians v Old Westminsters

Winner of Prelim (1) v Old Salopians

Winner of Prelim (2) v Old Foresters

Winner of Prelim (3) v Old Etonians

Winner of Prelim (4) v Old Carthusians

THE COMPETITION

Eight teams were selected to play in the preliminary round, including the holders of the Cup, Old Chigwellians. It was not to be Chigwellians' year though, as they lost 0 - 1 to Old Cholmeleians. Meanwhile, Old Reptonians showed the early form and trounced Old Eastbournians 12 - 0.

In the first round, Old Brentwoods had a good win (6 - 2) over Aldenhamians and Old Salopians won easily (7 - 2) over Old Haberdashers. Meanwhile, Old Carthusians just got the better of Old Cholmeleians at Highgate in a very tight game (4 - 3).

The draw for the second round set up some intriguing ties. Old Salopians were drawn against Old Westminsters, a repeat of the previous year when they had met in the same round, but on this occasion the game was played at Vincent Square.

In a very close game, Old Salopians played some very good football in the first period of the first half and looked as if they would score freely. However, after taking the lead they allowed Old Westminsters back into the game and were

grateful for the game to end 1 - 1. In the replay, Old Salopians were the stronger side as they won 3 - 0.

While Lancing overcame Old Brentwoods, Old Carthusians had a very hard tussle with Old Bradfieldians. There was some extra needle in this match as Tom Walker of Carthusians had to mark his friend and ex-flat-mate, Glynn Austen-Brown, who was playing up front for Bradfieldians. *"That resulted in both of us trying even harder to win, combined with the fact that we had beaten them in the final two years previously.*

In the first game, (at Charterhouse) we were winning and they scored a very late goal to take it to extra time....They equalised and then outplayed us in extra time and scored another goal. At the end of the second half of extra time, with almost the last kick of the game, we scored from a corner (by Henkes) to take the match to a replay. Neither side deserved to win in the end and a draw was a fair result.

The replay provided an equally competitive game going into extra time. During normal play, they went 1 - 0 up and we equalised from a lovely left foot volley by Frost. Then, during extra time, we managed a last-gasp goal from Leal to clinch the match after Bradfieldians had missed a couple of opportunities to score themselves" (Tom Walker, Old Carthusian captain).

The other second round game brought together one of the Cup's old stagers, Old Reptonians, who were in great form, and the competition newcomers, Old Haileyburians, who had previously shown no form at all. In the event, this tie was the game of the round. *"The first game was played at Repton School with the score 2 - 2 after extra time on a sunny winter afternoon. Reptonians took a 2 - 0 lead and appeared to be coasting to victory against opposition three divisions below in the League. Then we gave away a penalty. Haileyburians were back in the game and deserved to draw after a performance full of effort"* (Mike Cockcroft, Old Reptonians).

In the replay, there were nine goals, Haileyburians winning 5 - 4 after 90 minutes. *"It was a horrible day: wind and driving rain. The pitch was very muddy and probably the smallest we played on all season. The scoring sequence was quite tight all the way through, with one team going a goal up, and another coming back to equalise. I remember Haileyburians being 5 - 3 up, before our*

ABOVE: THE ANNUAL HANDBOOK, WHICH HAS BEEN PUBLISHED SINCE 1928.

fourth goal and a late rally meant an interesting end to the game". (Mike Cockcroft).

This set up a couple of fascinating semi-finals – Haileyburians, at this stage for the first time, would welcome Old Salopians, who were in confident form; Carthusians, who had been scraping through the early stages, would travel to Lancing, who were quietly progressing in the competition.

THE SEMI-FINALS

RIGHT: THE HAILEYBURIAN DEFENCE WAS NOT BROKEN UNTIL MID-WAY THROUGH THE SECOND HALF.

In the semi-final, Old Salopians were just a little bit stronger than the Old Haileyburians but it was not until mid-way through the second half that they scored their first goal and eventually won 2 - 0.

ABOVE: OLD HAILEYBURIANS CONGRATULATE OLD SALOPIANS ON THEIR 2 - 0 WIN.

RIGHT: SALOPIANS HAVE CONTROL IN THE CENTRE OF THE FIELD.

RIGHT: PRESSURE ON THE CARTHUSIAN GOAL.

In the other semi-final, Old Carthusians were quite lucky to overcome a strong Lancing Old Boys team 2 - 1 at Lancing. Tom Walker (Carthusian captain) saw the game slightly differently and remarked that *"during this game, we played some of the best football of our season and went 1 - 0 up. They then equalised in the second half to take the game into extra time. Matt Bailey (son of the school first XI coach) secured our win with a lovely left-foot shot from outside the area".*

BELOW: THE CARTHUSIANS WINNING GOAL.

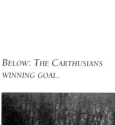

RIGHT: AERIAL COMBAT IN A STUNNING SETTING.

CENTENARY 2002 — 2003

THE CENTENARY DINNER

To mark this very special season, it was decided to hold a Centenary dinner. As on previous occasions, the New Connaught Rooms, Holborn, London were selected as the venue. And so, on 14th March 2003, over four hundred people assembled for a very special evening. Several generations of players mingled to renew old acquaintances, to remember old rivalries, and to check on the number of former colleagues who were now follicly challenged.

THE ARTHUR DUNN CUP

CENTENARY 2002 — 2003

THE DINNER
FRIDAY 14th MARCH 2003
NEW CONNAUGHT ROOMS

Also in the room were a number of special guests from the Football Association, the Amateur Football Association and particularly, Ned Boldero, the grandson of Arthur Dunn, Andrew Ross (great-grandson of Arthur Dunn), Ken Shearwood & John Dutchman. *The list of guests at the dinner is on page 181.*

After a splendid meal accompanied by some interesting wines, the assembled were treated to a trio of excellent speakers – Chris Saunders, Lancing Old Boys, Oxford University and Vice-President of The Football Association, Fred Woolley, Old Harrovian and Life Vice-President of the Arthurian League, and finally, Nick Coward, Old Salopian and Acting Chief Executive of The Football Association.

Toasts

THE QUEEN
R T H Wilson
Chairman of the Arthur Dunn Cup Committee

THE ARTHUR DUNN CUP

Proposed by C H Saunders
Oxford University and
Vice-President of The Football Association

Response by R H Woolley
Old Harrovian and
Life Vice-President of the Arthurian League

THE GUESTS

Proposed by R H Woolley

Response by N Coward
Acting Chief Executive of The Football Association

ABOVE: THE TOASTS PAGE FROM THE MENU.

FAR LEFT: THE CUP ON DISPLAY AT THE RECEPTION BEFORE THE DINNER.

LEFT: NICK COWARD PRESENTS AN ENGRAVED VASE TO THE ARTHUR DUNN CUP COMMITTEE CHAIRMAN RICHARD WILSON ON BEHALF OF THE FOOTBALL ASSOCIATION.

FAR LEFT BELOW (anti clockwise): THE SPEAKERS, CHRIS SAUNDERS, FRED WOOLLEY AND NICK COWARD BROUGHT A SMILE TO DAVID ROY.

LEFT CENTRE: NED BOLDERO, THE GRANDSON OF ARTHUR DUNN. LEFT: JAN BRIDLE, OLD MALVERNIAN. BELOW: LEE WALTON, OLD CARTHUSIAN POSES NEXT TO A PICTURE OF THE 1977 WINNERS, THAT HE CAPTAINED.

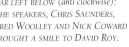

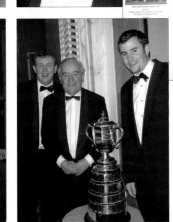

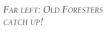

FAR LEFT: OLD FORESTERS CATCH UP!

LEFT CENTRE: ROBIN MOULSDALE, OLD SALOPIAN.

LEFT: DAVID ROY AND SONS ANGUS (left) AND EDWARD (OLD WESTMINSTERS) WITH THE ARTHUR DUNN CUP.

CENTENARY
2002   2003

ARTHUR DUNN CUP FINAL
CENTENARY
1903   2003
OLD CARTHUSIANS
v.
OLD SALOPIANS
AT
IMPERIAL COLLEGE SPORTS GROUND
COBHAM, SURREY
ON
SATURDAY 5th APRIL 2003
KICK-OFF 3.00pm
Preceded by a veterans game to commemorate
the 1903 final between
OLD CARTHUSIANS and OLD SALOPIANS at 1.15pm
PRESENTATION OF THE CUP BY
JANE SAWYER,
GRANDDAUGHTER OF THE LATE ARTHUR DUNN
ADULTS £2.00   CHILDREN 50p
THE PROCEEDS FROM TODAY'S FINAL
WILL BE DONATED TO CHARITY

5TH APRIL 2003

Three weeks later, a vociferous crowd, mainly of Salopians and Carthusians, assembled at the Imperial University Sports Ground at Stoke D'Abernon, Cobham for the Centenary Final.

This was the final that any neutral would have wanted for this centenary year. What could be better than the two teams that had met in the first final in 1903. They are also two of the most successful teams in the history of the competition. Yet, it had come about against all the odds. Salopians had showed some form but Carthusians were unlikely finalists.

It had already been decided that, as a precursor to the final, there should be a veterans' game, representing the 1903 finalists. What a spectacle this turned out to be! The attractive array of support-bandages was only outdone by the rosy-red faces of the participants.

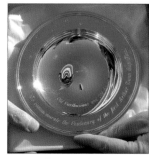

On the pitch were many players who had appeared in the Arthur Dunn Cup Finals. There was even a super-sub for Salopians, (Barry Burns) who appeared in devastating form for short periods in both halves. The bobbly surface did not suit many, and this led to a disjointed game which the Salopian team won 2 - 0.

The first goal was scored when the ball was aimed at the Carthusian goal, the goalkeeper, support-bandage and all, coming to meet it, only for it to bounce over his head and into the net.

TOP FAR RIGHT: 'ARMADA DISHES' WERE PRESENTED TO THE OLD SALOPIAN AND OLD CARTHUSIAN CLUBS TO COMMEMORATE 100 YEARS OF THE ARTHUR DUNN.

RIGHT: OLD SALOPIANS VETERANS TEAM.
(Back row)
S GOODMAN, C WARD, D SARGEANT, A POLLOCK, A WATERWORTH, J CLARK, D ARTHUR.
(Front row)
B BURNS, C EVANS, W RICHARDS, P DYKE, D LLOYD-JONES, D HONYCHURCH.

RIGHT: OLD CARTHUSIANS VETERANS TEAM.
(Back row)
J MERRICK, J KEMBALL, P GODBY, A STEWART, R FAULKER, S EASTON, J HOLDER, N BLANCHARD.
(Front row)
H PRATT, A ADOMAKOH, R OULTON, S AGER, J SCHOLFIELD, R FORD, T SMITH.

CENTENARY

2002   2003

*ABOVE: BARRY BURNS,
OLD SALOPIAN (SUPER-SUB).*

*ACTION FROM THE
VETERANS GAME.
SPOT THE BANDAGES
AND THE BECKHAM-LIKE
FREE KICK...*

CARTHUSIAN JEREMY KEMBALL FLOATS AROUND ANDY POLLOCK, SALOPIAN AND HON. TREASURER TO THE ARTHUR DUNN CUP, DURING THE VETERANS COMMEMORATIVE GAME.

CENTENARY

2002   2003

FAR LEFT: OH DEAR, MISSED THAT ONE...

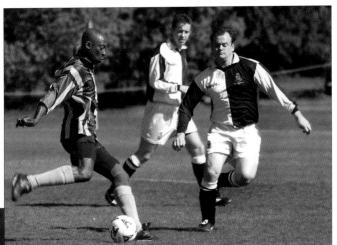

MORE ACTION PICTURES FROM THE VETERANS GAME.

THE TWO VETERAN TEAM CAPTAINS (FAR LEFT: DAVID HONYCHURCH, OLD SALOPIANS AND LEFT: NICK BLANCHARD, OLD CARTHUSIANS) RECEIVE THEIR 'ARMADA DISHES' FROM JANE SAWYER, GRANDDAUGHTER OF ARTHUR DUNN AND DAVID ROY, HON. SECRETARY OF THE ARTHUR DUNN CUP ON BEHALF OF THEIR CLUBS.

THE CENTENARY FINAL

And so to the final itself. The Times correspondent Mel Webb captured the moment: *"There was barely an example of facial adornment to be seen and the kit was of the 21st century, very different to the way it would have been 100 years ago, when burly moustaches and shorts that were anything but would have been the order of the day. Yet there was an appropriate feeling of déjà vu in the final…. in deepest Surrey on Saturday.*

The combatants in the centennial final at the Imperial Sports Ground in Stoke D-Abernon were, by serendipity, the same as they had been back then".

In a close first-half, Matthew Mitten scored for Carthusians and then Scott Ellis equalised for Salopians. Both these goals were the result of goalkeeper errors.

In the second half, however, Salopians were much the stronger in midfield despite sterling efforts by Tom Walker at the heart of the Old Carthusian defence to repel most of the Old Salopian attacks.

Eventually, the game was decided by a spectacular shot into the top corner of the goal by Ben Chesters, Salopians' star player and Man of the Match.

Despite all their efforts, Carthusians could not get an equalizer and so the Cup was heading for Shrewsbury. Tom Walker, the Carthusian captain, said: *"We didn't deserve to win. Salopians adapted far better to the conditions than we did. I know there was only one goal in it, but we were beaten fair and square".*

It was a deserved result and very gratifying for Salopians in this, their own Centenary year.

ABOVE: THE TWO CAPTAINS SHAKE HANDS AT THE START OF THE MATCH WATCHED BY THE REFEREE T ROWLEY AND THE ASSISTANT REFEREES D WOOLCOTT AND B HARVEY.

RIGHT: THE SALOPIANS GOAL COMES UNDER PRESSURE AT THE START OF THE MATCH.

RIGHT: OLD SALOPIANS 2003.
(Back Row)
P CURRAN, D M COOKSON, L BRIGGS, J A D LEACH, G R GOW, J D TAYLOR, P N THOMAS, B J CHESTERS, G R DAVIES.
(Front Row)
D J UMPLEBY, H E E RAVEN, S W K ELLIS, J JONES, R E COOKE.

CENTENARY
2002 2003

LEFT: DAVID WOOLCOTT THE
ASSISTANT REFEREE KEEPS A SHARP
EYE ON THE ACTION.

FAR LEFT: AERIAL ACTION.

LEFT: A SALOPIAN
BREAKTHROUGH.

LEFT: OLD CARTHUSIANS 2003.
(Back Row): H NASH, P S S LEAL,
W J S CLARK, M T BAILEY,
R TAYLOR, J E GREEN, M J MITTEN.
(Front Row): D C M STERN,
E J REES, J C GOLDER,
T E B WALKER, S HENKES,
G R C BROOKE, A J VIALL.

A COLLAGE OF PICTURES FROM THE CENTENARY FINAL.

THE PRESENTATION

There remained just one more ritual, the presentation of medals to the teams and the Cup to the winning captain. Once again, as she has done almost continuously for the last 44 years, Jane Sawyer, the granddaughter of Arthur Dunn, presented the 100 year old Cup to the Salopian Captain, Scott Ellis.

It was a fitting tribute to Arthur Dunn and the ideals that he espoused. The Cup competition is one hundred years young and long may it continue!

LEFT: THE OLD CARTHUSIANS COLLECT THEIR RUNNERS UP MEDALS.

ABOVE: JANE SAWYER IS THE GRANDDAUGHTER OF ARTHUR DUNN. SHE HAS PRESENTED THE CUP TO THE WINNING TEAM ALMOST EVERY SEASON OVER THE LAST 44 YEARS. SHE HERSELF WAS ONLY CONTINUING A TRADITION ESTABLISHED BY HER GRANDMOTHER, MRS ARTHUR DUNN, AND HER MOTHER, MRS ANDREW SHIRLEY.

LEFT: JANE SAWYER PRESENTS THE CUP TO SCOTT ELLIS, THE OLD SALOPIAN CAPTAIN.

LEFT: OLD SALOPIANS WINNERS 2003.
(Back Row): L BRIGGS, P N THOMAS, G R GOW, J A D LEACH, J D TAYLOR, H E E RAVEN, B J CHESTERS.
(Front Row): J JONES, P CURRAN, D M COOKSON, S W K ELLIS, R E COOKE, D J UMPLEBY, G R DAVIES.

Scott Ellis the Old Salopian Captain, holds up the Cup after winning the 2003 Centenary final.

HISTORY OF THE DUNN CLUBS

When the Arthur Dunn Cup started in 1902, there were just 14 clubs in the draw for the competition. Over the last 100 years, clubs have joined and withdrawn. There was an exodus particularly after the First World War when so many schools turned to rugby.

In all, 34 clubs have participated in the competition. Some have been spectacularly successful, some not so. Many have made an enormous contribution without ever winning the silverware.

The following pages outline the origins and history of each club that has played in the Arthur Dunn Cup and a little about the schools from which they get their life-blood.

CONTENTS

OLD ALBANIANS

There is no mention of exactly when the Old Albanian Football Club began but it was probably during 1902 just as the Arthur Dunn Cup began. Early games were played against such sides as The War Office, Stanmore and Old Quintinians, as well as Dunn sides like Old Cholmeleians, Old Westminsters and Old Foresters.

However, it was a further five years before they were admitted to the Dunn competition, by which time the club was having its difficulties e.g. for the 1908/09 season, they were struggling to obtain a suitable ground. At this time, a new football Club was formed in St Albans and, as a result, the Old Albanians lost the use of the Clarence Park Football Ground.

The argument was that the OA team was open to non-residents and therefore not entitled to use local facilities. This drew a vitriolic response from the OA secretary as follows:

"At any rate, every member of the OAFC has had some connection with the city in that he attended the School. How many of those who play for the first eleven of the new Club have any connection whatever with St Albans? Week after week we read in the local paper of 'the new goalkeeper from London' (the first one came from Watford!), the new half-back from somewhere else, and the last new player has (according to the same authority) been imported from 'the unknown!'. One is tempted to enquire what inducements are held out to persuade these 'aliens' to invade our city on Saturday afternoons".

The OAs eventually acquired a new ground but this did not lead to much success. In their first cup-tie in the 1908 AFA Senior Cup they lost to Old Cholmeleians 9 - 2 partly because one of their forwards did not turn up. Apparently, the new man had not played for the Club before, and *"is not likely to be asked to play again for a long time"*. He had *"sent a wire half an hour before the kick-off to say he was 'bilious!'. We hope he is still!"*.

In the 1910/11 season, the team achieved its only success in the Arthur Dunn competition when they defeated Old Ipswichians 5 - 4. Despite the lack of success, the club was re-formed after the First World War. But there were further problems as the school changed to rugby in 1920. This meant that the supply of recent school leavers to swell the ranks of Old Albanians dried up.

By 1923 the situation had become intolerable and reluctantly the Old Albanians scratched from the Arthur Dunn competition in the 1924/25 season.

PLAYING RECORD	
FC Club Founded:	1902
Season joined:	1908/9
Season left:	1924/25
Semi-finalists:	-
Times in Final:	-
Cup Winners:	-

OLD ALDENHAMIANS

Old Aldenhamians Football Club was officially founded in January 1905 when the Old Aldenhamian Society agreed to pay the entrance fee of £2.2.0d so that the Old Aldenhamians could play in the Arthur Dunn Cup in season 1905/06. It was also agreed that the committee could spend at their discretion the sum of ten guineas in aid of the team competing in the Arthur Dunn Competition.

The first season in the Arthur Dunn Cup was very successful. After wins over Bradfield Waifs (2 - 1), Old Citizens (6 - 1) and Old Wykehamists (6 - 0), Aldenhamians met the holders, Old Carthusians, in the semi-final. However, with the withdrawal of one player, injured just before the game, and an early injury to another, the nine men narrowly lost 1 - 0 to Carthusians who went on to win and retain the trophy.

The Club reached their first final in 1912/13. They were obviously a strong attacking side as they had scored 18 goals without conceding one in three games to reach the final. However, their opponents were Old Brightonians who, on the day, were the better side and won 2 - 1.

After the Great War, they only had to wait two seasons, until 1921, before they were in the final again and in fact they reached the final again in 1922. On both occasions they lost to Old Carthusians.

One of the half-backs for Old Aldenhamians, C F Etheridge, played in all three finals (1913, 1921 and 1922) - the only Old Aldenhamian to do so.

Twelve years were to pass (1934) before the Aldenhamians had another opportunity to win the trophy. On this occasion, Old Aldenhamians had the considerable benefit of the skills and presence of one E D R (Donald) Shearer. He captained the side and led from the front. He made goals for others and scored himself in the semi-final. In the final, at the Crystal Palace, *"he scored the important first goal early in the game, and thereafter his dash and clever passes always had the Wykehamists' defence in trouble"* (The Aldenhamian). The result was a 6 - 2 win for Aldenhamians. (This still remains the highest number of goals in total in a final and has only been equalled once in 1955 when Old Brentwoods and

Old Salopians drew 4 - 4).

Two years later, Shearer played for Great Britain in the 1936 Olympic Games in Berlin and was part of the team that refused to give the Nazi salute at the opening ceremony. That same year, he played for the Casuals when they won the Amateur Cup defeating Dulwich Hamlet and he scored one of the goals. Donald must be one of the best players who ever played in the Arthur Dunn Cup.

The other distinguished player of this era was C B G Hunter, an outstanding Corinthian and amateur international. He was later responsible for the football at Winchester and, indeed, sent his old colleagues some useful tips on the eve of the 1934 Arthur Dunn Final!

Since the Second World War, Aldenhamians have had only limited success. They did reach a semi-final in 1952

only to lose to an invigorated Old Etonian side. Twelve years later (1964), they got to the final again. Although Aldenhamians lost, the Times correspondent did not believe that the score (4 - 1) did justice to their efforts.

In 1979, Aldenhamians got another chance and, against all the odds, they beat the favourites, Old Brentwoods, with a solitary goal by Pickett near the end of the game.

PLAYING RECORD	
FC Club Founded:	1905
Season joined:	1905/06
Season left:	-
Semi-finalists:	14
Times in Final:	6
Cup Winners:	2

ARDINGLY College was the third of Nathaniel Woodard's schools and founded in Shoreham in 1858. It moved to its present site in mid-Sussex in 1870. Like so many schools that took up football in the early nineteenth century, Ardingly developed its own version, initially with 25 players a side. As late as 1880, they still had not adopted the FA rules and school teams were playing the Ardingly game with twelve players per side. Ardingly's greatest rivals are their near neighbours, Hurstpierpoint and Lancing.

OLD ARDINIANS

The earliest mention of an Old Ardinian Football Club was in 1887 when the school Annals reported that C G N Dearman was the secretary of the Club. However, only three matches were played that season and from later reports the Club did not prosper. With the formation of the Old Ardinian Club in 1906, a football club was formally organised by C T Squires and started playing in 1907.

The annual fixture against the School was now organised on a proper basis.

The Club joined the Amateur Football Association and supported itself through several fund-raising social events.

After the First World War, the Club was re-established at the Old Ardinian dinner of 1924 and rapidly achieved success in the Old Boys' Cup.

After a semi-final appearance in 1928, Ardinians reached the final in 1932, only to lose 4 - 5. In the following year, they finally won the Cup after a replay; in that season only one game was lost. Shortly after this the Club was invited to play in the Arthur Dunn Cup and this continued until 1999/2000.

During the 1950s, Ardinians reached the semi-final of the Arthur Dunn Cup on two occasions. And with such talented players as Brian Morris, Paul Kirk, Dick Joyce, Charlie Godwin and Bobby Barker, they reached three consecutive semi-finals in 1963, 1964 and 1965.

Apart from a good win in an early round in the 1969/70 season, there was not to be any further success for 15 years. It was 1991 before the team gained another victory; they beat Old Harrovians in the first round. This led to a quarter-final appearance where they lost to Old Salopians and was the last real success that the Club achieved.

PLAYING RECORD	
FC Club Founded:	1887
Season joined:	1933/34
Season left:	1999/2000
Semi-finalists:	5
Times in Final:	-
Cup Winners:	-

BERKHAMSTED *School was started in 1541 when John Incent, Dean of St Paul's, was granted a licence by Henry VIII to found a school in Berkhamsted, Incent's home town. A separate girls' school was founded in 1888 (and the two were combined into the Collegiate School in 1996). The school has a prestigious history, former pupils being Lady Churchill and Graham Greene. After initially playing soccer in the winter term, the school converted to rugby after the First World War.*

OLD BERKHAMSTEDIANS

At the suggestion of the Old Berkhamstedians Association, the Old Berkhamstedians Football Club was formed in 1906 so that they could compete against the other Public School Old Boys teams in the Arthur Dunn Cup. Arrangements were not in place for the 1906/07 season so a formal invitation was read out at the Old Berkhamstedian dinner in 1907 and they first entered the competition for the 1907/08 season.

Unfortunately, in the first round, they were pitted against Old Foresters and promptly lost 7 - 0. Berkhamstedians continue to participate in the competition until the First World War but with only limited success. In their second season, they got through the first round by beating an Old Harrovian team 3 - 1, but then came up against the formidable Salopians. On the Brentwood Cricket Club ground, Salopians were far superior and won 5 - 1.

After another visit to the second round in 1909/10, they made no further impression until the 1912/13 season when they trounced Old Ipswichians 9 - 0, only to lose 3 - 7 in the second round to Old Reptonians.

In 1915 the School took up rugger as well as football and though the club continued to play a little football, by 1918, it was no longer viable; there was just not the supply of new recruits from the school. So, in 1920 the Old Berkhamstedians Football Club was changed into an Old Boys Rugger Club.

PLAYING RECORD	
FC Club Founded:	1906
Season joined:	1907/08
Season left:	1913/14
Semi-finalists:	-
Times in Final:	-
Cup Winners:	-

BRADFIELD *College was founded 150 years ago by Thomas Stevens, Rector and Lord of the Manor of Bradfield. Bradfield developed its own form of football in the early nineteenth century and, unlikely as it may seem, this particular form of the game was taken to South Africa and adopted at "Bishops" College in Cape Town. Eventually, this led to a South African form of rugby football and the evolution of the great Springbok teams that have proved such great opponents for the home unions and the British Lions. Bradfield eventually adopted the association code as the winter sport and very soon an Old Bradfieldian football club was spawned.*

OLD BRADFIELDIANS

The first mention of Old Bradfieldian football was in the early 1860s, at a time when the players wore side-whiskers and a blue velvet cap with a silver tassel. But it was in 1875 that an Old Bradfieldian team played against anyone other than the School team. Thus it was that on Friday 17th December 1875, the Bradfield Waifs defeated the Swifts by four goals to nil.

The term *"waif"* is reputedly defined as *"that which comes along by chance"* and that is a good clue to the fortunes of the Bradfieldian club. There always seemed to be a difficulty in getting a team together. Maybe that was the reason that the Old Bradfieldians did not follow other Old Boy teams of the time and enter the fledgling FA Cup competition. Indeed, the best OBs of the time got their chances in the FA Cup by playing with other teams – e.g in the 1877/78 season, J W Guy and F G Guy (Old Foresters), W T Sale and E Watson (Swifts), S T Holland (Herts Rangers), A J Graves (High Wycombe), P J M Rogers (Oxford) and C A Denton (Wanderers).

So great was the continuing difficulty of making up teams that after 1892 any attempt at a regular fixture list was abandoned. The match against Hoddesdon was typical of this period: six Waifs only appeared on the ground, and understandably they were defeated by eight goals to nil.

Entry was made into the Amateur Cup and when the Arthur Dunn Cup started Old Bradfieldians were among the first entrants. But they were not in a position to respond. Year after year, they were knocked out in the first round. At the time, OBs held a joint tenancy of a ground at Norbury Park with Old Malvernians but as the OMs went from success to success, they commandeered the ground. Eventually, OBs received formal notice to quit.

From 1907 to 1918, they tried yet another strategy of arranging fixtures only in the varsity vacations. They soon achieved some success and one year they beat Old Radleians 7 - 0 in the first round of the Arthur Dunn. But it all fell apart as they lost 3 - 0 to the Old Citizens in the next round. Further losses led to a new approach – to encourage younger Old Bradfieldians to play regularly, it was decided that the train fares above 3 shillings should be paid for all players by the Club. New attractive fixtures were arranged, usually on opposing grounds or at the Elms, Walthamstow, or the Public School Sports Club at Wembley. But still players were difficult to get, so A N Other and B R Adfield often appeared.

The Inter-war period saw a revival of fortunes of the Club. On the field, the Club benefited from some very able people. Men like Keith Robinson, Philip Herbert and Jack Stewart provided the stability in the side, and in 1921 Dick Blundell made his first appearance at right-back against the Foresters. (By 1929, Blundell had appeared in 325 matches for the Club). Off the field, Jack Stewart also became Hon. Secretary. The 1922/23 season was described as *"one of the most successful seasons since the formation of the Club"*. 10 out of 20 matches were won, as against 9 defeats and Bradfield Waifs reached the semi-final of the Arthur Dunn Cup. Further improvements took place when a certain J R B Moulsdale arrived at Bradfield. Under his influence,

the standard of school teams improved and this eventually fed through to the newly-named Old Bradfieldians. Ultimately, this led to two Arthur Dunn finals in 1936 and 1937 but the team lost on both occasions (0 - 2 to Old Carthusians and then 1 - 4 to Old Salopians).

Unfortunately, it was over 30 years before the Club appeared in the Arthur Dunn final again, this time in the 1968/69 season losing 0 - 1 to Old Malvernians. A little under 10 years later, in 1977/78, the Club again lost to the same opponents by the larger margin of 1 - 4, giving the Malvernians their third win in four consecutive seasons.

The Old Bradfieldians have not been lucky enough to get their name on the Arthur Dunn Cup but they have consistently played an important part in the competition throughout its history.

PLAYING RECORD	
FC Club Founded:	1875
Season joined:	1902/03
Season left:	–
Semi-finalists:	17
Times in Final:	5
Cup Winners:	-

BRENTWOOD School, founded in 1557, teaches boys and girls separately from 11-16. Pupils enjoy a broad academic curriculum and extensive extra-curricular opportunities.

OLD BRENTWOODS

A Brentwood Alumni Football Club was formed in the Summer of 1906 but in September of that year, it was decided to be expedient to form an exclusively Old Brentwood Club. So, it was proposed that Brentwood Alumni FC should be amalgamated with the Brentwood Rovers FC, which consisted mainly of Old Brentwoods and that the Committee should have a majority of Old Brentwoods. Brentwood Rovers also had players from other schools which played in the Arthur Dunn Cup – Old Carthusians, Old Felstedians, Lancing Old Boys, Old Malvernians and Old Reptonians.

Old Brentwood Football Club was eventually founded in 1913 when they were invited to be one of the the original teams to enter the Old Boys Cup, which started in 1913/14. Their start was not very auspicious because they lost in the first round to Old Burians (Bury St Edmunds School) by three goals to one.

After several years of competing in the Old Boys Cup, the Club was formally invited to play in the Arthur Dunn Cup in the Autumn of 1939. Due to the outbreak of war, Old Brentwoods were unable to take up the invitation until 1946/47.

Their first success in the competition was in 1955. After good away wins over Ardinians and the Carthusians, Old Brentwoods met Old Salopians in the final at Tooting and Mitcham. In the first half, they raced to a 3 - 1 lead only to see this overhauled in the second half when Old Salopians themselves scored three goals. *"From this point, the suspense was agony for Old Brentwood's spectators until a last-minute goal resulted in 30 minutes more of nerve-shattering play, during which time, there was no further score"*. So the Cup was shared with a scoreline of 4 - 4 after extra time. The Old Brentwood team included the late Reg (Sinner) Vowells, an amateur international.

"After the final, the club held its Annual Supper at the Three Nuns Hotel and the emotional draw of the afternoon was relieved in an evening of hectic celebrations. The function was marred only by our President, Archie Turner, having his car stolen. However regrettable, the incident was not without humour for Archie, although indignant and worried by his loss, had no voice left to tell the police".

A further final appearance came in 1958/59 when Old Brentwoods lost to the Old Cholmeleians 1 - 3 at Plough Lane, Wimbledon. There were three amateur internationals in that side. *"After the game, the team and spectators met in the St Stephens Tavern, Westminster, which was a night to remember!"*.

The first outright success of the Old Brentwoods was in 1967 when they defeated the Old Malvernians 3 - 2 in the final at Crystal Palace, the winning goal being scored by Peter Allen (now of Radio 5 Live). The team also included well-known Old Brentwoods - Peter Clements, Pat Francis, Andrew Love and Tim Russell.

Further successes followed in 1972 with a win over Old Salopians 1 - 0 and in 1973 with a narrow victory over Old Malvernians 3 - 2. The most recent victory was a 1 - 0 defeat of the Old Cholmeleians in 1986.

The Old Brentwoods have appeared in fifteen finals but have only won five times. In fact, Don Cameron and John Davey have both appeared in at least five finals without success. It would appear that the club under-performs in finals as on several occasions the team on paper should have been considerably stronger than the opposition, but have failed to fulfil their promise.

As well as Reg Vowells, the club has fielded several other players of a high standard such as Micky Ryan, David and Gerry Harrison, Micky Walker, Simon Doran, and most recently Eddie Kirby who has played regularly for the AFA representative side.

PLAYING RECORD	
FC Club Founded:	1913
Season joined:	1946/47
Season left:	-
Semi-finalists:	29
Times in Final:	15
Cup Winners:	5

BRIGHTON *College was founded in 1845 by a consortium headed by William Aldwin Soames. From the beginning, the school adopted football; the earliest reference to College Football comes from 1852. However, it was a different form of the game – with 12 players in a team, and points awarded for "rouges", "rouge goals" and "kick goals" (a rouge was probably a kind of scrum). In 1873, Brighton, like other colleges, adopted association football, abandoning its own version. The new game caught on quickly and over the next ten years (1874-83), Brighton were highly successful, many of the participants progressing to win football blues and to play for England. Cotterill and Cooper captained Cambridge, Wilson did the same at Oxford; all three were Corinthians.*

OLD BRIGHTONIANS

On Boxing Day 1880, a team calling itself "Old Brightonians" played a match against South Norwood. The Brighton College magazine stated that *"the condition of the weather and the ground were execrable"* but despite this "Old Brightonians" won 5 - 0. A second game was played against the Pilgrims when the stars were two brothers, N and W Leete. Shortly afterwards, the Old Brightonian Association was formed officially.

It was not long before fixtures were arranged against teams like the Pilgrims and the Mosquitoes, as well as the Old Boys teams of other colleges. Old Brightonians adopted the ground at the Greyhound, Dulwich as their own.

Soon, entry was made into the Sussex Cup and the FA Cup competition but success was hard to come by. In late 1884, they did achieve a draw in an FA Cup match with Old Westminsters at Vincent Square and in the replay on the same ground *"only eight minutes had elapsed before Cotterill scored the first goal, by hustling Moon through the posts while the ball was in his hands"*. However, in the end, they lost the game 3 - 1. Indeed, on occasion the club found it difficult to raise a full team.

In a match against Somerset held at Wimbledon, it was reported that *"the ground was as usual in a frightfully rough state, and the grass about half a foot long"*. Old Brightonians could raise only nine men, as the Leete brothers were absent. *"Brealey, however, came to look on, and was pressed into requisition"*.

A month later, only seven players turned up for a game against Old Foresters. So Matthews, an Old Forester, played for Old Brightonians. So eight played ten – of the eight, four of them came from one family, the Muspratt's. The full team was: – A C Stone (goal), W Leete & J P Muspratt (backs), P C Muspratt (half-back), F C Muspratt, J H Matthews, C D Muspratt & J H Bennett (Capt.) (forwards). Notice the playing formation.

Things did not improve as was demonstrated in the first fixture against Brentwood Rovers. *"Owing to the awkward times of the trains, and the distance between the ground and the railway station, the match was commenced very late and finished in semi-darkness. We were not only one short throughout, but our goalkeeper foolishly missed his train (although he arrived at Liverpool Street in plenty of time for it), and consequently only turned up at half-time"*.

OLD BRIGHTONIANS 1903.

Of course, Old Brightonians achieved success in the early years of the Arthur Dunn Cup, being the first team to defeat Old Carthusians, and reached the 1907 final. In 1913, they won the trophy by beating Old Aldenhamians. But the writing was on the wall, for like other schools, Brighton gave up football in the 1917/18 season and so the supply of players for the Old Boys team dried up. Old Brightonians did not rejoin the Arthur Dunn competition after the first World War.

PLAYING RECORD	
FC Club Founded:	1880
Season joined:	1902/03
Season left:	1913/14
Semi-finalists:	4
Times in Final:	2
Cup Winners:	1 (1913)

OLD BRIGHTONIANS 1913.

CHARTERHOUSE *School can claim to have a unique place in the annals of football history. The school was originally based in the City of London and the boys started playing a form of "dribbling" game in the cloisters, later moving into the open air on the "Green". And this game died hard as a Charterhouse tradition. The last time it was played was on March 7th 1872, against the Old Boys. Indeed, it was so popular that when the school moved to Godalming, near Guildford, there were some who wanted to build the cloister on the new site.*

OLD CARTHUSIANS

There are no records to pinpoint the date that the Old Carthusian Football Club was formed. It is known that the School first selected a football eleven in 1861, and that the first school match took place against Westminster in 1863, the year the Football Association was formed. The first recorded match played by the Old Carthusians was on Saturday 25th November 1876 against the School on a very wet day. That date therefore has been taken as the one on which the Club was formed.

After that first match, the Club made dramatic strides and by 1879 rules had been produced, and it was decided that the Club colours should be brown, black and orange stripes, changed in 1880 to pink, dark blue and cerise, which colours have remained to this day. The club report for the 1879/80 season included the following words: *"The result of last year's matches was most satisfactory from a social point of view, but if we are to keep up our football reputation, individuals must make greater efforts to play regularly"* – familiar words to this day! Possibly spurred on by such words, on Saturday 9th April 1881, the Club took the first step of an amazing double by beating Old Etonians 3 - 0 in the final of the FA Cup. In 1894, the Casuals were beaten 2 - 1 in the first Amateur Cup Final, a record equalled only by the Royal Engineers and Wimbledon.

In fact, the end of the 19th Century saw the golden era of the Club, when most of the game's senior trophies were won. Each victory was reported in a telegram to the School. When this was produced by the then Headmaster, Dr William Haig-Brown, every boy knew its significance, and the news would be cheered *"till the roof rang"*, probably because of the ensuing half-holiday! Following the 1897 Amateur Cup victory against Stockton (4 - 1), the Club resolved to retire from the competition as the play of many of the competing sides was often *"not quite of the style which is expected in amateur football"*. The Club had ceased to compete in the FA Cup by 1894 because of the involvement of professional players. Thus it became necessary to re-create the true Amateur or Corinthian spirit that was the essence of the game in the 1860s and 1870s. The formation of both the Arthur Dunn Cup competition in 1902, and the Amateur Football Alliance in 1907 went a long way to achieving that end, and it is worth noting that the first President of the AFA was Lord Alvestone, an Old Carthusian.

Perhaps the most famous match played by the Club was in 1887 in the semi-final of the FA Cup against Preston North End. Preston had been undefeated in league matches during that season. W N Cobbold *"the Prince of Dribblers"*, and the greatest goalscorer of that era, gave the Club the lead in the second half. Preston equalised near the end of the game, and secured victory 2 - 1 in extra time. That match was regarded as the last great struggle by an Old Boys side to win the FA Cup, and the last time an amateur Club had any real chance of winning the trophy.

OLD CARTHUSIANS 1889.

Now to turn to the personalities of those years. A H Tod, a master at Charterhouse, is accepted as the first organiser, secretary and historian of the Club. W N Cobbold has been mentioned already, and he together with T W Blenkiron, A Amos, and A M Walters were members of the famous Cambridge University team of 1883. Those four not only founded the Corinthians, but with P M Walters (A M's brother) perfected the then *"modern"* theory of combined play for both the Corinthians and England. Through the ages, the name Wreford-Brown has been synonymous with Carthusian football. The quote by A H Tod in his early

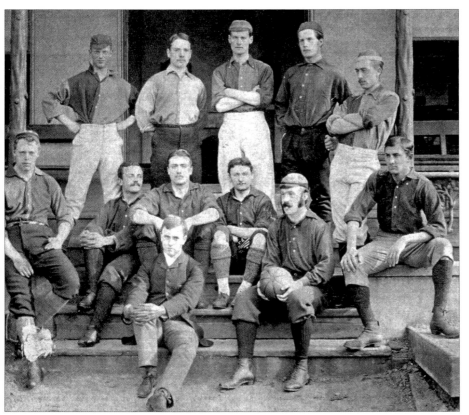

THE OLD CARTHUSIAN FA CUP WINNING TEAM OF 1881.

history of the game *"meanwhile in Old Carthusian Football to Wreford-Brown a Wreford-Brown succeeds"* was made on account of the fact that O E Wreford-Brown is considered the father of the game as we know it. His younger brother, C Wreford-Brown, remained the mainstay of the Club for many years until retiring from the game at the turn of the 20th century, after captaining England against Scotland (see profile of Charles Wreford-Brown in Chapter 2). Another family member, W J H Curwen, a brother-in-law to O E and C played in the first five Dunn finals. To complete the Wreford-Brown trio, A J Wreford-Brown (C's son) played in a number of winning sides both before and after the Second World War, whilst a master at the school.

Of course, the period between 1890 and the early part of the 20th Century was monopolised by the legendary G O Smith, who was capped 21 times for England, and is spoken of by many as the best centre-forward ever (see profile in Chapter 2). Together with C Wreford-Brown and W H Stanbrough, the side at the turn of the century could field three full England internationals.

In fact, it is worth a comparison, at this stage, of the Dunn teams of 1903 and 1951, for it tells much of the spread and development of the game in half a century. The first eleven contained 9 Blues (including the 3 internationals). Both of the players who failed to gain a Blue had played for *"unofficial"* English teams against Germany and South Africa.

The eleven which regained the Dunn Cup in 1951 contained 3 Blues, one of them (J D P Tanner) an amateur international. In 1903 ten Carthusians played in the Varsity match (7 for Oxford, and 3 for Cambridge). In the Arthur Dunn competition of 1951, 16 schools were represented, and in all they produced only 4 Blues in the Varsity match of that year (one each from Charterhouse, Shrewsbury, Bradfield and Brentwood).

The most capped player after G O Smith was A G (Baish) Bower (18) and he played well into the 1920s. He retired to Jersey and until his death in 1973, was a keen supporter of the Club on its Easter tours to that island. Another English international of that era was W E Gilliatt, and his sons I A W and J H H were distinguished Carthusian sportsmen of the 1920s and 1930s. His grandson R M C obtained an Oxford blue for cricket and football, captained

Hampshire at cricket in the 1970s and is now second master at the School. The club won the Arthur Dunn Cup six times in the first eight years of the Competition, with the goalkeeper T S Rowlandson playing in each final. A barren period followed until 1921 when J S F Morrison (a triple Oxford Blue at football, cricket and golf) teamed up with Baish Bower to form a formidable pair of backs in front of H C D Whinney in goal. Despite Bower's continuing enthusiasm, another lean period followed in the Dunn until, in 1936, G T (Gerry) Hollebone, the then Cambridge University captain, also took over the captaincy of the Club. He gathered together a formidable side that included J C and W F Moss, and R M Hollis a hard-tackling back whose motto was *"they shall not pass"*. He obtained an Oxford Blue and took over the captaincy after the Second World War, continuing the success started by Hollebone. Hollis sadly died in the late 1970s, but Hollebone is still alive and well, living in Suffolk, and he has been of considerable help in the writing of this short history.

The period following the Second World War was notable for the performances of J D P (John) Tanner (see Profile in Chapter 4, 1946-1964) who played in three winning Dunn teams with P B H May (see Profile in Chapter 4), his brother J W H May, D G W Goodliffe (who played for Millwall just after the War), and T R H Savill, these formed the backbone of the Club's successes in those years.

Another pair of brothers D B and J J M Lees played in the 1962 winning side, the former captaining the side. He represented the Army side during National Service.

Before the Second World War, the Club led a nomadic existence, but in the 1950s an agreement was reached with Hampstead Cricket Club in North-west London to use a pitch there from October to March.

This was to be the Club's home for over 20 years, but in 1970 a proposed rental of £400 for the season was considered too much by the Committee. Agreement was reached with the School for 2 pitches to be made available, and at the same time an Old Carthusian Clubroom incorporating a bar was created in the old tuck shop and pavilion.

At that time it was also agreed that the Club should have a formal constitution and at the first Annual General Meeting held at the Combined Universities Club, H C D Whinney was selected as the Club's first President. All these changes took place under the guidance of the Club's hard-working Chairman and Secretary of the time, J J Ullman and S J E Easton.

The Dunn had not been won since 1962, but under this new regime and the captaincy of L K (Lee) Walton victories followed in 1977 and 1982. Those sides included two outstanding forwards in I A Stewart, a Leeds United trialist and A A Y (Louis) Adomakoh, a Cambridge Blue who, extraordinarily came on as a substitute in the winning side of 2001 when well over 40! In 1982 the Club achieved the coveted double of League and Cup, a year in which, incidentally, the Old Carthusians won the Cricketer Cup and the Halford Hewitt, the Dunn equivalent in Cricket and Golf. This is a record equalled only by the Old Reptonians.

The 1990s saw the first decade when the Club failed to win the Arthur Dunn since its foundation. A final was lost in 1991 after a replay. However, 2001 saw the Club return to winning ways with a side captained by E J Rees, who represented the combined universities, and G R C Brooke, a former Cambridge University captain. Of course, the team under the captaincy of Tom Walker reached the centenary final in 2003.

The Club is as strong as it has ever been, fielding 3 teams regularly in the Arthurian League, and to show its strength in depth 5 sides are raised to play the School at the start of each season. This has been achieved by the hard work of many officers over the years to whom the Club is greatly indebted.

PLAYING RECORD	
FC Club Founded:	1876
Season joined:	1902/03
Season left:	–
Semi-finalists:	39
Times in Final:	25
Cup Winners:	19

W N COBBOLD "THE PRINCE OF DRIBBLERS".

CHIGWELL *School dates from 1619 when the Archbishop of York, Samuel Harsnett bought a "demesne and pightle of land" from a John Wroth for the sum of £16 10s. The first Headmaster, Peter Mease, a Dutchman, was installed in 1623 and the Foundation of the School was sealed in 1629. From the beginning "the scholars do every Thursday and Saturday, betwixt Three and Four of the Clock in the Afternoon, play of course". It seems that the School turned to Football in 1876 and inevitably Forest were soon their greatest rivals. The earliest Chigwell player to find fame was H A Swepstone who gained caps for England against Scotland, Wales and Ireland between 1880 and 1883.*

OLD CHIGWELLIANS

The formation of Old Chigwellians Football Club probably goes back over 100 years, to late Victorian times when a group would form a team with other like-minded young men. A team known as Old Chigwellians played in the Old Boys Cup, which began in 1913 but it was not until 1924, just over 75 years ago, that OCs were formally organised. An announcement appeared in the The Chigwellian as follows:

"For the last few years there had been a feeling at the OC Club that the Club should run permanent football sides, and at a recent meeting of the Club Committee, it was decided to do so as from next season.

Though the existence of the Emeriti, with which so many soccer-playing old boys have been happily associated since the War, there is available a sufficient number of them accustomed to playing together to render the moment a favourable one for the project in view, as they all indicated that they will support it. Details have yet to be arranged, but a scheme for running two XIs on similar lines to that of the Emeriti suggests itself, and Old Chigwellians desiring to play should communicate the fact to the Hon. Athletic Secretary of the Club without delay, if they have not already done so.

To the Emeriti will be due a large measure of the success which the OC XIs should obtain, and it appears fitting to record here the debt owed to many OCs to that Club and, in particular to its captain, H R Gross for the pleasant games and memories of the past four seasons".

Playing for the School that year was a boy named Ken Skinner, who was adjudged in the first XI appraisal to *"have done very well at left back, he has a strong kick and can tackle well".* Ken was an outstanding

footballer and played for the OCs for many years.

After the War, he was centre-half, the pillar of the defence, finally retiring from the Vets in the later 1960s, over 40 years from leaving School. Ken was a large and gentle man, a fine cricketer and footballer who survived over 3 years as a Japanese POW on the Burma railway, emerging weighing only 7 stone, something he would never talk about. Ken became the Club President and retired from OC football in 1968.

The OCs, like other Old Boys teams, did not play league football. However, there were Cup competitions such as the AFA Senior Cup as in 1928 when they lost to the Norsemen 3 - 1. Even in those days the Club ran 3 teams, a ground had been found near what is now Debden Station and there was an Easter tour in Kent. In 1932 the Club was in the Essex Senior Cup, and the AFA Senior Cup. The membership had then grown to over 50 and it was recorded that the Extra "B" had yet to lose a game. Impressive for a school of only 250 boys.

While the Club entered these Cup competitions from the very early times it was not until 1936 that the Club was invited to play in the Arthur Dunn Cup. The first round was against the Etonians resulting in an 11 - 2 win, followed in the next round by losing 3 - 5 to the Old Bradfieldians. Since then there were many years when they failed to get to the final although doing well in the earlier rounds. The Club would have to wait until 1980 to win the Cup, a timely reward with the opening of the new Clubhouse and ground.

In 1939 the war stopped the Club in its tracks. The 55 members were called up for military service and there was a break to July 1946 when the OCs had their first practice on their *"new ground"* at Buckhurst

Hill Cricket Club. The Cricket Club's second eleven grounds by the River Roding were to be the Football Club's home for the next 30 years.

By the early 1960s, the Club was running 7 teams. The Arthurian League was started and games became more competitive. With more active members, initial discussions were started to find its own ground. After many years of fund-raising, the Club in (1980) purchased and developed its current Clubhouse and grounds in Roding Lane, Chigwell. Before that date, the Club suffered massive under-achievement and the only notable events were being placed top of the Arthurian League First division in 1963 when the League was cancelled owing to bad weather and winning the Second Division Championship in 1966. However, in the 20 years or so from the opening of the new Clubhouse, the Club has more than made up for its previous record. In that time the 1st XI has won numerous Arthur Dunn Cups and Arthurian League Championships and the 2nd XI has won many second Division championships and junior League Cups. There have also been successes for the First, Second and Third XIs in the Essex AFA Cups and various Championship victories for the Third, Fourth and Fifth XIs. The Veterans have won the Veterans AFA Cup and Arthurian League Cup.

The Honours Board from 1980 is one to be proud of. In all, there are 43 Cup and League successes listed. From 1980 to 1990 the First and Second XIs won 8 league titles but perhaps the best years were 1990 and 1992 when the First XI did the double, winning both the Arthur Dunn Cup and the Arthurian Premier League. In 1994 they won the Cup again and the AFA Essex Senior Cup and the next year the Premier and Junior Leagues and the AFA Vets Cup. More recently, in 1998, the Vets won the Arthurian Vets Cup and in 1999 the First XI won the Premier League again.

Old Chigwellians beat Old Reptonians to win the Cup for the fifth time in 2002.

PLAYING RECORD	
FC Club Founded:	1924
Season joined:	1936/37
Season left:	–
Semi-finalists:	16
Times in Final:	6
Cup Winners:	5

HIGHGATE School dates from 1565 when it was founded by Sir Roger Cholmeley, knight and Lord Chief Justice. Highgate is unusual in that it gave up the rugby code and took to association football. Their records show that from 1862 to 1877 they played rugby XV matches against Merchant Taylor, Dulwich and Blackheath amongst others. Having taken up association football, the school was guided by that great player of the Edwardian era, Rev K R G Hunt. He arrived as a housemaster in 1908, the very year that he scored a goal for Wolverhampton Wanderers in the FA Cup Final and so helped them beat the mighty Newcastle United at the Crystal Palace. Hunt was followed by none other than A H Fabian who gained six amateur caps for England.

OLD CHOLMELEIANS

The Old Cholmeleian Club was constituted as a result of a meeting held on 16th December 1893 and the Club started in 1894. The Club did not enter the Arthur Dunn Cup in its first season but joined in 1903/04. Their first match was against the Old Carthusians who were the joint-holders of the Cup. The game was held at Highgate. They lost 4 - 1.

They made little progress until the 1913/14 season when they reached the final. Their opponents were Old Reptonians who had already won the Cup in a previous season. Cholmeleians were no match for their opponents. As the Sportsman reported:

"Had the winners enjoyed similar opportunities to their opponents to play together earlier in the season, there is little doubt that the losers would have been defeated rather more heavily. However, Bury for Cholmeleians was a tower of strength in the Cholmeleian defence". After the match, an informal dinner was held at the Florence Restaurant with a large number of OCs present.

Old Cholmeleians played in two finals between the Wars in 1933 & 1939. The Cholmeleian magazine reported in 1939,

"The Old Carthusians beat the Old Cholmeleians on Saturday March 25th by two goals to one, and so won the Arthur Dunn Cup for the eleventh time".

Carthusians scored their two goals in the first half but *"in the second half, there was a complete volte-face. The Dickensian wind grew stronger, roared 'Ho! Ho!' over the countryside, and obliterated the Old Carthusian attack, so that Stebbings was left standing in his goal, and like Mr Micawber, 'waiting for something to turn up.... Fabian and the wind were taking some beautiful corners from both sides of the field, and the former was doing a great amount of work".* Eventually a pass by Fabian gave Webster the opportunity to score.

A further visit to the final was achieved in 1948 but on this occasion they came up against a very powerful Wykehamist team.

By this time, Ocs were attempting to acquire a ground of their own. In the Old Cholmeleian magazine of June 1948, Ken Boustred, the Hon. Sec., requested any information from members of a ground that might be available. After a great deal of effort particularly by Ken Boustred, four years later, in 1952, a ground was found at Totteridge.

In 1957, the new Club President, Robert Hinton, stated in his inaugural speech, *"Why don't we win the Arthur Dunn Cup?"* At the time, no-one present would have dared to forecast the decisive reply he was to receive. Yet, the following year, the unbelievable happened. After an exciting semi-final against Old Foresters, the Cholmeleians had a convincing win over Old Reptonians in the final, and with virtually the same side they triumphed again in 1959.

Cholmeleians had to wait another twenty nine years before they achieved more success. Under the able captaincy of Doug Wainwright, the Club reached three successive finals between 1986 and 1988, finally winning the Cup in 1988 by beating Old Brentwoods 2 - 1.

Since that time, Cholmeleians have not reached the later stages of the competition.

PLAYING RECORD	
FC Club Founded:	1894
Season joined:	1903/04
Season left:	-
Semi-finalists:	27
Times in Final:	10
Cup Winners:	3

CITY OF LONDON School has its origins in the fifteenth century when John Carpenter, Town Clerk of London, made provision in his will for the education of poor men's sons. It was formally founded in 1834.

OLD CITIZENS

Old Citizens joined the Arthur Dunn Cup competition soon after it started.

They were invited to participate in the third season, 1904/05. They then continued to take part until the outbreak of the Second World War; at this point the school had converted to rugby. In the thirty-plus years up to 1939, Old Citizens reached the final of the competition in 1931, beaten 1 - 5 by Old Wykehamists who were playing in their fourth consecutive final.

During the 1980s the school once again turned to football and so in 1984/85

Old Citizens again joined the Dunn, unfortunately, they had little success, losing in the first game each season.

Due to the difficulty of raising a team, Old Citizens were forced to withdraw from the competition once again in 1990.

PLAYING RECORD	
FC Club Founded:	1903
Season joined:	1904/05, 1984/85
Season left:	1938/39, 1989/90
Semi-finalists:	3
Times in Final:	1
Cup Winners:	-

OLD CRANLEIGHANS

Old Cranleighans played association football initially and were invited to enter the Arthur Dunn Cup in 1903. They did not achieve any real success in the competition, their most successful season being in 1911/12 when they reached the semi-final. However, in 1916, the school moved to rugby football, apparently mainly driven by two members of the staff, J G Fawcus and L C Gower, and the Headmaster, the Reverend Herbert A Rhodes, known as *"Searchlights"* because of his piercing eyes.

Thus when the Great War ended, Cranleighans were one of those who could not raise a team and withdrew from the competition.

PLAYING RECORD	
FC Club Founded:	1903
Season joined:	1903/04
Season left:	1913/14
Semi-finalists:	1
Times in Final:	-
Cup Winners:	-

OLD EASTBOURNIANS

The Old Eastbournian Association was not founded until 1895, and the soccer club was founded in 1899. The team played in the Eastbourne Charity Cup competition, and against other clubs such as Surbiton Hill, London Hospital, Bexley, Guys Hospital, Old Brightonians, West Kent, Barts Hospital and Old Malvernians. Owing to the demise of soccer at the school, its last fixture for many years was played on 22nd March 1902 - a 1 - 0 defeat of the Old Malvernians in Norbury, London.

Things then went quiet for the next 65 years or so! Possibly in the wake of England's World Cup success in 1966, an unofficial soccer society emerged at the college in 1968. By 1974 there were enough interested and capable Old Boys to form a side to play against the school, which the former won 3 - 2. Also in 1974, a Cambridge blue, John Hargreaves arrived at Eastbourne, and soccer took on a more serious aspect, being granted the status of a minor sport. Under his guidance some fairly talented players emerged, and as they moved into OE ranks their thoughts turned towards the possibility of making the football club a more active concern. During the 1980/81 season, the club played 3 games in addition to the annual fixture against the school, and by the following year matches were played against Arthurian League sides, Old Wykehamists and Old Foresters. Christopher Ray and Philip Gearing had been instrumental in resurrecting the Old Eastbournian Football Club, but it was only with the additional energy of Peter Burt that a full fixture list of friendly matches was arranged and fulfilled, enabling the club to apply for membership of and to be admitted to the Arthurian League. In 1986/87 we played our first season of league fixtures in division 5. During the inaugural year, the OEs played 15 cup and league matches, scoring 100 goals and conceding just 22. In one match against a hapless and hopelessly outclassed Old Chigwellian fifth eleven, the referee abandoned the match after 59 minutes at the request of the opposition skipper, due to the *"overwhelming superiority of the opposition, who were leading 10 - 0 at the time"*.

The poor man was nearly suspended from the referee's panel for his *"humane"* decision! Needless to say the OEs won promotion as champions, having lost just one match to an Old Ardinian second eleven team that contained rather better quality personnel than we had faced in the first fixture against them! Since then however, the OEs have spent their time moving between Divisions 3 and 4 without threatening to reach a level from which they could advance to play in the First and Premier Divisions.

In 1990/91 the club was invited to play in the Arthur Dunn Cup Competition for the first time, and entertained our South Coast rivals Lancing Old Boys who were restricted to a single goal advantage at half time. Superior fitness and technique were much in evidence in the second half, and they ran out winners by six goals to nil. However this proved to be a memorable season, as we were rewarded with the Bill Chivers Sportsmanship Trophy at the end of it, and were promoted from Division 4 as runners-up.

In the cup the following season we lost by the same six goal margin to Old Westminsters, and although there have been slightly closer games against Old Reptonians (against whom we led for a short time before succumbing 1 - 4) and Old Carthusians (0 - 3), the disparity in footballing educations is all too apparent between the Old Eastbournians and Arthurian League sides at Premier level. Old Bradfieldians, Old Brentwoods and Old Wellingburians have subsequently enjoyed very comfortable preliminary or first round victories against us. Although in 1998 we did lead Old Haberdashers' 1 - 0 with 20 minutes of the game to play however finishing up losing 1 - 4 due to the usual superior fitness and skill.

Whilst Eastbourne College remains successful at schools level at rugby and hockey, the pro-football lobby cannot expect to increase the profile of soccer at the school from what is still minor sports status. Consequently the Old Boys are unlikely to improve their status in the Arthurian League, and will continue to struggle in the Cup which is for first eleven's only.

In the early 1980s the club played its home games at Whiteley Village, but for

our entry into the Arthurian League the home venue was moved to West End Lane in Esher, and then to Barnes in South London in 1992.

The geographical position of the school has also made it difficult to maintain sufficient numbers of Old Boys willing and able to play regular league football in and around London. The League Committee would not countenance our home ground being located near Eastbourne, but this is where a significant caucus of former day pupils continue to live, and the journey up to London just for home games has often proved to be an obstacle to recruiting

significant numbers of new club members.

Ian Raeburn, Tim Reading and Robin Burn have been enormous contributors to the club in recent years, most notably the latter who is almost certainly at the top of the appearance list for the OE football club.

PLAYING RECORD	
FC Club Founded:	1899
Season joined:	1990/91
Season left:	-
Semi-finalists:	-
Times in Final:	-
Cup Winners:	-

*E*TON *College is one of the oldest schools in the country having been founded by King Henry VI in 1440. Expanded in the time of King Henry VIII and again in the seventeenth century, the College has a long and famous tradition. During the 19th century, the pupils were encouraged to participate in sporting activities and the College created its own forms*

of football – the Wall game and the Field game. Indeed, these still take precedence over the association game. A number of Old Boys from Eton were instrumental in the creation of the association game and its standardisation with the formation of the Football Association in 1863. The Association's first president was an Old Etonian, Lord Kinnaird.

had a successful season. In 1951/52 they fought their way to the final itself but came up against a strong Old Salopian side that beat them 6 - 1. Over the next 30 years, Etonians only managed two semi-final appearances (1975 and 1985) only to come up against Old Foresters, who beat them on each occasion.

Their best achievement in modern times has been a second visit to the final in 1992 but on this occasion they were beaten by Old Chigwellians (3 - 1). So, after 100 years, Old Etonians are still looking for that Final victory.

OLD ETONIANS

Old Etonians have a unique place in the evolution of modern football. Six times between 1875 and 1883, Old Etonians reached the final of the FA Cup, winning the trophy on two of these occasions. Their finest victory was in 1882 against Blackburn Rovers but that effectively was the end of the amateur in the FA Cup competition. Between 1873 and 1903 Eton provided 55 Blues for Oxford and Cambridge and in roughly the same period, 39 full international caps were won. Indeed, the England side against Scotland in the first (unofficial) international of 1870 contained five Etonians.

Of course, Arthur Dunn himself was an Etonian and it was his contemporaries - Norman Malcolmson, Charles Wreford-Brown (Old Carthusian), Robert Gosling and others who were instrumental in the formation of the Arthur Dunn Cup. Old Etonians were thus founder members of the competition but surprisingly they have had very little success. Indeed, when so many Old Boy associations

found it difficult to raise teams after the First World War (due to wartime losses and schools changing to rugby) Etonians decided to withdraw from the competition. They agreed to rejoin in 1926/27 but it was the 1929/30 season before they were able to take up their place.

It was the early 1950s that Old Etonians

PLAYING RECORD	
FC Club Founded:	1878
Season joined:	1902/03, 1929/30
Season left:	1913/14
Semi-finalists:	4
Times in Final:	2
Cup Winners:	0

THE 1883 FINAL AT THE OVAL,
FROM THE ILLUSTRATED SPORTING AND DRAMATIC NEWS.
OLD ETONIANS WERE BEATEN 2 - 1 BY BLACKBURN OLYMPIC.

FELSTED *School. Felsted is a picturesque village in the north Essex countryside. Its history goes back to Roman times and it later featured in the Domesday Book. The school was founded in 1564. Oliver Cromwell's four sons were educated at Felsted. The modern school dates from 1851.The school expanded rapidly in both the size of its premises and pupil numbers in the 1860s. It was able to expand in subsequent years into the surrounding farmland. A school chapel was added in 1873. The school went fully co-educational in 1994. The school has a fine sporting tradition and has produced a number of first class Essex and England cricketers including in recent times Derek Pringle, Nick Knight and John Stephenson.*

OLD FELSTEDIANS

The club was formed in 1893 in response to a letter from Bertram Kirwan, later to become Lieutenant-General Sir Bertram Kirwan C.B., C.M.G., R.A., who was the club's first secretary. The club played its first game in the second round of the Arthur Dunn Cup (they had a w/o in the first round) on 24 January 1903 at Catford, a goalless draw against Old Carthusians (beaten 3 - 1 in the replay). Their final game in the competition was played in 1920, which was actually after the dissolution of the club, following the school changing code. The captain of the Felstedians in their final game was J W H T Douglas who had also played in their first game sixteen years earlier. Douglas was an all round sportsman who captain Essex and played for England against Australia. He was nicknamed *"Johnny Won't Hit Today"* by Australian supporters as a result of his dour batting style. He also won a boxing gold medal at the 1908 London Olympics in controversial circumstances. The referee of the middleweight contest was his father.

PLAYING RECORD	
FC Club Founded:	1893
Season joined:	1902/03
Season left:	1919/20
Semi-finalists:	-
Times in Final:	-
Cup Winners:	-

FOREST *School has a long tradition in association football. The School was founded in 1834 with just 22 pupils and took to football. This was at the time when football was starting to be organised and Forest were one of the first teams to take part in the FA Cup competition. Even though Donington school can claim to be the first school to be involved (they were invited to the first meeting of the FA but in the event they did not take part). Forest School entered a team for the FA Cup from 1876 to 1879 and they can claim to be the only school to compete in the same competition as the Old Boys team because Old Foresters also entered the 1876 campaign.*

OLD FORESTERS

The Old Foresters Club was constituted in 1876, the same year that the team entered the FA Cup competition. The team had been in existence for some years and had competed against the school, but in 1876 the arrangements were formalised. Between 1884 and 1894, the Club had a golden era, reaching the quarter-final of the FA Cup on two occasions and winning the Essex Cup several times.

When the Arthur Dunn Cup competition was started in 1902, Old Foresters were one of the original teams but their early results were not encouraging. Football historians have commented that the golden era of Old Foresters football had passed before the Dunn competition had started. E W Swanton writing in 1936 remarked that *"had the Dunn started a few years earlier, few could doubt that the Old Foresters would have been amongst the early victors"*. It was not to be, however, and most of the first half of the competition's history i.e. between the wars, in fact coincided with perhaps the leanest period of School and Club success.

In the post 1939 period, the improvement had much to do with the sheer growth in numbers at the school but success was slow in coming. There was one remarkable record for which Foresters were responsible.

In 1955/56 the team that played in one Dunn match had the distinction of including three sets of brothers - J & R Trimby, D & G Meister and the twins J & D Taylorson. The match against Old Wykehamists was lost 7 - 3.

Yet, it was that Old Foresters had to wait until 1958 to notch up a second semi-final appearance after a lapse of exactly 50 years. In the 1960s, the semi-final stage was reached only once. With the talent that was now available, it seemed incredible that a further 12 years would pass before the Club would reach its first Arthur Dunn Final.

Year after year, the first round would give rise to high hopes only for the second round to be played on a day when Corinthian-Casuals and Pegasus were involved in an FA Amateur Cup tie with the consequent loss of one or two outstanding players. In vain did veterans recall the days when players turned down invitations to be available for their old school in Arthur Dunn matches.

The advent of the Arthurian League provided regular league football for many who would formally have opted to play Isthmian League football for the Corinthian-Casuals, and that league is no longer amateur in the former sense. As a result, the former bone of contention of how far it was really worth disturbing the regular Saturday side to bring in *"stars"* for the Dunn fortunately disappeared and there was now little distinction between the club's league sides and Cup sides.

More years in the wilderness followed. But in 1970 everything changed. In that year, the Club reached the final – the first of its eight visits to this stage. The 1970 final was lost 1 - 2 but the Old Foresters have rarely played as well as they did in the first half of that final. However, with only one goal lead at half-time to show for their apparent superiority, as so often happens in Cup matches, a sudden break produced an unexpected equaliser, and a new found confidence gave Reptonians a narrow victory.

In the second appearance, in 1974, an extra time penalty goal was needed to bring the long-awaited first victory in the final. As the Brentwoods mounted attack after attack in the dying moments of that game, it seemed as if after a lifetime of absence, lady luck was with the Foresters at last.

The following season, 1974/75, the final was reached again, and again the Old Foresters dominated the first half, scored only one goal and let the Malvernians back into the game and victory was lost. Foresters met the Malvernians again in 1976, this time in the semi-final. Malvernians away at Malvern proved too great a hurdle.

A further decade was to pass before Foresters made any other impression on the competition. The final was reached again in 1985 only to result in a heavy loss (to Lancing Old Boys). Ten years later, in 1995, they did it again only to lose to Old Salopians. Two years later, the same two teams met in the final but this time Foresters got their revenge defeating Old Salopians 3 - 1. Foresters followed this up by retaining the Cup in 1998 by beating their local rivals, Old Brentwoods, in the final.

Foresters last appearance in the final was in the year 2000 when they met Lancing for the second time. Unfortunately on this occasion, they were no match for a good Lancing side.

PLAYING RECORD	
FC Club Founded:	1876
Season joined:	1902/03,
Season left:	-
Semi-finalists:	12
Times in Final:	8
Cup Winners:	3

P. C. ADAMS   J. D. TRIMBY   A. C. FORECAST   J. B. TAYLORSON   C. E. C. FOX   O. D. POLLARD

D. M. MEISTER   R. W. TRIMBY   D. R. TAYLORSON   J. M. RALPH   G. MEISTER
(CAPT.)

THE OLD FORESTERS TEAM OF 1955/56, WHICH INCLUDED THREE SETS OF BROTHERS.

HABERDASHERS' Aske's School was founded in 1690, its income arising from an estate left in trust to the Haberdashers' Company by Robert Aske, Citizen of London and liveryman of the Haberdashers' Company. In 1898 it was transferred from Hoxton to Hampstead and in 1961 to Aldenham Park, Elstree, Hertfordshire.

OLD HABERDASHERS'

The Old Haberdashers' AFC is probably the newest of the Old Haberdashers' Association's sporting ventures, having been set up as recently as 1993 by Andy Evans and Matt Regan. They became members of the Arthurian League in 1994 and were invited to join the Arthur Dunn Cup competition for the following season (1995/96).

They are yet to show any form as they have consistently lost in the early rounds. They did progress to the second round in 1999 and then fought in a tremendous tussle with Old Chigwellians. After drawing 4 - 4 in the first game, Chigwellians finally overwhelmed them 5 - 0 in the replay.

Two years ago, Haberdashers' participated in another high-scoring match in the preliminary round losing 3 - 4 to Old Cholmeleians.

PLAYING RECORD	
FC Club Founded:	1993
Season joined:	1995/96
Season left:	-
Semi-finalists:	-
Times in Final:	-
Cup Winners:	-

HAILEYBURY School, founded in 1862 when it occupied buildings by the East India Company's training college.

OLD HAILEYBURIANS

Old Haileyburians AFC started in 1961 through the initial efforts of several Old Boys, including Judge Detheridge, Morris Brown and Tom Fisher. They were invited to join the Arthur Dunn competition for the 1986/87 season but did not show any form until 2003. Until the 2002/03 season, they had not progressed beyond the first round. Indeed, they had been the recipients of some spectacular defeats, notably 1 - 9 in the first round against Bradfieldians (1996) and 0 - 8 against Brentwood in the first round of 1997. They had a spectacular win in 1990 when they beat St Edmund's Canterbury OBs 13 - 1 in the preliminary round only to lose 1 - 7 to Old Brentwoods in the next round.

As recently as the 2001/2 season, Haileyburians looked like a team without any luck as they crashed to a 2 - 14 defeat to Old Salopians. However, that all changed in the Centenary season as Haileyburians defied all the odds and raced through to the Arthur Dunn semi-final.

PLAYING RECORD	
FC Club Founded:	1961
Season joined:	1986/87
Season left:	-
Semi-finalists:	1
Times in Final:	-
Cup Winners:	-

HARROW School was founded in 1572 under the Royal Charter granted by Elizabeth I to John Lyon, a local farmer. His new School House was completed in 1615 and his School, beginning with one recorded pupil, settled into its gradual, if not uninterrupted, growth towards fame. By the beginning of the  *nineteenth century Joseph Drury could count among his pupils a quartet of future Prime Ministers. Harrow was one of the first schools to take up a form of football and it was here that C W Alcock, the father of the Football Association learned the game. Indeed, many of the elements of the Harrow Field game formed the basis for the rules formalised by the new FA.*

OLD HARROVIANS

Although it is now known that the Old Harrovian Football Club began life as early as 1859 - just 4 years after Sheffield, the first club to have been formed, and before the game itself acquired its first set of rules in 1863 - little is known about its activities as a club in the first 40 years of its existence. A clue as to the identity of its possible founder lies in the fact that 1859 was the year when one C W Alcock left the school. A member of Druries House, Alcock became an important influence in the early years of the game's development. His achievements were legion - on the field he was, in 1866, the first player ever to be ruled offside, and more auspiciously captained the first winners of the FA Cup - Wanderers - in 1872. (Sadly, he is emulated by modern day OH footballers in only one of these two respects). Off the field, he had become a member of the FA Committee and, in 1870, its secretary. It is a reasonable assumption that he was also the driving force behind the creation of the Old Boys Club.

Other OHs featured prominently at that time. Alongside Alcock in the Wanderers side for that first Cup Final were M P Betts (Head Master, 1862-65), W P Crake (West Acre 1866- 69) and R C Welch

THE HARROW FOOTERS TEAM 1871.

(Home Boarders 1864-71). Betts scored the only goal of the game. Crake also played in the first *"international"* fixture, for England against a team of London-based Scots in 1870. In the second FA Cup Final, contested by the Wanderers and Oxford University, Welch played for the Wanderers, and 2 other OHs, C J Longman (The Park 1864 -70) and W B Paton (Rendalls 1866-72) played for Oxford. The Wanderers won 2 - 0.

Harrow's involvement with the Arthur Dunn Cup commenced with the inception of that tournament in 1902. On Saturday 26th July of that year, a letter appeared in the School's bi-weekly magazine, The Harrovian, from one W F Sheridan of 22 Austin Friars, London, notifying *"fellows in the school"* of the proposal by the Old Etonians that the tournament should be established. Sheridan concluded his letter by *"trusting that it may be our good fortune to win"* the tournament and *"hoping that any one who wishes to play in these or other matches will write for a place, and not wait to be asked"*.

Modern-day secretaries will raise an eyebrow at an idea that anyone might *"write for a place, and not wait to be asked"*; but, whether or not that hope was vain, Sheridan's hope of success in the tournament certainly was. Harrow's record in the years up to the World War was, to put it bluntly, atrocious; played 11, lost 11, goals for 5, goals against an astonishing 52. Throw in a walkover to the Old Albanians in 1911 and a very sorry picture is completed.

This may have done more than merely dent the morale of those OHs unfortunate enough to have answered Sheridan's call. On 22nd November 1902, a correspondent calling himself *"Elaphos"* wrote to The Harrovian extolling the virtues of rugby over

"the now universal Association game". His reasoning, *"having played both games indiscriminately for many years"*, was that rugby kept a larger number more fully occupied, was more likely to be played after Harrovians left school, and was better suited to the Harrow pitches. On 20th December, *"Pithecos"* - the fashion in pseudonyms has changed as well - wrote taking up the call and citing *"the decisive defeat of the OHAFC in the Arthur Dunn Memorial Competition"* as *"surely another argument in favour of trying a different code of Rules in the Easter Term"*. The defeat in question was a 7 - 0 thumping by the Old Salopians, and the subsequent results cannot greatly have improved the bargaining position soccer afficionados had within the School.

After the First World War the OHAFC struggled on, and in 1923 achieved their first ever Dunn victory, defeating the Old Carthusians 4 - 1. There followed a relative purple patch, as the Club won 3 and drew 1 of their 10 Dunn ties between 1923 and 1928. Events elsewhere however were conspiring against the Club. At the School, the debate about the merits of the respective sports had raged for quarter of a century since Elaphos and Pithecos had set out their manifesto. Soccer was looked down upon because of its professionalisation and in 1927 Cyril Norwood, the Head Master, abolished it in favour of rugby. His decision attracted protest, but not because of the end of soccer; it was Harrow Football that was seen by his dissenters to be in jeopardy. In fact Harrow football survived and continues to survive; but soccer was not re-introduced until the late 1980s.

Unsurprisingly, this sounded the death knell for the OHAFC. In 1929/30 and 1930/31, walkovers were given to the Club's Dunn opponents, and not long afterwards it disbanded.

While it was perhaps not the most important footballing event of 1966, the re-entry of the Club to Dunn competition in that year was nonetheless enthusiastically undertaken for that. In fact, it had been around in its new incarnation for 2 or 3 seasons, the inaugural game of this phase of its history having been the 4 - 2 defeat of Lancing OBs

2nd XI on 5th October 1963. Of that game, Fred Woolley, the then co-founder and now President of the OHAFC, wrote that *"the spirit was willing but the flesh was all too evident"*, and it clearly took a couple of years for the appropriate degree of concealment to occur. When it did, and the Dunn Committee issued the invitation to rejoin the competition, the Club acquitted itself honourably, losing 2 - 3 to Old Brentwoods on 14th January 1967 in the last seconds of extra time. That Brentwoods went on to win the Cup that year is a mark of the quality of Harrow's performance. It is particularly remarkable that this, and other similar results (including the winning of the Arthurian League in 1977/8) were achieved by the Old Boys of a school where soccer continued, to put it mildly, to be discouraged. In his History of Harrow School (OUP 2000) Christopher Tyerman records a meeting of house masters on 30th January 1967 in which, according to the minutes, *"some discussion took place about the seeping and insidious threat of soccer"*. Not much joy there at the events at Wembley six months earlier.

It was to be another two seasons before the revitalised Club's inaugural Dunn victory, gained at the expense of Old Westminsters in 1969/70. Glory was short-lived however; on 7th February 1970 the Club lost a titanic second round struggle against Old Foresters 3 - 4. Perhaps for the reasons given above, these patchy performances have been typical of the Club's contribution to Dunn competition. The spirit has indeed been willing; in 1970-71 a spectator was persuaded to forego the comfort of the touchline after a dressing-room hamstring strain deprived the Club of a key member of the starting line-up, and in 1975-6 a former 1st XI captain interrupted his honeymoon to take the field against Lancing. Both acts of self-sacrifice were in vain; and so, all too often, it has continued.

On two occasions in the last 20 years the Club has reached the semi-finals. In 1983/84, victories over Chigwell and Eton led to a clash against Lancing. A 3 - 0 lead was established before the tide turned. Geoff Harrow, a talismanic centre forward, broke his leg, and Lancing eventually triumphed 5 - 3. In 2000/01, the Club saw off an awkward Winchester side before overwhelming Cholmeleians 8 - 2. The scale of this achievement is only increased by the consideration that fixture congestion required the game to be played the day after the Club's annual dinner! Perhaps preparation of a similarly unconventional kind would have helped for the semi-final; but a determined and well-organised Bradfield side contained the Harrovian normally potent attack and snatched a decisive first-half goal to win 1 - 0.

An Old Harrovian recalled in 2001, the sinking feeling regularly experienced at the opening draw in mid June, *"with monotonous regularity our willing but inexperienced teams (soccer continues only to occupy about half a term in the Harrow calendar) seem to have been paired against high-flying Premiership opposition who have gone on to bring our campaigns to premature ends. Lately, we have started to hold our own, betrayed only by a lack of self-belief; Carthusians in 1997/98 and*

Brentwood in 1998/99 both needed late goals to achieve 4 - 3 and 2 - 1 victories. Now the Club is competing with the best in the Arthurian League and is faced with a different kind of challenge, needing to dispatch teams from lower divisions with the same kind of efficiency which used so often to account for us a decade ago.

We have started the 2001/02 challenge by doing exactly that; drawing 1 - 1 with Old Malvernians with 5 minutes of extra time left, a late surge gave us a 4 - 1 victory. We go on to face our old friends and adversaries from Winchester in the first round proper".

(They beat them 6 - 0, but lost in the semi-final to Old Reptonians 3 - 2).

"We now need to compete with the biggest

clubs so as to mount a serious challenge for the Dunn as the competition enters its second century. I hope that I do not become a latter-day W F Sheridan in saying that I too trust that it may be our good fortune, one day, to win".

PLAYING RECORD	
FC Club Founded:	1859
Season joined:	1902/03; 1966/67
Season left:	1930/31
Semi-finalists:	3
Times in Final:	-
Cup Winners:	-

HURSTPIERPOINT *College was founded in 1849 by the Rev Canon Nathaniel Woodard and was the second of his foundation.*

OLD HURST-JOHNIANS

The Old Boys of St John's College, Hurstpierpoint formed their club in December 1912. In their first full season, they won the Old Boys' Cup 3 - 1, against Old Lawrentians. The club played in the Arthur Dunn Cup between 1919/20 and 1931/32.

Although they did not enjoy any great success in the Arthur Dunn competition, the Club and their players exemplified the spirit of the competition and AFA football. Take for example one Maurice Pitcher who, by February 1931, had played in 200 out of the 205 fixtures the club had played in since the First World War. He played in every position other than goalkeeper scoring 116 goals including

nine in one game. He also walked from London to Brighton in sixteen and quarter hours in 1924.

The school however gave up football in preference for rugby in 1925. By 1932 the lack of players meant their final fixture was played at the Crystal Palace on 10 December 1932 against the Corinthians 'A' team.

PLAYING RECORD	
FC Club Founded:	1912
Season joined:	1919/20
Season left:	1931/32
Semi-finalists:	-
Times in Final:	-
Cup Winners:	-

IPSWICH *School was founded in 1390 by the Ipswich Merchant Guild of Corpus Christi. Its first charter was granted by Henry VIII and confirmed by Queen Elizabeth I.*

OLD IPSWICHIANS

Old Ipswichians have a short history in the Arthur Dunn. The Club was formed in 1907 and within months were invited to join the Arthur Dunn competition in the 1907/08 season.

In the period up to the First World War, they played only 7 games and lost on each occasion. Nevertheless, when the competition restarted in 1920, Ipswichians continued. Sadly, their first

round opponents were a strong Old Reptonians side who promptly defeated them 8 - 1.

PLAYING RECORD	
FC Club Founded:	1907
Season joined:	1907/08
Season left:	1920/21
Semi-finalists:	-
Times in Final:	-
Cup Winners:	-

ST JOHN'S *School, Leatherhead was founded in 1851. Its founder Ashby Haslewood, was the vicar of St Mark's, St John's Wood, North London. His purpose was to offer free education for the sons of poor clergymen and to provide a choir for his large church. In 1854 the school moved to Kilburn, and three moves later, the school arrived at Leatherhead. The school began taking fee-paying pupils at the end of the nineteenth century and expanded during the first half of the twentieth century.*

OLD JOHNIANS

Old Johnians FC, joined the Arthur Dunn Cup for the third season (1904/05). In their first season, they were very successful, reaching the semi-final, with 4 - 0 and 5 - 0 victories over Felstedians and Wykehamists respectively. However, in the following seasons, they fell at the first hurdle.

Like so many other schools, St John's School changed to rugby after the First World War and Old Johnians were reluctantly forced to drop out of the competition.

PLAYING RECORD	
FC Club Founded:	1904
Season joined:	1904/05
Season left:	1913/14
Semi-finalists:	1
Times in Final:	-
Cup Winners:	-

LANCING *College was founded by the Rev Nathaniel Woodard, curate of Shoreham-by-sea in 1848. The founder's aim was "to provide a good and complete education ... of sound principle and sound knowledge, firmly grounded in the Christian faith". To further his ideals, he planned to create an educational network throughout the country. During the course of his life, he founded 11 schools. Now the Woodard Corporation is the largest group of Independent Schools in England and Wales, with 24 in full membership and 14 others associated to it.*

LANCING OLD BOYS

was another nine years before Lancing achieved more success.

The Lancing College Magazine reported in December 1883 that a Lancing Old Boys Club had been formed. The first President was Dr Sanderson with vice-presidents R H Birkett and J Kenrick, both of whom played for England, and the captain was P C Bated, late of Cambridge University FC. Initially, the team played only a few matches per season but by 1885 this had increased to a fixture list of 21 matches, several against "first-rate clubs". The Club also entered for the FA Cup.

When the Arthur Dunn Cup was started in 1902, Lancing Old Boys were invited to be one of the founder teams. However, it was some time before they achieved anything like success. In fact, it was 1929 before they reached a semi-final. In the first round, after a draw (2 - 2) with Old Harrovians, they won the thrilling replay 4 - 2 with two goals by G W Shaw. This was followed by a lucky victory over Old Citizens (3 - 1). Lancing were unfortunate to then come up against Old Carthusians in the semi-final and were soundly beaten 8 - 2.

A barren period followed and it

In the 1937/38 season, Lancing OBs met Old Etonians in the first round and trounced them 11 - 1. On a frozen ground, goals were scored by C R Heycock (5), G A K Collins (3), K A H Read (2) and F P H Pearse. In the second round, Lancing played Old Citizens at Hurlingham. The Citizens provided strong opposition and Lancing were two goals down after about 20 minutes but got a goal back before half-time. In the second half, however, the Lancing forwards took control and the final result was 4 - 2.

In the semi-final however, there was disappointment as Old Wykehamists won by the only goal of the game.

Lancing then went into another lean period and it was not until the late 1960s that they got into the later stages of the competition. In 1969 they had a magnificent win over Old Salopians in the second round (4 - 3) but this was the era when the competition was dominated by two teams – Reptonians and Malvernians – and it was Lancing's misfortune to meet Old Malvernians in the semi-final. The likes of Tolchard, Loader, Ryder-Smith and Illaszewicz were too strong and Malvernians ran out 5 - 1 winners.

In the next few years, Lancing reached the semi-final twice more (1972 and 1973) but by the late 1970s the work of Ken Shearwood, who had become master in charge of football at Lancing, was really beginning to pay dividends. The key breakthrough came in 1980 when the club made it to its first final. After wins over Cholmeleians, Foresters and a close 4 - 3 victory over Brentwoods in the semi-final, Lancing lost out in a thrilling final against Chigwellians (4 - 2 after extra time). After two more semi-finals, Lancing at last won the trophy in 1983. In a repeat of the 1980 final, Lancing gained a well-deserved victory over Chigwellians (2 - 0). On a hard and uneven surface at Champion Hill, Dulwich, Lancing were better at mastering the high-bouncing ball and the skills of Nigel Pitcher and Nigel Bennett proved decisive. Lancing actually got the ball in the net four times but on two occasions the goals were disallowed. However, Bennett scored in the first half, and then in the second half, *"...a faulty back pass, and there was Pitcher, quick as a flash, seizing the opportunity and from all of twenty yards, steadying himself, before chipping the advancing goalkeeper – while spectators held their breath as they watched the flight of the ball, finally and tantalisingly slowly, come to rest in the far corner of the Chigwell goal. And that was that".* (Lancing College Magazine).

This was the first of a trio of victories as Lancing went on to win the trophy again in 1984 and 1985. Prior to the 1984 final, Lancing had to beat Cholmeleians (5 - 3), Salopians (2 - 0 in a replay) and then Harrovians (5 - 3) in the semi-final. What a remarkable game this was! The Harrovians were captained by Geoff Harrow who gave his side a lead but then broke a leg in a challenge with S Bennett of Lancing. Nevertheless, Old Harrovians raced to a 3 - 0 lead. It is part of Lancing folklore how Nigel Pitcher led his team not only to claw back the three-goal deficit but to get two more goals in the last ten minutes to win the game. After that the final should have been easier but a game against Old Carthusians could never be underrated. It was to the credit of the Lancing players that they ran out 2 - 0 winners.

This same team completed the hat-trick of wins the following year when they decisively beat Old Foresters in the 1985 final. However, it was to be a different team that was to reach the final on the next occasion. After a semi-final loss in 1992, Lancing reached the final in 1993 beating Old Reptonians by a single goal. They reached the final again in 1996, initially this final did not go to plan because by half-time, Old Brentwoods were 1 - 0 up. However, *"four goals in the second half, all scored with dexterity, enabled Lancing Old Boys to win the Arthur Dunn Cup for the fifth time in 13 years"* (The Times). Ian Brown-Peterside scored two of the goals and the others came from the wingers, Martin Wyatt and Peter Alcock. And it was the nucleus of this team – Kelsey, Evans, Brown-Peterside, Gurney, Mercer, Alcock and Simpson – that formed the backbone of the side that reached another final in 1999. They followed this up by winning the trophy for the sixth time in 2000.

Lancing had another successful season in 2002/03 only narrowly losing to Old Carthusians 3 - 2 in the semi-final.

PLAYING RECORD	
FC Club Founded:	1883
Season joined:	1902/03
Season left:	-
Semi-finalists:	19
Times in Final:	8
Cup Winners:	6

MALVERN College was founded by a group of local businessmen in 1865 with 24 boys and 6 masters. Initially there were two houses but expansion was rapid and by 1877 there were six houses and 290 boys. In the 1890s the number of pupils nearly doubled and a further four houses were added. The College continued to expand in the first half of the twentieth century despite two periods of exile during the 1939-45 War, firstly to Blenheim Palace and then to Harrow School. The school is now co-educational with 350 pupils.

OLD MALVERNIANS

There had been OM football played before 1897; indeed there was quite an extensive fixture list. However, the first meeting to establish a club was on April 20th 1897 and the Rules were agreed in June of that year. This was ratified at a meeting the following year as well as the proposal to award presentation caps; 17 were awarded immediately.

The Club acquired the use of Norbury Park as a *"home"* ground, and sub-let 50 percent to the Bradfield Waifs for £25 for the season. The opening match of the club was against Wood Green on 25th September. In the opening season their run in the Amateur Cup was as follows:

QUALIFYING:
    beat Old Brightonians 9 - 0,
          Bradfield Waifs 3 - 2,
          London Welsh 5 - 1,
          Novacastrians 7 - 0
COMPETITION:
    beat King's Lynn 3 - 0,
          Maidenhead 3 - 2,
          Chesham Generals 4 - 2
SEMI FINAL:
    lost to Uxbridge 0 - 1

There was an amicable dispute about this result! Among the players G H Simpson and R E Foster who played cricket for England and C J Burnup and W L Foster who nearly did! At this time there was a well-established Cambridge OMFC with a long fixture list which included Cambridge Old Westminsters FC.

From the results that are known, it is evident that Malvernians had a strong and successful team. By 1902, the Club had won the Amateur Cup but at the fifth AGM on June 2nd 1903, it was proposed that the Club should now withdraw from the Amateur Cup competition as they were playing in the Arthur Dunn Cup.

Up to the First World War, Malvernians had won the Arthur Dunn Cup in 1909 and 1912, the FA Amateur Cup in 1902, the AFA Senior Cup in 1911 and the Eastbourne Charity Cup in 1913.

Like so many Clubs, there were problems arising from the loss of players due to the Great War and the spectre of rugby football being adopted by the School. However, in 1921, the then Headmaster, Mr Topping, assured the OMFC that there would be no question of Malvern going over to rugby as its main game whilst its rivals, Repton and Shrewsbury, continued to play soccer.

In 1922, Norman Beeson proposed the possibility of buying a football ground in Mitcham but unfortunately this was turned down. Also the Club passed a resolution that no boys still at school should be allowed to play for the Old Boys side in the Arthur Dunn Cup, which crops up from time to time. Although the minutes suggest the Club struggled along, as indeed they probably do today, the Club was enjoying one of its purple patches.

In 1922, the Club won the Essex AFA Senior Cup, and then won the Dunn Cup three times running from 1924 to 1926 and again in 1928. When the Arthur Dunn Cup was won, there were no shrinking violets in the OMs, all players in the winning side were awarded Presentation Caps. Tours at Christmas and Easter were organised on the South Coast or on the Continent. The Club was always trying to increase the membership and get more players and indeed more subscriptions during this period. The tone of the correspondence in those days varies little from today.

Malvernians reached the final again in 1938 where they met the Old Wykehamists, even extra time could not separate the teams and the Cup was shared. 1956 saw a repeat of 1938, again the match went to extra time but this time Malvernians were victorious. They retained the Cup the following year by beating Old Reptonians. The 1960s turned out to be another purple patch for the Club.

Another Malvern Lion, Ivor Norton, resigned at the AGM on 12th July 1971, having been Chairman for the previous ten years. The Club had had another purple patch, as Ivor reminded us in his

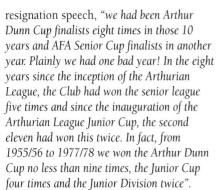

HARVEY CHADDER (1903 - 1995)

Harvey Chadder was educated at Taunton School. He went on to St John's College, Oxford and appeared in the varsity matches between 1923 and 1925.

He spent most of his professional life as a master at Malvern and for 20 years he was the master in charge of football. However, his claim to fame was as an ever-present member of the great Corinthian team that was the scourge of professional teams in the FA Cup between the two World Wars.

He was also a founder member of the Pegasus Football Club and he later succeeded another public school master, Rev K R G Hunt of Highgate, as President of Pegasus.

It was Chadder's influence that led Denis Saunders, captain in both Pegasus FA Amateur Cup victories, to Malvern to become the college's modern football guru.

DENIS SAUNDERS (1924 - 2003)

Denis Saunders went to Scarborough High School, where he was a keen rugby player. His enthusiasm for football was fuelled when he went up to Exeter College, Oxford. There he joined a group of relatively mature undergraduates, including Ken Shearwood, Tony Pawson and John Tanner. These four became the corner-stones of the Pegasus team which twice won the FA Amateur Cup.

By the time Saunders led the team to its second victory, over Harwich in 1953 he had become a geography master at Malvern, where he also took charge of football training. His influence was immediate. The school went unbeaten for four years and this led to the successful Old Malvernian team which won the Arthur Dunn Cup nine times between 1956 and 1978 (this team included Chadder's son, Richard).

Such was Saunders reputation that, in 1984, he was invited by the Football Association to be academic headmaster at their new school of excellence at Lilleshall.

resignation speech, *"we had been Arthur Dunn Cup finalists eight times in those 10 years and AFA Senior Cup finalists in another year. Plainly we had one bad year! In the eight years since the inception of the Arthurian League, the Club had won the senior league five times and since the inauguration of the Arthurian League Junior Cup, the second eleven had won this twice. In fact, from 1955/56 to 1977/78 we won the Arthur Dunn Cup no less than nine times, the Junior Cup four times and the Junior Division twice".*

The great OM teams of the 60s began to age a little – Williams, Theobald, Irvine, Costeloe, Dogsie Martin, wee Davy Loader, Roger Tolchard, Phil Hayden, Nick Stockbridge and Mike Murphy, but other players were coming through to bridge the 60s to the 70s. Ian Murray was already established as was Peter Townend, but in 74 a new crop headed by Chris Williams, Nick Williams, and the Denham brothers came together to support Richard Wilson, Mike Byers, Nick Stockbridge, Richard Whateley and the evergreen Jan Bridle. The two Murphy brothers also played their part, and the Dunn was won again in 1975, 1976 and 1978.

It was to be another 11 years before a Malvern side inspired a new generation of Giles King, Eddie Gilbert, Andy Temperton, Giles Lunt, Lawrence Lindsay, Douglas Pennant, Sam Harries, the Denhams and the fearsome Wills in goal.

PLAYING RECORD	
FC Club Founded:	1897
Season joined:	1902/03
Season left:	-
Semi-finalists:	48
Times in Final:	28
Cup Winners:	17

MILL HILL *School was set up in 1807 by a committee of non-conformist merchants and ministers. They decided to place their school outside of London because of the "dangers both physical and moral, awaiting youth while passing through the streets of a large, crowded and corrupt city". Their foresight has provided generations of Millhillians with quite unique surroundings, peaceful, secure and rural and yet within minutes of links to Central London.*

OLD MILLHILLIANS

Old Millhillians FC were founded in 1995. They quickly joined the Arthurian League and won the Division 4 title at the first attempt. This was followed by the Division 3 championship.

In 1998, Old Millhillians were invited to join the Arthur Dunn Cup competition and competed with little success for 2 seasons before folding.

PLAYING RECORD	
FC Club Founded:	1995
Season joined:	1998/99
Season left:	2000/01
Semi-finalists:	-
Times in Final:	-
Cup Winners:	-

RADLEY

RADLEY College was founded in 1847 by William Sewell, Fellow of Exeter College, Oxford, to provide an independent school education on the principles of the Church of England. Football has been played at Radley for a century and a half, and to three distinct codes. From 1847 to 1880 there was Radley football, a game unique to the College. The Rules of the Football Association were agreed in 1863 and of the Rugby Football Union in 1871. The school adopted Association football quite late, in 1881, and played it until 1913. From 1914 to the present day, the school has followed the rugby code.

OLD RADLEIANS

The Old Radleian Football Club was founded in 1898. Though the club was involved in the discussions about the formation of the Arthur Dunn Cup, it was decided not to participate in the first few seasons. However, after some criticism from some members of the club, it finally joined for the 1906/07 season.

Unfortunately, Radleians were not very successful. In the first game, they lost 0 - 9 to Old Westminsters, and the following year they went down 0 - 7 to Bradfieldians. In 1908/09, the club could not even manage to raise a team and so their opponents, Old Cranleighans, got a bye to the next round.

The first win came in 1912 when Radleians beat Cranleighans 4 - 0 only to lose 7 - 2 to Malvernians in the next round.

Again, like so many other Old Boys teams, with the school turning to rugby football after the First World War, Radleians found it difficult to raise a football team and so they did not enter the competition in 1919.

PLAYING RECORD	
FC Club Founded:	1898
Season joined:	1906/07
Season left:	1913/14
Semi-finalists:	-
Times in Final:	-
Cup Winners:	-

REPTON

REPTON School was founded in 1557, with the earliest mention of Football around 1837, at which time it appeared that most public schools played a game that is best described as a cross between soccer and rugby. This led to the adoption of a set of rules laid down by leading footballers from public schools at Cambridge in 1863, which appear to form the basis for the current FA. It was in 1877, some 3 years after the Oxford v Cambridge University match, that "The Kicking Game" was installed as the winter game to be played at Repton, thus heralding the beginning of Repton football.

OLD REPTONIANS

During the period 1880 to 1914, several Old Reptonians won International Honours, the most celebrated of these being C B Fry, who won England caps from 1891 to 1901, whilst appearing in the FA Cup Final for Southampton in 1902. Also, between 1874 and 1914, some 35 Old Reptonians played in the Varsity matches of that period, a figure surpassed during that period only by Charterhouse, Eton and Winchester. At this time, there being no organised Old Boys' football, most of the good players from all public schools played for either the Corinthians (forerunners to the Corinthian-Casuals) or the Norsemen.

When the Arthur Dunn Cup Competition started in 1902, the existence of the above mentioned quality Old Reptonian footballers gave the Old Reptonians a sound basis to perform strongly in this new competition and, between 1903 and 1914, they appeared in six finals, lifting the trophy in 1907, 1911 and 1914. It is perhaps interesting to note that, courtesy of the War starting in 1914 and the Dunn competition not resuming until 1920, the Club retained the trophy, albeit in the school library, for some 7 years! Distinguished amongst those Reptonians of this pre-war phase was the amateur international, R A (Dick) Young, who was alone in representing the ORs in all those six finals.

Preparing sides to compete in the Arthur Dunn Cup has always been a challenging issue, as Reptonians have tended to scatter across the country after leaving school. To address this problem, the OR Football Club was formed in 1925 to gather players together for training sessions, but the star players were often committed elsewhere and, while some success was achieved in the AFA Cup, an early exit from the Dunn was common.

After the Second World War, Reptonians reached the final of the Arthur Dunn again in 1947, the first year in which the competition had been revived, with Dick Sale as both moving spirit and organiser. The school's credit in the football world was best upheld at this stage by the appearance at Wembley of D B Carr in the successful Amateur Cup winning sides fielded by Pegasus in 1951 & 1953, and also by G C Citron, who represented Corinthian-Casuals in the drawn final against Bishop Auckland in 1956.

At the time, there was a view that, being a Midlands-based school, in an age where travel was not so easy, because most ORs returned to their mainly northern home areas on leaving school, the possibility of football in London, with a side playing together regularly, to provide a strong Dunn challenge was responsible for this drought. While there must be some truth in this, it has to be said that this did not prevent the Old Salopians and Old Malvernians from overcoming the same obstacle during this period! As the Dunn was basically a Southern Competition, this, combined with the unavailability of quite a few of the better players, conspired to produce weakened sides who came together on the day and were expected to gel immediately. It is a theme which has been echoed down the years until the Old Reptonians finally managed to raise enough support to enter the Arthurian League in 1967/68 - and beyond. Even then, the Dunn side was still mainly made up of *"non-Londoners"*, mostly playing for Clubs such as

CHARLES BURGESS FRY
OLD REPTONIAN

C B Fry was the supreme example of the all-round sportsman. Though born in Croydon (25th April 1872), his family hailed from Sussex. He was educated at Repton and gained a first at Oxford. Fry also has the distinction of being a triple blue – for football, athletics and cricket, and would have got a fourth, in rugby had he not been injured. He appeared for the Barbarians in 1894/95 and an injured thigh caused him to miss the University match after he had played in all the season's fixtures.

He was a fine cricketer. Despite occasional problems with his home county, (he and Ranjitsinjhi once went on strike) he was outstanding for Sussex. He is one of only a handful of batsmen to make six hundreds in successive Innings. His performances for England were mixed but he did eventually become captain of the side, his 287 against Australia at Sydney in 1903/04 remains the highest score by an Englishman in a Test in Australia. It was his first Test match.

He played football for Corinthians and represented his country in the England v Ireland International at the Dell in 1901. The following year he played for Southampton in the FA Cup Final. In athletics, his best event was the long jump and in 1892, while still at Oxford, he equalled the world record with a jump of 23 feet 5 inches, a record that was not broken until 1913.

Fry became a master at Charterhouse before turning to journalism and later taught at the training ship H M S Mercury (1908-1950).

He tried several times to become a member of Parliament but was unsuccessful. However, his involvement in politics led him on one occasion to be offered the throne of Albania, which he turned down as he felt he could not afford it.

He died in Hampstead on 7th September, 1956.

Liverpool Ramblers, Huddersfield Amateurs and Sheffield Falcons etc. It was therefore a pivotal moment in October 1974, when John McConville's report for the ORFC (London Branch) to the Terminal Letter (now re-named the OR Newsletter) announced with some pride that the London Club had provided no less than five members of the Dunn side, plus the 12th man. The London Branch of the Club had come a long way in a very short time. It should be noted that the setting up of regular OR football in London did not happen overnight. It is a tribute to the hard, often thankless work, put in initially by Philip Curtis up to 1957, when he was succeeded by John Chaumeton, who organised a number of games for ORs in London. The composition of these sides then would not have met with approval of the Arthurian League Committee, but it was a start!

In order to raise sides, friends from Corinthian-Casuals and the Norsemen (as mentioned earlier) were invited to make up the numbers. How difficult it must have been is shown by the fact that John eventually gave up the unequal struggle in 1958. During this period, the Captain and Secretary of the Club was Dick Sale,

himself an outstanding if uncompromising player, and the Terminal Letter of October 1959 records the entry *"Owing to lack of support, the London ORFC will not be functioning. The Hon. Sec., R Sale would be glad to hear from anyone prepared to run OR football matches in the North or South!"*. The challenge was enthusiastically taken up by John (Ginge) Hare and, while the possibility of entering the Arthurian League at its inception in 1963 was discussed, it took until 1967 for that to happen.

It is no coincidence that the 60s and 70s was another purple era for Reptonian football as the ORs and Old Malvernians dominated the Dunn during that period, more of which below. It is also perhaps significant that in 1968/69 the same two sides faced a final match to decide the Arthurian League 1st Division title - there was no Premiership at that stage.

The result was a sound thrashing for Reptonians (7 - 1) at Oatlands Park, but an underlying factor was that while Reptonians put out a (nearly full strength) League side, they were confronted by the might of the Malvernians Dunn side. Lesson learned, and it had a great influence on the development of OR football in London.

As ever, life is full of non-sequitors

though, since in the 1963 Dunn final, played in pouring rain at the Bank of England Ground, Roehampton, John Hare found himself short of four first-choice players (including the Captain, Pat Vaughan, who had decided to get married on that day) to face a strong Malvern side. Fielding two players fresh out of Repton the previous term (Barnwell & Rolfe) among the replacements, the ORs administered a 4 - 0 drubbing to their arch rivals!

Returning to London, the Club already had a good structure in place, with regular Committee meetings and a disciplinary section with fines to encourage players to be on time, but were still without a proper *"Home"* and short of funds, relying solely on Subscriptions (where collection was possible!), match fees (ditto) and a £50 annual grant from the Old Reptonian Society. It was only through the League's tolerance and dispensation that we were allowed to play our *"Home"* fixtures many miles out of London at Preston (Herts), which was a serious trek for some of the Essex Clubs - well, it cut both ways! Something had to be done so, in the mid-1970s the London Branch was restructured to have its own President (Peter Rolfe) and serious fund raising was started, in the form of social events and a 150 Club monthly prize draw. This, allied to the introduction of a newsletter, wittily produced by Kent Heller led to a real social scene in London and was, without question, responsible not only for the increase in membership but the feeling that Repton soccer now belonged well and truly in London.

Additionally, financial independence from the OR Society was established and the Club, while flirting briefly with 3 sides, now had 2 sides firmly established in the League, with the use of London pitches. It had taken a while, but the initial hard work of those already mentioned plus all subsequent Officers and Committee members, in particular Peter Rowland who headed up the initial committee when the Club finally entered the Arthurian League, had finally paid off. Mention should also be made of Ian Payne who has served the club non-stop from the seventies in many capacities, not least of which was to become the first London President to also hold the position of overall President of the ORFC, finally relinquishing all responsibilities (though not support) only this year. If the 2 President situation seems a slight anachronism, this leads nicely to the conclusion of this piece. The overall ORFC has always had a President appointed from within by the outgoing President with consultation with a committee of two. The title is basically an honour for contribution to OR football and has, since the London Branch has achieved its aim of providing all (or most) of the Dunn side, had little function other than to support that team. All the day to day work has, since the mid-seventies been carried out in London.

There have been therefore two AGMs, the full club meeting taking place on OR day in September, when the school play the Dunn side. This has regularly been attended by about 4 or 5 people (mainly officials) and the occasional dog! Meanwhile, the London Branch meeting takes place pre-season in July and, initially due to the showing of *"training films of a different nature"* but subsequently because of its venue (a Pub), attracts a far larger and more participating audience.

It seemed logical to combine the two, hopefully dropping the (rather Trades Union sounding) title of *"London Branch"* and complete the task of basing OR football in London, a conclusion which I believe would have been well received by the sadly late John Hare and Peter Rowland. It certainly has the full support of all current members who have been approached. Clearly, there can no longer be two Presidents but this will merely mean a change in title for the London President. It is perhaps appropriate that the first President of the new regime will, subject to the ratification at the AGM (rejection of which would be unthinkable) be Alan Basnett, one of Repton's finest footballers.

PLAYING RECORD	
FC Club Founded:	1879?
Season joined:	1902/03
Season left:	-
Semi-finalists:	37
Times in Final:	23
Cup Winners:	11

ROSSALL School was founded in 1844 and the School's Governing Body, the Corporation of Rossall School, was incorporated under Royal Charter in 1890. At this time, the School adopted Football as the Winter game.

OLD ROSSALLIANS

The Old Rossallian Football Club was officially inaugurated in 1891 although some matches had been played in the late 1880s. It prospered until 1914 and the Great War. Thereafter, it declined because the main school game became rugby. However, throughout the 1890s the club flourished. On April 14th 1891, a meeting was held at the Criterion Restaurant in London for the purpose of inaugurating the Old Rossallian Football Club. Mr F W Wright made a stirring speech, outlining the advantages of the Club: it would bring the school the reputation of being a nursery for football players, sportsmen and gentlemen: friendships, which had been formed at school, would be cemented: it would give men, fresh from school, an opportunity to play when otherwise they might not get a game. The rules of the club were formulated. The team colours were to be the same as those of Rossall, cerise and grey with OR on the pocket of the shirt. The cap was to be half and half with OR on it. Subscriptions were 10/6d for honorary members and 5/6d for playing members. They appointed Mr F W Wright as President and Messrs Bell and Toone, joint secretaries.

The General Meeting of 1892, held in the Dean's Yard, reported a surplus of £3/13s/5d and the best subscribers were the men of Cambridge. It was reported that the 1891 season had been successful because the ORs defeated the leading football Old Boys teams of the time - Old Carthusians, Old Foresters and Old Westminsters. The fixture list already numbered 25 matches and it was hoped to extend the list in the Manchester and Liverpool area. Most *"home"* games had been played at Cambridge. It was agreed, by one vote, to levy all subscriptions at 5/-. The 1893 General Meeting, held at Church House, Westminster, reported the healthy state of the finances but turning out a full strength team was proving difficult because the London-based players tended to play for their own clubs. There were three new fixtures, R I E C, Leatherhead and Repton. The most important news, however, was that a ground in Richmond had been secured for the 1894 season.

Despite the difficulties, the ORs managed to reach the final of the Arthur Dunn Cup in 1904 and 1910. In 1904 the ORs beat Old Cranleighans 4 - 2 and in the semi-final beat old Malvernians, 4 - 3. However, they lost in the final to Old Carthusians, 2 - 0. In 1910, the ORs beat Lancing in the second round, 3 - 2; the Old Cholmeleians 4 - 0 in the third round; the Old Wykehamists in the semis, 3 - 0 but succumbed to the Old Carthusians once again, 2 - 1 in the final. By 1913 letters were flowing into the Old Rossallian Magazine for and against rugby becoming the main school game. Much was written about tradition and our duty to support Repton and Charterhouse when the reputation of football was at a low ebb. Also mentioned was Rossall's contribution to the Arthur Dunn Cup and the *"varsity"* sides. One correspondent pointed out that within the Liverpool and Manchester areas there were only three teams with which Public School boys could be associated – *"there are no really nice soccer clubs outside London"*.

The Headmaster, Canon E J W Houghton announced in the April edition of the Rossallian that from Michaelmas Term, 1914, rugger would be the school game. And so ended Rossall's connection with Association Football. Rossall had produced several internationals: W Campbell (Cambridge and Ireland), G P Wilson (England), L I Scott (Ireland), E Mansfield (England), V Edwards (Wales) and H Thwaites (England). There were also many prominent blues one of whom was F H Mugliston who captained a Cambridge side that contained four other Rossallians. Another prominent player was G L Beardsley who kept goal for Corinthians when they beat Manchester United 11 - 3 in 1904.

PLAYING RECORD	
FC Club Founded:	1891
Season joined:	1903/04
Season left:	1913/14
Semi-finalists:	3
Times in Final:	2
Cup Winners:	-

ST EDMUND'S School, Canterbury dates back to 1749 and its foundation as the Clergy Orphan School.

ST EDMUND'S, CANTERBURY OLD BOYS

The St Edmund's Old Boys football team was founded in the early 1980s. Julian Ironside and Mike Green, who were both keen footballers, got together to raise a team specifically to enter the Dunn Cup competition. Mike Green and his brother, Oliver, were already heavily involved in arranging sports fixtures for the school Old Boys, mainly cricket and hockey.

A number of young players were recruited to play alongside the afore-mentioned and the club entered the Dunn in the 1984/85 season. Unfortunately, when the draw was made, St Edmund's first opponents were Lancing Old Boys. At the time, Lancing were having a good run in the competition and St Edmund's were knocked out at the first hurdle (2 - 6).

The following season, the first-round opponents were Old Harrovians and despite the fact that the game was played at Harrow, St Edmund's pulled off their first victory (2 - 1). The success was not followed up however.

They were beaten 6 - 1 by Old Cholmeleians, who were finalists that year.

For a number of years, St Edmund's continued to put together a team for the Arthur Dunn but it was always difficult to get players on a regular basis. So they achieved little success and after a 13 - 1 defeat to Old Haileyburians in 1989/90, the club reluctantly withdrew.

PLAYING RECORD	
FC Club Founded:	1984
Season joined:	1984/85
Season left:	1990/91
Semi-finalists:	-
Times in Final:	-
Cup Winners:	-

SHREWSBURY School was founded in 1551. Under the headmastership of Dr Kennedy, football was restored to Shrewsbury in 1836 and until 1870 was played under Dowling rules. Of course, in 1846, H de Winton and J C Thring, both Old Salopians, while at Cambridge and in the company of two Old Etonians, framed an original set of laws by which some form of standardisation of the various school games could be achieved.

OLD SALOPIANS

Although Salopians played a prominent part in the meetings to discuss a common set of Laws of the Game in the 1850s and 1860s, the origins of the Old Salopian Football Club are somewhat unclear, the club evolving rather than having any clear foundation date. 'Old Salopians' have appeared on the Shrewsbury School fixture list since the School first began to play 'Association Football' in the 1870s and former pupils played a prominent role in the foundation of Shrewsbury Town FC in 1886. Old Boys of the school played in the early years of the FA Cup but mostly for the winning Wanderers sides of the 1870s or for Shropshire Wanderers, rather than for the Old Salopians who scratched on the sole occasion they entered (1876/77).

The 1890s were a golden era for Shrewsbury football, with several Old Boys winning full international caps for England and Wales. Old Salopian football clubs existed at both Oxford and Cambridge Universities and regular matches were played against the School. However, it was the inauguration of the Arthur Dunn Cup in season 1902/03 that brought more organisation to the proceedings with the necessity of bringing together, not just 11 names, but the best available side. It was that first season of Arthur Dunn football, and the two memorable 2 - 2 draws in the final against the Carthusians, which began a Salopian obsession with the tournament that has survived throughout the first 100 years of Arthur Dunn history.

Many legendary stories surround that first final, not least that of the Morgan-Owen brothers, Morgan Maddox

and Hugh, both of whom were selected to play for Wales against Ireland in Belfast on 28th March, the same day as the final. Both brothers had no hesitation in declining the Welsh offer in order to turn out at the Crystal Palace for their old school against the Carthusians. Sadly, however, W J Oakley, Shrewsbury's greatest footballer of the era with 16 England caps, was unable to play in the match, having been forced to retire from the game in 1902 due to a heart condition. Instead, he acted as linesman and, coincidentally, he was later to join the great Carthusian G O Smith, an opponent

G E WILKINSON, CAPTAIN OF OLD SALOPIANS 1903.

M M Morgan-Owen scores for Oxford v Cambridge.

in the first final, in succeeding Arthur Dunn as Headmaster of Ludgrove School.

After such an auspicious start, subsequent Salopian performances in the Cup were disappointing, a 3 - 0 defeat to Malvern in 1909 being the only other appearance in the final until the late 1920s. Shrewsbury was too far for home games, which were played either in London or in Oxford until the 1950s. In 1926, however, the Salopians reached the final again and, although they lost narrowly 3 - 2 to the Malvernians, that disappointment was soon to be forgotten as they began an 11 year period of dominance between 1927 and 1937 during which the Cup was won on five occasions (1927, 1932, 1933, 1935 and 1937) with an additional runners-up position achieved in 1930.

The Salopian side during this period remained remarkably settled. Philip Snow, Alan Barber and Bill Blaxland played in all these finals but the key figure was unquestionably Blaxland, who was master in charge of football at Repton but who still found the time to take on the duties

of secretary of the OSFC and to mastermind the Arthur Dunn triumphs of this era. Both Barber and Blaxland regularly turned out for the Corinthians against Football League clubs and the Salopian half back line of Barber, Blaxland and Ranulph Waye was considered by many to be the key to their strength at this time. Other notable figures were inside forwards John Haslewood and Alan Barlow who both played in all four of the cup winning sides of the 1930s.

Following the Second World War, the Salopians again reached the final in 1949, losing to the Carthusians, before beginning another period of dominance between 1952 and 1955, helped by being able to play home matches at Shrewsbury for the first time. Cup Final victories over the Etonians (1952) and the Wykehamists (1953) were followed by finishing runners-up to the Carthusians in 1954 and then sharing the trophy with Old Brentwoods in 1955 after a remarkable 4 - 4 draw, a match described by The Times as *"quite one of the best and certainly the most exciting of Arthur Dunn Finals"*. The

architect of all these successes was Robin Moulsdale, captain of the outstanding School side of 1946 and now back in Shrewsbury as master in charge of football. Besides scoring seven goals in the three winning Cup Finals, he was the inspiration of the side, both as a scheming inside forward and as the captain and organiser off the field. Henry Oxenham, Miles Robinson, Jeremy Bretherton, Barry Pugh appeared in all three of those winning teams, along with centre forward Dick Rhys, regarded by many as one of the outstanding all-time Salopian footballers. The strength of Salopian football at this time is illustrated by the fact that Ken Shearwood, a regular in the Pegasus side that won the FA Amateur Cup at Wembley in 1951 and 1953, was available to the Salopians in 1952 & 1954.

The late fifties and early sixties were disappointing, with several early exits, but in 1964 Moulsdale was tempted out of retirement for one final Arthur Dunn adventure and it seemed almost inevitable that the Salopians again marched to the final where the Aldenhamians were defeated, Moulsdale typically scoring a trademark goal. In retrospect, however, that 1964 win masked a host of problems and a barren spell followed. The formation of the Arthurian League in London enabled many rivals to field their best teams on a regular basis whilst the Salopians, whose best players have not always lived in the capital, agonised over whether to pick the best players or be loyal to the regular league side which invariably languished outside the Arthurian Premier Division.

One glimmer of hope, an appearance in the 1972 final, was quickly extinguished when a young side that had played well in the earlier rounds went down 1 - 0 to the Old Brentwoods. At times it seemed that the Arthur Dunn Cup success was a thing of the past, a nostalgic memory never to return.

In 1993 David Honychurch was appointed captain. A prolific Arthur Dunn goalscorer over many years, he possessed infectious enthusiasm and made it clear

that he would pick the best players, wherever they came from, and brought down the average age of the side by picking a number of recent school leavers. Above all, he injected belief into the team and a desire to recapture the *"holy grail"*. In his first season in charge, the Salopians reached the final for the first time in 21 years and led the Chigwellians 2 - 0, only to surrender the lead and go down heavily in the replay - but the belief that victory was possible had returned.

The following season saw the Salopians reach the final once again and this time two Honychurch goals brought victory over the Foresters. There were more than a few moist eyes as the Cup returned to Shrewsbury for the first time in 31 years. A defeat in the final by the Foresters in 1998 was followed by victory over the Lancing Old Boys in the 1999 final under Hugh Raven's captaincy. Then Scott Ellis led the Salopians to a thirteenth success, appropriately over the Carthusians, in the

Centenary Final of 2003. Three victories, two further appearances in the final and two in the semi-finals in a period of just 10 years made the period 1994-2003 one to rival the 1930s and 1950s, with Hugh Raven and Rob Cooke achieving the notable distinction of appearing in all five finals during this period.

After the frustration of that 31 year barren spell, the Salopian love affair with the Arthur Dunn Cup has been well and truly restored and looks set to continue long into the tournament's second century.

PLAYING RECORD	
FC Club Founded:	1870s
Season joined:	1902/03
Season left:	-
Semi-finalists:	35
Times in Final:	21
Cup Winners:	13

WELLINGBOROUGH *School was first endowed in 1595 and granted Letters Patent in the reigns of Edward VI and Elizabeth I. The school moved to its present site in 1881.*

OLD WELLINGBURIANS

The first time that a team representing past pupils of the school is recorded was in 1884 when they competed against the School team. However, it was not until 1905 that Old Wellingburians were invited to join the Arthur Dunn Cup. There were a couple of notable wins in early rounds of the competition before the First World War (7 - 3 against Old Salopians in 1912/13 and 10 - 0 over Old Etonians in 1913/14) but they did not reach the later stages.

Between the Wars, there were two semi-final appearances (1922 and 1926) but, throughout this period, the team only played together once or twice per year. After the Second World War, this changed and the team played more frequently, mostly against College sides e.g. Oxford and Cambridge. The founders of this regular side were Garnett Scott (an Old Boy and a teacher at the School) and Sir Ray Whitney, the current Old Wellingburian president. This led to quick success and Wellingburians reached the Arthur Dunn semi-final in 1949, losing to Old Salopians, and progressed to the final in 1951, only to lose to Old Carthusians (4 - 2). The Wellingburian team on that day included John Riley and Leo Edon, an ex-schoolboy international.

Since then, Old Wellingburians have not progressed beyond the second round of the competition although they have achieved these second round appearances after some high-scoring games as follows:

1959/60 8 - 3 v Old Chigwellians
1965/66 6 - 1 v Old Etonians
1993/94 6 - 0 v Old Eastbournians.

In the late 1960s Old Wellingburians joined the Arthurian League and have put up one or two teams ever since.

Among the notable players in the OW team in the post-war period has been Peter Phillips, who was an England Amateur international, and a Cambridge blue scoring the winning goal in the Varsity match three years running. He also played for Luton and Cambridge. Unfortunately, he only played in a few Arthur Dunn matches and some games in the Arthurian League, at the end of his career.

Simon Marriott is notable because he started playing for Old Wellingburians in the 1970s and is still playing. In all, he has played 470 games in the Dunn and the Arthurian League.

PLAYING RECORD	
FC Club Founded:	1905?
Season joined:	1905/06
Season left:	-
Semi-finalists:	4
Times in Final:	1
Cup Winners:	-

WESTMINSTER School has roots as the medieval school of the Benedictine Abbey at Westminster. The modern school has a history dating back to the reforming of the school by Elizabeth I in 1560. The school has a fascinating history and has withstood attacks by a Puritan mob in 1642, Chartist rioters in 1848, and First World War shelling. Its main buildings were sadly destroyed in an air raid in 1941. Many important figures in British history were educated at Westminster. Names that leap from its records include Ben Jonson, Christopher Wren, John Dryden, Edward Gibbon and Jeremy Bentham. Amongst more recent former pupils are John Gielgud, Tony Benn, Adrian Boult, Norman Parkinson, Peter Ustinov, Nigel Lawson and Andrew Lloyd-Webber.

OLD WESTMINSTERS

The Old Westminster's Football club was founded in 1880 when it was decided that a team should be entered into the FA Cup which had started in 1871 with the first final being played in 1872. The Old Westminsters entered the FA Cup in 1882/83 and played in it until 1891/92, their best season was in 1886/87 when they reached the sixth round (quarter-finals) when they lost 5 - 1 to Glasgow Rangers. This was the last season Scottish clubs played in the competition.

Before the Club was formed Old Westminsters Boys had been playing for other teams in the FA Cup. Robert Vidal played in the first three FA Cup Finals, for The Wanderers when they won the first FA Cup Final in 1872. He was still at school that year and as far as can be ascertained, he is the only player to have won a FA Cup winners medal while still at school. Also for Oxford University in 1873 when they lost to The Wanderers and again for Oxford

University when they won in 1874.

In the 1874 FA Cup Final two other Old Westminsters were playing, the Rawson brothers, but played on opposing sides. W S Rawson played for Oxford University and H E Rawson played for the Royal Engineers. This is possibly the only time when two brothers have played against each other in the FA Cup Final.

In these early days of Association Football the Old Westminsters provided a good number of English Internationals the

more distinguished ones being R W Vidal, N C Bailey, H E and W S Rawson, R T Squire, who later became President of the Arthur Dunn Cup committee, J G Veitch, W R Moon and possible the finest Old Westminster of that generation was S S Harris who captained Cambridge University in 1903/04 and played six times for England between 1904-1906, three of these caps were against Scotland in 1904/05/06, by which time the game was dominated by the professional players.

R T Squire represented the Old Westminsters at the inaugural meeting of the Arthur Dunn Cup competition in 1902 and the Old Westminsters were one of the original fourteen sides, which entered the competition. R T Squire was President of The Arthur Dunn Cup Committee between 1929 until his death in 1944.

The Old Westminsters did not achieve great success in the competition and the only notable event was S S Harris scoring six goals against the Old Radleians in 1906.

Their first period of success came in the 1920s when they reached the semi-finals in 1923 and 1924. In 1925 they reached the final for their only appearance.

One of their players was R G H Lowe,

W S RAWSON IN 1877.

OLD WESTMINSTERS' FOOTBALL CLUB, 1920-21.

DAVID ROY
OLD WESTMINSTER

David Roy was an ever-present member of the Old Westminsters team from 1961 to 1975.
A nippy little winger, he was the scourge of defences in the Dunn. One of his adversaries during these years (Jeremy Tomlinson) remarked: "No-one has done more for Dunn football than David - a skillful, bustling player who had one knee or the other bandaged throughout his career - Was it always the same bandage?".

WESTMINSTER'S THIRD GOAL, SCORED BY D A ROY (CENTRE BACKGROUND) IN A 4 - 1 WIN OVER CHARTERHOUSE IN 1960.

who played for Cambridge University for four years from 1923-1926 and gained one Amateur International Cap against Scotland in 1927.

In the nineteen thirties the club reached the semi-finals of the Dunn in 1931, 1933 and 1935.

Another successful period was the late 1950s when they again reached the semi-finals of the Dunn in 1958 and 59, and in 1958 they reached the final of the AFA Surrey Senior Cup where they drew 2 - 2 with Carshalton and therefore shared the trophy.

The only other times that they have reached the semi-finals of the competition were in 1969 where the side was based on the successful school side of the late 1950s and early 60s, in 1984 when the side included Simon Craft who played for Oxford University in 1984 and 1985, and in more recent times in 2001 under the leadership of Nadar Fatemi.

PLAYING RECORD	
FC Club Founded:	1880
Season joined:	1902/03
Season left:	-
Semi-finalists:	11
Times in Final:	1
Cup Winners:	-

KING EDWARD'S School, Witley has its origins in the presentation of Bridewell Palace to the Lord Mayor and Commonalty of London by King Edward VI in 1553. This building had by this time become 'a wide, large, empty house... which would wonderfully serve to lodge Christ in'. The resultant foundation created the Bridewell Royal Hospital, and subsequently the School, which it still supports. Football has been played at King Edward's School, Witley since the 1880s. For fifty years, the School has possessed a first XI pitch whose surface is a delight to play on. In the early years, the first XI played matches against teams from local villages and from regiments stationed in the Aldershot area, teams travelling by horse-drawn brake or on foot against very local opposition.

OLD WITLEIANS

Before the formation of an Old Boys Football Club, the Old Boys had played friendly matches against opposition in the London area. They then became members of the London League before joining the Old Boys League in 1912. In the latter, they played as the Old Edwardians FC. The 1913/14 season, the last before young men volunteered for more serious business, was a good one for the young club. Alleyn's OBs were twice beaten by eight goals and Old Westminster Citizens were beaten 7 - 5 in a remarkable game. The Old Edwardians'

talents extended off the field into organising social evenings which drew attendances of about a hundred. At these Smoking Concerts, as there were termed, a number of Old Boys displayed a diversity of musical talents.

After the First World War, the Old Boys played only occasional friendly matches, although a number in the 1920s and 1930s adorned the ranks of senior amateur clubs such as Dulwich Hamlet. In 1952, the School became co-educational and soon after the Old Witleians Association succeeded the KES OBA. Several OWs played for Corinthian-Casuals, Chris Swain having the distinction of keeping goal

against the Arsenal in a Sheriff of London Shield Match. Another outstanding player, Harry Houghton, who had played for the Army, became a professional with Birmingham City and Oxford United. Since the 1960s KES has been represented in a number of Independent Schools' XIs. School colours: Oxford and Cambridge blue stripes.

In the 1980s, largely due to the enthusiasm of Philip Oakley and Paul Whittle, Old Witleians began to arrange regular fixtures in the London area and in season 1987/88 were highly honoured when they were invited to join the Arthurian League. This was followed in 1990 by an invitation to join the Arthur Dunn Cup competition. So far, their best showing has been three appearances in the second round, 1994/95, 1996/97 and in 2000/01 when they defeated the holders, Lancing Old Boys 2 - 0 in the first round.

PLAYING RECORD	
FC Club Founded:	1912
Season joined:	1990/91
Season left:	-
Semi-finalists:	-
Times in Final:	-
Cup Winners:	-

OLD WYKEHAMISTS

The possibility of the formation of an Old Wykehamist football team was discussed as early as 1876, not long after the establishment of the Old Wykehamist Club.

When the Arthur Dunn Cup began in 1902, Old Wykehamists FC were invited to join the other teams in the draw for the inaugural season. Some concern was expressed at the team's lack of success, blamed mainly on the inability of players to travel to games at distant locations. One correspondent in the Wykehamist noted that *"an absolutely unrepresentative team went down to Brighton and suffered defeat at the hands of the Old Brightonians by 5 - 0".*

The suggested solution was an annual subscription to provide for the payment of travelling expenses.

But success in the Arthur Dunn did not come too soon. Wykehamists did manage to reach the final in 1908 and two consecutive semi-finals in 1909 and 1910, but their first victory came in 1920. The critical difference was the arrival on the scene of a clutch of talented players, notably M Woosnam and Claude Ashton, who both gained full England caps in 1922 and 1926 respectively. Woosnam played many times for Manchester City as captain and centre-half and was an especially talented games player. When Claude Ashton and his two brothers, Hubert and Gilbert, were all together in the same

Cambridge team of 1920, the University side earned itself the nickname of *"Ashton Villa".*

With Claude Ashton particularly, a string of successes were soon to follow. After a runner-up spot in 1928, Wykehamists won the Arthur Dunn three times in a row (1929-31). They also reached the final again in 1934 and 1935, and in 1938 it was only a strong Old Malvernian team that prevented Wykehamists from winning the trophy outright (a tied game resulted in the Cup being shared).

After the Second World War, a new generation of stars, like H A Pawson, G H G Doggart and R P Hornby, took up the mantle and it led to immediate success. Wykehamists won the final of 1948 and again in 1950, to be followed by defeat in the finals of 1953 and 1956. Another glorious victory in 1961 has been followed by a dearth. Since then, Wykehamists have reached the semi-final stage just three times in 1977, 1990 and 1999.

PLAYING RECORD	
FC Club Founded:	1876
Season joined:	1902/03
Season left:	-
Semi-finalists:	24
Times in Final:	14
Cup Winners:	8

March. 12. 1902

An informal meeting of Old Boys interested in Amateur Football was held at the Sports Club on Wednesday March 12th 1902, at which most of the undermentioned Schools were represented, and the following resolutions were passed.

(1) That in the opinion of this meeting an annual competition under Association Football Rules, in the form of a cup contest, confined to the representatives of the chief public Schools. is desirable.

(2) That a trophy, to be called "The Arthur Dunn Memorial Cup" or by some such title, be provided for competition, to be held by the winners for one year.

(3) That the following schools be invited to appoint one representative to act on the general Committee :

Bradfield	Forest School	Repton
Brighton	Harrow	Rossall
Charterhouse	Lancing	Shrewsbury
Eton	Malvern	Westminster
Felsted	Radley	Winchester

N.B. The competition to be for the 'Old Boy' teams of the above schools.

Mr N. Malcolmson, hon.sec. of Old Etonians F.C was elected to the post of honorary secretary to the competition pro.tem.

The first meeting of the general Committee was fixed for Thursday. April 3rd.

The representatives present expressed their feelings in favour of the competition being run, so far as circumstances should permit, on the lines of devoting any surplus profit to charity.

THE MINUTES OF THE FIRST MEETING OF THE ARTHUR DUNN CUP COMMITTEE. INSET: THE COVER OF THE MINUTE BOOK.

THE ORIGINAL RULES
OF THE ARTHUR DUNN CUP

1. The Competition shall be called the *"Arthur Dunn Challenge Cup"*.

2. A General Meeting shall be held annually within one month of the Final Tie.

3. The General Meeting shall consist of one representative appointed by each of the Clubs competing during the previous season, together with the President, who shall be elected by the representatives, and the Committee. No member of such meeting shall be entitled to more than one vote.

4. The entire control and management of the Competition shall be vested in a Committee, limited to nine, consisting of the Secretary and not less than five others.

5. The Committee need not necessarily be elected from among the representatives mentioned in Rule 3.

6. Two members of the Committee shall retire annually in rotation, but shall be eligible for re-election at the General Meeting.

7. The Committee shall have power to fill up any vacancy in their number which may occur during the year, subject to confirmation at the next General Meeting.

8. Upon the requisition in writing of six representatives, the Secretary shall call a General Meeting, to be held within three weeks from the receipt of such requisition. At such Meeting any decision of the Committee may be reversed or amended by a three-fourths majority of those present.

9. The Competition shall be open to all Clubs consisting exclusively of past members of any one Public School which may be annually invited to compete by the Committee.

10. The invitations to compete shall be sent out on or before the end of January in every year. The Entrance Fee shall be Two Guineas, and shall be payable immediately on accepting, acceptance must be made at once.

11. The accepting Clubs shall be drawn by lot in couples.

12. Unless otherwise mutually arranged, the Club which is in each instance first drawn shall have choice of ground. In the case of replayed ties, the Club had not choice of ground in the first instance, shall have choice of ground for the replayed tie.

13. The competing Clubs may agree upon a referee. If, however, they should be unable to agree upon a referee, they shall apply to the Hon. Secretary six clear days before the match, to appoint one. Each Club may appoint a linesman.

14. The duration of each tie shall be one hour and a half, or such shorter period not less than one hour as the competing Clubs may agree upon. Extra time of not less than twenty minutes shall be played in the case of all drawn ties.

15. The Secretary of the winning Club shall send written notice of the result of each tie, with names and initials of the players of the winning Club, to the Hon. Secretary within three days of the tie, Sundays not included.

16. Where the colours of two competing Clubs are similar the home team must make a change.

17. The final tie shall be played on such ground as the Committee may determine.

18. Any matters not provided for by, and any alteration or addition to the foregoing rules, shall be decided by the Committee, whose decisions shall be accepted as final by all Clubs and players taking part in the Competition.

THE ARTHUR DUNN CUP FINALS

Year	Date		Venue	Finalists			
1903	28th March	at	Crystal Palace	Old Carthusians	2	Old Salopians	2
Replay	1st April	at	Ealing F.C.	Old Carthusians	2	Old Salopians	2
1904	19th March	at	Queens Club	Old Carthusians	2	Old Rossallians	0
1905	8th April	at	Queens Club	Old Carthusians	2	Old Reptonians	0
1906	31st March	at	Queens Club	Old Carthusians	2	Old Reptonians	0
1907	23rd March	at	Queens Club	Old Reptonians	4	Old Brightonians	1
1908	4th April	at	Queens Club	Old Carthusians	2	Old Wykehamists	1
1909	31st March	at	Leyton	Old Malvernians	3	Old Salopians	0
1910	9th April	at	Weybridge F.C.	Old Carthusians	2	Old Rossallians	1
1911	1st April	at	Ealing F.C.	Old Reptonians	1	Old Carthusians	0
1912	30th March	at	Merton	Old Malvernians	4	Old Reptonians	1
1913	5th April	at	Twickenham	Old Brightonians	2	Old Aldenhamians	1
1914	28th March	at	Merton	Old Reptonians	3	Old Cholmeleians	0
1920	17th April	at	Queens Club	Old Wykehamists	4	Old Malvernians	0
1921	12th March	at	Queens Club	Old Carthusians	2	Old Aldenhamians	0
1922	1st April	at	Leyton	Old Carthusians	2	Old Aldenhamians	1
1923	24th March	at	Spotted Dog, Forest Gate	Old Carthusians	5	Old Malvernians	1
1924	15th March	at	Crystal Palace	Old Malvernians	2	Old Reptonians	0
1925	4th April	at	Crystal Palace	Old Malvernians	3	Old Westminsters	0
1926	27th March	at	Crystal Palace	Old Malvernians	3	Old Salopians	2
1927	2nd April	at	Crystal Palace	Old Salopians	6	Old Malvernians	3
1928	31st March	at	Crystal Palace	Old Malvernians	3	Old Wykehamists	2
1929	13th April	at	Crystal Palace	Old Wykehamists	3	Old Carthusians	0
1930	29th March	at	Crystal Palace	Old Wykehamists	4	Old Salopians	1
1931	28th March	at	Crystal Palace	Old Wykehamists	5	Old Citizens	1
1932	2nd April	at	Crystal Palace	Old Salopians	6	Old Reptonians	1
1933	1st April	at	Crystal Palace	Old Salopians	3	Old Cholmeleians	1
1934	14th April	at	Crystal Palace	Old Aldenhamians	6	Old Wykehamists	2
1935	6th April	at	Crystal Palace	Old Salopians	3	Old Wykehamists	0
1936	28th March	at	Crystal Palace	Old Carthusians	2	Old Bradfieldians	0
1937	20th March	at	Hurlingham Club	Old Salopians	4	Old Bradfieldians	1
1938	26th March	at	Hurlingham Club	Old Wykehamists	2	Old Malvernians	2
1939	25th March	at	Hurlingham Club	Old Carthusians	2	Old Cholmeleians	1
1947	12th April	at	Lloyds Bank, Beckenham	Old Carthusians	3	Old Reptonians	1
1948	3rd April	at	Tooting & Mitcham	Old Wykehamists	5	Old Cholmeleians	1
1949	2nd April	at	Tooting & Mitcham	Old Carthusians	2	Old Salopians	0
1950	1st April	at	Tooting & Mitcham	Old Wykehamists	3	Old Carthusians	1
1951	31st March	at	Tooting & Mitcham	Old Carthusians	4	Old Wellingburians	2
1952	5th April	at	Tooting & Mitcham	Old Salopians	6	Old Etonians	1
1953	28th March	at	Tooting & Mitcham	Old Salopians	3	Old Wykehamists	1
1954	3rd April	at	Tooting & Mitcham	Old Carthusians	2	Old Salopians	0
1955	26th March	at	Tooting & Mitcham	Old Brentwoods	4	Old Salopians	4
1956	24th March	at	Tooting & Mitcham	Old Malvernians	3	Old Wykehamists	2
1957	23rd March	at	Wimbledon	Old Malvernians	3	Old Reptonians	1
1958	29th March	at	Wimbledon	Old Cholmeleians	2	Old Reptonians	0
1959	18th April	at	Wimbledon	Old Cholmeleians	3	Old Brentwoods	1

Year	Date		Venue	Finalists			
1960	26th March	at	Wealdstone	Old Reptonians	3	Old Malvernians	2
1961	15th April	at	Wealdstone	Old Wykehamists	4	Old Cholmeleians	2
1962	7th April	at	Wealdstone	Old Carthusians	2	Old Malvernians	1
1963	20th April	at	Bank of England	Old Reptonians	4	Old Malvernians	0
1964	11th April	at	Highgate School	Old Salopians	4	Old Aldenhamians	1
1965	27th March	at	Crystal Palace	Old Malvernians	2	Old Reptonians	1
1966	2nd April	at	Crystal Palace	Old Reptonians	4	Old Malvernians	3
1967	1st April	at	Crystal Palace	Old Brentwoods	3	Old Malvernians	2
1968	6th April	at	Crystal Palace	Old Malvernians	1	Old Reptonians	1
1969	29th March	at	Crystal Palace	Old Malvernians	1	Old Bradfieldians	0
1970	4th April	at	Crystal Palace	Old Reptonians	2	Old Foresters	1
1971	3rd April	at	Crystal Palace	Old Malvernians	4	Old Brentwoods	2
1972	8th April	at	Crystal Palace	Old Brentwoods	1	Old Salopians	0
1973	7th April	at	Crystal Palace	Old Brentwoods	3	Old Malvernians	2
1974	6th April	at	Crystal Palace	Old Foresters	2	Old Brentwoods	1
1975	5th April	at	Crystal Palace	Old Malvernians	2	Old Foresters	1
1976	10th April	at	Crystal Palace	Old Malvernians	5	Old Brentwoods	3
1977	2nd April	at	Crystal Palace	Old Carthusians	3	Old Brentwoods	0
1978	8th April	at	Crystal Palace	Old Malvernians	4	Old Bradfieldians	1
1979	7th April	at	Crystal Palace	Old Aldenhamians	1	Old Brentwoods	0
1980	12th April	at	Crystal Palace	Old Chigwellians	4	Lancing Old Boys	2
1981	11th April	at	Crystal Palace	Old Reptonians	3	Old Malvernians	3
Replay	15th April	at	Crystal Palace	Old Reptonians	1	Old Malvernians	0
1982	3rd April	at	Dulwich Hamlet	Old Carthusians	3	Old Malvernians	0
1983	16th April	at	Dulwich Hamlet	Lancing Old Boys	2	Old Chigwellians	0
1984	7th April	at	Dulwich Hamlet	Lancing Old Boys	2	Old Carthusians	0
1985	13th April	at	Dulwich Hamlet	Lancing Old Boys	5	Old Foresters	0
1986	12th April	at	Dulwich Hamlet	Old Brentwoods	1	Old Cholmeleians	0
1987	4th April	at	Motspur Park	Old Reptonians	2	Old Cholmeleians	2
Replay	4th May	at	Motspur Park	Old Reptonians	3	Old Cholmeleians	2
1988	9th April	at	Motspur Park	Old Cholmeleians	2	Old Brentwoods	1
1989	8th April	at	Motspur Park	Old Malvernians	3	Old Brentwoods	1
1990	7th April	at	Motspur Park	Old Chigwellians	1	Old Reptonians	1
Replay	5th May	at	Motspur Park	Old Chigwellians	3	Old Reptonians	2
1991	6th April	at	Motspur Park	Old Reptonians	1	Old Carthusians	1
Replay	20th April	at	Motspur Park	Old Reptonians	4	Old Carthusians	0
1992	4th April	at	Motspur Park	Old Chigwellians	3	Old Etonians	1
1993	3rd April	at	Motspur Park	Lancing Old Boys	1	Old Reptonians	0
1994	9th April	at	Motspur Park	Old Chigwellians	2	Old Salopians	2
Replay	23rd April	at	Motspur Park	Old Chigwellians	5	Old Salopians	1
1995	1st April	at	Motspur Park	Old Salopians	2	Old Foresters	1
1996	13th April	at	Motspur Park	Lancing Old Boys	4	Old Brentwoods	1
1997	5th April	at	Motspur Park	Old Foresters	3	Old Salopians	1
1998	4th April	at	Motspur Park	Old Foresters	3	Old Brentwoods	1
1999	10th April	at	Motspur Park	Old Salopians	3	Lancing Old Boys	1
2000	29th April	at	Motspur Park	Lancing Old Boys	3	Old Foresters	0
2001	7th April	at	Cobham	Old Carthusians	4	Old Bradfieldians	1
2002	6th April	at	Cobham	Old Chigwellians	2	Old Reptonians	0
2003	5th April	at	Cobham	Old Salopians	2	Old Carthusians	1

RESULTS AND ANALYSIS

The following pages list the results for each season over the last 100 years,
they show each stage of the competition, and detail each final, its location and
the goal-scorers. These are followed by the clubs playing record, analyses
of the results, plus some interesting facts and figures.

SALOPIANS
ARE RALLIED BY
MOULSDALE

FORESTERS DENY
BRENTWOODS IN
EXTRA TIME

MALVERNIANS
UNBRIDLED FURY

CHIGWELLIANS
MAKE HISTORY

WESTMINSTERS
FIND BEST FORM

CARTHUSIANS
INSPIRED BY TANNER

LANCING SCORE
5 IN 15 MINUTES

HARROVIANS
PROVE A POINT

CHOLMELEIANS
DOUBLE SAVER

REPTONIANS IN
STERN TUSSLE

ALDENHAMIANS
UPSET THE
FORM BOOK

METAXA BOYS
BOOST ETON

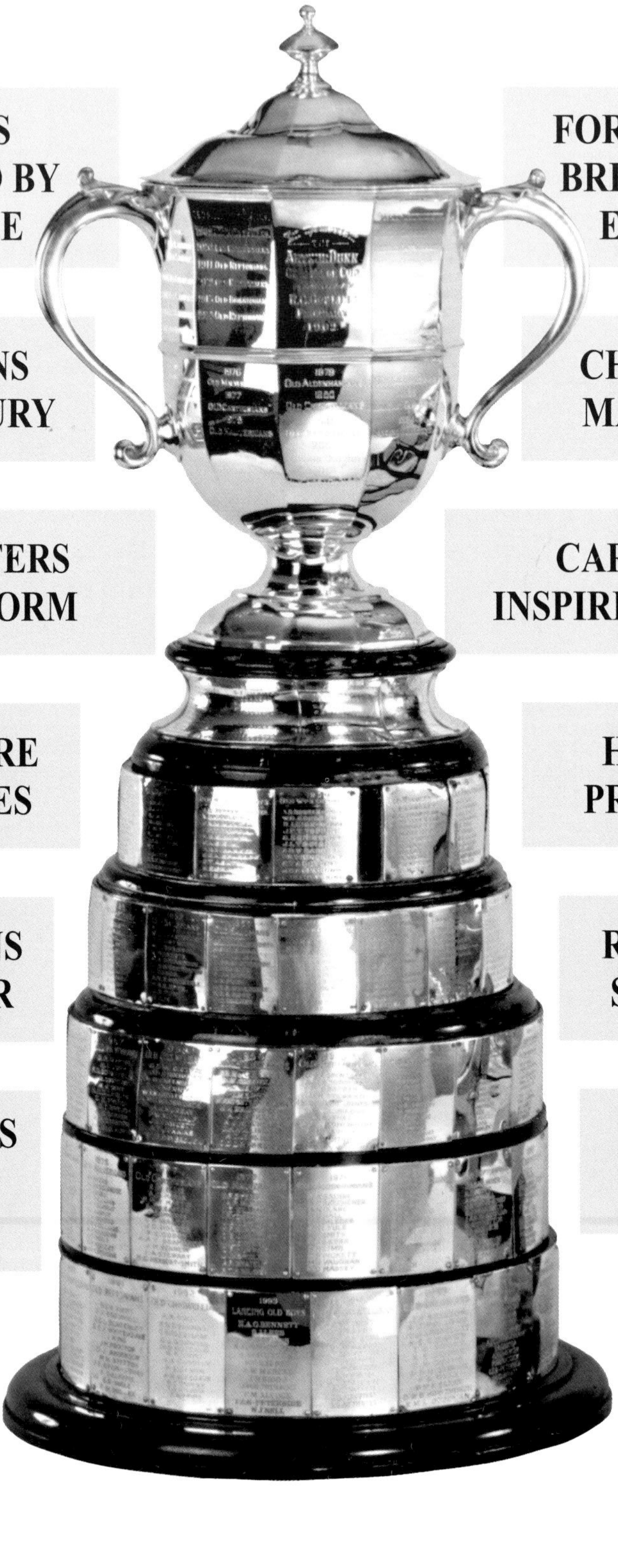

SEASON 1904 - 1905

SECOND ROUND	THIRD ROUND	SEMI FINAL	FINAL	WINNERS
Old Reptonians / Old Brightonians	Reptonians 7-1	Reptonians 4-0	Reptonians 5-3	
Old Etonians / Lancing Old Boys	Etonians 4-1			
Old Johnians / Old Felstedians	Johnians 5-0	Johnians 4-0		Carthusians 2-0
Old Wykehamists / Old Harrovians	Wykehamists 10-0			G O Smith, Vassall
Old Carthusians / Old Foresters	Carthusians 11-2	Carthusians 5-0	Carthusians 4-2	
Old Cholmeleians / Old Citizens	Cholmeleians 0-0, 4-0			
Old Malvernians / Old Salopians	Malvernians 3-0	Malvernians 7-2		
Old Rossallians / Old Cranleighans	Rossallians 2-0			

Played at Queens Club

FIRST ROUND   Old Carthusians 4 Bradfield Waifs 0, Old Malvernians 10 Old Westminsters 1

OLD CARTHUSIANS Winners 1905 - T S Rowlandson, I G Witherington, W U Timmis, W J H Curwen, C Wreford-Brown, O T Norris, G C Vassall, W F H Stanbrough, G O Smith, C F Ryder, W W Bruce.

OLD REPTONIANS Runners up 1905 - P Musker, F C V Smith, Rev. W Blackburn, R W D Wallis, T H Hughes, H Vickers, R E Hounsfield, F H Bryant, G S Harris, A H Birks, R A Young.

SEASON 1905 - 1906

SECOND ROUND	THIRD ROUND	SEMI FINAL	FINAL	WINNERS
Old Carthusians / Old Cranleighans	Carthusians 4-1	Carthusians 3-3, 3-0	Carthusians 1-0	
Old Westminsters / Old Foresters	Westminsters 7-1			
Old Aldenhamians / Old Citizens	Aldenhamians 6-1	Aldenhamians 6-0		Bence-Pembroke, Trechmann
Old Wykehamists / Lancing Old Boys	Wykehamists 3-1			Carthusians 2-0
Old Reptonians / Old Brightonians	Reptonians 8-0	Reptonians 3-0	Reptonians 7-1	
Old Wellingburians / Old Harrovians	Wellingburians 2-1			
Old Cholmeleians / Old Johnians	Cholmeleians 2-1	Cholmeleians 2-1		
Old Rossallians / Old Felstedians	Felstedians 4-1			

Played at Queens Club

FIRST ROUND   Old Carthusians 4 Old Malvernians 1, Old Cranleighans 2 Old Etonians 1, Old Westminsters 1 Old Salopians 0, Old Aldenhamians 2 Bradfield Waifs 1.

OLD CARTHUSIANS Winners 1906 - T S Rowlandson, W U Timmis, J C D Tetley, B Tuff, D Grahame, W J H Curwen, R A Bence-Pembroke, R H Allen, O L Trechmann, I E Snell, G C Vassall.

OLD REPTONIANS Runners up 1906 - F C Johnson, A S Bright, Rev. W Blackburn, F J Seedorff, E W Page, H Vickers, E R Hussey, F H Bryant, G S Harris, A H Birks, R A Young.

INAUGURAL SEASON 1902 - 1903

FIRST ROUND	SECOND ROUND	SEMI FINAL	FINAL	WINNERS
Bradfield Waifs (a bye)	Bradfield Waifs	Brightonians 6-1	Salopians 7-2	Edwards, H Morgan-Owen (R): C W Alexander, H Morgan-Owen
Old Brightonians / Old Wykehamists	Brightonians 5-0			
Old Malvernians (a bye)	Malvernians	Salopians 3-0		2-2 aet, and Replay Salopians drew with Carthusians (Cup held jointly).
Old Salopians / Old Harrovians	Salopians 7-0			
Old Reptonians / Old Westminsters	Reptonians 7-1	Reptonians 7-1	Carthusians 5-2	Haig-Brown, C F Ryder (R): G O Smith (2)
Old Etonians / Old Foresters	Etonians 4-1			
Old Carthusians / Lancing Old Boys	Carthusians 3-0	Carthusians 0-0, 3-1		
Old Felstedians / Old Rossallians	Felstedians w/o			

Played at Crystal Palace (Replay at Ealing FC)

OLD SALOPIANS Joint Winners 1903 - P Johnson, C L Alexander, J D Craig, J S D Rider, H N Edwards, H Morgan-Owen, H A Lowe, M M Morgan-Owen, G E Wilkinson, C W Alexander, S Evans.

OLD CARTHUSIANS Joint Winners 1903 - O T Norris, C H Wild, C F Ryder, A R Haig-Brown, T S Rowlandson, O E Wreford-Brown, W U Timmis, W F H Stanbrough, G O Smith, C Wreford-Brown, M H Stanbrough.

SEASON 1903 - 1904

FIRST ROUND	SECOND ROUND	SEMI FINAL	FINAL	WINNERS
Old Carthusians / Old Cholmeleians	Carthusians 4-1	Carthusians 2-0	Carthusians 5-0	
Old Salopians / Old Westminsters	Salopians 4-0			
Old Reptonians / Old Wykehamists	Reptonians 2-0	Reptonians 8-1		G O Smith (2)
Old Brightonians / Old Harrovians	Brightonians 2-1			Carthusians 2-0
Old Rossallians / Bradfield Waifs	Rossallians 4-2	Rossallians 4-2	Rossallians 4-3	
Old Cranleighans / Old Felstedians	Cranleighans 2-2, 3-0			
Old Malvernians / Lancing Old Boys	Malvernians 9-2	Malvernians 5-1		
Old Etonians / Old Foresters	Etonians 2-1			

Played at Queens Club

OLD CARTHUSIANS Winners 1904 - T S Rowlandson, O T Norris, W U Timmis, C H Wild, C Wreford-Brown, O E Wreford-Brown, A R Haig-Brown, W F H Stanbrough, G O Smith, C F Ryder, M H Stanbrough.

OLD ROSSALLIANS Runners up 1904 - G L Beardsley, A W Roberts, P P Burgess, C L Stocks, H E Beardsley, H Thwaites, H W Carrington, F B Roberts, G P Wilson, E W Moore, L Taylor.

SEASON 1908 - 1909

SECOND ROUND	THIRD ROUND	SEMI FINAL	FINAL	WINNERS
Old Malvernians / Old Westminsters	Malvernians 3-0	Malvernians 12-0		
Old Cranleighans / Old Cholmeleians	Cranleighans 3-1			
Old Carthusians / Old Etonians	Carthusians 7-2	Carthusians 11-1	Malvernians 2-1	
Old Wellingburians / Old Rossallians	Wellingburians 3-3, w/o			S H Day (2), Napier — **Malvernians 3-0**
Old Salopians / Old Berkhamstedians	Salopians 5-1	Salopians 5-0		*Played at Leyton*
Old Johnians / Lancing Old Boys	Johnians 2-0		Salopians 3-1	
Old Wykehamists / Old Reptonians	Wykehamists 4-2	Wykehamists 4-1		
Old Aldenhamians / Old Foresters	Aldenhamians 2-1			

FIRST ROUND Old Cranleighans w/o Old Radleians, Old Cholmeleians 3 Old Albanians 1, Old Salopians w/o Old Ipswichians, Old Berkhamstedians 3 Old Harrovians 1, Lancing Old Boys 1, 2 Old Bradfieldians 1, 1, Old Wykehamists 1, 2 Old Citizens 1, 1, Old Reptonians 2, 4 Old Felstedians 2, 2, Old Aldenhamians 6 Old Brightonians 3

OLD MALVERNIANS Winners 1909 - A P Day, C C Page, R N Balfour, F H Hooper, G B Canny, E H Cuthbertson, S E Day, S H Day, B S Foster, W W Lowe, L Napier.

OLD SALOPIANS Runners up 1909 - J A Appleton, R D Owen, F Vachell, R D Craig, M Morgan-Owen, Rev. E M Cooke, J O Hughes, F J Roberts, H Morgan-Owen, F W Roberts, N Wells.

SEASON 1909 - 1910

SECOND ROUND	THIRD ROUND	SEMI FINAL	FINAL	WINNERS
Old Carthusians / Old Westminsters	Carthusians 4-1	Carthusians 2-0.		
Old Aldenhamians / Old Berkhamstedians	Aldenhamians 4-2		Carthusians 5-2	
Old Reptonians / Old Radleians	Reptonians 7-0	Reptonians 4-1		Curwen, Vassall — **Carthusians 2-1** — Crummack
Old Citizens / Old Johnians	Citizens 4-2			*Played at Weybridge FC*
Old Rossallians / Lancing Old Boys	Rossallians 3-2	Rossallians 1-1, 4-0		
Old Cholmeleians / Old Malvernians	Cholmeleians 1-0		Rossallians 3-0	
Old Wykehamists / Old Salopians	Wykehamists 3-1	Wykehamists 3-2		
Old Brightonians / Old Foresters	Brightonians 8-0			

FIRST ROUND Old Westminsters 5 Old Harrovians 0, Old Aldenhamians 4 Old Etonians 2, Old Reptonians 3 Old Bradfieldians 2, Lancing Old Boys 1, 4 Old Ipswichians 1, 1, Old Cholmeleians 1, 3, 3 Old Felstedians 1, 3, 1, Old Malvernians 5 Old Cranleighans 1, Old Brightonians 5 Old Wellingburians 1, Old Foresters 3 Old Albanians 0

OLD CARTHUSIANS Winners 1910 - T S Rowlandson, J C D Tetley, R L L Braddell, Rev. J G Birch, D Grahame, J B Bickersteth, A A Tyler, W J H Curwen, R M Weeks, G C Vassall, L R Burrows.

OLD ROSSALLIANS Runners up 1910 - E H Holmes, F H Mugliston, F W Stevens, R C Cutter, A E Herman, A L F Addie, J Hollingsworth, V Edwards, R W Crummack, P Lancaster, H B Edwards.

SEASON 1906 - 1907

SECOND ROUND	THIRD ROUND	SEMI FINAL	FINAL	WINNERS
Old Reptonians / Old Malvernians	Reptonians 4-1	Reptonians 7-0		
Bradfield Waifs / Old Aldenhamians	Bradfield Waifs 1-0		Reptonians 4-1	
Old Rossallians / Old Salopians	Rossallians 6-3	Rossallians 4-3		Birks (3), Hughes — **Reptonians 4-1** — Hoffmeister
Old Cranleighans / Old Citizens	Cranleighans 3-2			*Played at Queens Club*
Old Brightonians / Old Foresters	Brightonians 3-2	Brightonians 5-4		
Old Carthusians / Old Wykehamists	Carthusians w/o		Brightonians 4-2	
Old Cholmeleians / Old Felstedians	Cholmeleians 3-0	Cholmeleians 4-2		
Old Westminsters / Old Radleians	Westminsters 9-0			

FIRST ROUND Old Aldenhamians 7 Old Harrovians 1, Old Citizens 2 Old Etonians 1, Old Brightonians 5 Lancing Old Boys 3, Old Foresters 4 Old Johnians 0, Old Westminsters 8 Old Wellingburians 1

OLD REPTONIANS Winners 1907 - F Trotter, I C V Smith, A S Bright, H Vickers, T H Hughes, F J Seedorff, R A Young, A H Birks, C S Harris, F H Bryant, T C Davis.

OLD BRIGHTONIANS Runners up 1907 - B W V King, G Belcher, C L A Smith, E C Turner, F L King, A I Carr, H D Wright, C E Hoffmeister, A H Belcher, F P Klinkhardt, S C Hellings.

SEASON 1907 - 1908

SECOND ROUND	THIRD ROUND	SEMI FINAL	FINAL	WINNERS
Old Malvernians / Lancing Old Boys	Malvernians 5-0	Malvernians 3-0		
Old Reptonians / Old Cholmeleians	Reptonians 4-1		Carthusians 2-0	
Old Carthusians / Old Johnians	Carthusians 9-1	Carthusians 2-1		Grahame, Vassall — **Carthusians 2-1** — Pidcock
Old Salopians / Old Rossallians	Salopians 7-1			*Played at Queens Club*
Old Foresters / Old Wellingburians	Foresters 6-0	Foresters 2-1		
Old Citizens / Bradfield Waifs	Citizens 3-0		Wykehamists 3-1	
Old Wykehamists / Old Felstedians	Wykehamists 7-1	Wykehamists 2-0		
Old Aldenhamians / Old Harrovians	Aldenhamians 2-0			

FIRST ROUND Old Reptonians 2 Old Brightonians 1, Old Cholmeleians 1 Old Ipswichians 0, Old Carthusians 13 Old Etonians 0, Old Salopians 9 Old Cranleighans 1, Old Foresters 7 Old Berkhamstedians 0, Old Wellingburians 3 Old Westminsters 1, Old Citizens 7 Old Albanians 0, Bradfield Waifs 0, 7 Old Radleians 0, 0

OLD CARTHUSIANS Winners 1908 - T S Rowlandson, W U Timmis, J C D Tetley, W J H Curwen, D Grahame, I E Snell, C E Deacon, H K Waller, O L Trechmann, B Tuff, G C Vassall.

OLD WYKEHAMISTS Runners up 1908 - G E Fawcus, W J L Wallace, F C Stocks, E L Wright, G K Molineux, H C McDonell, A G L Clarke, S S Jenkyns, E Hain, R G Pidcock, E Benson.

SEASON 1912 - 1913

SECOND ROUND	THIRD ROUND	SEMI FINAL	FINAL	WINNERS
Old Brightonians / Old Foresters	Brightonians 2-2, 10-3	Brightonians 3-1	Brightonians 1-0	
Old Wellingburians / Old Salopians	Wellingburians 7-3			
Old Malvernians / Old Radleians	Malvernians 7-2	Malvernians 5-3		Havelock-Davies, Clarke
Old Felstedians / Old Cholmeleians	Felstedians 6-3			Brightonians 2-1
Old Citizens / Old Westminsters	Citizens 4-3	Citizens 5-2		Deakin
Old Reptonians / Old Berkhamstedians	Reptonians 7-3		Aldenhamians 5-0	*Played at Twickenham*
Old Aldenhamians / Old Albanians	Aldenhamians 7-0	Aldenhamians 6-0		
Old Etonians / Lancing Old Boys	Etonians 1-0			

FIRST ROUND — Old Malvernians 10 Old Johnians 0, Old Radleians 4 Old Cranleighans 1, Old Felstedians 3 Old Rossallians 1, Old Cholmeleians 3 Old Bradfieldians 1, Old Citizens 4 Old Wykehamists 0, Old Westminsters 8 Old Harrovians 0, Old Reptonians 2 Old Carthusians 1, Old Berkhamstedians 9 Old Ipswichians 0

OLD BRIGHTONIANS Winners 1913 - A D Cave, A R G Roberson, G Belcher, G M Dawbarn, W S Ross, L F Dower, A J Murdock, P Havelock-Davies, M H Clarke, C E Hoffmeister, W R Dower.
OLD ALDENHAMIANS Runners up 1913 - E A Brock, C H Gimingham, P C Sainsbury, Rev. E M Hacking, A F White, C F Etheridge, E E A Collisson, E E Paget-Tomlinson, F W H Hirsch, C J K Deakin, W E Goodyear.

SEASON 1913 - 1914

SECOND ROUND	THIRD ROUND	SEMI FINAL	FINAL	WINNERS
Old Reptonians / Old Citizens	Reptonians 5-0	Reptonians 13-0	Reptonians 4-1	
Old Wellingburians / Old Etonians	Wellingburians 10-0			
Old Brightonians / Old Bradfieldians	Brightonians 8-1	Brightonians 4-0		Richardson, Foster (2)
Lancing Old Boys / Old Harrovians	Lancing 3-1			Reptonians 3-0
Old Cholmeleians / Old Malvernians	Cholmeleians 3-3, 3-1	Cholmeleians 2-0		
Old Wykehamists / Old Carthusians	Wykehamists 2-1		Cholmeleians 3-3, 3-0	*Played at Merton*
Old Aldenhamians / Old Felstedians	Aldenhamians 3-0	Aldenhamians 5-4		
Old Cranleighans / Old Radleians	Cranleighans 4-1			

FIRST ROUND — Old Reptonians 8 Old Berkhamstedians 0, Old Citizens 4 Old Johnians 0, Old Etonians 4 Old Foresters 3, Old Brightonians w/o Old Rossallians, Old Cholmeleians 5 Old Westminsters 2, Old Carthusians 1, 2 Old Salopians 1, 1, Old Aldenhamians w/o Old Ipswichians, Old Cranleighans 10 Old Albanians 3

OLD REPTONIANS Winners 1914 - N V C Turner, A M Wilkinson, 1 P F Campbell, R F Popham, A T Sharp, H A Hewitt, E G G Cockburn, M Howell, A W Foster, J N Richardson, R A Young.
OLD CHOLMELEIANS Runners up 1914 - R B Critall, M Rabone, H V Bury, L T Leaver, P C Kay, G D Loup, G S Smith, W G Kay, N J Cox, P R Phillips, H S Maclure.

SEASON 1910 - 1911

SECOND ROUND	THIRD ROUND	SEMI FINAL	FINAL	WINNERS
Old Harrovians / Old Reptonians	Reptonians 3-0	Reptonians 1-0	Reptonians 3-0	
Old Cholmeleians / Old Westminsters	Cholmeleians 1-0			
Old Malvernians / Old Aldenhamians	Malvernians 4-0	Malvernians 2-1		Birks
Old Citizens / Old Foresters	Citizens 3-2			Reptonians 1-0
Old Carthusians / Old Wykehamists	Carthusians 4-0	Carthusians 4-0		
Old Albanians / Old Ipswichians	Albanians 5-4		Carthusians 2-1	*Played at Ealing FC*
Old Salopians / Old Etonians	Salopians 4-0	Salopians 7-1		
Old Brightonians / Old Bradfieldians	Brightonians 5-1			

FIRST ROUND — Old Reptonians 4 Old Berkhamstedians 0, Old Westminsters 5 Old Wellingburians 0, Old Malvernians 5 Old Felstedians 1, Old Aldenhamians 2, 1 w/o Old Cranleighans 2, 1, Old Carthusians 4 Old Rossallians 0, Old Ipswichians 2 Old Radleians 0, Old Citizens 4 Old Johnians 3, Old Brightonians 3 Lancing Old Boys 0

OLD REPTONIANS Winners 1911 - N V C Turner, 1 P F Campbell, A S Bright, L H Lang, A C Kirby, E W Page, A E Cardew, C E Squire, R A Young, A H Birks, C Law.
OLD CARTHUSIANS Runners up 1911 - E R Newman, J C D Tetley, R L L Braddell, S Powell, Rev. J G Birch, R M Weeks, W Steer, W J H Curwen, I K Snell, A A Tyler, R E Norris.

SEASON 1911 - 1912

SECOND ROUND	THIRD ROUND	SEMI FINAL	FINAL	WINNERS
Old Westminsters / Old Malvernians	Malvernians 4-1	Malvernians 7-0	Malvernians 2-0	
Lancing Old Boys / Old Citizens	Lancing 3-1			
Old Cholmeleians / Old Wykehamists	Cholmeleians 6-3	Cholmeleians 6-4		S H Day; S E Day; Vidal (2)
Old Salopians / Old Wellingburians	Salopians w/o			Malvernians 4-1
Old Reptonians / Old Ipswichians	Reptonians w/o	Reptonians 2-1		Young
Old Aldenhamians / Old Rossallians	Aldenhamians 3-1		Reptonians 2-1	*Played at Merton*
Old Cranleighans / Old Foresters	Cranleighans 5-1	Cranleighans 9-1		
Old Etonians / Old Albanians	Etonians 1-1, 2-1			

FIRST ROUND — Old Malvernians 5 Old Brightonians 3, Old Citizens 3 Old Felstedians 1, Old Cholmeleians 5 Old Bradfieldians 1, Old Ipswichians 2 Old Berkhamstedians 0, Old Aldenhamians 4 Old Radleians 1, Old Cranleighans 4 Old Carthusians 3, Old Foresters 4 Old Johnians 1, Old Albanians w/o Old Harrovians

OLD MALVERNIANS Winners 1912 - L E Langley, R G Thompson, J W Stretton, F H Hooper, G N Foster, R C Cross, S E Day, S H Day, L A Vidal, L Simpson, J D Moore.
OLD REPTONIANS Runners up 1912 - N V C Turner, A S Bright, 1 P F Campbell, R F Popham, A C Kirby, E W Page, A E Cardew, C E Squire, R A Young, A H Birks, C Law.

SEASON 1919 - 1920

SECOND ROUND	THIRD ROUND	SEMI FINAL	FINAL	WINNERS
Old Wykehamists / Old Albanians	Wykehamists 4-1			
Old Reptonians / Old Carthusians	Reptonians 2-1	Wykehamists 2-1		
Old Salopians / Old Aldenhamians	Salopians 3-1		Wykehamists 2-0	H Ashton (3), C T Ashton → Wykehamists 4-0
Old Hurst-Johnians / Old Wellingburians	Hurst-Johnians 2-0	Salopians 4-0	*Played at Queens Club*	
Old Malvernians / Old Foresters	Malvernians 8-2			
Old Citizens / Old Bradfieldians	Citizens 3-0	Malvernians 4-2		
Old Cholmeleians / Old Westminsters	Cholmeleians 4-1		Malvernians 5-0	
Old Felstedians / Lancing Old Boys	Felstedians w/o	Cholmeleians 3-1		

FIRST ROUND — Old Albanians w/o Old Ipswichians, Old Hurst-Johnians w/o Old Harrovians, Old Wellingburians w/o Old Cranleighans, Old Foresters w/o Old Brightonians, Old Citizens w/o Old Etonians, Old Felstedians w/o Old Johnians.

OLD WYKEHAMISTS Winners 1920 - D R Jardine, W M Leggatt, G D Huband, A C Stanley-Clarke, M Woosnam, H M Watt, J Toppin, H Ashton, G Ashton, C T Ashton, J E Frazer.

OLD MALVERNIANS Runners up 1920 - A H Hughes, J W Stretton, G N Foster, R T Lee, W C M Berridge, F H Hooper, J D Moore, R J B Brooke, H W Beeson, D J Knight, W C Stuart-Low.

SEASON 1920 - 1921

FIRST ROUND	SECOND ROUND	SEMI FINAL	FINAL	WINNERS
Old Aldenhamians / Old Westminsters	Aldenhamians 5-4			
Old Wykehamists / Old Albanians	Wykehamists 7-2	Aldenhamians 3-2		
Old Malvernians / Old Salopians	Malvernians 5-2		Aldenhamians 2-1	
Old Bradfieldians / Old Foresters	Bradfieldians 3-2	Malvernians 2-1	*Played at Queen's Club*	Carthusians 2-0; J G Williams, Reiss
Old Carthusians / Old Wellingburians	Carthusians 7-2			
Old Cholmeleians / Old Citizens	Cholmeleians 4-1	Carthusians 4-1	Carthusians 3-1	
Old Reptonians / Old Ipswichians	Reptonians 8-1			
Lancing Old Boys / Old Hurst-Johnians	Lancing 4-1	Reptonians 10-2		

OLD CARTHUSIANS Winners 1921 - H C D Whinney, A G Bower, J S F Morrison, P Fraser, A G H Butcher, J Pollock, R T Thorne, J G Williams, P Q Reiss, H R H Williams, R H Whalley.

OLD ALDENHAMIANS Runners up 1921 - G R Stopford, H J Gibbon, P C Sainsbury, F J Heaton, C B J Hunter, P G R Whalley, M Stoner, C R Pollitt, C F Etheridge, W L Nelson, H L Nelson.

SEASON 1921 - 1922

FIRST ROUND	SECOND ROUND	SEMI FINAL	FINAL	WINNERS
Old Carthusians / Old Malvernians	Carthusians 6-2			
Old Reptonians / Old Hurst-Johnians	Reptonians 5-4	Carthusians 6-1		
Old Wellingburians / Old Albanians	Wellingburians 3-1		Carthusians 2-0	H R H Williams, Thorne-Thorne → Carthusians 2-1
Old Foresters / Old Bradfieldians	Bradfieldians 4-2	Wellingburians 5-2		
Lancing Old Boys / Old Westminsters	Westminsters 2-0		*Played at Leyton*	Sainsbury
Old Aldenhamians / Old Harrovians	Aldenhamians 3-0	Aldenhamians 4-1		
Old Wykehamists / Old Salopians	Wykehamists 3-2		Aldenhamians 2-0	
Old Citizens / Old Cholmeleians	Citizens 2-0	Citizens 2-1		

OLD CARTHUSIANS Winners 1922 - H M Ward-Clarke, A G Bower, J S F Morrison, G W Shilcock, B C A Patchitt, P Rucker, R Thorne-Thorne, J G Williams, H R H Williams, B G Bearman, D L M Thompson.

OLD ALDENHAMIANS Runners up 1922 - J R Stopford, H J Gibbon, P C Sainsbury, P J Heaton, G H G Hunter, C F Etheridge, L F Partridge, C R Pollit, E A Hayes, W L Nelson, H L Nelson.

SEASON 1922 - 1923

FIRST ROUND	SECOND ROUND	SEMI FINAL	FINAL	WINNERS
Old Wykehamists / Old Foresters	Wykehamists 7-2			
Old Malvernians / Old Hurst-Johnians	Malvernians 3-2	Malvernians 4-0		
Old Cholmeleians / Old Albanians	Cholmeleians 5-1		Malvernians 1-0	N E Partridge
Old Aldenhamians / Old Bradfieldians	Bradfieldians 1-0	Bradfieldians 2-0		
Lancing Old Boys / Old Wellingburians	Wellingburians 3-2		*Played at Spotted Dog Forest Gate*	Carthusians 5-1; H R H Williams (3), J G Williams, Bearman
Old Carthusians / Old Reptonians	Carthusians 2-1	Carthusians 3-1	Carthusians 6-0	
Old Citizens / Old Harrovians	Citizens 5-0			
Old Westminsters / Old Salopians	Westminsters 3-2	Westminsters 1-0		

OLD CARTHUSIANS Winners 1923 - H M Ward-Clarke, A G Bower, J S F Morrison, F E Powell, B C A Patchitt, G Shilcock, I A W Gilliat, J G Williams, H R H Williams, R H Whalley, B G Bearman.

OLD MALVERNIANS Runners up 1923 - R A Parry, H A Pridham, R A Orchard, R T Lee, N W Beeson, R N Stone, W C Stuart-Low, D M Smith, G B Partridge, N E Partridge, W Marlow.

SEASON 1925 - 1926

FIRST ROUND	SECOND ROUND	SEMI FINAL	FINAL	WINNERS
Old Harrovians / Old Reptonians	Harrovians 4-2	Malvernians 4-2	Malvernians 5-3	Partridge, Robson, Holmes
Old Malvernians / Old Bradfieldians	Malvernians 6-5			
Lancing Old Boys / Old Aldenhamians	Aldenhamians 4-3	Wykehamists 3-2		
Old Wykehamists / Old Westminsters	Wykehamists 7-3			
Old Salopians / Old Cholmeleians	Salopians ?	Salopians 2-1	Salopians 3-2	
Old Citizens / Old Hurst-Johnians	Hurst-Johnians 4-2			
Old Foresters / Old Wellingburians	Wellingburians 10-0	Wellingburians 6-1		
Old Carthusians (a bye)	Carthusians			

Malvernians 3-2 — Watson, Lewis
Played at Crystal Palace

OLD MALVERNIANS Winners 1926 - W R T Picton-Warlow, H A Pridham, E R T Holmes, C G W Robson, T B G Welch, D B Campbell, R N Stone, C F Morice, W C Stuart-Low, G L Miller, G B Partridge.

OLD SALOPIANS Runners up 1926 - J D Deuchar, R Heslop, L A B Morris, R C Lancaster, L B Blaxland, A T Barber, J M Peterson, L Band, H G Lewis, G S Watson, J T Bush.

SEASON 1926 - 1927

FIRST ROUND	SECOND ROUND	SEMI FINAL	FINAL	WINNERS
Old Malvernians / Old Hurst-Johnians	Malvernians 5-1	Malvernians 3-2	Malvernians 4-2	Picton-Warlow, Robson, Fielden
Old Reptonians / Old Foresters	Reptonians 10-5			
Old Cholmeleians / Lancing Old Boys	Cholmeleians 5-1	Cholmeleians 4-3		
Old Bradfieldians / Old Etonians	Bradfieldians w/o			
Old Westminsters / Old Wykehamists	Wykehamists 5-1	Aldenhamians 1-0	Salopians 2-1	
Old Harrovians / Old Aldenhamians	Aldenhamians 4-0			
Old Citizens / Old Wellingburians	Wellingburians 5-0	Salopians 3-0		
Old Salopians / Old Carthusians	Salopians 3-2			

Salopians (2-2), 6-3 aet — Lewis, Peterson, Bush, Newton (3)
Played at Crystal Palace

OLD SALOPIANS Winners 1927 - J D Deuchar, P S Snow, R Heslop, R C Lancaster, L B Blaxland, A T Barber, J M Peterson, H V Newton, H G Lewis, G S Watson, J T Bush.

OLD MALVERNIANS Runners up 1927 - J H Mears, I Begbie, G L Miller, R N Stone, N W Beeson, S S Fielden, H C D Abrams, C G Toppin, G B Partridge, C G W Robson, W R T Picton-Warlow.

SEASON 1923 - 1924

FIRST ROUND	SECOND ROUND	SEMI FINAL	FINAL	WINNERS
Lancing Old Boys / Old Foresters	Lancing 8-1	Westminsters 2-1	Reptonians 7-4	N E Partridge, G B Partridge
Old Albanians / Old Westminsters	Westminsters w/o			
Old Harrovians / Old Carthusians	Harrovians 4-1	Reptonians 7-4		
Old Citizens / Old Reptonians	Reptonians 4-2			
Old Aldenhamians / Old Wykehamists	Wykehamists 5-1	Wykehamists 4-2	Malvernians 2-1	
Old Salopians / Old Cholmeleians	Salopians 6-3			
Old Bradfieldians / Old Hurst-Johnians	Hurst-Johnians 3-1	Malvernians 9-2		
Old Malvernians / Old Wellingburians	Malvernians 3-1			

Malvernians 2-0
Played at Crystal Palace

OLD MALVERNIANS Winners 1924 - A E Mackinnon, H A Pridham, G L Miller, R N Stone, N W Beeson, C F Morice, W C Stuart-Low, G B Partridge, N E Partridge, W R T Picton-Warlow, W Marlow.

OLD REPTONIANS Runners up 1924 - J E Hadfield, C K Part, N C E Ashton, H C Boddington, A G German, T H M Sharpley, H M Morris, M Howell, E K M Hilleary, F M Cardew, R F Griffin.

SEASON 1924 - 1925

FIRST ROUND	SECOND ROUND	SEMI FINAL	FINAL	WINNERS
Lancing Old Boys / Old Harrovians	Harrovians 4-2	Westminsters 3-2	Westminsters 3-1	Picton-Warlow (2), Holmes
Old Citizens / Old Westminsters	Westminsters 4-0			
Old Albanians / Old Reptonians	Reptonians w/o	Reptonians 4-3		
Old Carthusians / Old Wellingburians	Carthusians 2-1			
Old Aldenhamians / Old Foresters	Aldenhamians 2-0	Malvernians 6-0	Malvernians 2-1	
Old Cholmeleians / Old Malvernians	Malvernians 4-2			
Old Hurst-Johnians / Old Salopians	Salopians 4-1	Salopians 4-1		
Old Wykehamists / Old Bradfieldians	Wykehamists 5-0			

Malvernians 3-0
Played at Crystal Palace

OLD MALVERNIANS Winners 1925 - A E Mackinnon, H A Pridham, G L Miller, R N Stone, N W Beeson, C F Morice, W C Stuart-Low, G B Partridge, E R T Holmes, C G W Robson, W R T Picton-Warlow.

OLD WESTMINSTERS Runners up 1925 - W N McBride, E F Lutyens, G B Keily, A Chisholm, D A Radmacher, P E McJ Mellor, N P Andrews, K Brodie, W E Newall, R G H Lowe, W S Harris.

SEASON 1929 - 1930

FIRST ROUND	SECOND ROUND	SEMI FINAL	FINAL	WINNERS
Old Westminsters / Old Wykehamists	Wykehamists 6-0	Wykehamists 5-0	Wykehamists 1-0	Ashton, Kingsley; Barty-King, Sparrow
Old Aldenhamians / Old Citizens	Aldenhamians 7-3			
Old Cholmeleians / Old Foresters	Cholmeleians 7-0	Cholmeleians 2-1		
Old Malvernians / Old Wellingburians	Malvernians 6-3			
			Wykehamists 4-1 — Lewis	
			Played at Crystal Palace	
Old Etonians / Lancing Old Boys	Lancing 4-2	Bradfieldians 0-0,3-2	Salopians 4-0	
Old Hurst-Johnians / Old Bradfieldians	Bradfieldians 5-1			
Old Carthusians / Old Reptonians	Carthusians 3-0	Salopians 4-3		
Old Salopians / Old Harrovians	Salopians w/o			

OLD WYKEHAMISTS Winners 1930 - A D Bonham-Carter, W B Goulding, R Leigh-Wood, J L T Guise, G S Grimston, J F T Toppin, A R V Barker, P G T Kingsley, C T Ashton, J H Sparrow, G I Barty-King.

OLD SALOPIANS Runners up 1930 - B C Lee, P S Snow, H F Robinson, L B Blaxland, G A R Green, A T Barber, G S Watson, J S Haslewood, H G Lewis, D N Moore, R F Skelton.

SEASON 1930 - 1931

FIRST ROUND	SECOND ROUND	SEMI FINAL	FINAL	WINNERS
Old Bradfieldians / Old Reptonians	Bradfieldians 3-2	Westminsters 4-2	Wykehamists 2-0	Ashton (2), Toppin (2), Grimston
Old Westminsters / Old Etonians	Westminsters 5-0			
Old Salopians / Old Aldenhamians	Salopians 4-1	Wykehamists 2-2,2-1		
Old Wykehamists / Old Cholmeleians	Wykehamists 4-0			
			Wykehamists 5-1 — Broughton	
			Played at Crystal Palace	
Old Harrovians / Old Foresters	Foresters w/o	Citizens 3-1	Citizens 4-2	
Old Citizens / Old Carthusians	Citizens 5-4			
Lancing Old Boys / Old Hurst-Johnians	Lancing 2-1	Malvernians 5-4		
Old Malvernians / Old Wellingburians	Malvernians 4-1			

OLD WYKEHAMISTS Winners 1931 - A D Garrow, G S Grimston, G R M Ricketts, J L T Guise, A R V Barker, P G T Kingsley, C T Ashton, J F T Toppin, C R V Bell, M B S Bower, J W M Mansel.

OLD CITIZENS Runners up 1931 - F E Jarvis, D L Collier, C C Taylor, A A E Moore, F C Hawker, L E Youngman, L W Barnett, F Pearson, E D S Offord, A R Fulford, E C W Broughton.

SEASON 1927 - 1928

FIRST ROUND	SECOND ROUND	SEMI FINAL	FINAL	WINNERS
Old Cholmeleians / Old Bradfieldians	Bradfieldians 2-2,5-2	Bradfieldians 5-2	Malvernians 1-0	Pyne, Toppin, Robson
Old Harrovians / Old Foresters	Harrovians 3-0			
Lancing Old Boys / Old Reptonians	Lancing 2-1	Malvernians 2-0		
Old Salopians / Old Malvernians	Malvernians 5-0			
			Malvernians (2-2), 3-2 aet — Ashton, Bower	
			Played at Crystal Palace	
Old Aldenhamians / Old Wykehamists	Wykehamists 4-0	Wykehamists 3-2	Wykehamists 2-1	
Old Etonians / Old Westminsters	Westminsters w/o			
Old Citizens / Old Hurst-Johnians	Citizens 4-3	Carthusians 4-2		
Old Carthusians / Old Wellingburians	Carthusians 2-1			

OLD MALVERNIANS Winners 1928 - J H Mears, H A Pridham, G L Miller, W J Goldsmith, F W A Carter, C F Morice, H C D Abrams, C G Toppin, J M Pyne, C G W Robson, J W Greenstock.

OLD WYKEHAMISTS Runners up 1928 - A D Bonham-Carter, R W Maxwell-Gumbleton, R Leigh-Wood, P J T Kingsley, M B S Bower, G A Sim, R Pinney, A R V Barker, C T Ashton, F H Sparrow, R A Jerome.

SEASON 1928 - 1929

FIRST ROUND	SECOND ROUND	SEMI FINAL	FINAL	WINNERS
Old Citizens / Old Hurst-Johnians	Citizens 3-3,0-0,2-1	Lancing 3-1	Carthusians 8-2	
Old Harrovians / Lancing Old Boys	Lancing 2-2,4-2			
Old Carthusians / Old Foresters	Carthusians 11-1	Carthusians 3-1		
Old Wellingburians / Old Westminsters	Wellingburians 2-0			
			Wykehamists 5-1 — Ashton, Grimston, Sparrow	
			Played at Crystal Palace	
Old Reptonians / Old Wykehamists	Wykehamists 1-0	Wykehamists 2-1	Wykehamists 5-1	
Old Salopians / Old Aldenhamians	Aldenhamians 2-1			
Old Malvernians / Old Bradfieldians	Malvernians 7-2	Malvernians 4-2		
Old Cholmeleians (a bye)	Cholmeleians			

OLD WYKEHAMISTS Winners 1929 - A D Bonham-Carter, J W Mansel, W B Goulding, G A Sim, M B S Bower, J F T Toppin, G I Barty-King, G S Grimston, C T Ashton, J H Sparrow, A R V Barker.

OLD CARTHUSIANS Runners up 1929 - H M Ward-Clarke, A G Bower, J H G Gilliat, F H D Pritchard, T C Johnson, R B Beare, J C Cornell, J N Carter, G D Kemp-Welch, G S Fletcher, J T R Groves.

SEASON 1933 - 1934

FIRST ROUND	SECOND ROUND	SEMI FINAL	FINAL	WINNERS
Old Salopians / Old Reptonians	Salopians 1-0	Bradfieldians 1-1, 2-1	Aldenhamians 2-1	P R Hardman (3), C R Hardman, Sparke, Shearer
Old Etonians / Old Bradfieldians	Bradfieldians 7-1			
Old Carthusians / Old Aldenhamians	Aldenhamians 3-3,1-0	Aldenhamians 6-2		
Old Wellingburians / Lancing Old Boys	Lancing 1-0			Aldenhamians 6-2 — Ashton, Barker
Old Cholmeleians / Old Malvernians	Cholmeleians 4-1	Cholmeleians 4-2	Wykehamists 4-1	
Old Westminsters / Old Citizens	Citizens 4-2			
Old Ardinians / Old Foresters	Foresters 2-1	Wykehamists 2-0		
Old Wykehamists (a bye)	Wykehamists			

Played at Crystal Palace

OLD ALDENHAMIANS Winners 1934

L R Kent, A W S Sim, P J Hardie, M Lampard, M A Nelson, N S Smith-Spark, P R Hardman, D J Sparke, E D R Shearer (Capt.), C R Hardman, R B Morton.

OLD WYKEHAMISTS Runners up 1934

R C White, M B S Bower, R G Tindall, A D Garrow, J A Darwall-Smith, P G T Kingsley, A R V Barker, C T Ashton (Capt.), G W White, R de W K Winlaw, G I Barty-King.

SEASON 1931 - 1932

FIRST ROUND	SECOND ROUND	SEMI FINAL	FINAL	WINNERS
Old Hurst-Johnians / Old Citizens	Hurst-Johnians 3-1	Wykehamists 2-0	Salopians 4-3	Moxon (3), Haslewood, Skelton, Barber
Old Malvernians / Old Wykehamists	Wykehamists 6-2			
Old Wellingburians / Old Salopians	Salopians 6-1	Salopians 5-3		Salopians 6-1 — R H C Human
Old Cholmeleians / Old Carthusians	Carthusians 2-0			
Old Westminsters / Old Aldenhamians	Aldenhamians 5-2	Aldenhamians 4-2	Reptonians 4-1	
Lancing Old Boys / Old Etonians	Lancing 4-1			
Old Bradfieldians / Old Foresters	Bradfieldians 6-0	Reptonians 2-1		
Old Reptonians (a bye)	Reptonians			

Played at Crystal Palace

OLD SALOPIANS Winners 1932 F A K Green, P S Snow, C Mason, A T Barber, L B Blaxland, R Waye, A F A Fairweather, J S O Haslewood, G R Moxon, E A Barlow, R F Skelton.

OLD REPTONIANS Runners up 1932 J D H Gilbert, E E N Causton, I P Rayner, G Willatt, J H Vaughan, J S Lark, J H Human, R H C Human, A C J German, B H Valentine, J C Dodds.

SEASON 1932 - 1933

FIRST ROUND	SECOND ROUND	SEMI FINAL	FINAL	WINNERS
Old Cholmeleians (a bye)	Cholmeleians	Cholmeleians 3-2	Cholmeleians 5-4	McFarlane
Old Citizens / Old Wykehamists	Wykehamists 7-0			
Old Malvernians / Old Wellingburians	Malvernians 14-0	Reptonians 3-2		Salopians 3-1 — Moxon, Haslewood, Skelton
Old Carthusians / Old Reptonians	Reptonians 3-0			
Old Salopians / Old Bradfieldians	Salopians 4-1	Salopians 2-0	Salopians 8-3	
Old Aldenhamians / Old Foresters	Aldenhamians 4-1			
Old Etonians / Lancing Old Boys	Etonians 5-2	Westminsters 2-0		
Old Westminsters (a bye)	Westminsters			

Played at Crystal Palace

OLD SALOPIANS Winners 1933 F A K Green, P S Snow, A G Strasser, A T Barber, L B Blaxland, R Waye, J J Adie, J S O Haslewood, G R Moxon, E A Barlow, R F Skelton.

OLD CHOLMELEIANS Runners up 1933 J G E Stevens, G W Russell, G H Tidswell, R L Clarke, G H Adlard, A B Kyd, F K Reeves, A H Fabian, K H McFarlane, W H Webster, R W V Robins.

SEASON 1935 - 1936

FIRST ROUND	SECOND ROUND	SEMI FINAL	FINAL	WINNERS
Old Foresters	Foresters 2-1	Salopians 0-0, 2-0	Bradfieldians 3-2	Carthusians 2-0
Old Reptonians				
Old Westminsters	Salopians 4-3			Dunbar (2)
Old Salopians				
Old Citizens	Bradfieldians 1-1,2-1	Bradfieldians 1-1,3-1		
Old Bradfieldians			*Played at Crystal Palace*	
Old Malvernians	Malvernians 8-0			
Lancing Old Boys				
Old Ardinians	Wykehamists 4-1	Cholmeleians 3-0	Carthusians 5-1	
Old Wykehamists				
Old Etonians	Cholmeleians w/o			
Old Cholmeleians				
Old Carthusians	Carthusians 2-2,5-4	Carthusians 3-0		
Old Aldenhamians				
Old Wellingburians (a bye)	Wellingburians			

OLD CARTHUSIANS Winners 1936

(Back Row)
J C Moss, J L Field, H M Mitton, J G Dunbar, S C Gillchrest, R M Hollis.

(Front Row)
D A Pott, W F Moss, G T Hollebone, K P S Caldwell, A J Wreford-Brown.

OLD BRADFIELDIANS Runners up 1936

M C C Higgins, J G Stevenson, F M Webb, D R Fussell, P H Williams, I H G Gilbert, F H M Murdoch, R W E Groves, L L le P Gardner, R N Rayne, I M Sorensen.

SEASON 1934 - 1935

FIRST ROUND	SECOND ROUND	SEMI FINAL	FINAL	WINNERS
Old Bradfieldians	Bradfieldians 3-1	Bradfieldians 3-2	Salopians 3-0	Salopians 3-0
Old Reptonians				Roberts (2), Booker
Old Citizens	Citizens 5-1			
Old Etonians				
Old Ardinians	Malvernians 8-1	Salopians 5-2	*Played at Crystal Palace*	
Old Malvernians				
Lancing Old Boys	Salopians 1-0			
Old Salopians				
Old Carthusians	Aldenhamians 3-1	Wykehamists 4-0	Wykehamists 5-2	
Old Aldenhamians				
Old Wykehamists	Wykehamists 6-1			
Old Cholmeleians				
Old Foresters	Wellingburians 6-0	Westminsters 6-5		
Old Wellingburians				
Old Westminsters (a bye)	Westminsters			

OLD SALOPIANS Winners 1935

(Back Row)
F A K Green, A G Strasser, R Waye, G R G Roberts, M L Booker.

(Front Row)
J S O Haslewood, R E Skelton, A T Barber, L B Blaxland (Capt.), P S Snow, E A Barlow.

OLD WYKEHAMISTS Runners up 1935

R C White, A J N Young, R G Tindall, A D Garrow, J A Darwall-Smith, J L T Guise, H S Scott, G W White, C T Ashton (Capt.), P G T Kingsley, P A T Holme.

SEASON 1937 – 1938

FIRST ROUND	SECOND ROUND	SEMI FINAL	FINAL	WINNERS
Old Ardinians	Citizens 3-1			
Old Citizens		Lancing 4-2		
Old Etonians	Lancing 11-1			
Lancing Old Boys			Wykehamists 1-0	
Old Carthusians	Carthusians 4-1			
Old Reptonians		Wykehamists 2-0		
Old Chigwellians	Wykehamists 2-2,7-1			
Old Wykehamists				Wykehamists 1-0
Old Salopians	Aldenhamians 2-0			Scott, A B Kingsley
Old Aldenhamians		Aldenhamians 4-1		
Old Wellingburians	Cholmeleians 2-1			
Old Cholmeleians			Malvernians 2-2, 2-0	Wykehamists and Malvernians (2-2), 2-2 aet
Old Bradfieldians	Bradfieldians 3-1			
Old Westminsters		Malvernians 5-1		Simson (og), Jacomb
Old Malvernians	Malvernians 5-1			
Old Foresters				

Played at Hurlingham Club

OLD MALVERNIANS
Joint Holders 1938

(Back Row)
A H Brodhurst, E D W B Hirst, G N Cronhelm, B L Jacomb, H R Townend, J N Cronhelm, J C N Burrow.

(Front Row)
N W Beeson E O W Hunt, R G Stainton (Capt.), F E H Gibbens, D Cook.

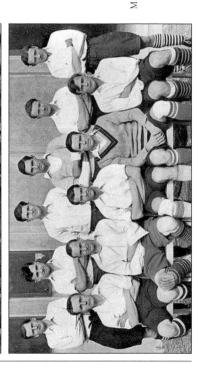

OLD WYKEHAMISTS
Joint Holders 1938

(Back Row)
W E D Paul, S W Clayton, A B Kingsley, H A S Disney, H S Scott, C P Greenway.

(Front Row)
M R F Simson, J A Darwall -Smith, P G T Kingsley (Capt.), G I Barty-King, R G Tindall.

SEASON 1936 – 1937

FIRST ROUND	SECOND ROUND	SEMI FINAL	FINAL	WINNERS
Old Foresters	Bradfieldians 4-1			
Old Bradfieldians		Bradfieldians 5-3		
Old Chigwellians	Chigwellians 11-2			
Old Etonians			Bradfieldians 1-0	
Old Westminsters	Westminsters 4-2			
Old Wellingburians		Wykehamists 4-2		
Lancing Old Boys	Wykehamists 7-0			
Old Wykehamists				Salopians 4-1
Old Cholmeleians	Carthusians 2-0			Sorensen
Old Carthusians		Aldenhamians 2-1		
Old Ardinians	Aldenhamians 5-0			
Old Aldenhamians			Salopians 5-3	Haslewood, Roberts (2), Singleton
Old Reptonians	Salopians 4-2			
Old Salopians		Salopians 6-0		
Old Citizens	Citizens 1-1, 3-0			
Old Malvernians				

Played at Hurlingham Club

OLD SALOPIANS
Winners 1937

(Back Row)
W H H Allon, M L Booker, A G Strasser, G M Thornycroft, R Waye, G R G Roberts, A P Singleton.

(Front Row)
J S O Haslewood, A T Barber, L B Blaxland (Capt.), P S Snow, E A Barlow.

OLD BRADFIELDIANS
Runners up 1937

(Back Row)
P W Sedgwick, F O Faulkner, F M Webb, F E Templer, P H Williams, H A Davies, W R Evans, R W E Groves, D R Fussell, L L le P Gardner, I M Sorensen.

147

SEASON 1946 - 1947

FIRST ROUND	SECOND ROUND	SEMI FINAL	FINAL	WINNERS
Old Ardinians / Old Wykehamists	Wykehamists 3-0	Carthusians 4-2	Carthusians 5-0	Wreford-Brown, Tanner (2)
Old Carthusians / Old Aldenhamians	Carthusians 4-1			
Old Westminsters / Old Brentwoods	Brentwoods 4-1	Salopians 7-3		
Old Foresters / Old Salopians	Salopians 4-2			Carthusians 3-1 — Hill
Old Wellingburians / Old Chigwellians	Chigwellians 4-3	Reptonians 2-1	Reptonians 1-0	
Old Cholmeleians / Old Reptonians	Reptonians 3-0			
Old Bradfieldians / Lancing Old Boys	Bradfieldians 6-0	Bradfieldians 3-2		
Old Malvernians / Old Etonians	Malvernians w/o			

Played at Lloyds Bank, Beckenham

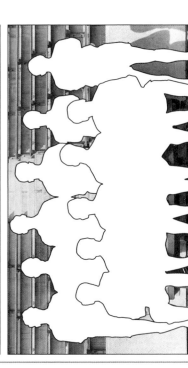

OLD CARTHUSIANS Winners 1947

(Back Row)
D P Rowat, F A Peet, H P Cunningham, A K Hughes, J G Larking, G L Howard.

(Front Row)
J D P Tanner, K P S Caldwell, R M Hollis (Capt.), A J Wreford-Brown, J C Daukes.

OLD REPTONIANS Runners up 1947

I L Ferguson, A P H Durham, B Pownall, J W R Smith, R Sale, G L Willatt, D Carr, P F Hill, R L Lowcock, P C Curtis, R J Norton.

SEASON 1938 - 1939

FIRST ROUND	SECOND ROUND	SEMI FINAL	FINAL	WINNERS
Old Ardinians / Old Wykehamists	Wykehamists 4-0	Carthusians 2-1	Carthusians 2-2,1-0	Wreford-Brown, Field
Old Carthusians / Old Foresters	Carthusians 3-0			
Old Bradfieldians / Old Malvernians	Bradfieldians 3-0	Bradfieldians 5-2		
Old Salopians / Old Etonians	Salopians 6-1			Carthusians 2-1 — Webster
Old Chigwellians / Old Cholmeleians	Cholmeleians 3-3,1-1,5-0	Cholmeleians 4-1	Cholmeleians 3-1	
Lancing Old Boys / Old Citizens	Citizens 3-1			
Old Westminsters / Old Aldenhamians	Aldenhamians 5-0	Aldenhamians 2-0		
Old Reptonians / Old Wellingburians	Reptonians 1-1,3-2			

Played at Hurlingham Club

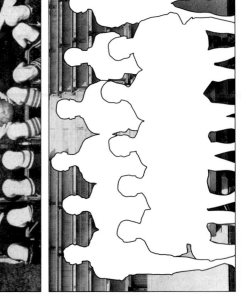

OLD CARTHUSIANS Winners 1939

(Back Row)
E H Ades, A J Wreford-Brown, J B Lyon, A R Woods, P L Richards, S C Gillchrest,

(Front Row)
J L Field, K P S Caldwell, G T Hollebone (Capt.), W F Moss, R M Hollis.

OLD CHOLMELEIANS Runners up 1939

W H Webster, G Newton, K A F Frost, A H Fabian, J K G Webb, A G A Turnbull, D N Broad, M H Webb, G G Harris, J K C Scott, H P Stebbings.

SEASON 1948 - 1949

FIRST ROUND	SECOND ROUND	SEMI FINAL	FINAL	WINNERS
Old Foresters / Old Salopians	Salopians 1-1, 6-1	Salopians 5-1	Salopians 2-1	Carthusians 2-0
Old Westminsters / Old Reptonians	Reptonians 6-1			P C G Larking, Goodridge
Old Malvernians / Old Ardinians	Malvernians 6-0	Wellingburians 2-1		
Old Wellingburians / Old Aldenhamians	Wellingburians 6-1			
Lancing Old Boys / Old Carthusians	Carthusians 3-1	Carthusians 2-1	Carthusians 5-1	
Old Etonians / Old Wykehamists	Wykehamists w/o			
Old Cholmeleians / Old Bradfieldians	Bradfieldians 4-3	Bradfieldians 6-2		
Old Chigwellians / Old Brentwoods	Brentwoods 4-3			

Played at Tooting & Mitcham

OLD CARTHUSIANS Winners 1949

(Back Row)
D L Benke, P C G Larking, P B H May, V R Goodridge, A Hastings, K R Dolleymore.

(Front Row)
M J Rimell, A J Wreford-Brown, R M Hollis (Capt.), J G Larking, P Bennett.

OLD SALOPIANS Runners up 1949

(Back Row)
R W Painter, J B Pugh, M Robinson, C R Thompson, J Bretherton, J Clegg.

(Front Row)
W E Rhys, A T G Groves, K A Shearwood (Capt.), M G Crawford, H R S Rhys.

SEASON 1947 - 1948

FIRST ROUND	SECOND ROUND	SEMI FINAL	FINAL	WINNERS
Old Wellingburians / Old Chigwellians	Chigwellians 5-2	Chigwellians 6-2	Cholmeleians 3-0	Wykehamists 5-1
Old Ardinians / Old Malvernians	Malvernians 2-1			Thornton, Doggart (2), Abbott (2), Tillard
Lancing Old Boys / Old Foresters	Foresters 2-1	Cholmeleians 3-1		
Old Cholmeleians / Old Etonians	Cholmeleians w/o			
Old Brentwoods / Old Carthusians	Carthusians 7-2	Salopians 2-0	Wykehamists 2-1	
Old Reptonians / Old Salopians	Salopians 5-1			
Old Wykehamists / Old Aldenhamians	Wykehamists 3-1	Wykehamists 4-1		
Old Bradfieldians / Old Westminsters	Bradfieldians 2-0			

Played at Tooting & Mitcham

OLD WYKEHAMISTS Winners 1948

(Back Row)
T J Drury, E L Ashton, M F C Pickett, J R Tillard, W W Slack, M Maynard.

(Front Row)
D B Abbott, H A Pawson, M R F Simson (Capt.), R P Hornby, G H G Doggart.

OLD CHOLMELEIANS Runners up 1948

(Back Row)
M L Freegard, N S Boggon, J B Woodward, J D Cairns, J K W Webb, M G Kingston-Jones, S S Rogers, A H Fabian, D H Thornton, W H Webster, R A Stillman.

SEASON 1950 - 1951

FIRST ROUND	SECOND ROUND	SEMI FINAL	FINAL	WINNERS
Old Westminsters / Old Ardinians	Ardinians 1-1, 4-0	Reptonians 8-0	Carthusians 4-1	Savill (2), Tanner, Williams
Old Reptonians / Old Foresters	Reptonians 5-0			
Old Carthusians / Old Brentwoods	Carthusians 5-0	Carthusians 6-3		
Old Salopians / Old Cholmeleians	Salopians 10-1		Carthusians 4-2	Belton, Riley
Lancing Old Boys / Old Aldenhamians	Aldenhamians 6-1	Wellingburians 4-2		
Old Wellingburians / Old Bradfieldians	Wellingburians 7-1		Wellingburians 3-1	
Old Chigwellians / Old Malvernians	Malvernians 0-0, 1-0	Malvernians 2-1		
Old Etonians / Old Wykehamists	Wykehamists 4-4, 6-3			

Played at Tooting & Mitcham

SEASON 1949 - 1950

FIRST ROUND	SECOND ROUND	SEMI FINAL	FINAL	WINNERS
Lancing Old Boys / Old Cholmeleians	Cholmeleians 3-2	Carthusians 4-0	Carthusians 2-0	May
Old Carthusians / Old Salopians	Carthusians 3-1			
Old Aldenhamians / Old Bradfieldians	Bradfieldians 2-1	Reptonians 3-2		
Old Reptonians / Old Ardinians	Reptonians 4-1		Wykehamists 3-1	T W Slack, Doggart (pen), Hornby
Old Foresters / Old Wykehamists	Wykehamists 4-0	Wykehamists 6-2		
Old Chigwellians / Old Wellingburians	Chigwellians 3-3, 2-1		Wykehamists 4-2	
Old Etonians / Old Brentwoods	Brentwoods w/o	Brentwoods 2-1		
Old Westminsters / Old Malvernians	Malvernians 7-1			

Played at Tooting & Mitcham

SEASON 1952 - 1953

FIRST ROUND	SECOND ROUND	SEMI FINAL	FINAL	WINNERS
Old Brentwoods / Old Bradfieldians	Bradfieldians 4-2	Salopians 4-0	Salopians 4-1	Salopians 3-1
Lancing Old Boys / Old Salopians	Salopians 8-0			Moulsdale (2), Pugh
Old Westminsters / Old Malvernians	Malvernians 2-1	Malvernians 2-2,2-1,6-1		
Old Aldenhamians / Old Chigwellians	Aldenhamians 4-2			
Old Reptonians / Old Foresters	Reptonians 8-0	Carthusians 4-1	Wykehamists 3-2	Abbott
Old Wellingburians / Old Carthusians	Carthusians 2-2,5-1			
Old Cholmeleians / Old Wykehamists	Wykehamists 5-3	Wykehamists 5-0		
Old Etonians / Old Ardinians	Ardinians 4-0			

Played at Tooting & Mitcham

OLD SALOPIANS Winners 1953

(Back Row)
D Cox, J E S Bretherton, H B Oxenham, M L Charlesworth, S Jackson, J C Walker, R H Crawford.

(Front Row)
G Roberts, H R S Rhys, A R B Moulsdale (Capt.), M T Robinson, J B Pugh.

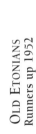

OLD WYKEHAMISTS Runners up 1953

(Back Row)
E B Trubshaw, J R S Maclure, I P E Gay, J Robertson, D A N C Miers, D W R Bedford, R J Foster.

(Middle Row)
D B Abbott, H A Pawson, G H G Doggart (Capt.), R P Hornby, W W Slack.

(Front Row)
J R M Millar, M Maynard.

SEASON 1951 - 1952

FIRST ROUND	SECOND ROUND	SEMI FINAL	FINAL	WINNERS
Old Chigwellians / Lancing Old Boys	Lancing 2-1	Aldenhamians 4-0	Etonians 2-1	Salopians 6-1
Old Aldenhamians / Old Bradfieldians	Aldenhamians 3-1			Faber
Old Etonians / Old Foresters	Etonians 4-1	Etonians 3-1		Moulsdale (3), Rhys (2), Clegg
Old Westminsters / Old Wykehamists	Wykehamists 5-1			
Old Salopians / Old Carthusians	Salopians 4-0	Salopians 3-0	Salopians 2-0	
Old Ardinians / Old Brentwoods	Brentwoods 5-1			
Old Wellingburians / Old Reptonians	Reptonians 4-0	Reptonians 6-0		
Old Malvernians / Old Cholmeleians	Malvernians 2-1			

Played at Tooting & Mitcham

OLD SALOPIANS Winners 1952

(Back Row)
D Cox, H B Oxenham, G Roberts, M L Charlesworth, J B Pugh, M T Robinson.

(Front Row)
J Clegg, K A Shearwood, A R B Moulsdale (Capt.), H R S Rhys, J E S Bretherton.

OLD ETONIANS Runners up 1952

M M G Naylor-Leyland, C P Parnell, A R Davey, G X Constantinidi, D H Macindoe, W N Coles, O W T W Fiennes, N C Wadham, M L O Faber, P D S Blake (Capt.), A J Butterwick.

SEASON 1954 - 1955

FIRST ROUND	SECOND ROUND	SEMI FINAL	FINAL	WINNERS
Old Brentwoods / Old Westminsters	Brentwoods 4-1	Brentwoods 2-1	Brentwoods 3-2	Harrison, Skeate, Horrex (2)
Old Ardinians / Old Wykehamists	Ardinians 3-2			
Old Aldenhamians / Old Chigwellians	Chigwellians 4-1	Carthusians 4-2		Brentwoods and Salopians (4-4), 4-4 (Cup held jointly). aet
Old Bradfieldians / Old Carthusians	Carthusians 2-0			
Lancing Old Boys / Old Etonians	Etonians 4-2	Salopians 6-1	Salopians 5-2	Bretherton, Moulsdale (2), Rhys
Old Malvernians / Old Salopians	Salopians 2-0			
Old Foresters / Old Reptonians	Reptonians 2-0	Cholmeleians 1-0		
Old Cholmeleians / Old Wellingburians	Cholmeleians 2-0			

Played at Tooting & Mitcham

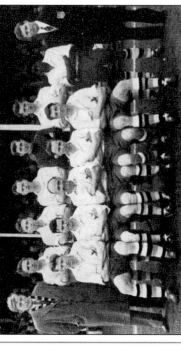

OLD BRENTWOODS Joint Holders 1955

(Back Row) B Buitenhuis, D B Coull, G W Horrex, J R B Meehan, R C Malyon, D L Nissim, S E Odamtten, D L Stacey.

(Front Row) R C Vowells, F J Skeate, D H Langridge (Capt.), B S Corker, D G Harrison.

OLD SALOPIANS Joint Holders 1955

(Back Row) D H Lanyon, H B Oxenham, J N Webb, B M Smallwood, J E S Bretherton, G Roberts.

(Front Row) J Clegg, H R S Rhys, A R B Moulsdale (Capt.), M T Robinson, J B Pugh.

SEASON 1953 - 1954

FIRST ROUND	SECOND ROUND	SEMI FINAL	FINAL	WINNERS
Old Westminsters / Old Brentwoods	Westminsters 4-3	Carthusians 4-3	Carthusians 3-0	Savill, Whinney
Lancing Old Boys / Old Carthusians	Carthusians 0-0, 6-0			
Old Wellingburians / Old Reptonians	Reptonians 3-0	Reptonians 5-1		Carthusians 2-0
Old Ardinians / Old Malvernians	Ardinians 2-1			
Old Bradfieldians / Old Chigwellians	Chigwellians 2-0	Chigwellians 6-0	Salopians 2-0	
Old Aldenhamians / Old Wykehamists	Wykehamists 1-1, 4-0			
Old Salopians / Old Etonians	Salopians 3-1	Salopians 4-1		
Old Cholmeleians / Old Foresters	Foresters 1-1, 3-2			

Played at Tooting & Mitcham

OLD CARTHUSIANS Winners 1954

(Back Row) A G Williams, M H D Whinney, J N Fair, M G Varcoe, G Clarke, J W H May.

(Front Row) J D P Tanner, D H G Goodliffe, T R H Savill (Capt.), J G Larking, G L Howard.

OLD SALOPIANS Runners up 1954

J N Webb, H B Oxenham, M T Robinson, J E S Bretherton, K A Shearwood, P Jackson, J Clegg, A R B Moulsdale (Capt.), H R S Rhys, G Roberts, J B Pugh.

SEASON 1956 - 1957

FIRST ROUND	SECOND ROUND	SEMI FINAL	FINAL	WINNERS
Lancing Old Boys / Old Ardinians	Ardinians 4-1	Malvernians 2-1	Malvernians 3-0	Malvernians 3-1
Old Wellingburians / Old Malvernians	Malvernians 6-2			Brough, MacLaurin, Garner
Old Westminsters / Old Carthusians	Carthusians 4-3	Carthusians 7-2		
Old Aldenhamians / Old Cholmeleians	Aldenhamians 1-1, 3-2		*Played at Wimbledon*	
Old Foresters / Old Bradfieldians	Foresters 3-2	Brentwoods 4-3	Reptonians 1-0	
Old Brentwoods / Old Salopians	Brentwoods 2-2, 3-1			Gillard
Old Wykehamists / Old Reptonians	Reptonians 3-2	Reptonians 3-2		
Old Etonians / Old Chigwellians	Etonians 4-3			

OLD MALVERNIANS Winners 1957
(Back Row)
D M French, M M D Laidlaw, J M Costeloe, J M Garner, I C MacLaurin, F D Scholefield.
(Front Row)
R H Chadder, M J Gent, D W T Brough (Capt.), H I Jory, D R Martin.

OLD REPTONIANS Runners up 1957
(Back Row)
P A Trott, J J Black, B R T Smith, A W S.Robinson, P J Barber, R G Gillard.
(Front Row)
G C Citron, R Sale, D B Carr (Capt.), D B Wilkinson, M R Steward.

SEASON 1955 - 1956

FIRST ROUND	SECOND ROUND	SEMI FINAL	FINAL	WINNERS
Old Reptonians / Old Cholmeleians	Reptonians 2-2, 5-4	Reptonians 2-1	Malvernians 3-1	
Old Aldenhamians / Old Wellingburians	Aldenhamians 4-1			Farrer-Brown (2), R Jory
Old Etonians / Old Brentwoods	Brentwoods 4-1	Malvernians 1-0		Malvernians (1-1), 3-2 aet
Old Malvernians / Old Chigwellians	Malvernians 1-0		*Played at Tooting & Mitcham*	
Old Foresters / Old Wykehamists	Wykehamists 7-3	Wykehamists 5-2	Wykehamists 3-0	Maclure (2)
Old Salopians / Old Carthusians	Salopians 5-2			
Lancing Old Boys / Old Westminsters	Westminsters 4-3	Ardinians 6-4		
Old Ardinians / Old Bradfieldians	Ardinians 8-1			

OLD MALVERNIANS Winners 1956
(Back Row)
R P D Jory, F D Scholefield, D R Martin, R L Cooper, G Farrer-Brown, A W Beeson.
(Front Row)
D W T Brough, M J Gent, H I Jory (Capt.), R M S George, R H Chadder.

OLD WYKEHAMISTS Runners up 1956
(Back Row)
M Maynard, M Morse, J Robertson, D McCarthy, R Barbour, I Gay.
(Front Row)
T Slack, H Pawson, D Abbott (Capt.), D Bedford, J Maclure.

SEASON 1958 - 1959

FIRST ROUND	SECOND ROUND	SEMI FINAL	FINAL	WINNERS
Old Brentwoods / Old Wykehamists	Brentwoods 5-4	Brentwoods 3-2	Brentwoods 8-2	Cholmeleians 3-1
Old Reptonians / Old Wellingburians	Reptonians 2-1			Coull
Old Bradfieldians / Old Foresters	Foresters 4-1	Westminsters 3-2		A Jenkins, Murray, Hollinrake
Old Westminsters / Old Aldenhamians	Westminsters 4-2		*Played at Wimbledon*	
Old Chigwellians / Lancing Old Boys	Chigwellians 5-4	Cholmeleians 3-1	Cholmeleians 4-2	
Old Etonians / Old Cholmeleians	Cholmeleians 7-3			
Old Salopians / Old Malvernians	Malvernians 5-3	Malvernians 3-2		
Old Ardinians / Old Carthusians	Carthusians 4-2			

SEASON 1957 - 1958

FIRST ROUND	SECOND ROUND	SEMI FINAL	FINAL	WINNERS
Old Ardinians / Old Wykehamists	Wykehamists 4-0	Reptonians 4-3	Reptonians 7-1	Cholmeleians 2-0
Old Reptonians / Old Malvernians	Reptonians 4-2			Drybrough, Fawcett
Lancing Old Boys / Old Westminsters	Westminsters 2-0	Westminsters 3-2	*Played at Wimbledon*	
Old Brentwoods / Old Wellingburians	Brentwoods 4-1			
Old Aldenhamians / Old Foresters	Foresters 4-3	Foresters 5-2	Cholmeleians 3-1	
Old Carthusians / Old Bradfieldians	Carthusians 2-2, 4-0			
Old Salopians / Old Chigwellians	Chigwellians 3-0	Cholmeleians 3-1		
Old Etonians / Old Cholmeleians	Cholmeleians 4-0			

OLD CHOLMELEIANS Winners 1959
(Back Row)
D Holland, R W Greenslade, G Jenkins, R MaC Clyde, M Wadsworth, J Merry, A Murray.

(Front Row)
A Mitchell, D A Hollinrake, W Knightley-Smith (Capt.), A Jenkins, C Drybrough.

OLD BRENTWOODS Runners up 1959
(Back Row)
M A Ryan, B S Corker, R Cook, R C Vowells, D G Harrison, M A Reis.

(Front Row)
L Atkins, G P Harrison, B R Taylor (Capt.), P Griffiths, D B Coull.

OLD CHOLMELEIANS Winners 1958
(Back Row)
P Metcalf, C Drybrough, J K Fawcett, J Merry, A Murray, M Wadsworth.

(Front Row)
A Jenkins, C D MaC Clyde, W Knightley-Smith (Capt.), J Buchanan, R Greenslade.

OLD REPTONIANS Runners up 1958
(Back Row)
W A S Wesson, A R Turl, B R T Smith, R G Gillard, P J Barber, A W S Robinson, P A Trott.

(Front Row)
M R Steward, R Sale, D B Carr (Capt.), D B Wilkinson, G C Citron.

SEASON 1960 - 1961

FIRST ROUND	SECOND ROUND	SEMI FINAL	FINAL	WINNERS
Old Carthusians / Old Westminsters	Carthusians 6-2	Cholmeleians 4-1		
Old Ardinians / Old Cholmeleians	Cholmeleians 2-1			
Old Salopians / Lancing Old Boys	Salopians 2-1	Malvernians 4-0	Cholmeleians 2-0	A T Jenkins, Fawcett
Old Malvernians / Old Wellingburians	Malvernians 4-1			
Old Wykehamists / Old Chigwellians	Wykehamists 4-2	Wykehamists 4-0		
Old Foresters / Old Bradfieldians	Foresters 4-1		Wykehamists 3-1	Smith (2), Patrick, Maclure
Old Brentwoods / Old Reptonians	Brentwoods 3-1	Brentwoods 2-1		
Old Etonians / Old Aldenhamians	Etonians 3-0			

Played at Wealdstone

WINNERS: Wykehamists 4-2

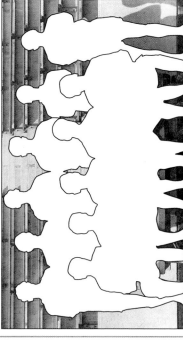

OLD CHOLMELEIANS Runners up 1961
R McC Clyde, L J Hughs, R W Greenslade, J Merry, W Knightley-Smith (Capt.), A T Jenkins, I G Jenkins, P W Metcalf, J K Fawcett, A J Murray, C D Drybrough.

SEASON 1959 - 1960

FIRST ROUND	SECOND ROUND	SEMI FINAL	FINAL	WINNERS
Old Malvernians / Old Salopians	Malvernians 5-3	Malvernians 6-2		
Old Wykehamists / Old Etonians	Wykehamists 2-0			
Old Chigwellians / Old Wellingburians	Wellingburians 8-3	Bradfieldians 4-1	Malvernians 5-0	Williams, MacLaurin
Old Bradfieldians / Lancing Old Boys	Bradfieldians 1-0			
Old Carthusians / Old Cholmeleians	Carthusians 3-2	Ardinians 4-1		
Old Brentwoods / Old Ardinians	Ardinians 6-3		Reptonians 4-2	Citron (2), Tomlinson
Old Westminsters / Old Reptonians	Reptonians 2-2, 5-3	Reptonians 3-3, 4-2		
Old Aldenhamians / Old Foresters	Foresters 5-0			

Played at Wealdstone

WINNERS: Reptonians 3-2

OLD REPTONIANS Winners 1960
(Back Row)
D C M Vaughan, C P Waddilowe, A W S Robinson, J J W Tomlinson, S B Webb-Jones, D J T Shentall.
(Front Row)
A R Turl, M R Steward, P J Barber (Capt.), G C Citron, P H Vaughan.

OLD MALVERNIANS Runners up 1960
(Back Row)
M J Theobald, J G S Woods, P G Jagger, D R Martin, A K Williams, H D Loader.
(Front Row)
J M Costeloe, D W T Brough, A W Beeson (Capt.), R H Chadder, I C MacLaurin.

SEASON 1962 - 1963

FIRST ROUND	SECOND ROUND	SEMI FINAL	FINAL	WINNERS
Old Westminsters / Old Carthusians	Carthusians 2-2,3-1	Malvernians 5-4	Malvernians 3-2	Reptonians 4-0 — Barnwell (2), Allen, Waite
Old Aldenhamians / Old Malvernians	Malvernians 7-2			
Old Chigwellians / Old Cholmeleians	Cholmeleians 4-3	Foresters 2-1		
Old Foresters / Old Wellingburians	Foresters 4-3			
Lancing Old Boys / Old Etonians	Lancing 1-1,4-0	Ardinians 3-1	Reptonians 4-2	
Old Bradfieldians / Old Ardinians	Ardinians 1-0			
Old Brentwoods / Old Wykehamists	Brentwoods 4-3	Reptonians 6-1		
Old Reptonians / Old Salopians	Reptonians 6-3			

Played at Bank of England

OLD REPTONIANS Winners 1963
(Back Row) A W Allen, A P Basnett, D C M Vaughan, L M L Barnwell, T J Waite, P W Rolfe.
(Front Row) J J W Tomlinson, A W S Robinson, B J Hare (Capt.), P W S Rowland, C P Waddilove.

OLD MALVERNIANS Runners up 1963
(Back Row) C E Wilson, G H Irvine, D R Martin, J W Illaszewicz, H D Loader, A G Theobald.
(Front Row) A K Williams, R H Chadder, A W Beeson (Capt.), J M Costeloe, P G Jagger.

SEASON 1961 - 1962

FIRST ROUND	SECOND ROUND	SEMI FINAL	FINAL	WINNERS
Lancing Old Boys / Old Wykehamists	Wykehamists 2-0	Wykehamists 4-2	Malvernians 6-2	Carthusians (1-1), 2-1 aet — Costeloe; Jakobson, Savill
Old Westminsters / Old Etonians	Westminsters 2-1			
Old Salopians / Old Malvernians	Malvernians 3-2	Malvernians 3-2		
Old Wellingburians / Old Reptonians	Reptonians 2-1			
Old Chigwellians / Old Foresters	Foresters 3-2	Carthusians 2-0	Carthusians 3-2	
Old Aldenhamians / Old Carthusians	Carthusians 2-1			
Old Ardinians / Old Cholmeleians	Cholmeleians 5-0	Cholmeleians 3-1		
Old Brentwoods / Old Bradfieldians	Brentwoods 8-1			

Played at Wealdstone

OLD CARTHUSIANS Winners 1962
(Back Row) J M Lees, D S Mace, A T C Allom, R F Buckley, J N Garrow, A P Blumer.
(Front Row) D H Goodliffe, F E Kung, D B Lees (Capt.), T R H Savill, T R Jakobson.

OLD MALVERNIANS Runners up 1962
(Back Row) A G Theobald, P G Jagger, C E Wilson, C W Stevens, I Ryder-Smith, J W Illaszewicz.
(Front Row) A K Williams, R H Chadder, A W Beeson (Capt.), D R Martin, J M Costeloe.

SEASON 1964 - 1965

FIRST ROUND	SECOND ROUND	SEMI FINAL	FINAL	WINNERS
Old Ardinians / Old Etonians	Ardinians 4-0	Ardinians 3-0	Reptonians 7-0	
Old Wellingburians / Old Aldenhamians	Wellingburians 3-1		*Hare*	
Old Wykehamists / Old Reptonians	Reptonians 9-2	Reptonians 4-0		Malvernians 2-1
Old Foresters / Lancing Old Boys	Foresters 3-0			*Williams, Theobald*
Old Malvernians / Old Brentwoods	Malvernians 3-0	Malvernians 4-3	Malvernians 1-1, 6-1	
Old Carthusians / Old Westminsters	Westminsters 3-2			
Old Bradfieldians / Old Chigwellians	Chigwellians 3-1	Chigwellians 2-1		
Old Cholmeleians / Old Salopians	Cholmeleians 4-2			

Played at Crystal Palace

OLD MALVERNIANS Winners 1965

(Back Row)
A G Theobald, D Bailey, I Ryder-Smith, D G H Marnham, A K Williams, J W Illaszewicz.

(Front Row)
H D Loader, A W Beeson, R H Chadder (Capt.), J M Costeloe, C W Stevens.

OLD REPTONIANS Runners up 1965

(Back Row)
P W S Rowland, R M Stockdale, A P Basnett, J L Hutton, M H Overend, T M Arden.

(Front Row)
J J W Tomlinson, B J Hare (Capt.), R G Gillard, D C M Vaughan, P H Vaughan.

SEASON 1963 - 1964

FIRST ROUND	SECOND ROUND	SEMI FINAL	FINAL	WINNERS
Old Wellingburians / Old Cholmeleians	Cholmeleians 1-0	Cholmeleians 2-2, 1-0	Salopians 2-2, 2-1	
Old Malvernians / Old Foresters	Foresters 3-0			Salopians 4-1
Old Westminsters / Old Salopians	Salopians 3-2	Salopians 4-2		*Moulsdale, Sargeant (2), Walls*
Old Reptonians / Old Brentwoods	Reptonians 3-2			
Old Carthusians / Old Wykehamists	Carthusians 6-0	Ardinians 2-1	Aldenhamians 3-1	*King*
Old Ardinians / Lancing Old Boys	Ardinians 3-2			
Old Aldenhamians / Old Bradfieldians	Aldenhamians 1-1, 4-2	Aldenhamians 2-1		
Old Etonians / Old Chigwellians	Chigwellians 2-0			

Played at Highgate School

OLD SALOPIANS Winners 1964

(Back Row)
J S Ker, D H Sargeant, A J M Walls, J L Osborne, D L Wright, D J Platt, J G Alexander.

(Front Row)
J E Burns, A R B Moulsdale (Capt.), F W Cooper, L G Parry.

OLD ALDENHAMIANS Runners up 1964

(Back Row)
R A R Arthur, G M Chapman, J F R Stainer, P Benjamin, D H King, P H C Holloway.

(Front Row)
C D Riley, S T Adams, S J Murray (Capt.), D R Barker, P K Smith.

SEASON 1966 - 1967

FIRST ROUND	SECOND ROUND	SEMI FINAL	FINAL	WINNERS
Old Harrovians / Old Brentwoods	Brentwoods 3-2	Brentwoods 5-0	Brentwoods 2-0	Francis, Allen, Thomas
Old Ardinians / Old Bradfieldians	Ardinians 3-2			
Old Westminsters / Old Cholmeleians	Cholmeleians 2-1	Cholmeleians 6-1		Brentwoods 3-2
Old Chigwellians / Old Aldenhamians	Chigwellians 3-1		*Played at Crystal Palace*	Illaszewicz, Ryder-Smith (pen)
Old Wykehamists / Old Etonians	Wykehamists 2-1	Malvernians 4-0	Malvernians 4-0	
Old Reptonians / Old Malvernians	Malvernians 6-2			
Old Carthusians / Old Wellingburians	Carthusians 3-2	Carthusians 2-0		
Old Salopians / Lancing Old Boys	Lancing 2-0			

PRELIMINARY ROUNDS — Old Brentwoods 2, 3 Old Foresters 2, 2

OLD BRENTWOODS
Winners 1967

A Guyver, B Maguire,
A Love, J Churchill (Capt.),
P Thomas, T Russell,
P Clements, P Francis,
P Allen, G Harvey,
G Bowman.

OLD MALVERNIANS
Runners up 1967

(Back Row)
P M Townend, J W Illaszewicz,
D Bailey, A K Williams,
R W Tolchard, P Hayden.

(Front Row)
H D Loader, C W Stevens,
I Ryder-Smith (Capt.),
R H Chadder, A W Beeson.

SEASON 1965 - 1966

FIRST ROUND	SECOND ROUND	SEMI FINAL	FINAL	WINNERS
Old Salopians / Old Reptonians	Reptonians 5-1	Reptonians 1-1,8-0	Reptonians 5-0	Basnett (2), Tomlinson, Gillard
Old Etonians / Old Wellingburians	Wellingburians 6-1			
Old Carthusians / Old Westminsters	Carthusians 2-1	Carthusians 5-2		Reptonians 4-3
Old Bradfieldians / Old Cholmeleians	Cholmeleians 0-0,5-1		*Played at Crystal Palace*	Ryder-Smith (pen), Stevens, Illaszewicz
Old Wykehamists / Old Ardinians	Ardinians 2-1	Malvernians 3-0	Malvernians 4-1	
Old Aldenhamians / Old Malvernians	Malvernians 4-2			
Lancing Old Boys / Old Brentwoods	Brentwoods 2-2,4-2	Brentwoods 2-1		
Old Foresters / Old Chigwellians	Foresters 5-3			

OLD REPTONIANS
Winners 1966

(Back Row)
D C M Vaughan, C B Ellis,
G C Turner, P H Vaughan,
P W S Rowland, L M L Barnwell.

(Front Row)
A P Basnett, R G Gillard,
B J Hare (Capt.), J J W Tomlinson,
J D Harrison.

OLD MALVERNIANS
Runners up 1966

(Back Row)
P A Walton, A W Beeson,
A G Theobald, J M Costeloe,
I Ryder-Smith, H D Loader.

(Front Row)
J W Illaszewicz, A K Williams,
R H Chadder (Capt.), P Hayden,
C W Stevens.

SEASON 1968 - 1969

FIRST ROUND	SECOND ROUND	SEMI FINAL	FINAL	WINNERS
Old Westminsters / Old Cholmeleians	Westminsters 2-0	Westminsters 2-1	Bradfieldians 2-1	Malvernians 1-0
Old Ardinians / Old Chigwellians	Chigwellians 3-3,4-1			Driver
Old Bradfieldians / Old Wykehamists	Bradfieldians 4-2	Bradfieldians 1-1,5-4		
Old Aldenhamians / Old Carthusians	Aldenhamians 2-0			
Old Malvernians / Old Reptonians	Malvernians 3-2	Malvernians 1-0	Malvernians 5-1	
Old Wellingburians / Old Brentwoods	Brentwoods 4-0			
Lancing Old Boys / Old Foresters	Lancing 3-2	Lancing 4-3		
Old Etonians / Old Salopians	Salopians 3-2			

Played at Crystal Palace

PRELIMINARY ROUNDS: Old Harrovians 1 Lancing Old Boys 4

OLD MALVERNIANS Winners 1969
(Back Row)
R W Tolchard, P M Townend, T M P C Begg, M A Walker-Smith, R D Erhardt, M S Driver.
(Front Row)
P Hayden, H D Loader, I Ryder-Smith (Capt.), A K Williams, J W Bridle.

OLD BRADFIELDIANS Runners up 1969
(Back Row)
J McClaren, I Buckley, I Simpson, G Roope, K Pink, K Michel.
(Front Row)
J Gregory, D Shilton, C Gorringe (Capt.), N Fyler, N Loman.

SEASON 1967 - 1968

FIRST ROUND	SECOND ROUND	SEMI FINAL	FINAL	WINNERS
Old Malvernians / Old Harrovians	Malvernians 6-0	Malvernians 6-2	Malvernians 1-0	Williams
Old Westminsters / Old Wellingburians	Wellingburians 4-3			Malvernians and Reptonians (1-1),1-1 aet (Cup held jointly).
Old Foresters / Lancing Old Boys	Foresters 4-0	Brentwoods 2-1		P H Vaughan
Old Brentwoods / Old Salopians	Brentwoods 3-2			
Old Cholmeleians / Old Aldenhamians	Cholmeleians 3-1	Cholmeleians 2-1	Reptonians 2-0	
Old Chigwellians / Old Ardinians	Ardinians 2-1			
Old Carthusians / Old Etonians	Carthusians 5-1	Reptonians 2-0		
Old Bradfieldians / Old Reptonians	Reptonians 5-0			

Played at Crystal Palace

PRELIMINARY ROUNDS: Old Salopians 3 Old Wykehamists 0

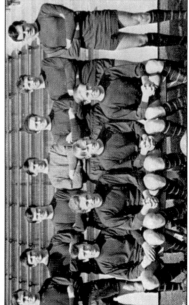

OLD MALVERNIANS Joint Holders 1968
(Back Row)
R D Erhardt, J W Illaszewicz, D Bailey, P M Townend, H D Loader, J M M Vaughan.
(Front Row)
A K Williams, R H Chadder, I Ryder-Smith (Capt.), C W Stevens, P Hayden.

OLD REPTONIANS Joint Holders 1968
(Back Row)
J J W Tomlinson, P N Gill, J D Harrison, D C M Vaughan, P W Rolfe, C P Waddilove, G C Turner.
(Front Row)
P H Vaughan, P W S Rowland, B J Hare (Capt.), R G Gillard.

SEASON 1970 - 1971

FIRST ROUND	SECOND ROUND	SEMI FINAL	FINAL	WINNERS

Lancing Old Boys
Old Cholmeleians } Lancing 4-3

Old Malvernians
Old Wellingburians } Malvernians 2-2, 3-1 } Malvernians 5-4

Old Bradfieldians
Old Carthusians } Carthusians 1-0 } Carthusians 3-0 } Malvernians 6-2

Old Reptonians
Old Salopians } Reptonians 2-1

Old Brentwoods
Old Ardinians } Brentwoods 3-1 } Brentwoods 5-0

Old Wykehamists
Old Etonians } Wykehamists 4-2 } Brentwoods 2-0

Old Harrovians
Old Foresters } Foresters 4-1 } Chigwellians 1-0

Old Westminsters
Old Chigwellians } Chigwellians 1-1, 4-0

Malvernians 4-2 — Stevens (og), Ryan

Played at Crystal Palace

Williams, Murray, Bridle (2)

OLD MALVERNIANS Winners 1971

(Back Row)
M F Murphy (sub), R D Erhardt, P Hayden, N H Stockbridge, I A R Murray, P M Townend.

(Front Row)
J W Bridle, D Bailey, H D Loader, I Ryder-Smith (Capt.), A K Williams, C W Stevens.

OLD BRENTWOODS Runners up 1971

(Back Row)
R Baker, M A J Ryan, D Anderson, R Deasley, R Barker, B Baker.

(Front Row)
H Maguire, D Cameron, P Thomas, P Clements (Capt.), M Tack, J Harris.

SEASON 1969 - 1970

FIRST ROUND	SECOND ROUND	SEMI FINAL	FINAL	WINNERS

Old Wellingburians
Old Aldenhamians } Wellingburians 3-3, 5-3

Old Reptonians
Old Chigwellians } Reptonians 2-0 } Reptonians 3-1

Old Bradfieldians
Old Brentwoods } Brentwoods 3-0 } Brentwoods 5-4 } Reptonians 4-2

Lancing Old.Boys
Old Ardinians } Ardinians 3-0

Old Cholmeleians
Old Etonians } Cholmeleians 2-0 } Cholmeleians 7-4

Old Malvernians
Old Salopians } Salopians 4-0 } Foresters 6-2

Old Harrovians
Old Westminsters } Harrovians 2-0 } Foresters 4-3

Old Foresters
Old Wykehamists } Foresters 2-0

Reptonians 2-1 — Rogers

Played at Crystal Palace

Gill, Tomlinson

OLD REPTONIANS Winners 1970

M Stockdale, B J Hare, A C Borrett (sub), P H Vaughan, P N Gill, A C Whitehead, P W Rolfe, G C Turner, J J W Tomlinson, J D Harrison (Capt.), P R Smith, P W S Rowland.

OLD FORESTERS Runners up 1970

G Peacock, R Hayes, R Dunn, G Green, C Smith, R Wheeler, L Beschizza, D Wilson, R Marshall, M Rogers, S Duncombe.

SEASON 1972 - 1973

FIRST ROUND	SECOND ROUND	SEMI FINAL	FINAL	WINNERS
Old Chigwellians / Old Etonians	Chigwellians 1-1, 6-1	Chigwellians 4-3		
Old Ardinians / Old Bradfieldians	Bradfieldians 2-0		Malvernians 2-0	
Old Reptonians / Old Carthusians	Reptonians 2-0	Malvernians 2-1		Andrew, Bridle
Old Malvernians / Old Salopians	Malvernians 2-1			
Old Cholmeleians / Old Wellingburians	Cholmeleians 2-1	Brentwoods 2-1		Brentwoods (2-2), 3-2 aet
Old Brentwoods / Old Foresters	Brentwoods 3-2		Brentwoods 3-1	N Harris, Francis, Thomas
Old Harrovians / Old Aldenhamians	Harrovians 2-1	Lancing 7-3		
Old Wykehamists / Lancing Old Boys	Lancing 0-0, 3-1			

Played at Crystal Palace

PRELIMINARY ROUNDS   Old Westminsters 2 Old Wellingburians 3

OLD BRENTWOODS Winners 1973

(Back Row)
T Russell, R Baker, D Anderson, P Thomas, A Guyver, J Harris, N Harris (sub).

(Front Row)
H Maguire, P Needham, B Baker (Capt.), M Tack, P Francis.

OLD MALVERNIANS Runners up 1973

(Back Row)
W F MacNaught, M F Murphy, M A Walker-Smith, R T H Wilson, R J Andrew.

(Front Row)
I A R Murray, P Hayden, J W Bridle, I Ryder-Smith (Capt.), H D Loader, N H Stockbridge.

SEASON 1971 - 1972

FIRST ROUND	SECOND ROUND	SEMI FINAL	FINAL	WINNERS
Old Carthusians / Old Brentwoods	Brentwoods 3-2	Brentwoods 2-0		
Old Chigwellians / Old Bradfieldians	Bradfieldians 2-1		Brentwoods 3-0	
Old Foresters / Old Aldenhamians	Foresters 4-2	Malvernians 2-1		J Harris
Old Malvernians / Old Wykehamists	Malvernians 3-2			
Old Wellingburians / Old Westminsters	Wellingburians 1-0	Salopians 2-1		Brentwoods 1-0
Old Reptonians / Old Salopians	Salopians 3-2		Salopians 2-0	
Old Ardinians / Lancing Old Boys	Lancing 1-0	Lancing 4-2		
Old Etonians / Old Harrovians	Etonians 1-0			

Played at Crystal Palace

PRELIMINARY ROUNDS   Old Reptonians 1 Old Cholmeleians 0

OLD BRENTWOODS Winners 1972

(Back Row)
P Wright (sub), D Anderson, R Deasley, A Guyver, T Russell, R Baker,

(Front Row)
N Harris, H Maguire, P Thomas, P Clements (Capt.), B Baker, J Harris.

OLD SALOPIANS Runners up 1972

(Back Row)
R H Gilkes, R A S Weetch, J G Sale, W A Tutton, G B Kendrew (sub), I R Short.

(Front Row)
R T Tudor, S K Jones, J G Alexander, A J M Walls, P St J Worth, C J Rowlinson.

SEASON 1974 - 1975

FIRST ROUND	SECOND ROUND	SEMI FINAL	FINAL	WINNERS
Old Westminsters / Old Foresters	Foresters 3-0	Foresters 2-0		
Lancing Old Boys / Old Wellingburians	Lancing 3-1			
Old Salopians / Old Harrovians	Salopians 3-3,4,6-3	Etonians 2-1	Foresters 3-1 (Hassid)	
Old Cholmeleians / Old Etonians	Etonians 2-1		*Played at Crystal Palace*	**Malvernians 2-1** (Murray; Bridle)
Old Brentwoods / Old Carthusians	Brentwoods 3-0	Bradfieldians 2-1		
Old Ardinians / Old Bradfieldians	Bradfieldians 3-1		Malvernians 1-0	
Old Wykehamists / Old Malvernians	Malvernians 2-1	Malvernians 2-1		
Old Reptonians / Old Chigwellians	Chigwellians 4-2			

PRELIMINARY ROUNDS: Old Aldenhamians 1 Old Chigwellians 4

OLD MALVERNIANS Winners 1975

M R Byers, R T H Wilson, P Hayden, N E Williams, I A R Murray, M F Murphy, P M Townend, C G J Williams, N H Stockbridge, J W Bridle, A R Whately, J A C Denham (sub).

OLD FORESTERS Runners up 1975

(Back Row) C B Smith(sub), J F Morley, S B Duncombe, G F Peacock, R B Hayes, R J Moss.

(Front Row) R S Wheeler, L P Beschizza, G S Green (Capt.), R S Marshall, M P Hassid.

SEASON 1973 - 1974

FIRST ROUND	SECOND ROUND	SEMI FINAL	FINAL	WINNERS
Old Carthusians / Old Cholmeleians	Carthusians 3-2	Carthusians 2-1		
Old Chigwellians / Old Bradfieldians	Bradfieldians 2-0		Brentwoods 4-1	
Old Harrovians / Old Wykehamists	Harrovians 3-2	Brentwoods 3-1		Foresters (1-1), 2-1 aet
Old Brentwoods / Old Malvernians	Brentwoods 4-3		*Played at Crystal Palace*	(Forbes, Wilson (pen))
Lancing Old Boys / Old Etonians	Lancing 2-0	Reptonians 5-2		
Old Reptonians / Old Aldenhamians	Reptonians 4-0		Foresters 3-0 (Cameron)	
Old Foresters / Old Westminsters	Foresters 4-1	Foresters 3-0		
Old Salopians / Old Wellingburians	Salopians 2-0			

PRELIMINARY ROUNDS: Old Ardinians 0 Old Etonians 3

OLD FORESTERS Winners 1974

(Back Row) S B Duncombe, R B Hayes, R S Marshall, G F Peacock, C S Forbes, J F Morley, D Wilson.

(Front Row) S W Balme (sub), C B Smith, L P Beschizza, G S Green (Capt.), R S Wheeler.

OLD BRENTWOODS Runners up 1974

(Back Row) K H Boon (Chairman), P Francis, B Baker, N Harris, J Kilmartin, R Deasley, N Bunter (sub).

(Front Row) N Parsons, P Needham, D Anderson (Capt.), D Cameron, H Maguire, R Baker.

162

SEASON 1976 - 1977

FIRST ROUND	SECOND ROUND	SEMI FINAL	FINAL	WINNERS
Old Westminsters / Lancing Old Boys	Lancing 3-2	Carthusians 6-1	Carthusians 5-1	Carthusians 3-0
Old Harrovians				
Old Bradfieldians / Old Carthusians	Carthusians 6-1			
Old Wykehamists / Old Aldenhamians	Wykehamists 1-1,5-1	Wykehamists 4-1		
Old Ardinians / Old Wellingburians	Wellingburians 1-1,3-2			
Old Harrovians / Old Foresters	Foresters 2-2,4-1	Brentwoods 2-1	Brentwoods 1-0	
Old Brentwoods / Old Salopians	Brentwoods 2-1			
Old Chigwellians / Old Malvernians	Malvernians 1-0	Malvernians 3-0		
Old Reptonians / Old Cholmeleians	Reptonians 5-3			

Walton, Bennett (pen), Holder

Played at Crystal Palace

PRELIMINARY ROUNDS   Old Etonians 3 Old Brentwoods 4

OLD CARTHUSIANS Winners 1977

(Back Row)
M Herbert-Smith (sub), J M Bennett, S J E Easton, H M Martin, J D Holder, K R Ellis.

(Front Row)
A D Marks, I A Stewart, A Adomakoh, L K Walton (Capt.), P C Godby, C Comninos.

OLD BRENTWOODS Runners up 1977

(Back Row)
M Tack (sub), M Walker, D Cameron, J Kilmartin, D Anderson, B Baker.

(Front Row)
N Parsons, I Baker, P Needham, J Harris (Capt.), S Boon, R Deasley.

SEASON 1975 - 1976

FIRST ROUND	SECOND ROUND	SEMI FINAL	FINAL	WINNERS
Lancing Old Boys / Old Harrovians	Lancing 3-2	Malvernians 4-3	Malvernians 4-1	Malvernians 5-3
Old Malvernians / Old Chigwellians	Malvernians 2-1			
Old Foresters / Old Cholmeleians	Foresters 3-1	Foresters 3-2		
Old Bradfieldians / Old Ardinians	Bradfieldians 5-1			
Old Reptonians / Old Aldenhamians	Aldenhamians 3-2	Salopians 0-0,2-2,3-2	Brentwoods 7-3	
Old Salopians / Old Westminsters	Salopians 6-1			
Old Wellingburians / Old Etonians	Wellingburians 1-0	Brentwoods 5-3		
Old Wykehamists / Old Brentwoods	Brentwoods 4-2			

Murray (2), Saunders, Murphy (og)

Needham, Walker, Deasley

Played at Crystal Palace

PRELIMINARY ROUNDS   Old Salopians 1, 2 Old Carthusians 1, 1

OLD MALVERNIANS Winners 1976

(Back Row)
P M Townend, J A C Denham (sub), I A R Murray, M R Byers, N E Williams, M J Saunders, C G J Williams.

(Front Row)
J W Bridle, A R Whately, P Hayden (Capt.), M F Murphy, N H Stockbridge.

OLD BRENTWOODS Runners up 1976

(Back Row)
J Kilmartin, D Cameron, N Bunter, R Deasley, D Anderson, M Walker, B Baker.

(Front Row)
N Parsons, H Maguire, J Harris (Capt.), P Needham, I Baker (sub).

SEASON 1978 - 1979

FIRST ROUND	SECOND ROUND	SEMI FINAL	FINAL	WINNERS
Old Aldenhamians / Old Etonians	Aldenhamians 3-2	Aldenhamians 3-2		
Old Reptonians / Old Bradfieldians	Reptonians 2-0		Aldenhamians 3-1	
Old Chigwellians / Old Foresters	Chigwellians 2-1	Cholmeleians 2-1		
Old Ardinians / Old Cholmeleians	Cholmeleians 3-1			Aldenhamians 1-0
Old Brentwoods / Lancing Old Boys	Brentwoods 3-0	Brentwoods 3-2		*Pickett*
Old Westminsters / Old Malvernians	Malvernians 1-0		Brentwoods 2-0	
Old Harrovians / Old Wellingburians	Harrovians 3-1	Salopians 2-1		
Old Salopians / Old Carthusians	Salopians 2-1			

Played at Crystal Palace

PRELIMINARY ROUNDS: Old Cholmeleians 2, 3 Old Wykehamists 2, 1

OLD ALDENHAMIANS Winners 1979

(Back Row)
R C Beechener, S D Massey (sub), J R Baugh, M Vaughan, D R Pickett, P S S Kerr, J D L Yule.

(Front Row)
R D Hall, P K Smith, A N Clare (Capt.), A R Limb, S Rohleder.

OLD BRENTWOODS Runners up 1979

(Back Row)
K Fenwick, J Herlighy, J Harris, S Boon, A Guyver, M Walker, D Cameron.

(Front Row)
H Maguire (sub), I Baker, P Francis (Capt.), P Needham, N Harle.

SEASON 1977 - 1978

FIRST ROUND	SECOND ROUND	SEMI FINAL	FINAL	WINNERS
Old Brentwoods / Old Etonians	Brentwoods 4-1	Brentwoods 2-1		
Lancing Old Boys / Old Foresters	Lancing 2-1		Malvernians 5-4	
Old Harrovians / Old Malvernians	Malvernians 2-1	Malvernians 4-1		
Old Carthusians / Old Ardinians	Carthusians 3-1			Malvernians 4-1
Old Cholmeleians / Old Salopians	Cholmeleians 2-0	Chigwellians 1-0		*Ryder-Smith (2) (1 pen.), Bridle (2)*
Old Wykehamists / Old Chigwellians	Chigwellians 3-1		Bradfieldians 2-1	*Fyler (pen)*
Old Reptonians / Old Westminsters	Reptonians 4-1	Bradfieldians 2-2, 2-0		
Old Bradfieldians / Old Aldenhamians	Bradfieldians 2-1			

Played at Crystal Palace

PRELIMINARY ROUNDS: Old Chigwellians 2 Old Wellingburians 1

OLD MALVERNIANS Winners 1978

(Back Row)
I M Denham, N E Williams, J A C Denham, C F Murphy, M R Byers, R T H Wilson (sub), C G J Williams.

(Front Row)
M F Murphy, I Ryder-Smith, I A R Murray (Capt.), J W Bridle, A R Whately.

OLD BRADFIELDIANS Runners up 1978

(Back Row)
M Chapple, S Denehy, R Carne, R Blaskey, S Bodkin, R Thornton, N Fyler (sub).

(Front Row)
J Gregory, I Buckley, D Manners (Capt.), K Michel, N Colman.

SEASON 1980 - 1981

FIRST ROUND	SECOND ROUND	SEMI FINAL	FINAL	WINNERS
Old Wellingburians / Old Foresters	Foresters 4-3	Carthusians 1-0	Reptonians 5-3	Reptonians 3-3,1-0
Old Ardinians / Old Carthusians	Carthusians 4-2			Scott, Peacock (2) (R): Stretton
Old Aldenhamians / Old Cholmeleians	Cholmeleians 3-1	Reptonians 3-1		
Old Wykehamists / Old Reptonians	Reptonians 2-1			
Old Etonians / Lancing Old Boys	Lancing 3-0	Lancing 1-0	Malvernians 4-3	Smith, Saunders. Denham
Old Salopians / Old Chigwellians	Chigwellians 4-0			
Old Malvernians / Old Harrovians	Malvernians 6-0	Malvernians 4-2		
Old Bradfieldians / Old Brentwoods	Brentwoods 2-1			

Played at Crystal Palace

PRELIMINARY ROUNDS   Old Westminsters 0 Old Reptonians 5

OLD REPTONIANS Winners 1981

(Back Row)
J D E Wood, M N Stretton, S A H Blackburn, A H Cowell, J Ballinger, M J Beckett, D J Widdowson, T P Harrison.

(Front Row)
J R Eifion-Jones, R S Scott, R G Body (Capt.), T D R Peacock, T P Turner.

OLD MALVERNIANS Runners up 1981

(Back Row)
B P Dafforn-Jones, R Trotter, M J Saunders, M D K Wills, D F Moore, N E Williams, S Smith.

(Front Row)
A R Whately, J A C Denham, R T H Wilson (Capt.), M F Murphy, I M Denham.

SEASON 1979 - 1980

FIRST ROUND	SECOND ROUND	SEMI FINAL	FINAL	WINNERS
Old Salopians / Old Etonians	Salopians 0-0, 3-1	Salopians 3-1	Chigwellians 2-0	Chigwellians (2-2), 4-2 aet
Old Wellingburians / Old Wykehamists	Wykehamists 5-3			Redrup (2), Dutchman (2) (1 pen)
Old Westminsters / Old Bradfieldians	Bradfieldians 2-1	Chigwellians 1-0		
Old Chigwellians / Old Aldenhamians	Chigwellians 2-1			
Old Reptonians / Old Malvernians	Malvernians 3-2	Brentwoods 4-2	Lancing 4-3	Pitcher, Brooking
Old Carthusians / Old Brentwoods	Brentwoods 5-2			
Old Foresters / Old Harrovians	Foresters 3-1	Lancing 4-1		
Old Cholmeleians / Lancing Old Boys	Lancing 5-1			

Played at Crystal Palace

PRELIMINARY ROUNDS   Old Ardinians 1 Old Malvernians 4

OLD CHIGWELLIANS Winners 1980

(Back Row)
A Speed, S Day, S Redrup, H Burbidge, A Bone, M Taylor, G Inch (sub).

(Front Row)
D Dutchman, H Berndes (Capt.), S Phelps, R Berndes, M Brett.

LANCING OLD BOYS Runners up 1980

(Back Row)
N Grainger, R Brodhurst, N Bennett, C Sutherland, M Wyatt, N Triggs, A Brooking (sub).

(Front Row)
J Todd, M Todd, J Wood (Capt.), N Pitcher, P Stallibrass.

SEASON 1982 - 1983

FIRST ROUND	SECOND ROUND	SEMI FINAL	FINAL	WINNERS
Lancing Old Boys / Old Cholmeleians	Lancing 4-1	Lancing 2-1	Lancing 4-2	Lancing 2-0
Old Wykehamists / Old Harrovians	Harrovians 3-0			N Bennett, Pitcher
Old Salopians / Old Etonians	Salopians 6-0	Salopians 2-1		
Old Reptonians / Old Carthusians	Reptonians 1-1,1-0			
Old Ardinians / Old Chigwellians	Chigwellians 3-1	Chigwellians 3-0	Chigwellians 3-1	
Old Westminsters / Old Bradfieldians	Westminsters 4-1			
Old Brentwoods / Old Aldenhamians	Brentwoods 4-2	Brentwoods 5-4		
Old Malvernians / Old Wellingburians	Malvernians 4-0			

Played at Dulwich Hamlet

PRELIMINARY ROUNDS — Old Foresters 3 Old Bradfieldians 6

LANCING OLD BOYS Winners 1983

(Back Row) R W D Stallibrass (sub), C C Beale, N A O Bennett, C A Sutherland, S C O Bennett, M O Wyatt, R C C H Brodhurst.

(Front Row) A M F Todd, J K I Wood, N B Pitcher (Capt.), N G W Triggs, G J Sheridan.

OLD CHIGWELLIANS Runners up 1983

(Back Row) M West, G Inch, G Burbidge, J Connolly, J Payton, A Speed (sub), S Redrup.

(Front Row) S Phelps, R Berndes, H Berndes (Capt.), M Taylor, D Dutchman.

SEASON 1981 - 1982

FIRST ROUND	SECOND ROUND	SEMI FINAL	FINAL	WINNERS
Old Carthusians / Old Ardinians	Carthusians 7-0	Carthusians 7-1	Carthusians 2-1	Carthusians 3-0
Old Reptonians / Old Bradfieldians	Reptonians 3-2			Oulton, Pratt, Stewart
Old Wykehamists / Old Brentwoods	Brentwoods 1-0	Brentwoods 2-1		
Old Westminsters / Old Wellingburians	Westminsters 3-1			
Old Malvernians / Old Cholmeleians	Malvernians 2-0	Malvernians 3-2	Malvernians 4-3	
Old Aldenhamians / Old Chigwellians	Chigwellians 2-1			
Old Etonians / Old Salopians	Salopians 3-1	Lancing 4-2		
Lancing Old Boys / Old Foresters	Lancing 1-0			

Played at Dulwich Hamlet

PRELIMINARY ROUNDS — Old Harrovians 0 Lancing Old Boys 3

OLD CARTHUSIANS Winners 1982

(Back Row) I A Stewart, T C R Whalley, K R Ellis, M W G Doggart, G D T Pride, J D Holder (sub), H E Pratt.

(Front Row) M G Herbert-Smith, L K Walton, R A C Oulton (Capt.), P C Godby, S J E Easton.

OLD MALVERNIANS Runners up 1982

(Back Row) R Andrew (sub), R Trotter, M Holliday, M D K Wills, M J Saunders, B Horton, S Smith.

(Front Row) I Denham, J W Bridle, R T H Wilson (Capt.), J A C Denham, D F Moore.

SEASON 1984 - 1985

FIRST ROUND	SECOND ROUND	SEMI FINAL	FINAL	WINNERS
Old Malvernians Old Cholmeleians	Malvernians 5-1	Malvernians 2-1		
Old Bradfieldians Old Citizens	Bradfieldians 4-2		Lancing 3-0	
St. Edmund's O.B. Lancing Old Boys	Lancing 6-2	Lancing 2-2,1-1,4-0		N Bennett (2), Pitcher, Sheridan, Beale
Old Carthusians Old Wellingburians	Carthusians 1-0			Lancing 5-0
Old Aldenhamians Old Ardinians	Aldenhamians 5-2	Old Etonians 2-1	*Played at Dulwich Hamlet*	
Old Etonians Old Salopians	Etonians 3-1		Foresters 6-2	
Old Foresters Old Chigwellians	Foresters 1-1, 2-1	Foresters 3-0		
Old Reptonians Old Brentwoods	Reptonians 3-2			

PRELIMINARY ROUNDS Old Reptonians 5 Old Harrovians 0, Old Westminsters 0 Old Carthusians 2, Old Wykehamists 1 Old Bradfieldians 1, 2

LANCING OLD BOYS
Winners 1985

(Back Row)
J H Todd, G J Sheridan,
N J Bell (sub), S C O Bennett,
C A Sutherland,
R W D Stallibrass, C C Beale.

(Front Row)
R C C H Brodhurst, N B Pitcher,
N A O Bennett (Capt.),
M O Wyatt, N G W Triggs.

OLD FORESTERS
Runners up 1985

(Back Row)
R Harnack, P Andriesz,
T Chard, N Francis,
C Elliott, K Parsley,
I Crossley.

(Front Row)
S Balme, M Robinson,
L Beschizza (Capt.),
M Hassid (sub), T Hendrick.

SEASON 1983 - 1984

FIRST ROUND	SECOND ROUND	SEMI FINAL	FINAL	WINNERS
Old Etonians Old Harrovians	Harrovians 4-0	Harrovians 2-1		
Old Chigwellians Old Bradfieldians	Chigwellians 2-1		Lancing 5-3	
Old Wykehamists Old Salopians	Salopians 1-1, 2-0	Lancing 2-0		Wyatt, Pitcher
Old Cholmeleians Lancing Old Boys	Lancing 5-3			Lancing 2-0
Old Wellingburians Old Ardinians	Wellingburians 2-0	Carthusians 3-0	*Played at Dulwich Hamlet*	
Old Carthusians Old Brentwoods	Carthusians 4-3		Carthusians 2-1	
Old Reptonians Old Westminsters	Westminsters 2-1	Westminsters 2-2,1-0		
Old Aldenhamians Old Foresters	Aldenhamians 2-1			

PRELIMINARY ROUNDS Old Malvernians 2, 0 Old Brentwoods 2, 3

LANCING OLD BOYS
Winners 1984

(Back Row)
A J Hodgkinson, N J Bell (sub),
M O Wyatt, C A Sutherland,
R C C H Brodhurst, G J Sheridan,
J H Todd.

(Front Row)
P M Stallibrass, A M F Todd,
N B Pitcher (Capt.),
N A O Bennett, N G W Triggs.

OLD CARTHUSIANS
Runners up 1984

(Back Row)
K R Ellis, M W G Doggart,
M G Herbert-Smith, P C Godby,
T C R Whalley, G D T Pride,
H E Pratt (sub).

(Front Row)
A Adomakoh, L K Walton,
R A C Oulton (Capt.),
S J E Easton, I A Stewart.

167

SEASON 1986 - 1987

FIRST ROUND | SECOND ROUND | SEMI FINAL | FINAL | WINNERS

Old Reptonians / Old Ardinians → Reptonians 1-0
Old Haileyburians / Old Harrovians → Harrovians 3-2
— Reptonians 5-0

Old Aldenhamians / Old Brentwoods → Brentwoods 3-0
Old Malvernians / Old Westminsters → Malvernians 2-0
— Malvernians 1-1,1-0

FINAL: Reptonians 2-0

Old Chigwellians / Old Wykehamists → Chigwellians 5-0
Old Foresters / Old Bradfieldians → Bradfieldians 5-3
— Chigwellians 4-0

Lancing Old Boys / Old Cholmeleians → Cholmeleians 2-2,3-2
Old Carthusians / Old Salopians → Carthusians 3-0
— Cholmeleians 1-0

FINAL: Cholmeleians 2-1

WINNERS: Reptonians (1-1), 2-2*, 3-2
Stretton, Wale, (R): Stretton, Eifion-Jones, Cowell
M Halstead, Walton
(R): Wainwright, Walton
*aet

Played at Motspur Park

Old Chigwellians 9 St Edmund's 0, Old Citizens 1 Old Brentwoods 2.
Old Etonians 1 Lancing Old Boys 5, Old Wellingburians 1 Old Salopians 2

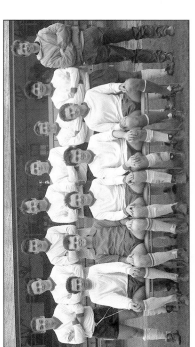

OLD REPTONIANS Winners 1987

(Back Row)
E G Wale (sub), J H Proctor, M R Batey, M S H Smith, G C L Blakesley, R N Miller, J M G Willatt.

(Front Row)
J S Frost, N C Walford, M N Stretton (Capt.), J R Eifion-Jones, A H Cowell.

OLD CHOLMELEIANS Runners up 1987

(Back Row)
W Wawn, P Sylvester, P Ambrose, H Olivere, S Halstead (sub), N Gray, A Savva, G Stempell.

(Front Row)
F Kyriacou, M Smith, D Wainwright (Capt.), M Halstead, M Walton.

SEASON 1985 - 1986

FIRST ROUND | SECOND ROUND | SEMI FINAL | FINAL | WINNERS

Old Citizens / Old Brentwoods → Brentwoods 4-1
Old Etonians / Old Wykehamists → Etonians 2-1
— Brentwoods 3-2

Lancing Old Boys / Old Ardinians → Lancing 3-0
Old Carthusians / Old Bradfieldians → Carthusians 2-1
— Carthusians 1-1,1-0

FINAL: Brentwoods 1-1, 2-0

St. Edmund's O.B. / Old Harrovians → St. Edmund's 2-1
Old Cholmeleians / Old Westminsters → Cholmeleians 3-0
— Cholmeleians 6-1

Old Chigwellians / Old Salopians → Chigwellians 1-0
Old Malvernians / Old Reptonians → Malvernians 3-0
— Malvernians 1-0

FINAL: Cholmeleians 5-3

WINNERS: Brentwoods 1-0
Dixon

Played at Dulwich Hamlet

Old Cholmeleians 1 Old Aldenhamians 0, Lancing Old Boys 6 Old Foresters 5, Old Wellingburians 0 Old Ardinians 4

OLD BRENTWOODS Winners 1986

(Back Row)
G Lockhart, S Doran, A Pears, P Smaje, D Mackay, C Pemberton (sub).

(Front Row)
P Preston, R Dixon, S Boon, K Fenwick (Capt.), P Needham, J Herlihy.

OLD CHOLMELEIANS Runners up 1986

(Back Row)
J Green, I Amstad, H J Olivere, M Walton, M Smith, S P Savva, G Stempel.

(Front Row)
F J Kyriacou, N Gray, E J Gray (sub), M Collins (Capt.), A P Savva, D B Wainwright.

SEASON 1988 - 1989

FIRST ROUND	SECOND ROUND	SEMI FINAL	FINAL	WINNERS
Old Westminsters / Old Salopians	Salopians 5-0	Carthusians 1-0		
Old Haileyburians / Old Carthusians	Carthusians 4-0		Malvernians 5-3	
Old Malvernians / Old Ardinians	Malvernians 5-1	Malvernians 0-0, 2-1		Malvernians (1-1), 3-1 aet
Old Reptonians / Old Harrovians	Reptonians 4-0			Harris, Temperton, I Denham / Needham
Old Wellingburians / Old Chigwellians	Chigwellians 2-2, 1-0	Cholmeleians 3-2		
Old Foresters / Old Cholmeleians	Cholmeleians 2-1		Brentwoods 4-2	
Old Etonians / Lancing Old Boys	Etonians 3-0	Brentwoods 2-1		
Old Brentwoods / St Edmund's O.B.	Brentwoods w/o			

Played at Motspur Park

PRELIMINARY ROUNDS   Old Bradfieldians 0 Old Salopians 5, Old Etonians 4 Old Aldenhamians 2, Old Cholmeleians 7 Old Citizens 1, Old Wykehamists 0 Old Chigwellians 3

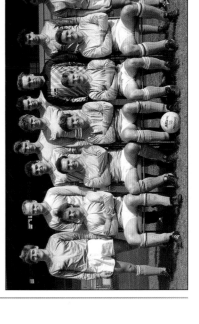

OLD MALVERNIANS Winners 1989

(Back Row) G N Lunt, R S Harris, A D C Ferguson, G E A King, L S Lindsay (sub), H C Douglas-Pennant, A P Temperton.

(Front Row) M D K Wills, I M Denham, J A C Denham (Capt.), E H Gilbert, P J Clare-Hunt.

OLD BRENTWOODS Runners up 1989

(Back Row) C Rowe, C Longden, S Moore, D Mackay, P Smaje, C Jarvis, N French, A Herbert, J Davey.

(Front Row) J Lockhart, K Fenwick, S Doran (Capt.), P Needham, S Boon.

SEASON 1987 - 1988

FIRST ROUND	SECOND ROUND	SEMI FINAL	FINAL	WINNERS
Old Bradfieldians / Old Etonians	Bradfieldians 3-2	Salopians 2-1		
St. Edmund's O.B. / Old Salopians	Salopians 4-1		Cholmeleians 1-0	
Old Aldenhamians / Lancing Old Boys	Lancing 2-2, 5-0	Cholmeleians 3-2		Cholmeleians 2-1
Old Citizens / Old Cholmeleians	Cholmeleians 6-1			Halstead (pen), Walton / Allden
Old Wellingburians / Old Malvernians	Malvernians 4-1	Malvernians 3-0		
Old Foresters / Old Chigwellians	Foresters 5-3		Brentwoods 3-0	
Old Brentwoods / Old Wykehamists	Brentwoods 3-1	Brentwoods 1-1, 3-1		
Old Westminsters / Old Reptonians	Reptonians 4-0			

Played at Motspur Park

PRELIMINARY ROUNDS   Old Ardinians 1, 2 Old Westminsters 1, 3, Old Foresters 5 Old Carthusians 2, Old Haileyburians 0 Old Malvernians 2, Old Harrovians 2 Old Reptonians 5

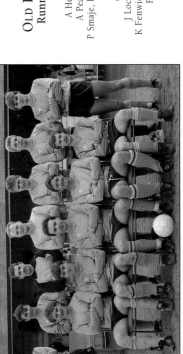

OLD CHOLMELEIANS Winners 1988

(Back Row) N J D Gray (sub), F J Kyriacou, H J Olivere, M Collins, M H Walton, M Lindstrom, J A Green.

(Front Row) N Rathbone, M R Smith, D B Wainwright (Capt.), M J Halstead, P G Lusardi.

OLD BRENTWOODS Runners up 1988

(Back Row) A Herbert, J Davey, A Pears, C Longden, P Smaje, R Wooldridge (sub), P Allden.

(Front Row) J Lockhart, S Doran, K Fenwick (Capt.), S Boon, P Needham.

SEASON 1990 - 1991

FIRST ROUND	SECOND ROUND	SEMI FINAL	FINAL	WINNERS
Old Foresters / Old Reptonians	Reptonians 3-2	Reptonians 2-0		
Old Aldenhamians / Old Wykehamists	Aldenhamians 2-2,1-0			
Old Eastbournians / Lancing Old Boys	Lancing 6-0	Lancing 2-1	Reptonians 2-0	Wale (R): Stretton, Gillespie (2), Wale
Old Cholmeleians / Old Etonians	Etonians 2-0			
Old Wellingburians / Old Westminsters	Wellingburians 2-1	Carthusians 2-1		Reptonians (1-1),1-1*, 4-0, Kerevan *aet
Old Carthusians / Old Salopians	Carthusians 1-0			*Played at Motspur Park*
Old Bradfieldians / Old Haileyburians	Bradfieldians 2-1	Brentwoods 3-1	Carthusians 2-1	
Old Brentwoods / Old Malvernians	Brentwoods 5-4			

PRELIMINARY ROUNDS Old Ardinians 0 Old Reptonians 3, Old Bradfieldians 2 Old Harrovians 1, Old Foresters 6 Old Chigwellians 3, Old Wirtleians 0 Old Etonians 1

OLD REPTONIANS Winners 1991
(Back Row) I King, P Gillespie, M R Batey, M S H Smith, S Whitehouse, G C L Blakesley.
(Front Row) D Anderson, P Brownhill, J H Procter, M N Stretton (Capt.), J R Eifion-Jones, E G Wale, (Absent: R N Miller).

OLD CARTHUSIANS Runners up 1991
(Back Row) A Viall, J Kemball, N Waters, J Aubrey, M Kerevan, R Faulkner, C May.
(Front Row) M G Herbert-Smith, A Adomakoh, J Golder (Capt.), K R Ellis, R A C Oulton.

SEASON 1989 - 1990

FIRST ROUND	SECOND ROUND	SEMI FINAL	FINAL	WINNERS
Old Bradfieldians / Old Wykehamists	Wykehamists 0-0, 3-2	Wykehamists 2-1		
Old Citizens / Old Harrovians	Harrovians w/o			
Old Salopians / Old Wellingburians	Wellingburians 4-2	Chigwellians 4-1	Chigwellians 2-0	Tapper (R): Tapper (2) Quill
Old Chigwellians / Old Cholmeleians	Chigwellians 3-2			
Old Brentwoods / Old Haileyburians	Brentwoods 7-1	Brentwoods 3-2		Chigwellians (1-1),1-1*, 3-2 *aet
Old Foresters / Old Aldenhamians	Aldenhamians 2-0			*Played at Motspur Park*
Old Ardinians / Old Reptonians	Reptonians 4-1	Reptonians 4-1	Reptonians 3-2	Stretton (R): Black, Wale
Old Malvernians / Old Etonians	Etonians 2-1			

PRELIMINARY ROUNDS Old Brentwoods 6 Old Carthusians 2, Old Haileyburians 13 St. Edmund's O.B. 1, Lancing Old Boys 1 Old Malvernians 3, Old Wellingburians 2 Old Westminsters 1

OLD CHIGWELLIANS Winners 1990
(Back Row) C M Batt, C Sydenham, I D Grover, D J Quill, A R Jefcoate, A J Brandon, J J Payton.
(Front Row) P N Burbidge, R C Tapper, M D Partridge (Capt.), G R Bryce, F B Davis (sub).

OLD REPTONIANS Runners up 1990
(Back Row) P Brownhill, A White, S Black, M S H Smith, S Whitehouse, D Anderson.
(Front Row) N J Walford, E G Wale, M N Stretton (Capt.), J S Frost, G C L Blakesley.

SEASON 1992 - 1993

FIRST ROUND	SECOND ROUND	SEMI FINAL	FINAL	WINNERS
Lancing Old Boys / Old Etonians	Lancing 3-1	Lancing 4-2	Lancing 3-2	Lancing 1-0 *(Alcock)*
Old Foresters / Old Malvernians	Foresters 3-2			
Old Aldenhamians / Old Chigwellians	Chigwellians 3-0	Chigwellians 3-0		
Old Westminsters / Old Harrovians	Harrovians 4-2			
Old Eastbournians / Old Reptonians	Reptonians 4-1	Reptonians 2-0	Reptonians 3-1	
Old Carthusians / Old Wykehamists	Carthusians 2-0			
Old Salopians / Old Brentwoods	Brentwoods 4-3	Brentwoods 1-0		
Old Cholmeleians / Old Wellingburians	Wellingburians 2-0			

Played at Motspur Park

PRELIMINARY ROUNDS: Old Bradfieldians 1 Old Brentwoods 2, Old Carthusians 3 Old Witleians 1, Old Etonians 3 Old Haileyburians 1, Lancing Old Boys 3 Old Ardinians 1

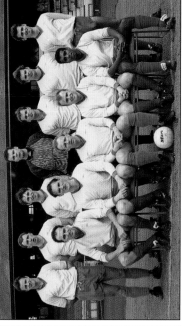

LANCING OLD BOYS Winners 1993
(Back Row) A J Cunningham, I Z B-Peterside, N J Bell, N A O Bennett, A J Lutwyche, S J Lees, S D Kelsey.
(Front Row) P M Alcock, B H Evans, A W Mercer (Capt.), J B Higgo, J D Robinson.

OLD REPTONIANS Runners up 1993
(Back Row) D Anderson, I King, P Gillespie, M Smith, R Basnett, S Black, S Jordan.
(Front Row) G Blakesley, S Whitehouse, M Stretton (Capt.), E Wale, N Sreevalsan.

SEASON 1991 - 1992

FIRST ROUND	SECOND ROUND	SEMI FINAL	FINAL	WINNERS
Old Chigwellians / Old Cholmeleians	Chigwellians 7-1	Chigwellians 4-2	Chigwellians 2-1	Chigwellians 3-1 *(Tapper (2), Davis)*
Old Aldenhamians / Old Bradfieldians	Aldenhamians 2-0			
Old Ardinians / Old Harrovians	Ardinians 2-1	Salopians 1-0		
Old Salopians / Old Haileyburians	Salopians 1-0			
Old Brentwoods / Old Foresters	Foresters 3-3	Lancing 5-2	Etonians 3-2	
Lancing Old Boys / Old Reptonians	Lancing 3-2			
Old Etonians / Old Witleians	Etonians 4-1	Etonians 4-3		*(Giles)*
Old Westminsters / Old Carthusians	Carthusians 5-1			

Played at Motspur Park

PRELIMINARY ROUNDS: Old Aldenhamians 2 Old Malvernians 1, Old Salopians 3 Old Wellingburians 2, Old Westminsters 6 Old Eastbournians 0, Old Wykehamists 0 Old Cholmeleians 7

OLD CHIGWELLIANS Winners 1992
(Back Row) F B Davis, D J Goddard, A R Jefcoate, J J Conolly, C Sydenham, A R Sweet, P S Elvin.
(Front Row) M D Hutchin, P N Burbidge, G R Bryce (Capt.), R C Tapper, I D Grover.

OLD ETONIANS Runners up 1992
(Back Row) C J Barnes, M Armander, N N H Matterson, C Yorke, K J Angeline Hurl, N R Hurd, D. Lewis.
(Front Row) D K Howell, J T N Scobie, J E J N Giles (Capt.), J P Ashmore, R N Gladstone.

SEASON 1994 - 1995

FIRST ROUND	SECOND ROUND	SEMI FINAL	FINAL	WINNERS
Lancing Old Boys / Old Chigwellians	Chigwellians 0-0,1-0	Chigwellians 5-1		
Old Witleians / Old Etonians	Witleians 1-0		Salopians 1-0	
Old Carthusians / Old Salopians	Salopians 1-0	Salopians 2-1		Honychurch (2)
Old Bradfieldians / Old Malvernians	Malvernians 2-1			Salopians 2-1
Old Harrovians / Old Reptonians	Reptonians 6-0	Reptonians 2-1		Pratt
Old Brentwoods / Old Cholmeleians	Brentwoods 3-1		Foresters 3-1	*Played at Motspur Park*
Old Ardinians / Old Foresters	Foresters 7-1	Foresters 7-1		
Old Wykehamists / Old Westminsters	Wykehamists 4-1			

PRELIMINARY ROUNDS: Old Bradfieldians 2 Old Haileyburians 1, Old Brentwoods 5 Old Aldenhamians 1, Old Cholmeleians 8 Old Eastbournians 0, Lancing Old Boys 3 Old Wellingburians 0

OLD SALOPIANS Winners 1995

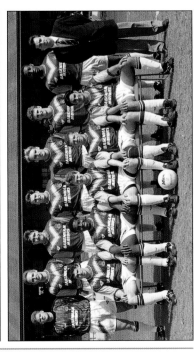

(Back Row)
R E Cooke, H E E Raven,
M J Lascelles, S W K Ellis,
J A Skelton, T G Cooke,
S M K Goodman.

(Front Row)
P L Dyke, D R G Arthur,
D W W Honychurch (Capt.),
P R Deans, A J Pollock.

OLD FORESTERS Runners up 1995

(Back Row)
M Butler, C Elliott,
N Francis, A Heyes,
M Shepherd, J Banks,
B Barnett, M Robinson.

(Front Row)
D Pratt, S Yankson,
R Harnack (Capt.),
L Douris, C Hossain.

SEASON 1993 - 1994

FIRST ROUND	SECOND ROUND	SEMI FINAL	FINAL	WINNERS
Old Chigwellians / Old Reptonians	Chigwellians 4-0	Chigwellians 2-0		Grover (2)
Old Malvernians / Old Haileyburians	Malvernians 6-0		Chigwellians 5-2	(R): Bryce, Jones, Sydenham, Brandon (2)
Old Etonians / Old Cholmeleians	Cholmeleians 1-0	Cholmeleians 2-1		Chigwellians (2-2),2-2*, 5-1
Old Eastbournians / Old Wellingburians	Wellingburians 6-0			Pollock, Dyke
Old Carthusians / Old Aldenhamians	Carthusians 3-2	Carthusians 1-1,1-0		(R): Pollock
Lancing Old Boys / Old Brentwoods	Lancing 2-1		Salopians 2-1	*Played at Motspur Park*
Old Witleians / Old Bradfieldians	Bradfieldians 2-1	Salopians 3-0		*aet
Old Salopians / Old Ardinians	Salopians 26-0			

PRELIMINARY ROUNDS: Old Foresters 1 Old Chigwellians 2, Old Harrovians 1 Old Reptonians 5, Old Malvernians 2 Old Wykehamists 0, Old Salopians 3 Old Westminsters 1

OLD CHIGWELLIANS Winners 1994

(Back Row)
S S Harding, D J Goddard,
I D Grover, D R Evans,
A R Sweet, S J Grover,
R K Jones, A R Jeffcoate,
A J Brandon.

(Front Row)
G R Bryce, M D Hutchin,
R C Tapper (Capt.),
J Legon, C Sydenham.

OLD SALOPIANS Runners up 1994

(Back Row)
R Cooke, O L Brown,
J J Clark, H E E Raven,
M J Lascelles, G P J Bowden,
P L Dyke, I R Stanley.

(Front Row)
A I Pollock, P R Deans,
D W W Honychurch (Capt.),
D J Saunders, S M K Goodman.

SEASON 1996 - 1997

FIRST ROUND	SECOND ROUND	SEMI FINAL	FINAL	WINNERS
Old Wellingburians / Old Reptonians	Reptonians 4-1	Foresters 2-0	Foresters 3-1	
Old Cholmeleians / Old Foresters	Foresters 2-2, 3-1			Foresters 3-1 — Francis, Elliott, Gray
Old Haileyburians / Old Brentwoods	Brentwoods 8-0	Brentwoods 2-0		Cookson
Old Harrovians / Old Witleians	Witleians 3-3, 2-1			
Lancing Old Boys / Old Westminsters	Lancing 13-2	Malvernians 2-1	Salopians 4-0	
Old Carthusians / Old Malvernians	Malvernians 2-0			
Old Etonians / Old Chigwellians	Chigwellians 2-1	Salopians 1-1, 0-0 (5-4 pens)		
Old Haberdashers' / Old Salopians	Salopians 8-1			

Played at Motspur Park

PRELIMINARY ROUNDS
Old Cholmeleians 3 Old Aldenhamians 0, Old Foresters 11 Old Eastbournians 0 Old Brentwoods 10, Old Haberdashers' 5 Old Ardinians 1, Old Wellingburians 2, 2 Old Bradfieldians 2, 1, Old Wykehamists 0 Old Chigwellians 5

OLD FORESTERS Winners 1997

(Back Row)
L Douris, M Kendall, A Heyes, C Elliott, M Butler, S Yankson, R Harnack, J Banks, A Smith.

(Front Row)
C Hossain. M Robinson, N Francis (Capt.), P Risby, J Gray.

OLD SALOPIANS Runners up 1997

(Back Row)
M R A Bailey, D J Saunders, R E Cooke, S W K Ellis, P E Hollands, T G Cooke, T W Onions, A P Clarke, D M Cookson.

(Front Row)
P L Dyke, P R Deans, D W W Honychurch (Capt.), M J Lascelles, H E E Raven.

SEASON 1995 - 1996

FIRST ROUND	SECOND ROUND	SEMI FINAL	FINAL	WINNERS
Lancing Old Boys / Old Wellingburians	Lancing 8-0	Lancing 2-1	Lancing 2-1	
Old Cholmeleians / Old Reptonians	Reptonians 1-0			Lancing 4-1 — Brown-Peterside (2), Wyatt, Alcock
Old Carthusians / Old Eastbournians	Carthusians 4-0	Carthusians 4-1		Sullivan
Old Chigwellians / Old Wykehamists	Chigwellians 4-0			
Old Bradfieldians / Old Haileyburians	Bradfieldians 9-1	Bradfieldians 2-1	Brentwoods 3-1	
Old Foresters / Old Witleians	Foresters 4-3			
Old Haberdashers' / Old Brentwoods	Brentwoods 5-0	Brentwoods 5-0		
Old Aldenhamians / Old Etonians	Aldenhamians 3-2			

Played at Motspur Park

PRELIMINARY ROUNDS
Old Carthusians w/o Old Ardinians, Old Foresters 11 Old Westminsters 0, Old Malvernians 3 Old Etonians 5, Old Salopians 0 Old Reptonians 1, Old Witleians 4 Old Harrovians 2

LANCING OLD BOYS Winners 1996

(Back Row)
S D Kelsey, M O Wyatt, J R Dexter, A J Cunningham, M Moulding, B H Evans, I Z B-Peterside.

(Front Row)
D A O Gurney, S J Lees, A W Mercer (Capt.), P M Alcock, J C Simpson.

OLD BRENTWOODS Runners up 1996

(Back Row)
C Rowe, D Gilbert, B Tappin, S McMillan, C Beale, R McMillan, M Shattock.

(Front Row)
D Mathieson, J Davey, P Sullivan (Capt.), J Cameron, T Clements.

SEASON 1998 - 1999

FIRST ROUND	SECOND ROUND	SEMI FINAL	FINAL	WINNERS
Old Reptonians / Old Salopians	Salopians 1-0	Salopians 3-2	Salopians 3-1	Westerman, Curran, Ellis
Old Foresters / Old Etonians	Foresters 1-0			
Old Chigwellians / Old Malvernians	Chigwellians 3-0	Chigwellians 4-4, 5-0		Salopians 3-1
Old Witleians / Old Haberdashers'	Haberdashers' 1-0			
Old Haileyburians / Old Wykehamists	Wykehamists 3-2	Wykehamists 1-0	Lancing 2-2, 2-0	Brown-Peterside
Old Cholmeleians / Old Carthusians	Cholmeleians 4-1			
Lancing Old Boys / Old Bradfieldians	Lancing 3-1	Lancing 4-1		
Old Harrovians / Old Brentwoods	Brentwoods 2-1			

Played at Motspur Park

PRELIMINARY ROUNDS: Old Aldenhamians 1 Old Brentwoods 3, Old Chigwellians 3 Old Wellingburians 1, Old Cholmeleians 2 Old Ardinians 0, Old Haberdashers' 4 Old Eastbournians 1, Old Wykehamists 5 Old Westminsters 0

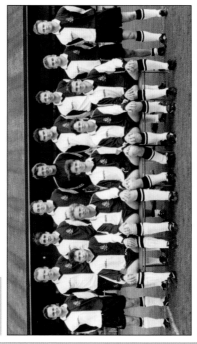

OLD SALOPIANS Winners 1999

(Back Row) D M Cookson, C J Brierley, J A D Leach, S W K Ellis, G R Gow, P R Westerman, S M K Goodman, P Curran, K M Cornwall-Legh.

(Front Row) D W W Honychurch, M J Lascelles, H E E Raven (Capt.), R E Cooke, T G Cooke.

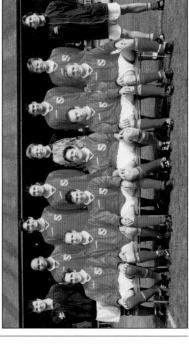

LANCING OLD BOYS Runners up 1999

(Back Row) B T C Walls, I Z B-Peterside, R J Moulding, A J Lutwyche, S Allen, D L Moulding, S J Lees, W Rum.

(Front Row) B H Evans, J C Simpson, A W Mercer, S D Kelsey (Capt.), P M Alcock, D A Gurney.

SEASON 1997 - 1998

FIRST ROUND	SECOND ROUND	SEMI FINAL	FINAL	WINNERS
Old Reptonians / Old Foresters	Foresters 2-0	Foresters 2-0	Foresters 2-1	Yankson, Elliott, Risby
Old Cholmeleians / Old Ardinians	Cholmeleians 13-0			
Lancing Old Boys / Old Wellingburians	Lancing 4-1	Lancing 9-0		Foresters 3-1
Old Haberdashers' / Old Wykehamists	Wykehamists 5-1			
Old Westminsters / Old Aldenhamians	Westminsters 2-0	Salopians 4-1	Brentwoods 2-0	Sansome
Old Salopians / Old Chigwellians	Salopians 3-1			
Old Bradfieldians / Old Eastbournians	Bradfieldians 9-0	Brentwoods 5-2		
Old Carthusians / Old Brentwoods	Brentwoods 4-1			

Played at Motspur Park

PRELIMINARY ROUNDS: Old Etonians 1 Old Foresters 3, Old Haileyburians 1 Lancing Old Boys 4, Old Harrovians 3 Old Carthusians 4, Old Malvernians 0 Old Salopians 1, Old Reptonians w/o Old Witleians

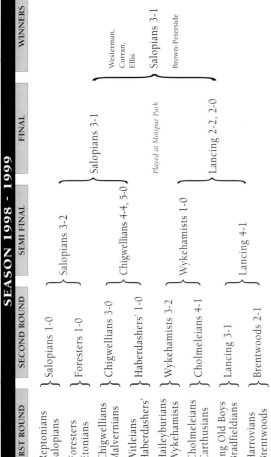

OLD FORESTERS Winners 1998

(Back Row) C Hossain, J Bannister, P Alexander, R Harnack, M Butler, C Elliott, N Keaveney, J Banks, P Risby.

(Front Row) A Heyes, L Douris, A Smith (Capt.), S Yankson, B Murphy.

OLD BRENTWOODS Runners up 1998

(Back Row) S Dick, B Noaks, A Sansome, A Martin, R McMillan, E Kirby, S Keane, D Mathieson, D Gilbert.

(Front Row) J Marsh, T Clements, C Beale (Capt.), J Davey, P Sullivan.

SEASON 2000 - 2001

FIRST ROUND	SECOND ROUND	SEMI FINAL	FINAL	WINNERS
Old Aldenhamians / Old Foresters	Foresters 10-0	Westminsters 2-1	Carthusians 4-2	Carthusians 4-1 — Golder, Mitten, Nash, Webb
Old Malvernians / Old Westminsters	Westminsters 3-0			
Old Salopians / Old Carthusians	Carthusians 2-1	Carthusians 4-2		
Lancing Old Boys / Old Witleians	Witleians 2-0			
Old Wykehamists / Old Harrovians	Harrovians 4-1	Harrovians 8-2	Bradfieldians 1-0	Bradfieldians — Austin-Brown
Old Etonians / Old Cholmeleians	Cholmeleians 3-0			
Old Haileyburians / Old Reptonians	Reptonians 6-0	Bradfieldians 4-0		
Old Bradfieldians / Old Brentwoods	Bradfieldians 3-1			

Played at Cobham

PRELIMINARY ROUNDS   Old Eastbournians 0 Old Bradfieldians 8, Old Foresters 8 Old Wellingburians 0, Old Haberdashers' 3 Old Cholmeleians 4, Old Millhillians w/o Old Westminsters, Old Wykehamists 2 Old Chigwellians 1

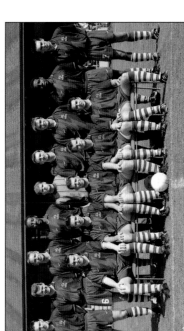

OLD CARTHUSIANS Winners 2001

(Back Row)
L J Webb, H Nash, M J Mitten, W R Frost, R Taylor, M T Bailey, J A Jarvis.

(Front Row)
T E B Walker, A A Y Adomakoh, J C Golder, E J Rees (Capt.), N P Waters, G R C Brooke, D C M Stern.

OLD BRADFIELDIANS Runners up 2001

(Back Row)
S Archer, A White, J Khaksar, T Dellor, S Seymour, A Jeffries, C Gent.

(Front Row)
S Dennis, J Lee, W. Robinson, R Oscroft (Capt.), P Begley, W Oscroft, G Austin-Brown.

SEASON 1999 - 2000

FIRST ROUND	SECOND ROUND	SEMI FINAL	FINAL	WINNERS
Old Eastbournians / Old Bradfieldians	Bradfieldians 7-1	Bradfieldians 2-0	Lancing 3-0	Lancing 3-0 — Brown-Peterside (3)
Old Cholmeleians / Old Ardinians	Cholmeleians w/o			
Lancing Old Boys / Old Millhillians	Lancing 3-2	Lancing 2-0		
Old Haberdashers' / Old Salopians	Salopians 6-0			
Old Foresters / Old Carthusians	Foresters 3-0	Foresters 5-3	Foresters 2-0	
Old Wellingburians / Old Westminsters	Westminsters 3-0			
Old Wykehamists / Old Reptonians	Reptonians 9-2	Reptonians 0-0, 2-1		
Old Brentwoods / Old Chigwellians	Chigwellians 2-1			

Played at Motspur Park

PRELIMINARY ROUNDS   Old Carthusians 3 Old Aldenhamians 0, Old Brentwoods 7 Old Malvernians 2, Old Etonians 1 Old Reptonians 4, Old Foresters 3 Old Harrovians 1, Old Haileyburians 0 Lancing Old Boys 5, Old Witleians 2 Old Salopians 3

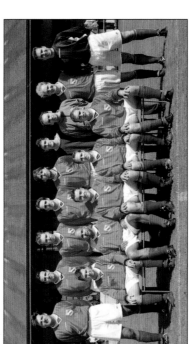

LANCING OLD BOYS Winners 2000

(Back Row)
S D Kelsey, A Rum, J Davies, B H Evans, W Rum, J Forbes-Wilson, P M Alcock, A J Cunningham, N A O Bennett.

(Front Row)
A W Mercer, I Z B-Peterside, A Pierce (Capt.), J C Simpson, D A Gurney.

OLD FORESTERS Runners up 2000

(Back Row)
N Keaveney, R Harnack, C Elliot, B Barnett, M Butler, J Banks, P Alexander, S Yankson, J Dunn.

(Front Row)
A Heyes, A Smith, L Douris (Capt.), B Murphy, P Hooper.

CENTENARY SEASON 2002 - 2003

FIRST ROUND	SECOND ROUND	SEMI FINAL	FINAL	WINNERS
Old Reptonians / Old Foresters	Reptonians 1-0	Haileyburians 2-2, 5-4		
Old Haileyburians / Old Witleians	Haileyburians 2-1		Salopians 2-0	
Old Malvernians / Old Westminsters	Westminsters 3-1	Salopians 1-1, 3-0		Salopians 2-1
Old Haberdashers' / Old Salopians	Salopians 7-2			
Old Aldenhamians / Old Brentwoods	Brentwoods 6-2	Lancing 3-2		
Old Harrovians / Lancing Old Boys	Lancing 3-2		Carthusians 2-1	
Old Cholmeleians / Old Carthusians	Carthusians 4-3	Carthusians 3-3, 2-1		
Old Bradfieldians / Old Etonians	Bradfieldians 3-1			

Ellis, Chesters (Salopians 2-0)

Mitten (Carthusians 2-1)

Played at Cobham

PRELIMINARY ROUNDS: Old Eastbournians 0 Old Reptonians 12, Old Bradfieldians 4 Old Wykehamists 2, Old Chigwellians 0 Old Cholmeleians 1, Old Wellingburians 2 Old Haberdashers' 3

OLD SALOPIANS Winners 2003

(Back Row)
P Curran, D M Cookson, L Briggs, J A D Leach, G R Gow, J D Taylor, P N Thomas, B J Chesters, G R Davies.

(Front Row)
D J Umpleby, H E E Raven, S W K Ellis (Capt.), J Jones, R E Cooke.

OLD CARTHUSIANS Runners up 2003

(Back Row)
H Nash, P S S Leal, W J S Clark, M T Bailey, R Taylor, J E Green, M J Mitten.

(Front Row)
D C M Stern, E J Rees, J C Golder, T E B Walker (Capt.), S Henkes, G R C Brooke, A J Viall.

SEASON 2001 - 2002

FIRST ROUND	SECOND ROUND	SEMI FINAL	FINAL	WINNERS
Old Salopians / Old Cholmeleians	Salopians 6-1	Salopians 4-0		
Old Brentwoods / Old Westminsters	Westminsters 4-4, 7-0		Chigwellians 1-1, 3-1	
Old Etonians / Old Foresters	Etonians 3-2	Chigwellians 3-0		Chigwellians 2-0
Old Chigwellians / Old Millhillians	Chigwellians w/o			
Old Wellingburians / Old Reptonians	Reptonians 8-1	Reptonians 5-0		
Old Bradfieldians / Old Haberdashers'	Bradfieldians 2-1		Reptonians 2-1	
Old Carthusians / Old Eastbournians	Carthusians w/o	Harrovians 3-2		
Old Harrovians / Old Wykehamists	Harrovians 6-0			

Landsman, Mahoney (Chigwellians 2-0)

Played at Cobham

PRELIMINARY ROUNDS: Old Carthusians 1, 2 Lancing Old Boys 1, 1, Old Etonians 1 Old Witleians 0, Old Haileyburians 2 Old Salopians 14, Old Harrovians 4 Old Malvernians 1, Old Aldenhamians 0 Old Brentwoods 3

OLD CHIGWELLIANS Winners 2002

(Back Row)
M C Witzenfeld, L J Mines, O M Compton, D R Evans, A R Sweet, A J Brandon, D J Goddard.

(Front Row)
J A Gordon, J D Webber, P S Landsman, D Cathcart (Capt.), T Compton, J D Mahoney, J R Longman.

OLD REPTONIANS Runners up 2002

(Back Row)
M Cockcroft, J Webster, A Merry, S Craig, M Smith, A Kington, J Cockcroft, N Rushton, A Callander, E Freer.

(Front Row)
N Sreevalsan, R Basnett, D Anderson (Capt.), C Divall, M Stretton, R Brownlee.

ARTHUR DUNN CUP COMPETITION – CLUB PLAYING RECORDS

Team	to 1913/14			to 1938/39			to 1959/60			to 1969/70			to 1979/80			to 1989/90			to 1999/2000			to 2002/03		
	P	W	Pos.	P	W	Pos.	P	W	Pos.	P	W	Pos.	P	W	Pos.	P	W	Pos.	P	W	Pos.	P	W	Pos.
Old Bradfieldians	16	2	17	65	25	8	89	34	8	105	37	8	127	48	8	144	53	8	165	63	8	176	70	8
Old Brightonians	29	17	5	29	17	15	29	17	17=	29	17	18=	29	17	19	29	17	19	29	17	19	29	17	19
Old Carthusians	44	33	1=	92	63	1	134	92	1	156	104	2	175	113	2	205	129	2	229	141	3	241	149	2
Old Etonians	20	7	11=	30	8	14	46	13	14	58	14	14	74	18	14	90	24	15	107	31	15	112	33	15
Old Felstedians	20	3	11=	21	3	18	21	3	21	21	3	21	21	3	21	21	3	21	21	3	21	21	3	21=
Old Foresters	19	6	15	42	8	12=	66	15	10=	89	26	9=	112	39	9	129	45	10	160	64	10	165	66	10
Old Harrovians	11	-	20	24	4	16	24	4	19	29	5	18=	45	8	18	59	12	18	71	13	17	79	18	17
Lancing Old Boys	18	4	16	50	15	11	66	16	10=	83	21	11	107	34	10	140	55	9	177	82	7	183	84	7
Old Malvernians	34	23	4	90	61	2	126	82	2	161	108	1	194	134	1	228	155	1	243	160	1	246	160	1
Old Reptonians	44	34	1=	79	48	4	122	75	3	150	95	3	169	103	3	202	122	3	230	139	2	240	145	3
Old Rossallians	20	9	11=	20	9	19	20	9	22	20	9	22	20	9	22	20	9	22	20	9	22	20	9	23
Old Salopians	25	11	7	78	46	5	115	69	5	133	77	5	161	89	4	181	98	4	214	121	4	225	128	4
Old Westminsters	20	7	11=	52	19	10	74	25	9	89	29	9=	100	29	11	117	34	12	130	37	13	139	41	13
Old Wykehamists	23	11	8	84	54	3	118	74	4	134	81	4	151	85	5	166	87	6	183	92	6	187	93	6
Old Cholmeleians	35	18	3	75	35	7	103	48	6	131	64	6	147	69	6	173	84	5	192	92	5	198	95	5
Old Cranleighans	22	9	9	22	9	17	22	9	20	22	9	20	22	9	20	22	9	20	22	9	20	22	9	20
Old Citizens	21	10	10	59	24	9	59	24	13	59	24	13	59	24	17	64	24	17	64	24	18	64	24	18
Old Johnians	13	3	18=	13	3	21=	13	3	24=	13	3	24=	13	3	24=	13	3	24=	13	3	25=	13	3	26=
Old Aldenhamians	28	16	6	76	42	6	100	48	7	117	52	7	134	57	7	149	60	7	164	64	9	167	64	9
Old Wellingburians	13	4	18=	42	12	12=	64	18	12	80	22	12	96	26	12	110	29	13	125	33	14	128	33	14
Old Radleians	9	1	21=	9	1	24=	9	1	26=	9	1	26=	9	1	26=	9	1	26=	9	1	29=	9	1	30=
Old Albanians	9	1	21=	13	1	21=	13	1	24=	13	1	24=	13	1	24=	13	1	24=	13	1	25=	13	1	26=
Old Berkhamstedians	9	2	21=	9	2	24=	9	2	26=	9	2	26=	9	2	26=	9	2	26=	9	2	29=	9	2	30=
Old Ipswichians	7	2	24	8	2	26	8	2	28	8	2	28	8	2	28	8	2	28	8	2	32	8	2	32
Old Hurst-Johnians				19	4	20	19	4	23	19	4	23	19	4	23	19	4	23	19	4	23	19	4	24
Old Ardinians				6	-	27	30	9	16	50	19	16	61	19	16	73	20	16	82	21	16	82	21	16
Old Chigwellians				7	1	23	32	10	15	48	15	17	73	29	15	101	45	14	134	65	12	140	68	12
Old Brentwoods							29	14	17=	56	30	15	93	59	13	127	80	11	156	99	11	162	101	11
St. Edmund's Cant. O.B.																7	1	29	7	1	33	7	1	33
Old Haileyburians																5	1	30	15	1	24	21	3	21=
Old Eastbournians																			10	-	28	12	-	29
Old Witleians																			13	3	25=	17	4	25
Old Haberdashers'																			9	3	29=	13	4	26=
Old Millhillians																			2	-	34	2	-	34

Ranked by games played.

177

ANALYSIS AND FACTS

ANALYSIS OF FINALISTS from 1903-1953

Club	Times in Final	Won
Old Carthusians	17	14
Old Salopians	12	8
Old Wykehamists	12	7
Old Malvernians	10	7
Old Reptonians	9	3
Old Aldenhamians	4	1
Old Brightonians	2	1
Old Cholmeleians	4	–
Old Bradfieldians	2	–
Old Rossallians	2	–
Old Westminsters	1	–
Old Citizens	1	–
Old Wellingburians	1	–
Old Etonians	1	–

NOTES: In 1902/03, when the Cup was founded, the Final twice resulted in a draw and the Cup was held jointly.

In 1937/38 the Final resulted in a draw after extra time and the Cup was held jointly.

ANALYSIS OF FINALISTS from 1953-2003

Club	Times in Final	Won
Old Malvernians	18	10
Old Reptonians	14	8
Lancing Old Boys	8	6
Old Brentwoods	15	5
Old Salopians	9	5
Old Carthusians	8	5
Old Chigwellians	6	5
Old Foresters	8	3
Old Cholmeleians	6	3
Old Wykehamists	2	1
Old Aldenhamians	2	1
Old Bradfieldians	3	–
Old Etonians	1	–

NOTES: In 1954/55 & 1967/68 the Final resulted in a draw after extra time and the Cup was held jointly.

ANALYSIS OF FINALISTS from 1903-2003

Club	Times in Final	Won
Old Carthusians	25	19
Old Malvernians	28	17
Old Salopians	21	13
Old Reptonians	23	11
Old Wykehamists	14	8
Lancing Old Boys	8	6
Old Brentwoods	15	5
Old Chigwellians	6	5
Old Cholmeleians	10	3
Old Foresters	8	3
Old Aldenhamians	6	2
Old Brightonians	2	1
Old Bradfieldians	5	–
Old Rossallians	2	–
Old Etonians	2	–
Old Westminsters	1	–
Old Citizens	1	–
Old Wellingburians	1	–

OLD BRENTWOODS V OLD MALVERNIANS

In the 20 seasons between 1964/65 and 1983/84 when both the Old Brentwoods and Old Malvernians were strong sides they met on seventeen occasions, the Old Brentwoods won nine and Old Malvernians eight.

In this period, the Old Malvernians appeared in twelve finals winning seven, the Old Brentwoods appeared in eight finals winning three.

The Old Malvernians appeared in successive finals between 1965 and 1969 and the Old Brentwoods appeared in successive finals between 1971 and 1974.

More amazing was the fact that between season 1966/67 and 1979/80 except for season 1969/70 the Old Malvernians either won the Cup or were beaten by the Old Brentwoods either in the final or in an earlier round.

RESULTS 1964/65 – 1983/84

1964/65 (1st R)	Old Malvernians 3	Old Brentwoods 0	Old Malvernians won Cup
1965/66 (SF)	Old Malvernians 4	Old Brentwoods 1	Old Malvernians lost Final
1966/67 (F)	Old Brentwoods 3	Old Malvernians 2	Old Brentwoods won Cup
1967/68 (SF)	Old Malvernians 1	Old Brentwoods 0	Old Malvernians shared Cup
1968/69 (2nd R)	Old Malvernians 1	Old Brentwoods 0	Old Malvernians won Cup
1970/71 (F)	Old Malvernians 4	Old Brentwoods 2	Old Malvernians won Cup
1971/72 (SF)	Old Brentwoods 3	Old Malvernians 0	Old Brentwoods won Cup
1972/73 (F)	Old Brentwoods 3	Old Malvernians 2	Old Brentwoods won Cup
1973/74 (1st R)	Old Brentwoods 4	Old Malvernians 3	Old Brentwoods lost Final
1974/75			Old Malvernians won Cup
1975/76 (F)	Old Malvernians 5	Old Brentwoods 3	Old Malvernians won Cup
1976/77 (SF)	Old Brentwoods 1	Old Malvernians 0	Old Brentwoods lost Final
1977/78 (SF)	Old Malvernians 5	Old Brentwoods 4	Old Malvernians won Cup
1978/79 (2nd R)	Old Brentwoods 3	Old Malvernians 2	Old Brentwoods lost Final
1979/80 (2nd R)	Old Brentwoods 4	Old Malvernians 2	
1980/81 (2nd R)	Old Malvernians 4	Old Brentwoods 2	Old Malvernians lost Final
1981/82			Old Malvernians lost Final
1982/83 (2nd R)	Old Brentwoods 5	Old Malvernians 4	
1983/84 (Pre Rd)	Old Brentwoods 2, 3	Old Malvernians 2, 0	

ADCC FACTS

The leading goal scorers in Arthur Dunn Cup Finals are:

J W Bridle	Old Malvernians	8
A R B Moulsdale	Old Salopians	8
C T Ashton	Old Wykehamists	7
I Brown-Peterside	Lancing Old Boys	5
G O Smith	Old Carthusians	5
M N Stretton	Old Reptonians	5 ·
R C Tapper	Old Chigwellians	5

The first penalty to be scored in a final was in 1950 by Hubert Doggart for the Old Wykehamists. The leading penalty scorer in final ties is Ian Ryder-Smith (Old Malvernians) with three.

The highest scoring finals in normal time were:

1934	Old Aldenhamians	6	Old Wykehamists	2
1955	Old Brentwoods	4	Old Salopians	4
1976	Old Malvernians	5	Old Brentwoods	3

The 1927 final saw nine goals when Old Salopians overcame Old Malvernians 6 - 3 but five of these came in extra time.

Of the 14 clubs that played in the inaugural season 1902/03, 11 competed in the 2002/03 centenary competition; Old Bradfieldians (known as the Bradfield Waifs in 1902), Old Carthusians, Old Etonians, Old Foresters, Old Harrovians, Lancing Old Boys, Old Malvernians, Old Reptonians, Old Salopians, Old Westminsters and Old Wykehamists.

Old Brightonians, Old Felstedians and Old Rossallians were unable to field sides after their respective schools took up rugby during the First World War.

The largest entries in the competition were in the seasons 1907/08 to 1913/14 when 24 teams per season entered the competition. The smallest entry was in the inaugural season, with 14 clubs taking part.

The highest score in a single game occurred in the first round in 1993/94. The result: Old Salopians 26 Old Ardinians 0.

Eight players have scored a hat trick in the final, but only one in the last 50 years. They are:

A H Birks	Old Reptonians	1907
H Ashton	Old Wykehamists	1920
H R H Williams	Old Carthusians	1923
H V Newton	Old Salopians	1927
G R Moxon	Old Salopians	1932
P R Hardman	Old Aldenhamians	1934
A R B Moulsdale	Old Salopians	1952
I Brown-Peterside	Lancing Old Boys	2000

CUP WINNING RECORDS

FA AMATEUR CUP		LONDON SENIOR CUP	
Old Carthusians	1894	Old Foresters	1885
Old Carthusians	1897	Old Westminsters*	1887
Old Malvernians	1902	Old Westminsters	1888
		Old Westminsters	1890
ESSEX SENIOR CUP		Old Westminsters	1892
Old Foresters	1885	Old Westminsters	1893
Old Foresters	1886	Old Foresters	1894
Old Foresters	1887	Old Carthusians	1895
		Old Carthusians	1896
LONDON CHARITY CUP		Old Carthusians	1897
		Old Carthusians	1899
Old Westminsters	1889	Old Malvernians	1903
Old Carthusians	1896	* Joint holders with Casuals	

FA CUP FACTS

The following Arthur Dunn sides played or entered the FA Cup:

Old Brightonians	1884/85	–	1888/89
Old Carthusians	1879/80	–	1889/90
Old Etonians	1873/74	–	1887/88
Old Foresters	1877/78	–	1887/88
Old Harrovians	1876/77	–	1887/88
Lancing Old Boys	1885/86	–	1887/88
Old Salopians	1887/88	–	(scratched)
Old Westminsters	1882/83	–	1891/92
Old Wykehamist	1876/77	–	1887/88

The first was Old Etonians who drew in the first round 0 - 0 with Swifts on 5 November 1874, and the last Dunn team to play in the competition were Old Westminsters who lost 3 - 2 to West Bromwich Albion in the first round of the 1891/92 competition. The only other Dunn team apart from Etonians and Carthusians to reach a semi-final were Old Harrovians who were defeated by the Royal Engineers on 16 March 1878.

Robert Vidal (Old Westminsters), played in the first three FA Cup Finals, for The Wanderers when they won the first FA Cup Final in 1872. He was still at school that year and as far as can be ascertained, he is the only player to have won an FA Cup winners medal while still at school. He played for Oxford University in 1873 when they lost to The Wanderers, and again for Oxford University when they won in 1874.

The last all amateur FA Cup Final was the game between Old Carthusians and Old Etonians in 1881. One of the Old Carthusians team was James Prinsep. He held, at this time, the distinction of being the youngest-ever player to appear in the FA Cup Final and to play for England. He was in the Clapham Rovers side that lost the 1879 FA Cup Final. A week later, he played for England against Scotland when he was only 17 years 252 days old.

Although Old Etonians appeared in six FA Cup Finals, and one replay, winning the competition on two occasions, they only managed to score four goals in total. They were the last Arthur Dunn side to win the FA Cup in 1882. They defeated Blackburn Rovers 1 - 0. This was Blackburn Rovers first FA Cup Final appearance; the club having been formed in 1875 by two Old Salopians, John Lewis and Arthur Constantine.

It is interesting to note that they all ceased playing at about the same time – about the time that the Football League was started.

DID YOU KNOW?

The Old Etonians have the unusual record of having appeared in more FA Cup Finals than Arthur Dunn finals. The club won the FA Cup in both 1879 and 1882 and were runners up on four occasions. They have appeared in just two Dunn finals in 1952 and 1992.

DID YOU KNOW?

Old Carthusians and Wimbledon are the only clubs to have won both the FA Cup and the FA Amateur Cup. The only sides to come close to joining them are Middlesbrough, Amateur Cup winners in 1895 and 1898, Cup Finalists in 1997 and Wycombe Wanderers, Amateur Cup winners in 1931 and Cup semi-finalists in 2001.

THE DINNERS

22nd April 1953.

14th March 1963.

List of Guests

The Head Masters of the following Schools :—
   Charterhouse, Shrewsbury, Highgate, Brentwood, Bradfield,
   Westminster, Forest, Chigwell, Ardingly.

A. G. Doggart, Chairman, The Football Association.
D. Follows, Secretary, The Football Association.
Dr. A. W. Barton, The Football Association.
S. C. Griffith, Secretary of the M.C.C.
H. L. Lewis, Chairman of The Hockey Association.
Colonel A. D. C. Macaulay, Secretary of All England
   Lawn Tennis Club.
G. R. Bristowe, Honorary Secretary, Halford Hewitt Cup.
C. C. Oakes, A.F.A.
L. Hutchinson, A.F.A.
Dr. H. W. Thompson, Oxford University, A.F.C.
C. J. Turnbull, Cambridge University, A.F.C.
W. D. Wickson, Corinthian Casuals F.C.
C. J. Weir, Pegasus F.C.
K. E. Wiltshire, Wealdstone F.C.
T. J. R. Dashwood, Secretary, The Public Schools Club.
J. Hennessy, *The Times.*
G. A. R. Green, *The Times.*
C. F. James, *The Daily Telegraph.*
H. J. Mackintosh, Old Boys Cup.
E. D. Boldero, Grandsons of Arthur Dunn.

Toasts

THE QUEEN

THE ARTHUR DUNN CUP

Proposed by G. A. R. Green
(OLD SALOPIANS)

Response by R. S. Blundell
HON SECRETARY ARTHUR DUNN CUP

THE GUESTS

Proposed by A. L. Hilder
HON. TREASURER ARTHUR DUNN CUP

Response by Sir Stanley Rous
SECRETARY FOOTBALL ASSOCIATION

Toasts

THE QUEEN

THE ARTHUR DUNN CUP

Proposed by S. C. Griffith
SECRETARY OF THE M.C.C

Response by R. S. Blundell
HON. SECRETARY ARTHUR DUNN CUP

THE GUESTS

Proposed by A. L. Hilder
HON. TREASURER ARTHUR DUNN CUP

Response by B. M. Young, M.A.
HEAD MASTER OF CHARTERHOUSE

10th March 1978.

12th March 1993.

14th March 2003.

Toasts

THE QUEEN

THE ARTHUR DUNN CUP

Proposed by Professor Sir Harold Thompson
CHAIRMAN THE FOOTBALL ASSOCIATION

Response by R. Sale
VICE-PRESIDENT OF THE ARTHUR DUNN AND HEADMASTER
OF BRENTWOOD SCHOOL

THE GUESTS

Proposed by R. Sale

Response by D. Miller
OLD CARTHUSIAN

Toasts

THE QUEEN

The Arthur Dunn Cup
Proposed by K. A. Shearwood
OXFORD UNIVERSITY AND PEGASUS

Response by G. H. G. Doggart
VICE-PRESIDENT OF THE ARTHUR DUNN AND
CAMBRIDGE UNIVERSITY

THE GUESTS

Proposed by G. H. G. Doggart

Response by F. Crozier
EX-BRITISH BROADCASTING CORPORATION

Toasts

THE QUEEN

R T H Wilson
Chairman of the Arthur Dunn Cup Committee

THE ARTHUR DUNN CUP

Proposed by C H Saunders
Oxford University and
Vice-President of The Football Association

Response by R H Woolley
Old Harrovian and
Life Vice-President of the Arthurian League

THE GUESTS

Proposed by R H Woolley

Response by N Coward
Acting Chief Executive of The Football Association

THE GUESTS AT THE CENTENARY DINNER

Adams S.	Old Aldenhamians	Carter E.	Referee
Adams P.C.	Old Foresters	Cathcart D.I.	Old Chigwellians
Adomakoh L.	Old Carthusians	Charlesworth M.L.	Old Salopians
Akker B.	Old Carthusians	Cheshire C.S	Old Radleians
Alcock R.H.	Old Salopians	Chicken C.B.O.	Old Cholmeleians
Alexander J.G.	Old Salopians	Chown C.	Old Haileyburians
Ambrose P.	Old Cholmeleians	Clare A.	Old Aldenhamians
Anderson C.D.	Old Reptonians	Clegg J.	Old Salopians
Anderson D.	Old Reptonians	Coccozza T.	Old Aldenhamians
Antrobus P.O.	Old Brentwoods	Cockcroft M.J.	Old Reptonians
Arthur D.R.G.	Old Salopians	Colman N.	Old Bradfieldians
Arthur J.	Old Salopians	Comninos C.	Old Carthusians
Ashmore J.	Old Etonians	Connell P.	Old Foresters
Askhom M.	Old Wellingburians	Conolly J.	Old Chigwellians
Ayliott J.	Old Haileyburians	Conolly R.	Old Chigwellians
Bailey M.	Old Carthusians	Cooper F.W.	Old Salopians
Bailey D.	Old Malvernians	Costeloe M.J.	Old Malvernians
Baker N.	Old Aldenhamians	Cottingham N.	Old Reptonians
Baker J.	Old Wellingburians	Cotton R.L.	Referee
Baker Q.	Old Harrovians	Coward N.	Acting Chief Executive of FA
Baker B.L.	Old Brentwoods	Cox M.	Old Aldenhamians
Ballinger J.	Old Reptonians	Crerar D.	Old Harrovians
Banks R.W.G.	Old Foresters	Cripps D.H.R.	Old Brentwoods
Banner F.J.	President of AFA	Davies J.L.	Old Aldenhamians
Bannister R.	Old Aldenhamians	Davies N.l.	Old Aldenhamians
Barber G. W.	Old Etonians	Davies N.	Old Chigwellians
Barbour W.	Old Carthusians	Davies P.G.H.	Old Cholmeleians
Barnes I.	Old Westminsters	Dawson A.J.N.	Old Etonians
Basnett A.P.	Old Reptonians	Denham I.M.	Old Malvernians
Basnett R.	Old Reptonians	Denham A.	Old Malvernians
Baugh J.	Old Aldenhamians	Dennis B.	Old Cholmeleians
Baylis N.	Old Haileyburians	Denton N.	Old Bradfieldians
Beckett M.	Old Reptonians	Dickson M.D.	Old Etonians
Beeson A.W.	Old Malvernians	Dodd S.L.	Old Haileyburians
Bennett J.	Old Carthusians	Doggart M.	Old Carthusians
Bennett N.	Lancing Old Boys	Doran S.	Old Brentwoods
Berndes F.H.	Old Chigwellians	Dowlen A.D.	Old Cholmeleians
Berndes R.	Old Chigwellians	Driver M.	Old Malvernians
Bevan I.	Historian/Publisher	Duncombe S.	Old Foresters
Birn L.	Old Aldenhamians	Durden-Smith N.	Old Aldenhamians
Black J.J.	Old Reptonians	Dutchman J.	Pegasus
Body R.	Old Reptonians	Dyke P.L.	Old Salopians
Boggis A.	Old Foresters	Easton S.	Old Carthusians
Boldero E.D.	Grandson of Arthur Dunn	Edwards D.	Lancing Old Boys
Boon K.H.	Old Brentwoods	Eggelden I.	Old Aldenhamians
Booth R.	Old Cholmeleians	Eifion-Jones J.R.	Old Reptonians
His Honour Judge		Elliott C.	Old Foresters
Booth, A.S.	Old Salopians	Ellis K.	Old Carthusians
Boustred R.	Old Cholmeleians	Ellis S.F.D.	Old Salopians
Bowers I.	Old Wellingburians	Ellis R.	Old Salopians
Bretherton J.E.S.	Old Salopians	Emery K.	Old Brentwoods
Bridle J.	Old Malvernians	Emmerson D.	Old Foresters
Broadhurst C.J.	Old Westminsters	Evans A.	Old Chigwellians
Brooke G.	Old Carthusians	Evans N.	Lancing Old Boys
Brooke-Smith R.	Old Salopians	Evans D.	Old Chigwellians
Brown E.N.W.	Old Westminsters	Farrar J.	Old Malvernians
Brown R.C.	Old Westminsters	Feldman P.A.	Old Cholmeleians
Brown M.L.	AFA Company Secretary	Fyler N.	Old Bradfieldians
Bryant M.J.	Old Chigwellians	Gilbert S.A.J.	Old Foresters
Bryce G.	Old Chigwellians	Gilbert M.A.	Historian/Publisher
Burne G.F.H.	Old Bradfieldians	Giles M.	Old Etonians
Burns F.B.	Old Salopians	Gillard R.	Old Reptonians
Burrowes P.	Referee	Gladstone R.	Old Etonians
Butler A.	Old Harrovians	Godby P.	Old Carthusians
Callander A.A.	Old Reptonians	Godby J.A.	Old Salopians
Capon M.	Old Aldenhamians	Godolphin P.	Old Aldenhamians
Captain of Football	Old Haileyburians	Golder J.	Old Carthusians
Carr P.A.M.	Old Salopians	Gooch D.	Old Aldenhamians

Goodbody J.B.	The Times
Goodfellow S.	Old Aldenhamians
Goodman S.	Old Salopians
Gordon G.	Old Reptonians
Gordon C.E.	Old Reptonians
Goss D.	Referee
Goss W.P.	Life Vice-President of AFA
Gray J.A.B.	Old Cholmeleians
Gray N.	Old Cholmeleians
Green H.G.D.	Old Wykehamists
Green G.	Old Foresters
Greene S.	Old Chigwellians
Greves A.E.	Old Ardinians
Grimmer D.	Referee
Groves S.	Old Bradfieldians
Gurney D.	Lancing Old Boys
Hall R.	Old Aldenhamians
Hall T.	Old Foresters
Harding J.	Corinthian-Casuals
Harling N.	Old Westminsters
Harnack R.	Old Foresters
Harris N.	Old Foresters
Harris J.	Old Brentwoods
Harrison J.D.	Old Reptonians
Harrison P.	Old Reptonians
Harvey B.	Old Brentwoods
Hassid M.P.	Old Foresters
Hayes R.B.	Old Foresters
Hays M.	Old Cholmeleians
Henchley A.	Old Aldenhamians
Henderson I.	Old Reptonians
Henkes S.	Old Carthusians
Herbert A.	Old Brentwoods
Hetherington M.	Old Aldenhamians
Hewer J.M.	Old Chigwellians
Hewitson G.	Old Wykehamists
Hewitt R.I.C.	Old Ardinians
Heyes A.	Old Foresters
Heyes M.	Old Foresters
Hibberd J.S.	Historian/Publisher
Holder J.	Old Carthusians
Honeyfield J.S.	Old Ardinians
Honychurch D.	Old Salopians
Hornby D.	Old Wykehamists
Hornby J.	Old Wykehamists
Horne C.	Old Etonians
Hoyle W.	Old Malvernians
Humble R.G.	Old Salopians
Hutchin M.C.G.	Old Chigwellians
Hutchin M.	Old Chigwellians
Hutton J.	Old Reptonians
Irvine G.	Old Malvernians
Jackson R.	Old Wellingburians
Jameson R.D.	Old Chigwellians
Jarvis J.	Old Carthusians
Jenkins G.	Old Cholmeleians
Jones S.K.	Old Salopians
Keegan D.	Old Brentwoods
Keenan M.	Old Harrovians
Kemball J.	Old Carthusians
Kentfield G.	Historian/Publisher
Ker, Major J.S.	Old Salopians
Kerr P.	Old Aldenhamians
Kilmartin J.R.	Old Brentwoods
King G.E.A.	Old Malvernians
Kitson J.	Old Cholmeleians
Knapman J.	Old Chigwellians
Kyriacou F.	Old Cholmeleians

181

Lambert A.H.	Old Cholmeleians	Pollard O.D.	Old Foresters
Lanyon D.H.	Old Salopians	Pollock A.J.	Old Salopians
Lauder J.A.	Old Westminsters	Pollock W.A.J.	Old Salopians
Lee T.	Old Etonians	Porter A.L.J.	Old Salopians
Legge I.A.T.	Old Salopians	Procter J.H.	Old Reptonians
Lewis R.	Old Carthusians	Purser I.	Old Wykehamists
Lewis R.	Referee	Purser H.	Old Wykehamists
Liddell M.	Old Bradfieldians	Pyrke M.G.	Old Cholmeleians
Limb A.	Old Aldenhamians	Ralphs G.	Old Reptonians
Littmoden R.C.	Old Brentwoods	Raven R.N.E.	Old Salopians
Littmoden C.	Old Brentwoods	Raven H.E.E.	Old Salopians
Loader N.J.	Old Brentwoods	Raymond D.	Old Chigwellians
Longrigg D.J.F.	Old Salopians	Redrup S.J.	Old Chigwellians
Luddy J.	Old Reptonians	Rees E.	Old Carthusians
Lyon G.	Old Foresters	Richardson J.F.G.	Old Westminsters
Lythgue K.	Old Haileyburians	Ridgewell R.W.	Old Cholmeleians
Maddison B.	Old Foresters	Rimmer N.	Lancing Old Boys
Maguire H.J.	Old Brentwoods	Roberts G.	Old Salopians
Maiterson N.	Old Etonians	Robinson A.W.S.	Old Reptonians
Marks T.	Old Carthusians	Robinson M.	Old Foresters
Marks L.G.	Old Westminsters	Robson M.	Old Haileyburians
Marriott S.	Old Wellingburians	Rodgers F.	Old Aldenhamians
Martin H.	Old Carthusians	Rodgers M.	Old Foresters
Massey D.	Old Aldenhamians	Rohleder S.	Old Aldenhamians
Massey C.	Old Aldenhamians	Rolfe P.W.	Old Reptonians
Mathieson S.	Old Brentwoods	Ross J.M.	Old Reptonians
McArthur S.	Old Reptonians	Ross A.	Great Grandson of Arthur Dunn
McConville J.	Old Reptonians	Rowe I.	Old Brentwoods
McLaren J.	Old Bradfieldians	Rowlinson C.J.	Old Salopians
Mellstrom B.	Old Carthusians	Roy A.D.	Old Westminsters
Mercer A.	Lancing Old Boys	Roy E.D.	Old Westminsters
Michel K.	Old Bradfieldians	Roy D.A.	Old Westminsters
Miller D.	Old Carthusians	Rundle R.I.	The Old Boys Cup
Milligan T.	Old Wykehamists	Russell F.	Old Reptonians
Mitchell K.B.	Old Chigwellians	Russell T.	Old Brentwoods
Mitten M.	Old Carthusians	Ryder-Smith I.	Old Malvernians
Molloy P.	Old Harrovians	Sainsbury J.	Old Aldenhamians
Moore D.	Old Malvernians	Sale C.	Old Reptonians
Morley J.F.	Old Foresters	Sale J.G.	Old Salopians
Morrison D.N.	Old Chigwellians	Samuel M.	President of Arthurian League
Moulsdale A.R.B.	Old Salopians	Sargeant D.N.	Old Salopians
Muir I.	Old Aldenhamians	Sarre C.	Old Harrovians
Murphy Dr.M.F.	Old Malvernians	Saunders C.J.	Vice-President of FA
Murphy C.	Old Malvernians	Savva A.	Old Cholmeleians
Murray S.	Old Aldenhamians	Scannell A.	Old Brentwoods
Murray K.	Old Aldenhamians	Scholfield J.	Old Carthusians
Nash H.	Old Carthusians	Scobie J.	Old Etonians
Needham P.V.	Old Brentwoods	Sears R.	Old Wellingburians
Nicholls J.	Old Wykehamists	Shannon P.	Old Foresters
Noble R.	Old Carthusians	Shearwood K.	Pegasus, Old Salopians
O'Toole B.V.	Referee	Sherlock P.	Old Brentwoods
Oulton R.	Old Carthusians	Shilton D.	Old Bradfieldians
Parry L.G.	Old Salopians	Simpson I.	Old Bradfieldians
Patel J.	Old Foresters	Smallwood B.M.	Old Salopians
Paul G.	Old Harrovians	Smith M.S.H.	Old Reptonians
Payne I.R.	Old Reptonians	Smith J.E.	Old Chigwellians
Peace N.B.	Old Chigwellians	Smith S.E.H.	Old Malvernians
Pegler M.	Old Carthusians	Smith C.B.	Old Foresters
Penn J.J.	Old Salopians	Smith D.M.B.	Referee
Pepper C.	Old Reptonians	Speed A.	Old Chigwellians
Phelps S.N.P.	Old Chigwellians	Speller G.R.	Old Foresters
Phipps P.	Old Wellingburians	St George C.	Old Etonians
Pickett D.	Old Aldenhamians	Stephenson M.G.	Old Brentwoods
Piggott K.	Old Ardinians	Stern D.	Old Carthusians
Pike C.L.	Old Westminsters	Stevens C.W.	Old Malvernians
Pink K.	Old Bradfieldians	Stewart A.	Old Carthusians
Pluck M.	Old Chigwellians	Stockbridge N.	Old Malvernians

Stockdale M.	Old Reptonians
Stratford J.E.	Old Brentwoods
Stretton M.N.	Old Reptonians
Sumner E.	Old Harrovians
Sweet A.R.	Old Chigwellians
Sweet D.	Old Chigwellians
Sydenham C.	Old Chigwellians
Syrett N.	Cricketer Cup
Taylor R.	Old Carthusians
Taylor L.	Lancing Old Boys
Taylor J.	Lancing Old Boys
Taylor A.	Old Foresters
Taylor N.	Old Brentwoods
Thom F.	Old Chigwellians
Thomas S.	Old Etonians
Thwaites C.	Old Aldenhamians
Tom D.	Old Cholmeleians
Tomlinson J.J.W.	Old Reptonians
Toone M.	Old Wykehamists
Trimby R.W.	Old Foresters
Trott Dr.P.A.	Old Reptonians
Tudor R.T.	Old Salopians
Turl A.R.	Old Reptonians
Tweddle C.	Old Harrovians
Tyrrell J.	Old Bradfieldians
Ullstein A.	Old Bradfieldians
Urwin R.	Old Haileyburians
Vandome M.	Old Foresters
Vaughan M.	Old Aldenhamians
Vaughan P.H.	Old Reptonians
Vaughan D.C.M.	Old Reptonians
Wainwright D.B.	Old Cholmeleians
Wakefield J.B.	Corinthian-Casuals
Walford C.	Old Reptonians
Walford N.C.	Old Reptonians
Walker T.	Old Carthusians
Walker J.C.	Old Salopians
Walker M.A.T.	Old Salopians
Wallis S.R.D.	Old Salopians
Walls B.	Lancing Old Boys
Walton L.	Old Carthusians
Walton P.	Old Malvernians
Warner N.	Old Harrovians
Webb L.	Old Carthusians
Webb J.N.	Old Salopians
Webb R.E.W.	Old Salopians
West I.R.	Old Brentwoods
Wheeler M.	Old Wykehamists
Whittingham L.N.	Old Salopians
Willatt J.M.G.	Old Reptonians
Williams E.B.	Old Bradfieldians
Williams A.K.	Old Malvernians
Willoughby J.	Old Westminsters
Willoughby A.J.T.	Old Westminsters
Wilson P.	Old Westminsters
Wilson R.T.H.	Old Malvernians
Wilson-Soppitt I.	Old Aldenhamians
Winter H.O.	The Daily Telegraph
Woods J.G.S.	Old Malvernians
Woolcott D.A.	Hon. Referee's Secretary
Woolley R.H.	Old Harrovians
Worth P.St J.	Old Salopians
Wright D.L.	Old Salopians
Wyatt J.	Old Bradfieldians
Wynn-Evans J.	Old Harrovians
Yule J.	Old Aldenhamians

BIBLIOGRAPHY

The principal publications consulted were as follows:

ANNUALS AND BOOKS:

A History of Felsted School. – Michael Craze 1955.

Arthur Dunn Cup Yearbooks.

Association Football and the men who made it – Gibson & Pickford 1906.

Association Football (Volume 2) - Caxton series. 1960.

A History of Merton and Morden – Evelyn Jowett 1951.

C B Fry – Iain Wilton (Richard Cohen Books) 1999.

Corinthians and Cricketers – Edward Grayson.

England: The Official History, RFU History – Rugby Football Association 1999.

Football at Radley - Tony Money (Archivist, Radley College).

Football Grounds of England & Wales – Simon Inglis (Willow Books) 1983.

From little acorns (a centennial review of the Old Foresters) – P C Adams.

Hardly a Scholar – Ken Shearwood An Autobiography (Tiger & Tyger 1999).

History of the Corinthians – F N S Creek (Longmans) 1933.

Men were different – Shane Leslie 1937.

Minutes of the meetings of the Arthur Dunn Cup Committee 1902 – 2002.

Old Malvernian Handbook.

Pegasus - Ken Shearwood (Oxford University Press 1975).

Shrewsbury School Football and the Old Salopian FC – Michael Charlesworth, Robin Moulsdale, Robin Trimby, Mark Dickson, Christopher Sturdy.

Soccer the World Game – Geoffrey Green 1954.

The Badminton Series (Football) 1899.

The Film of Memory - Shane Leslie 1937.

The History of Felsted – John Dury 2000.

The History of the Old Bradfieldian Football Club 1875 – 1949 – C E Nicholl, H M Bathurst, A R Wathen, J R B Moulsdale, F E Templer.

The Non League Football Grounds of Great Britain – Tony Williams 1990.

The Official Illustrated History of the FA Cup – Bryon Butler (Headline) 1996.

To the Palace for the Cup – Ian Bevan, Stuart Hibberd, Michael Gilbert (Replay Publishing) 1999.

Weybridge Past – Neil White (Phillimore) 1999.

NEWSPAPERS AND PERIODICALS:

The Daily Telegraph.

Illustrated Sporting and Dramatic News.

Surrey Advertiser.

The Sphere.

The Sportsman.

The Times.

Wimbledon Borough News.

SCHOOL MAGAZINES:

The Albanian.

The Aldenhamian.

Old Ardinian Society Handbook.

Berkhamsted School Magazine.

The Brentwoodian.

Brighton College Magazine.

The Carthusian.

The Cholmeleian.

The Elizabethan (Westminster).

Eton College Magazine.

The Felstedian.

The Harrovian.

Ipswich School Magazine.

Lancing College Magazine.

Old Malvernian.

The Reptonian.

The Wykehamist.

+ Various School and Club websites.

PICTURE CREDITS

Alastair Mercer: 94bl, b & br.

Aldenham School: 106b.

Alex Keighley (Felsted School): 117t.

Andy George: 126.

Angus Roy: 82tr.

Ardingly School: 107.

Arthur Dunn Cup archive: 18 inset, 37 all except tl, 38, 39c, 39c inset, 40 all except tl, 41 all, 42 all except tl, 42b, 44 all except bl, 45t, 45c inset, 45c, 46, 47 all, 48, 49t, 49b, 54, 55, 56, 57t, 59 all, 63, 68tl, 145 – 176.

BBC: 83tr inset.

Ben Gurr (Times): 90c.

Bill Maddison (Old Foresters): 66.

Book of Football: 20tl, 23bl, 25bl, 124cr.

Brian Pearce: 21c.

Caxton press: 14b, 23tl, 25tr, 29t, 43tl, 112.

Charterhouse Archives: 40t, 111 all.

Chigwell School: 113.

City of London School: 114b.

Cranleigh School: 115t.

David Roy: 27, 53tr, 53cr, 68cl, 69, 72, 73b, 74, 75, 76tl, 76cl, 77, 79b, 81tr, 81c, 82cl, 83tr except inserts, 83cr, 85tc, 85cr, 88tr, 90bl, 94tr, 94cl, 94c, 100b.

Dunn family archive: 10, 11cl, 14tc, 15tl, 42tl.

Eastbourne College: 115c.

Edward Grayson: 24b.

Essex County Cricket Club: 26t.

Eton College: 11tr, 19cr, 116c.

Football Association: 29b, 31t, 45br, 53tc, 71b.

Football Museum: 120.

Forest School: 117c.

Geoff Kentfield: 95bl.

Haberdashers' Aske's School: 119t.

Haileybury School: 119c.

Hurstpierpoint College: 121cl.

Ian Bevan: 100tl, 100c.

Illustrated Sporting & Dramatic News: 116b.

Ipswich School: 121bl.

ITV: 83tr inset.

J Mullins (Highgate School): 114t.

Jane Sawyer: 11t.

John Cassidy: 92, 96c, 96b, 97 all except t & bc, 98, 99 all, 101 all except b, 102 all, 103c, 103b, 105.

Ken Shearwood: 43c.

Kevin Kelly: 76b.

King Edward's School, Witley: 132c.

Lancing School Magazine: 73tr, 73c.

Lloyds Bank: 39b.

Ludgrove School: Cover, 11br, 12cr, 12bl, 13tc, 13tr, 13c, 13b.

Malvern College: 123.

Mark Aspland: (Times) 86tl, 86tr, 86cr, 86b.

Mark Dixon (Old Salopians): 65t, 84b, 85c, 85bl, 85br, 128br, 129.

Michael Gilbert: 11cr, 13cr, 15cr, 15b, 16, 18, 33t, 60, 79cl, 81br, 90br, 91 all, 95 all except bl, 96tr, 97tc, 97bc, 101b, 103tc, 103tr, 110tc, 122c, 134.

Mill Hill School: 124b.

Norman Rosser (Malvern College): 28, 31b, 32t, 32bl, 58 all, 62 all.

Old Brightonians: 26b, 110cr, 110b.

Old Carthusians: 19t, 20b, 21b, 36tl, 36cl, 36bc, 36br, 37tl, 39t.

Old Foresters: 87cl, 87b.

Old Malvernians: 50c, 50b.

Old Reptonians: 71t.

Oliver Pollard (Old Foresters): 118.

Oxfordshire Photographic Archive: 131bl.

Radley College: 125t.

Replay Publishing: 19b, 21t, 23br, 24t, 25br, 31c, 57b, 70.

Repton School: 125c.

Rossall School: 127.

Jennifer Wood (Brentwood School): 109.

John Plowright (Repton School): 32br.

Ralph Thompson (Harrow School): 119b.

Richard Chadder: 124tl.

Roger Boustred: 78.

St Albans School: 106t.

St Edmund's School, Canterbury: 128t.

St John's School, Leatherhead: 122t.

Shrewsbury School: 128c.

Simon Inglis: 51tr.

Simon Marriott (Old Wellingburians): 44bl.

Talbot Collection: 30b, 33bl, 33br, 34t, 34c, 34b, 35t, 35c, 35b, 36tr.

The Field: 65c.

The Sphere: 132tl, 132tc.

Timothy Morgan-Owen: 20cr.

Tom Hevezi (Times): 80, 88b, 89 all.

Twickenham Museum: 26c.

Wellingborough School: 130.

Westminster School: 131t, 131br.

Winchester College: 30t, 33c, 133.

Numbers refer to pages
t: top   b: bottom   r: right   l: left   c: centre

While every effort has been made to trace the owners of photographs used, this has sometimes proved impossible and copyright owners are invited to contact the publishers.

INDEX